Plasticity

Plasticity
The Promise of Explosion

Catherine Malabou

Edited by Tyler M. Williams

EDINBURGH
University Press

Edinburgh University Press is one of the leading university presses in the UK. We publish academic books and journals in our selected subject areas across the humanities and social sciences, combining cutting-edge scholarship with high editorial and production values to produce academic works of lasting importance. For more information visit our website: edinburghuniversitypress.com

© Catherine Malabou
© editorial matter and organisation Tyler M. Williams, 2022

Edinburgh University Press Ltd
The Tun – Holyrood Road
12(2f) Jackson's Entry
Edinburgh EH8 8PJ

Typeset in 11/13.5 Bembo by
IDSUK (DataConnection) Ltd

A CIP record for this book is available from the British Library

ISBN 978 1 4744 6211 2 (hardback)
ISBN 978 1 4744 6214 3 (webready PDF)
ISBN 978 1 4744 6212 9 (paperback)
ISBN 978 1 4744 6213 6 (epub)

The right of Catherine Malabou to be identified as the author of this work has been asserted in accordance with the Copyright, Designs and Patents Act 1988, and the Copyright and Related Rights Regulations 2003 (SI No. 2498).

The right of Tyler M. Williams to be identified as the editor of this work has been asserted in accordance with the Copyright, Designs and Patents Act 1988, and the Copyright and Related Rights Regulations 2003 (SI No. 2498).

Contents

Acknowledgements — vii
Introduction — 1
  by Ian James

Part One: Philosophical Heritages
1. An Eye on the Edge of Discourse: Speech, Vision, Idea — 15
2. Following Generation: Biological and Poetic Cloning — 27
3. Philosophy in Erection: Derrida's Columns — 39
4. The Possibility of the Worst: On Faith and Knowledge — 49
5. Before and Above: Spinoza and Symbolic Necessity — 63
6. Can We Relinquish the Transcendental? — 89
7. Is Science the Subject of Philosophy? Miller, Badiou and Derrida Respond — 101

Part Two: Masks
8. The Crowd: Figuring the Democracy to Come — 115
9. Life and Prison — 131
10. Odysseus's Changed Soul: A Contemporary Reading of the Myth of Er — 141
11. Epigenesis of the Text: New Paths in Biology and Hermeneutics — 157
12. Reading Lázló Földényi's 'Dostoyevsky Reads Hegel in Siberia and Bursts into Tears' — 167
13. Philosophy and the Outside: Foucault and Decolonial Thinking — 179

Part Three: Psyches, Brains, Cells
14. The Brain of History, or, The Mentality of the Anthropocene — 189
15. Whither Materialism? Althusser/Darwin — 203
16. Philosophy and Anarchism: Alternative or Dilemma? — 215

17 One Life Only: Biological Resistance, Political Resistance	227
18 Philosophers, Biologists: Some More Effort if You Wish to Become Revolutionaries!	237
19 How is Subjectivity Undergoing Deconstruction Today? Philosophy, Auto-Hetero-Affection and Neurobiological Emotion	243
20 Floating Signifiers Revisited: Poststructuralism Meets Neurolinguistics	253

Part Four: Destructive Forms

21 Is Retreat a Metaphor?	265
22 Plasticity and Elasticity in Freud's *Beyond the Pleasure Principle*	275
23 Are There Still Traces? Memory and the Obsolescence of the Paradigm of Inscription	287
24 Phantom Limbs and Plasticity: Merleau-Ponty and Current Neurobiology	297
25 The Example of Plasticity	309
Works Cited	321
Index	332

Acknowledgements

Several of the chapters included in this volume have appeared previously in various journals and edited volumes. The author and editor thank the following publishers for permission to reprint copyright material. Chapter 1 previously appeared as 'An Eye at the Edge of Discourse', *Communication Theory* 17 (2007): 16–25, and is reprinted with the permission of Oxford University Press. Chapter 2 previously appeared as 'Following Generation', *Qui Parle* 20.2 (2012): 19–33, and is reprinted with the permission of Duke University Press. Chapter 3 previously appeared as 'Philosophy in Erection', *Paragraph* 39.2 (2016): 238–48, and is reprinted with the permission of Edinburgh University Press. Chapter 4 previously appeared in *Umbr(a): A Journal of the Unconscious* and is reprinted with the permission of the journal's founder, Joan Copjec. Chapter 5 previously appeared as 'Before and Above: Spinoza and Symbolic Necessity', *Critical Inquiry* 43 (2016): 84–109, and is reprinted with the permission of the University of Chicago Press. Chapter 6 previously appeared as 'Can We Relinquish the Transcendental?', *Journal of Speculative Philosophy* 28.3 (2014): 242–55, and is reprinted with the permission of Pennsylvania State University Press. Chapter 7 previously appeared as 'The Subject of Science: Badiou, Derrida, and Miller', in *Thinking Catherine Malabou: Passionate Detachments*, ed. Thomas Wormald and Isabell Dahms (Lanham, MD: Rowman and Littlefield, 2018), and is reprinted with the permission of Rowman and Littlefield publishers. Chapter 8 previously appeared as 'The Crowd', *Oxford Literary Review* 31.1 (2015): 25–44, and is reprinted with the permission of Edinburgh University Press. Chapter 10 previously appeared in *Contemporary Encounters with Ancient Metaphysics*, ed. Abraham Jacob Greenstein and Ryan J. Johnson (Edinburgh: Edinburgh University Press, 2017), and is reprinted with the permission of Edinburgh University Press. Chapter 14 previously appeared as 'The Brain of History, or, the Mentality of the Anthropocene', *South Atlantic Quarterly* 116.1 (2017): 39–53, and is reprinted with the permission of Duke University Press. Chapter 15 previously appeared as 'Whither Materialism?', in *Plastic Materialities: Politics,*

Legality, and Metamorphosis in the Work of Catherine Malabou, ed. Brenna Bhandar and Jonathan Goldberg-Hiller (Durham, NC: Duke University Press, 2015), and is reprinted with the permission of Duke University Press. An earlier version of that same essay previously appeared as 'Darwin and the Social Destiny of Natural Selection', *theory@buffalo* 16, trans. Lena Taub and Tyler M. Williams. Chapter 17 previously appeared as 'One Life Only: Biological Resistance, Political Resistance', *Critical Inquiry* 42 (2016): 429–38, and is reprinted with the permission of the University of Chicago Press. Chapter 18 previously appeared as 'Philosophers, Biologists: Some More Effort If You Wish to Become Revolutionaries!', *Critical Inquiry* 43 (2016): 200–6, and is reprinted with the permission of the University of Chicago Press. Chapter 19 previously appeared as 'How Is Subjectivity Undergoing Deconstruction Today?', *Qui Parle* 17.2 (2009): 112–22, and is reprinted with the permission of Duke University Press. Chapter 21 previously appeared as 'Is Retreat a Metaphor?', *PUBLIC: Art, Culture, Ideas* 25.50 (2014): 35–42, and is reprinted with the permission of York University. Chapter 22 previously appeared as 'Plasticity and Elasticity in Freud's *Beyond the Pleasure Principle*', *Diacritics* 37.4 (2007): 78–85, and is reprinted with the permission of Johns Hopkins University Press. Chapter 24 previously appeared as 'Phantom Limbs and Plasticity: Merleau-Ponty and Current Neurobiology', *Chiasmi* 17 (2015). Oliver Bernard's translation of Guillaume Apollinaire's 'Autumn Crocuses', in *Selected Poems* (London: Anvil, 2004), is reprinted in Chapter 3 of this volume with the permission of Carcanet.

Editor's Acknowledgements

The editor wishes to thank, first and foremost, Catherine Malabou for her indispensable enthusiasm for this project. Without her openness and generosity, her patience, friendship and confidence, *Plasticity: The Promise of Explosion* obviously would have never come to fruition. From its earliest stages, Ian James expressed keen interest in this project, and his introduction makes an impactful contribution to its entirety. Much gratitude is also due to James Godley, who helped standardise citations from Freud's *Standard Edition*. The laborious task of translation often goes unnoticed and unappreciated, so a special acknowledgement is due to Malabou's many translators. Not every text included in this volume is a translation, but individual acknowledgement of each translator's work appears at the end of the translated chapters. Last but certainly not least, at Edinburgh University Press, Carol Macdonald's care and vision made this project possible, and her confidence in the volume sustained it throughout.

Introduction

Ian James

A newcomer to Catherine Malabou's philosophical writings might find themselves a little daunted by the scope, range and interdisciplinary breadth of her engagements. Given this, they might also find it a challenge to situate her thinking or to categorise it within the well-established traditions of so-called 'continental' philosophy or 'French theory'. On the one hand, she clearly works in the wake of Derridean deconstruction and also offers landmark readings and reformulations of Kantian, Hegelian and Heideggerian philosophy. Her writing can therefore most obviously be situated within the legacy of transcendental, phenomenological and post-phenomenological thought. On the other hand, her work brings together diverse and at times seemingly incompatible contexts. Engagements with neurology, neuroscience and cognitive psychology sit alongside discussions of psychoanalysis, aesthetics and politics. The philosophical negotiation with all of these contexts also unfolds within a sustained critical response to some of the most significant theoretical trends of twentieth-century and contemporary continental thought: structuralism, poststructuralism, biopolitics and speculative realism, to name but a few. At times, Malabou also writes very self-consciously as a female philosopher whose concerns are never far from those of feminism and of a feminist critique of the European philosophical tradition.

Faced with such diversity, newcomers and initiates alike might be tempted to categorise Malabou's thinking according to one or other of its most notable defining aspects. So her work could be pigeonholed, variably, as post-deconstructive, as Hegelian, as a philosophy of biology or of neuroscience, or as a variant of recently prominent trends such as 'new materialism'. Yet none of these somewhat reductive labels quite does justice to the scope, power and originality of what is, ultimately, a unique contribution to contemporary philosophy, one that both bridges and works between all these distinct and very different traditions.

The selection of essays and unpublished writings gathered together in this volume covers the full range of these diverse contexts and concerns, and they can all be shown, to one degree or another, to explore, elaborate and further interrogate what is indisputably the guiding concept and central concern of Malabou's philosophy: plasticity. From her earliest exploration of the concept in relation to Hegel's phenomenology through to its most recent elaboration in the context of Kant's transcendental thought, the science of epigenetics and the domain of artificial intelligence, 'plasticity' is the single sustained preoccupation that can be shown to give unity to Malabou's work over the last two decades or more. It occupies a central role in all her original reformulations of metaphysics, politics, neurology, psychoanalysis and aesthetics. Spanning the length of her career to date, the essays presented in *Plasticity: The Promise of Explosion* demonstrate both the sustained and persistent centrality of plasticity in her writing and its variable inflections in different domains.

The concept itself has been extensively glossed or commented upon in the burgeoning scholarship and critical-philosophical engagement with Malabou's thought, and is, as has been indicated, ceaselessly elaborated and re-elaborated throughout her work.[1] Defined, initially at least, as being 'at once capable of receiving and of giving form' (Malabou 2005: 8), the 'plastic' here is not just concerned with the emergence and dissolution of forms, either biological, material, symbolic or conceptual, but also and decisively informs the capacity of forms to be exchanged or transformed from one regime to another, that is to say, from the biological to the symbolic or from the material to the conceptual. So, plasticity in Malabou is not simply a concept to be worked out within the heterogeneous domains of biology, neurology, metaphysics, psychoanalysis, politics and so on. It is also and perhaps most importantly a means by which the relation of these different domains to each other can be thought. This is to say that cerebral- or neuroplasticity are not simply analogous to the plasticity of concepts or of consciousness in general, but rather that plasticity such as it is thought by Malabou can allow us to think, in a rigorous and highly original manner, the *passage* from biological or neurological form to conceptual and mental form. Perhaps the most singularly important and original contribution of Malabou's philosophy is to give us the means to think the continuity and possibilities of transition between biological and symbolic life. It is this that gives such a strong coherence and synthetic force to her diverse philosophical engagements across disciplines which span the sciences, social sciences and the arts.

Contexts

A brief overview of the intellectual-historical and philosophical contexts that frame Malabou's thinking can shed more light on its originality and singularity.

INTRODUCTION

Her philosophical formation within the context of Derridean deconstruction is evident (she was one of Derrida's doctoral research students). Yet the doctoral dissertation that eventually became her first philosophical work is so much more than a 'deconstructive' reading of the Hegelian philosophical system. Set within the trajectory of the twentieth-century French reception of Hegel, a vast and complex negotiation that begins in the 1920s and is defining for so much French intellectual life in the interwar and post-war years, Malabou's *The Future of Hegel* is both a major milestone and a point of rupture or innovation.[2] Broadly speaking, in the post-war decades of the 1950s, 1960s and 1970s a picture of Hegelian thought emerged in France that characterised it as a totalising system according to which all that is other, heterogeneous or different is more or less violently appropriated and assimilated into a logic of identity, homogeneity and sameness.[3] In this context, Hegel emerges as a 'totalitarian' thinker whose logic of self-fashioning subjectivity and absolute knowledge are, at best, retrospectively tainted by the historical events of Stalinism, National Socialism and European fascism. Based on a very detailed and meticulous reading of the figure of plasticity within the Hegelian text itself (*Plastizität* in German), Malabou's *The Future of Hegel* roundly challenges this view of the dialectic of subjectivity and the passage towards absolute knowledge in the *Phenomenology*.

What emerges in this context is an understanding of the Hegelian subject as always oriented towards, and exposed to, a futurity that is without identity and whose dialectical transformations are a ceaseless process constituted in the explosive deformation and solidifying reformation of forms. Hegel's philosophical thought appears here not as a speculative rationality for which absolute knowledge is an identifiable aim, telos or endpoint that the philosophical subject can grasp in advance, or whose perspective can somehow be adopted in anticipation of its eventual fulfilment. The Hegelian text itself emerges as a plastic form, one whose dialectical operations give rise to the very conceptual movement and process of thinking. This movement should be understood as the giving, receiving and transformation of the form of philosophical subjectivity as such, and as a ceaseless process that is without orientation towards any instance of final identity or absolute fulfilment.

Malabou's reading here not only marks the eclipse of what in many ways had always been something of a reductive caricature of the Hegelian system within certain strands of post-war French thought; it also signals a distinctive evolution of Derridean deconstruction. Malabou shifts Derrida's core emphasis on 'arche-writing', graphic inscription and the 'trace' to the question of *form* and the manner in which forms survive their deconstruction and both persist or are transformed in excess of any logic or possibility of self-identity or presence.[4]

Even at this stage, and perhaps because of this shift in emphasis towards the plasticity of forms, there is a questioning of the way in which conceptual form and empirical form can shape each other. Indeed, alongside the capacity to give and receive form, this, Malabou tells us, is the second principal meaning of plasticity that she derives from her reading of Hegel, that is to say, 'a mutual giving of form between the empirical and the noetic' (Malabou 2005: 45).

The thinking that is opened up here of a reciprocal donation of form between the empirical (or the material) and the noetic (or the mind) is no doubt one of the most significant achievements of *The Future of Hegel*. For it opens the way, from the earliest stages of Malabou's philosophical writing, for a rethinking of the relation between the regimes of the biological and of consciousness, or what she will later call the mental and the neuronal. Already, in her very first major work, Malabou is able to note the significance of the fact that it 'is not by chance that the notion of plasticity today operates in the domain of cell biology and neurobiology' (2005: 192). The key insight here is that no system, no form and no regime of being is ever closed or self-sufficient. All are constitutively open to and affected by the other systems, forms or regimes to which they are necessarily related and are so in such a way as to ensure that they will always have a capacity to modify or transform themselves. This would include, say, the transformation from one neuronal, conceptual or symbolic form into another, but also the transformation of neuronal *to* conceptual or symbolic forms and vice versa.

From the perspective of this inaugural moment of Malabou's thinking, it should be clear that her later engagements with neuroscience and epigenetics are not and cannot be judged simply to be some variant on the philosophy of biology. Rather, what is at stake is the question of the transformability of and transition between different regimes of form, and with this also a fundamental reworking of the status of philosophical conceptuality as such, and of its relation to the discourse of science in general and of biology in particular. To this extent, her work can also be placed in the context of a long-standing trajectory within the French philosophical tradition, where engagements with biology are central to the fundamental ontological and epistemological commitments of philosophy itself. One might cite in this regard the nineteenth-century French spiritualist tradition as represented by key figures such as Félix Ravaisson, whose commitment to vitalism drew on biological theories of its day.[5] Henri Bergson, Ravaisson's student, of course engaged critically with the legacy of Darwinian theory in the context of his thinking of *élan vital* and of creative evolution. Later thinkers such as Georges Canguilhem, one of the most influential mid-twentieth-century French philosophers and a key influence on Foucault and the development of structuralism in the 1960s, centred his thinking on his engagements with medical science, cell biology, and a refusal of mechanistic or reductivist approaches within biology more generally. And in the wake of Canguilhem, a whole host of greater or lesser known French philosophers give engagements with or interpretations of biology a central place at key moments in the development of their thinking, for example Gilles Deleuze and Henri Atlan. Many others could be cited, of course, but it should be clear that Malabou's original engagement with biology and neuroscience is by no means marginal or unique and can be situated within the very clearly established contexts that are central to the modern French philosophical tradition.

What may be surprising, however, is the fact that Malabou engages with biology and neuroscience from a very specific post-phenomenological and post-deconstructive perspective, which might appear, on the face of it at least, to be incompatible with or antithetical to the perspectives of empirical science and the reductivist approaches that often inform biological understanding. As a distinctive evolution of Derridean deconstruction, her philosophy might not be expected to have such a heavy investment in biology and neuroscience. Whereas a thinker such as Deleuze builds upon and is greatly influenced by Bergson and can thus be seen to stand already in a tradition of philosophical responses to the biological sciences, Derrida, whose earliest work is rooted in his meticulous readings of Edmund Husserl's phenomenology, cannot be so easily aligned with the perspectives of empirical scientific inquiry. This is because Husserl himself, formed in the ambient neo-Kantianism of the late nineteenth and early twentieth centuries, predicated his thinking on what he called the suspension of the natural attitude. Rather than taking the presence of things in the world around us as simple empirical givens, phenomenological thought needs to begin by suspending our common-sense beliefs about the simple reality of these things and interrogating the ways in which they are constituted in and by acts of intentional consciousness that are directed towards the world, and are so on the basis of horizons of sense and meaning that are themselves constitutive. Husserlian thought is thus a transcendental mode of inquiry that interrogates the conditions of possibility of the appearance or manifestation of things (phenomena) to consciousness, and thus stands in a direct lineage with Kantian transcendental philosophy.

To this extent, although it is by no means opposed to science (indeed Husserl, like Kant, sought to lay a more solid and universal ground for scientific knowledge), the operations of the phenomenological method are radically different from those knowledge discourses that ground themselves in empiricism. At the beginning of his career, Derrida's close readings of Husserl yield a deconstruction of the immediacy and self-identity of phenomenological presence, intentional consciousness and sense constitution, and thereby open the way for all the later developments of deconstructive thinking. Derridean deconstruction is therefore closely bound to the legacy of Kantian and Husserlian transcendentalism in ways Malabou herself will interrogate both in some of the essays included in this volume and elsewhere in her work. As she puts it in one of her most recent works, *Before Tomorrow*, a work in which Kant himself is read closely in order to develop insights into the contemporary science of epigenetics and its implications for neurobiology, 'the neurobiological viewpoint simply erases the transcendental' (Malabou 2016: 152). The problem, then, with bringing transcendental phenomenological or quasi-transcendental Derridean deconstructive thought into such a close engagement with biological science may be that their approaches simply preclude each other and that, therefore, such a bringing together cannot be carried out in any philosophically plausible or coherent manner.

Whereas Husserl at least sought to establish a transcendental ground for our knowledge of phenomena and the world and thus to secure scientific knowledge, Heidegger's existential phenomenology and rethinking of being is profoundly antagonistic to biological or bio-anthropological accounts of consciousness and worldly existence. All the more surprising, then, that Malabou's development of Derridean deconstruction in the wider context of an engagement with biology should also have been further developed in a major work on Heideggerian ontology and Heidegger's destruction or overcoming of metaphysics.

What is so striking and distinctive about Malabou's reading of Heidegger in her second major work, *The Heidegger Change* (2011), is that she reads him, somewhat against the grain, with a desire to render him unrecognisable in relation to any existing 'Heideggerianism' and as a thinker of the transformability of ontological regimes. What matters in this reading of Heidegger is not exactly his overcoming and destruction of metaphysics or onto-theology through a rethinking of being either as Dasein's 'being-in-the-world' or, later, as the originary giving or saying of 'Beyng'.[6] Rather, what matters here is the way in which the Heideggerian destruction of metaphysics shows us that the onto-theological understanding of being is liable to transform into another ontological form or regime. Malabou avoids treating Heidegger's own reformulations of the thinking of being as ends in themselves to be post-metaphysically consecrated as a new beginning for thought, and thereby treated as the sole idiom according to which thought can henceforth proceed. What she demonstrates in her reading of Heidegger as a thinker of ontological change is that the most fundamental concepts, horizons and images we have of being are just as plastic and as susceptible to transformation, deformation and reformation as any other form.

INTRODUCTION

So, once again, plasticity emerges as the guiding concept and core preoccupation of Malabou's philosophical writing, and Heidegger, read now as a thinker of ontological change and of the transformability of regimes of being, emerges as a further resource by which the possibility of transformation and transition between the empirical and the noetic or the biological and the symbolic can come to be thought. It should be clear from this the extent to which Malabou's reading of both Heidegger and Hegel is decisive for her reorientation of Derridean deconstruction towards the question of form and the manner in which forms survive or are transformed by their deconstruction. It should also be clear that these readings are decisive for the way in which she opens Derridean thought on to biology, neuroscience and later epigenetics. In this regard, it is perhaps not by chance that her seminal work *What Should We Do With Our Brain?* appeared in French in the very same year that *The Heidegger Change* was also first published (2004).

Plasticity and Politics

The stakes of thinking the transformability and transition between the biological and the symbolic are unequivocally philosophical, engaging as they do the long-standing fundamental question of the relation between mind and body, or, more precisely, of phenomenological consciousness to the neurobiological substratum of the brain. The possibility of renewing a radical materialism hangs in the balance here. As I have argued elsewhere, what is also at play is the possibility of developing something like a post-continental naturalism.[7] Yet the stakes here are also quite profoundly political, engaging questions of individual and collective identity, determinism and freedom, and ultimately also political and social organisation. Such stakes are addressed perhaps obliquely in books such as *The New Wounded* (2012), a work that questions the rival paradigms of neuroscience and psychoanalysis, their potential reconciliation, and the implications of 'destructive plasticity', a quality discernible in the neurological damage suffered by Alzheimer's patients. In interrogating biological corporeal and cerebral life, Malabou is in fact never far from political considerations.[8] This is most evident from her first book devoted to the question of brain plasticity: *What Should We Do With Our Brain?*

The political implications of neuroplasticity can be discerned on the most fundamental level in relation to philosophical questions of determinism and freedom conceived in relation to both the individual and the collective. In the context of biology, what plasticity in general, and neuroplasticity in particular,

7

indicates is that determinism – evolutionary, genetic or even environmental – cannot be the primary principle or factor that shapes what we are and what we can or will become. If the neural networks that constitute the cerebral base of our thought, consciousness and capacity for acting in one way or another are all formed within and by our lifelong experiences and interactions with our environment, then there is no sense in positing an essentialist notion of self and its behaviours that would be exclusively grounded in a personal genetic coding or species-level evolutionary psychology. Biological structures and the diverse forms and possibilities of consciousness and behaviour would emerge in a process of reciprocal donation and receiving of form in a complex dynamic of interaction which easily offers scope for some kind of agency, or indeed freedom, to emerge, since no instance of form is ever grounded in an exclusively determinate cause or plural constellation of causes. All of Malabou's arguments in *What Should We Do With Our Brain?* firmly point in this direction, as do her more recent writings around the question of epigenesis and the science of epigenetics.

At the very same time, Malabou elucidates the political implications of plasticity in relation to questions of neural, but also social and organisational, structure. She points out that, with the rise of cybernetic systems and computer technologies in the middle and second half of the twentieth century, there was a widespread tendency to understand the brain by analogy with these technologies. The understanding of the brain as a computational machine and as a centre of command and control in relation to the body arguably continues a long-standing tradition of using forms derived from our external technical milieus to articulate theoretical or philosophical conceptualisations of much more complex internal biological structures.[9] The image of the brain as a centralised command and control structure, Malabou argues, nevertheless became obsolete in the later twentieth and early twenty-first centuries with the development of a more complex understanding of neural systems as networked, as operationally parallel and, of course, as plastic. This development was itself paralleled by the rise of management theories that similarly laid a key emphasis on decentralisation and organisational participation or involvement. Malabou discerns a different kind of mirroring between our understanding of brain structure and our externalised modes of organisation, now understood as a convergence between contemporary neurobiological science and the management theories of late capitalism.

The political stakes of this come to the fore when one considers once again that the more fundamental philosophical issues of determinism and freedom are at play. This is because, ideologically speaking, the tendency is always to appeal to and to instrumentalise biological structures in order to naturalise and therefore justify in essentialist terms our surrounding social and political structures. In this context, Malabou further discerns a misappropriation of biological plasticity in the demand made by contemporary managerial organisation that labour forces be 'flexible' in their response to the demands made by markets, economic forces and so on. The language of flexibility implies that we should mould ourselves responsively to the external demands and pressures collectively placed upon us by the impersonal market forces of late modern capitalist production and consumption. In this context, the demand for flexibility, embedded as it is in the convergence between the contemporary image of plastic neural organisation and the contemporary image of management organisation, might appear as a purely natural rather than as a political or an ideological demand. And yet what the language of flexibility, in its insistence on passive receptivity with regard to externally imposed forms, neglects or represses is the fundamental quality of plasticity as (as Malabou never ceases to reiterate) the reciprocal receiving *and giving* of form. Malabou's gambit is to suggest, with some degree of polemical force, that if we understand fully the implications of plasticity for our neural and social political organisation, then this plasticity can be called upon as a resource for an active politics of resistance to our current political forms and for the creation of new alternative forms. Far from having to mould ourselves to social and economic structures which, by way of analogy with biological structures, would seek to impose themselves as somehow 'natural', plasticity can open up possibilities for the affirmation of free agency and for the renewal or transformation of those very structures.

In this way, the emphasis on the self-fashioning of consciousness, subjectivity or selfhood that lies at the centre of Hegel's phenomenology and Malabou's early-career rereading of Hegel can be shown to play out throughout the further development of her philosophical thinking conjointly and in an interrelated manner across the realms of neurobiology, culture, politics and social organisation.

Openings

The myriad ways in which the concept of plasticity opens on to different domains of interrogation and inquiry is reflected in the breadth and diversity of the essays collected in this volume. Divided into four parts, the collection clearly demonstrates that this diversity, however initially daunting in its scope, range and interdisciplinary breadth, finds a coherent articulation in the resonance that each of the parts has with the other.

The essays included in Part One interrogate the operation of plasticity across what might be called Malabou's philosophical heritage, a canon of

European thinkers that includes Derrida, Levinas, Lyotard, Hegel, Kant, Freud and Spinoza. At the same time, plasticity is engaged within the realm of biology and with regard to the question of heredity itself, and is so in a manner that allows the relation of philosophy to science to be questioned and thought anew. Central here is the status of the transcendental in philosophical thinking (that is to say, the ultimate conditions of possibility of thought) and Malabou's demonstration that the transcendental is not in any way an intrinsic or immutable element, but rather is itself a material instance at once liable to transformation and able to integrate its own plastic or epigenetic development. In this context, contemporary attempts in philosophical debate to jettison or abandon the transcendental moment of thought are shown to be at best questionable and at worst untenable.[10]

Part Two explores the political implications of the operations of plasticity, further developing the scope of the discussions in Part One. So, for instance, in her engagement with the discourse of biopolitics, Malabou elucidates the dynamic evolution of biological phenomena in their response to environments. In so doing, she re-poses the questions of freedom, determination and the political dimension of these in ways that recall the discussion of plasticity and politics above. The image of science that biopolitics presupposes, she argues, is one of a knowledge discourse that is calcified and instrumentalised for the purposes of furthering and supporting mechanisms of power. The renewed understanding of biological life and agency that Malabou's thinking of neuroplasticity and epigenetics offers produces a much more open and fluid image of biology and of biological life. It thereby also demonstrates the extent to which biological life resists instrumentalisation and ideological appropriation by power and by the historically contingent constructions of sovereignty through which power is wielded.

Part Three returns this renewed understanding of biology to a reworking of conceptions of subjectivity in order to widen the scope of questioning and to take in the much broader philosophical problems that lie at the heart of contemporary theoretical debate. The originality of Malabou's thinking here once again lies in her insistence that we need to engage philosophically and reflectively with all the latest developments in neuroscience and epigenetics and not to take them as neutral or as being without prior embedded assumptions that are themselves philosophical and therefore open to challenge. Such a renewed and critical philosophical engagement with contemporary science can be shown to yield results which oblige us to question some of the most important horizons of understanding that inform our current era: issues relating to freedom and determinism once again, but also to our collective understanding of the boundaries between sense and life, or between the human and the non-human.

The essays included in Part Four of this volume constitute an important self-questioning on Malabou's part in relation to the fundamentals of her thought and what one might call the darker side of plasticity. If the emphasis has hitherto been on the productive, transformative and 'freeing' capacities of plasticity, here the question of its destructive power is posed, including whether destruction itself can be said to have a form. Annihilation, erasure and therefore the negativity that was always at the beginning a key operation of the Hegelian dialectic now come directly into the foreground. For a new form to emerge, any prior given form must necessarily be erased. This question is posed in relation to the conceptual forms of thinkers on whom Malabou draws (Derrida and Freud), but also more generally in relation to the fundamental implications of plasticity for ontology. For, Malabou argues, there can be no promise of the creation, transformation or renewal of forms without something like a 'plastic explosion' and, with this, the annihilation of any ontological ground or foundation for form as such and in general.

Taken together, what the essays collected in this volume demonstrate is that philosophy, above all, has the ability and responsibility to respond to all the diverse forms that are both contemporary with it and that precede it in an anterior tradition or horizon that makes it possible as philosophy. These forms will be philosophical, of course, but they are also biological, social, political, cultural and aesthetic, and it is at the interrogation of the limits of such forms that philosophy may discern the potential for, or actuality of, renewal, transformation or indeed explosion. In this context, plasticity emerges not just as the key theme or motif of Malabou's thinking, but also as its core operation. Plasticity operates in all the forms of life and at the boundaries that separate or distinguish these forms each from the other. In this way, the material and the conceptual, the biological and the cultural, the human and the non-human can all be understood both in their specificity and distinctness, but also in their interrelation and in their liability to form and be formed each in relation to the other.

Notes

1 See, for example, Martinon (2007), James (2012; 2016; 2019), Wormald and Dahms (2018), Lawtoo (2017) and Williams (2013).
2 For general accounts of the twentieth-century French reception of Hegel in France, see Baugh (2003), Gutting (2001: 109–13) and Schrift (2006).

3 The most obvious example of this tendency in relation to Hegel would be the philosophy of Emmanuel Levinas in works such as *Totality and Infinity* (1969), and Gilles Deleuze's account of non-logical difference given in *Difference and Repetition* (1984).
4 Derrida himself would be rather sceptical of this renewed focus on form, as it might appear to reintroduce a more traditional philosophical category and risk a return to the logic of presence. On this, see James (2012: 85).
5 It is not by chance that Malabou wrote the preface to the English translation of Ravaisson's *Of Habit* (2008).
6 See in particular Heidegger (2010; 1999).
7 See James (2019).
8 See Malabou and Butler (2010), Malabou and Emmanuelli (2009). See also Malabou (2011a; 2019).
9 See Borck (2018).
10 See Meillassoux (2009).

Part One

Philosophical Heritages

1

An Eye on the Edge of Discourse: Speech, Vision, Idea

> If one looks at the etymology, one finds that to denote directed vision French resorts to the word *regard* [gaze], whose root originally referred not to the act of seeing but to expectation, concern, watchfulness, consideration, and safeguard, made emphatic by the addition of a prefix expressing a redoubling or return. *Regarder* [to look at, to gaze upon] is a movement that aims to recapture, *reprendre sous garde* [to place in safekeeping once again]. (Starobinski 1989: 2)

I'd like to talk about a strange state of vision: *the vision of thought*. What is it to *see* a thought? To see a thought coming? To be present at its emergence, at the moment when it is still no more than a promise, a plan, or sketch, but is already strong enough to live? What is it to see before writing, when a brand-new thought can already be apprehended sensibly, sensually, like a body? How should we approach that strange state of half-carnal, half-intelligible vision that oversees the torments of the text even as it establishes the suspended spatial presence of the text?

I am interested in the *schema* of discourse, where *schema* is understood in terms of the famous meaning Kant gives it as 'a general procedure of the imagination for providing a concept with its image' (1998: 273). What I want to explore first of all are the processes by which a thought, an idea or an intellectual motive allows itself to be figured before adhering to a definitive form. The second objective of this analysis is to explore these processes in the light of a philosophical fracture prevalent throughout the twentieth century among thinkers who questioned a particular conception of the connection between the idea and the sensible, between idealisation and writing, or between concept and text.

French philosophers such as Lyotard, Deleuze, Derrida and Levinas, as well as writers such as Blanchot, to cite only a few, consider the question of the space and time of thought, as well as the sensibility of the idea, as central to their work, even as they redefine the notion of intellectual visibility. In the philosophical tradition, to see thought designates the actual act of contemplation. This is the Platonic meaning of *theoria*: the idea, by definition, is that which allows itself to be seen as an image (*eidos*) and the soul is the eye that apprehends it, in other words, receives it without ever inventing, creating or forming it. In the traditional conception of thought, the visibility of thought is defined in terms of transcendence: the Idea is visible because it comes from elsewhere to impose itself on the mind as a phenomenon that the mind must welcome, interiorise and make its own.

What happens to the possibility of seeing thought when this conception of transcendence, which implies that the ideal object is given as an absolute referent outside the intellect, is faced with a radical challenge? What happens when the visibility of thought is no longer ontologically guaranteed by the transcendence of the object? What happens when vision is enclosed by the limits of discourse and writing, with no real outside? How does thought figure itself when the figurable and thinkable, to draw a distinction between them, are nonetheless *coalescent*?[1]

We must assume that there is an eye 'on the edge of discourse', to borrow an expression from Jean-François Lyotard's book *Discourse, Figure* (2010: 128). This eye is not mine, nor is it yours; it is not the eye of a subject or of a subject able to see herself think. Instead, the eye is the eye of discourse itself, an optical arrangement that language brings up to its edge through its structure, so that talking gives birth to the visibility of its subject matter. The eye that borders discourse does see something other than discourse, but this 'other thing' can only be envisaged as a function of discourse. This is another way of saying that language actually opens and founds that from which all too often it is thought to derive: namely, referentiality. The word that destines saying and seeing to each another is inscribed originally in their regard for each other. Thus, as Lyotard claims, 'Language is not a homogenous environment: it is divisive because it exteriorizes the sensory into a vis-à-vis' (2010: 7–8). The distance that both separates and brings together language and subject matter is, therefore, not a distance prior to language; it is not the pre-linguistic gap regulating the relation of word to thing outside of language and without it. The distance is in fact given with language, from the outset. '[I]f the world is a function of language, language possess a world-function, as it were: out of what it designates, every utterance makes a world, a thick object waiting to be synthesized, a symbol to be deciphered' (Lyotard 2010: 83).

However, this is not to say that language has the power to make things exist. Its demiurgical powers are not of this order. In fact, language begins by making things disappear, since to speak is to reveal the possibility of naming things in their absence, while also naming the absence. To speak is to lose. But in this instance, to be able to lose is also to be able to see, to be able to see what one loses, and to be able to say that one sees it. The 'world-function' of discourse, which ensures the constancy and possible evanescence of the world itself, is thus precisely what Lyotard means by the 'distance in which the eye settles on the edge of discourse' (2010: 128).

Before returning to our topic, other elements of the analysis are required. What is it to see a thought? How does a thought announce itself sensibly? To start with, it is worth noting that if the eye that settles at the edge of discourse comes from discourse, then to see another thought must designate one of the ways in which language both sees and schematises itself. The question is then that of knowing how – and here we grasp the full meaning of Lyotard's title *Discourse, Figure* – language renders itself both discourse *and* figure, and how it unfolds in both linguistic *and* figural space.

Lyotard insists that it is a matter of unfolding. From the opening lines of his book, he shows that to recognise the presence of an eye in discourse in no way implies that 'the given [is] a text' (2010: 3) or that the world is a book that can be reduced to linguistic units that simply await decoding. Far from it. The claim that language renders visible that to which it refers implies – and this is the function of this strange, foreign, external eye – that what is irreducibly given is the heterogeneity (call it a different nature, if you like) of discourse and figure, saying and form. Language involves a necessary spatial manifestation, but Lyotard says that this 'cannot incorporate without being shaken' (2010: 7). If the figure is not outside discourse, in the transcendent sense referred to above, it nevertheless constitutes the other of discourse within discourse, 'an exteriority it cannot interiorize as *signification*' (2010: 7). This exteriority, which is the thickness of the figural, is the sensible, opaque expanse in which thought is formed. The figural never offers itself as a simple signifier, the sensible reflection of ideality. Its very dependence makes it autonomous in relation to discourse, inasmuch as it is never more than *another* mode of being of the idea.

There is, therefore, an originary violence at work in language, causing an irremissible schism between discourse and figure, sense and sensible, and idea and flesh. Given this, when we ask what it means 'to see a thought', we must examine the distortion between the sayable and the unsayable, rent at the edge of language, and sound out the power of the eye, which is both language and look, without being more than the other. To see a thought rise, to stand on the edge of its creation, to watch the figure of a new idea necessarily amounts to an intensification of the originary spectacle of language, to an opening of the eye twice by attempting to localise the eye of discourse, to give it form – the form of style, writing and volume. Thus, Lyotard says that art generally goes 'from within discourse [. . .] into the figure' (2010: 7, translation modified). 'The [artistic] figure is a deformation that imposes another form on the layout of linguistic units' (2010: 60). Lyotard shows that this other form is expressed in an infinite variety of forms in painting, fiction, poetry and pure energy, 'which folds and crumples the text and makes an artwork out of it' (2010: 9).

If one sticks to the presence of the idea in writing, one might then wonder how, by envisaging itself, thought can figure its own gaze. In *Difference and Repetition*, Deleuze presents this figuring as a *mise-en-scène*, a *dramatisation*. Essentially, he says that the schema is a 'dramatization of the Idea' whose goal is to 'specify' and 'incarnate' it (1984: 218).[3]

To see a thought is thus to specify it in the figural. But just as there is an irreducible distortion in language between discourse and figure, as I explained above, there is also an irreducible distortion between thought and form. In other words, there is neither speculation nor reflection between the two. Instead, the mirroring is breached, there is a breach of reflexivity, to the point that when thought allows itself to be seen, it is always revealed as unrecognisable, unknowable, taking the form of an outside whose face is not an immediately identifiable reflection, even though it is visible; hence the invariable angst of writing.

Nevertheless, to see a thought is really to face a mirror game in which the relation between seeing and seen moves very quickly. In *The Space of Literature*, Blanchot describes this movement as the opening of the realm of *fascination*. It is true that when thought allows itself to be seen, the eye of discourse catches sight of itself between the word and figure, thus reflecting itself. As Blanchot says, it is precisely 'the mirror image' grasping 'one's own look' (1989: 32), and thus 'a vision that never comes to an end', 'what one sees seizes sight and renders it interminable [. . .] the gaze coagulates into light, [and] light is the absolute gleam of an eye one doesn't see but which one doesn't cease to see' precisely because it is the 'mirror image of own's own look' (1989: 32–3). The space between our eye and what it sees, in other words once again, between our eye and itself, is the milieu of fascination. 'Of whoever is fascinated it can be said that he doesn't perceive any real object, any real figure, for what he sees does not belong to the world of reality, but to the indeterminate milieu of fascination' (1989: 32).

In some respects, to see a thought amounts to seeing, to figuring absence, because a thought, as Blanchot puts it, 'points us constantly back to the presence of absence [. . .] to absence as its own affirmation' (1989: 30). Perhaps, then, the idea, the very process of thought, consists in nothing more than this fascinating materialisation of absence, which gives the impression that when one is thinking, *someone* is there; that the eye, at the edge of discourse, sees someone's face:

> When I am alone, I am not alone, but, in this present, I am already returning to myself in the form of Someone. Someone is there, where I am alone. The fact of being alone is my belonging to this dead time which is not my time, or yours, or the time we share in common, but Someone's time. Someone is what is still present when there is no one. (Blanchot 1989: 31)

Idealisation appears as presence, in solitude, of solitude. What the eye sees at the edge of discourse is the essence of solitude, namely a gaze fascinated by the fact of being captured by itself alone. At the same time, this presence, this someone, is a paradoxical figure of anonymity and impersonality. To see thought as someone is to see absence in person; that is, as much as it is to see no one, it is also to touch the limits of the figurable.

Consequently, this speculative dissymmetry, where the eye is not pointed back to something but instead is pointed to its own mirage, that is, to the impossibility of the face – caricature, Levinas would say (1999b: 121–30) – inverts the seeing and the seen. In the end, how do we know that it is not the idea that gazes upon us at the very moment we think we see it? Could we write without feeling gazed upon? The staring function of thought could be called the *superego*. How can we have ideas without satisfying the demands of the ideal self? A psychic function could be assigned to this searching power of the idea through which the eye of discourse in some senses turns back against its subject. But it is not clear that this spying scenario translates so easily, as it deconstitutes the subject instead of constituting it, thereby introducing into the narcissistic loop the sharp edge of a blade that threatens to take out the subject's eyes.

Thus, the starting *idée fixe* deconstitutes the subject. What does this mean? One might think that the original question, 'What is it to see a thought?', implies analysing a process of becoming, describing a thought's movement of maturation, indissociable from figurability. But in fact it looks as if even as the thought is born, it was always more mature than us, which is why it stares at us. Furthermore, even when we think that we are modelling it, it has the power to deform or deface us. Scrutinised by the idea, we unfurl ourselves before it, returning to a liminal, embryonic, pre-subjective state through the very activity of thinking or creating. In *Difference and Repetition*, Deleuze claims,

> It is true that every Idea turns us into larvae, having put aside the identity of the I along with the resemblance of the self. This is badly described as a matter

of regression, fixation, or arrestation of development, for we are never fixed at a moment or in a given state but always fixed by an Idea as though in the glimmer of a look, always fixed in a movement that is under way. (1984: 219)

The stare of the idea is, therefore, not only a gaze but is truly a process of fixing, a sight taken of the becoming of one who thinks, a sight that momentarily fixes the thinker in an identity without simultaneously sending it back a self-image, that is, without giving it the possibility of saying *I* or *me*; it is even less a superego.

There is so much to say about this moment before the subject, the moment of these identity limbos to which the idea binds us with its stare. Inevitably, it evokes childhood. Doesn't one always feel infantilised on seeing a thought? Doesn't one always feel unmasked as the child one always was? And doesn't the idea always have our mother's eyes? Blanchot writes,

> Perhaps the force of the maternal figure receives its intensity from the very force of fascination, and one might say then, that if the mother exerts this fascinating attraction it is because, appearing when the child lives altogether in fascination's gaze, she concentrates in herself all the powers of enchantment. It is because the child is fascinated that the mother is fascinating, and that is also why all the impressions of early childhood have a kind of fixity which comes from fascination. (1989: 33)

Blanchot describes the bond connecting the fascination of childhood with the fascination of writing; even if it is maternal, the face of the idea is no less impersonal:

> Whoever is fascinated doesn't see, properly speaking, what he sees. Rather, it touches him in an immediate proximity; it seizes and ceaselessly draws him to a close, even though it leaves him absolutely at a distance. Fascination is fundamentally linked to neutral, impersonal presence, to the indeterminate They, the immense, faceless Someone. (1989: 33)

The figure of the mother in the idea is always the photograph of an absence. Like my mother, the idea gazes at me, starting from the possibility of her disappearance, for we are always as afraid of losing an idea as we are of losing our mother.

Perhaps also, like a mother, the idea always threatens us with its disappointment. When we feel her harsh stare and regress before it, falling back into childhood, isn't that because we are as afraid of disappointing our idea as we were and will always be of disappointing our mother? A passage from *In Search of Lost Time* comes to mind. The hero is in Venice with his mother. She is waiting for him at the hotel, and from the balcony she sees him returning from a walk. Her anxious face appears behind the 'multicoloured' marble balusters, as if framed by a window, or rather, an arch. When the hero sees his mother looking at him like this, he is taken back to his childhood, which is also to return to the impossibility of writing. His mother's eyes harbour tenderness and disappointment at once. Tenderness:

> as soon as I called to her from the gondola, she sent out to me, from the bottom of her heart, a love which stopped only where there was no longer any corporeal matter to sustain it, on the surface of her impassioned gaze which she brought as close to me as possible. (Proust 1993: 847)

Disappointment:

> Of this sort was the window in our hotel behind the balusters of which my mother sat waiting for me, gazing at the canal with a patience which she would not have displayed in the old days at Combray, at a time when, cherishing hopes for my future which had never been realised, she was unwilling to let me see how much she loved me. Nowadays she was well aware that an apparent coldness on her part would alter nothing, and the affection she lavished upon me was like those forbidden foods which are no longer withheld from invalids when it is certain that they are past recovery. (1993: 845–6)

The idea stares hard at us, with the cruelty of disappointed love, but without this cruelty it is impossible to write. For it is impossible to think without feeling helpless, that is, stripped naked by a gaze. This ravishing, this capturing of the I, which skins it, also results from the fact that even as she feels herself gazed at by that which she tries to see and figure, the child subject does not really see that which looks at her. Thus, the principle behind all writing, in its ideality as well as in its figurability, is the *confession*, whose form and paradox was expressed so powerfully by St Augustine: Why should I confess to God if he already knows everything? Augustine's question shows that although God is watching me, I do not see him looking at me, which is why I confess to him, and why, in the end, I am and remain a child. All imaginative writing processes must therefore take the form of a *blind* figuration, that of a blind person who cannot see what is staring at her even as she feels stripped naked by a gaze. All confessions assume that the Other, someone, already knows what I am going to say and that I am egged on to say it, so to speak, without being able to turn round. The idea watches me from behind, at my back, because as we know since Hegel, all conscience is constituted and deconstituted precisely by this *a tergo* perspective. This explains why Blanchot describes the writer as Orpheus, as the one who cannot turn back. In the night of hell, the impossibility of turning round renders 'distance sensible'. Yet Orpheus is also the one who cannot not turn back. Essentially fallible, he gives in exactly to the temptation of the desire to see that which fascinates him, the desire to figure the eye that sees him, and the desire to stand face-to-face with him, and it is this specular weakness that kills him.

The attempt to see thought can also be seen as leading to the figuration of a secret. One can only write once that which is our most personal possession – our ideas, our plans – actually become secret, hidden from ourselves. It is worth recalling that, etymologically, secret means 'separated', 'withdrawn', 'hidden from sight'. The secret of the eye at the edge of discourse, the secret that the eye jealously guards by giving it form, is therefore that which is both closest and farthest from the one who tries to see the thought or to see herself think. Derrida devoted some essential analyses to the problem of the secret, in which he suggests that the writer or thinker is carried – put into gear, into action – by the secret of her own work, which is both unknown and unknowable to her.

To write always amounts, therefore, to simultaneously revealing and keeping the secret. It reveals the secret because one can only write under its dictation; yet writing also keeps the secret, as the revelation does not exhaust and cannot dry up the mystery of the eye that looks, but that one cannot see. The more the secret is revealed, made manifest, the more it is kept – in the same way that a criminal or suspect feels protected in the public space of a crowd.

The inherent, well-known paradox of the secret, that one is never better hidden than by the visible, inevitably raises the ethical question of *responsibility*. Let us start again from the impossible face-to-face encounter between the eye on the edge of discourse that looks and one that tries to look to see the thought. There is no speculation, no reflection between them. I see nothing. Yet from this non-vision or lack of foresight, one might say, responsibility is born, in the strict sense of the possibility of responding. To keep and to reveal a secret is always to respond: to answer *it* by revealing it, to answer *for it* by keeping it. To try to see the thought, thus, always results in seeing the structure of responsibility, in its very invisibility. Analysing the structure of compassion, Derrida writes,

> [An eye] looks at me and I don't see him and it is on the basis of this gaze that singles me out [*ce regard qui me regarde*] that my responsibility comes into being. Thus is instituted or revealed the 'it concerns me' or 'it's my lookout'

[*ça me regarde*] that leads me to say, 'it is my business, my affair' [. . .] that will nevertheless be mine and which I alone will have to answer for. (1995a: 91)

So, 'it's my concern'. This gaze that gazes at me without my knowing what it sees, at the very moment when I am trying to see it, this gaze that is the gaze of the idea, with the double meaning of the genitive: the idea watched and the idea watching. This gaze of the idea makes me responsible for the idea at the very moment that the gaze frees me of responsibility, as this eye is not mine, it is always that of another, of the Other. Derrida asks,

> How can another see into me, into my most secret self, without my being able to see in there myself and without my being able to see him in me? And if my secret self, that which can be revealed only to the other, to the wholly other, to God if you wish, is a secret that I will never reflect on, that I will never know or experience or possess as my own, then what sense is there in saying that it is 'my' secret [. . .]? (1995a: 92)

Indeed, if the eye stares at me although I am unable to envisage it, then my thought is not mine, it is not my own. At the same time, because it is not mine, because it belongs to the Other, I must keep it as my own, as a treasure in transit, as if I had to hand it in, give it back before leaving, return it to the Other, in other words, make it public. This then is my responsibility.

I'll conclude by asking again: What is it to see a thought? What should I call this embryo of form, which exists without existing, which starts to live, and which scrutinises everything even as it hides itself? As we know, Levinas calls this strange presence of absence, or presence of the Other, a *face*. The meaning he gives this concept enables the joining of the two axes I have shown in relation to the vision of thought. On the one hand, it is the speaking being, as a thinker, who sees what he thinks starting from an eye at the edge of discourse. For Levinas in *Totality and Infinity*, as for Lyotard, discourse shows and thereby shows *itself*: 'Better than comprehension, *discourse* relates with what remains essentially transcendent' (Levinas 1969: 195). Discourse puts thought outside itself, thus allowing thought to see itself. At the same time, by throwing thought out, discourse separates itself from thought in an absolute manner, digging an irreducible distance between thought and that which it figures in the distance: 'Absolute difference, inconceivable in terms of formal logic, is established only by language. Language accomplishes a relation between terms that breaks up the unity of a genus' (1969: 195). Thought, therefore, sees itself as another. On this basis, it succeeds in putting itself at a distance, as if it were objectivising itself. But in separating itself in this manner, it also loses itself. Its own epiphany or revelation is its face. *Its own face*, but also thereby necessarily *a* face staring at it, which is no longer its own, but that of an other, that of the Other. The face appears; yet one cannot grasp it. It reveals itself but prohibits the face-to-face encounter or symmetry. It is a phenomenon, yet exceeds any image. It refuses to be possessed. It escapes my vision, yet looks at me and calls me to the highest responsibility: 'the other absolutely other – the Other [. . .] [calls for] responsibility' (1969: 197). Levinas concludes that this structure of visibility–invisibility is *the very structure of ethics*.

To formulate my question, I began by unfolding discourse and figure. This led me to understand their proximity and distance within face. The answer to my opening question is now clear: What the eye of discourse sees, what it sees of thought, is a particular figure, namely a face. It is a complex figure, which imagines and stares; which is someone, yet is no one; which is both me and other; which is secret and public; which withdraws (to hell, for example), yet which is in the world. It calls me to answer. The figure is the face of alterity. Before concluding, however, I ask myself, do *figure* and *face*[4] designate the *same* thing? I have shifted between one and the other – discourse-figure, discourse-face – as if they were one and the same. But even in the introduction to his book, Lyotard differentiates the concept of *figure* from the concept of *face*. Levinas too is careful to draw a rigorous distinction between figure and face. What is at stake is the meaning of *form*. For Lyotard, the face as defined by Levinas lacks form; it appears as a pure event without a contour and hence in the end without materiality. In *Totality and Infinity*, Levinas says, 'the face [. . .] breaks through the form that nevertheless delimits it' (1969: 198). The face 'explodes form', that is, the contours of figure and face that we usually take as synonymous with it. If indeed the face sees the eye of discourse when it tries to look at thought, then it is possible that it sees nothing and that in the end all thought dissipates. As Lyotard says in the opening section of *Discourse, Figure*: 'Wanting to promote oneself as a partisan of the event, or to predispose oneself to the event, is still an ethical delusion. It is a property of the bestowal to dispossess us – one cannot predispose oneself to dispossession' (2010: 18). In other words, not to want to figure or not to want to take the Other in form amounts to missing the Other.

Does the eye that sees thought see a figure or a face? The development of this single question has led me to posit the apparently irreconcilable difference between the two concepts, as if they are indeed two concepts. Does the eye of thought see a form, or does it just see something that starts from the explosion of all form?

I have not spoken about what I might name, pretentiously, my own thought. Nor shall I talk about it; I only mention it in conclusion. I am working on the concept of plasticity, which refers to both the formation of the figure and the explosion of all form. Should we not turn to this concept to attempt to think through figure and face together, to try to see thought in the process of grasping itself? This is an open-ended question, to which I shall not respond, as it is no doubt too early to do so, for I have only just begun to be able to see myself think.

Translated by Carolyn Shread

Notes

1 Coalescence: from the Latin *coalescere*, 'to grow with'. The knitting of two tissue surfaces that are in contact (for instance, two lips of a wound). A state of liquid particles in suspension joined in larger droplets. Contraction of two or more phonic elements in a single element (*Le Robert Dictionary* 1994: 395).
2 An intentional choice was made to use *herself* rather than the gender-neutral *himself or herself*. This is a political move, intended to inscribe both author and translator as women in the text; furthermore, given the personal voice of the essay, this choice also made stylistic sense –Translator.
3 Deleuze explains further that it is a 'pure staging without author, without actors and without subjects' (1984: 219).
4 In French, *figure* and *visage* have the same general meaning, but *face* is less 'plastic' than *figure*, which means something more designed, more shaped (as in painting), than does *face*. This is why Levinas always uses *face* and never *figure*.

2

Following Generation: Biological and Poetic Cloning

You're reading 'Autumn Crocuses', that Apollinaire poem. You didn't notice anything special, you didn't see anything, you passed right by it. There is, in lines 10–11, a small mystery. This mystery is held in the little phrase that runs: 'autumn crocuses which are like their mothers / Daughters of their daughters'. Now admit that you've never asked yourself what this could really mean, these 'mothers / Daughters of their daughters'. You're going to do just that right now, you're going to ask yourself that question now. Now? Yes, now, which is to say, afterwards.

Following in his footsteps, after him, 'he' being Lévi-Strauss, one of the first to have felt the need to investigate, concerning 'Autumn Crocuses', the mystery of 'A Small Mythico-Literary Puzzle' (a text published in *The View from Afar*). Lévi-Strauss does not present a reading of Apollinaire's entire poem, but only of this 'detail that has remained enigmatic to commentators. Why does the poet equate with autumn crocuses the epithet *mères filles de leurs filles* ("mothers daughters of their daughters")' (1985a: 211)? You are about to discover this enigma, after Lévi-Strauss.

You are, we are, part of the 'generation following' structuralism. The 'generation following' structuralism, its 'following generation', means, first of all, the descendants, the inheritors, the sons and daughters. Next, it means the process of education [*formation*], of engendering, of constituting the *following* itself, the form of posterity. 'Following generation' invites a reflection not only on what it might mean to inherit, but also on the shaping [*formation*] of the inheritance by its inheritor, on the fact that an inheritance – no matter what it may be – far from being entirely constituted, must again, in some way, be engendered, shaped, regenerated to be what it is – to be something given. This double game of passivity and of activity or spontaneity in inheritance will once more evoke the menacing motif of autumn crocuses, the mute cry of these flowers that arrive to interrupt the sequence of filiation and education

PLASTICITY

Les Colchiques	Autumn Crocuses
Guillaume Apollinaire	Trans. Oliver Bernard (2004: 36)
Le pré est vénéneux mais joli en automne	The meadow is poisonous but pretty in the autumn
Les vaches y paissant	The cows that graze there
Lentement s'empoisonnent	Are slowly poisoned
Le colchique couleur de cerne et de lilas	Meadow-saffron the colour of lilac and of shadows
Y fleurit tes yeux sont comme cette fleur-la	Under the eyes grows there your eyes are like those flowers
Violâtres comme leur cerne et comme cet automne	Mauve as their shadows and mauve as this autumn
Et ma vie pour tes yeux lentement s'empoisonne	And for your eyes' sake my life is slowly poisoned
Les enfants d l'école viennent avec fracas	Children from school come with their commotion
Vêtus de hoquetons et jouant de l'harmonica	Dressed in smocks and playing the mouth-organ
Ils ceuillent les colchiques qui sont comme des mères	Picking autumn crocuses which are like their mothers
Filles de leurs filles et sont sont couleur de tes paupières	Daughters of their daughters and the colour of your eyelids
Qui battent comme les fleurs battent au vent dément	Which flutter like flowers in the mad breeze blown
Le gardien du troupeau chante tout doucement	The cowherd sings softly to himself all alone
Tandis que lentes et meuglant les vaches abandonnent	While slow moving lowing the cows leave behind them
Pour toujours ce grand pré mal fleuri par l'automne	Forever this great meadow ill flowered by the autumn

Figure 2.1

so as to poison the order of succession. Here, in the fields of the poem, in its meadowlands, daughters are before mothers, sons before fathers.

But what does 'structuralism' mean? Without seeming to, that is fundamentally what Lévi-Strauss is asking himself here. The phrase 'mothers daughters of their daughters' corresponds to no existing kinship structure, no facts of lineage that the anthropologist might be able to study. Which is to say that, by building this phrase into the nucleus of the poem, Lévi-Strauss designates this imaginary family tie as a structure to come. The structure will come after, will follow kinship. This structure will certainly be one of new relationships between mothers and daughters, mothers and sons, mothers and fathers. Now, as you will see, by thus opening structure on to its future, Lévi-Strauss anticipates the very deconstruction of structuralism.

Afterwards you will no longer be able to come from, to follow from, to return to a tradition, to return to (your) reading in a state of perfect peace. You will no longer know what to keep and what to reformulate or recreate in an inheritance. You will no longer be certain of coming afterwards, of following, and of making up the posterity of these reading traditions that directly influenced your generation: structuralism, deconstruction, the thought (or thoughts) of difference. To read or understand a text may very well mean, *even today*, drawing out its structural nucleus. But this structure, as we will know forevermore, is not originary; it erupts in the text as a result, as the result of its own deconstruction. Structure, or the structural nucleus, thus arrives in some sense after that which it structures. Structure would then be that which remains of a text *after* its deconstruction. Structure therefore names that element of a text that survives its own deconstruction, something I call form, and that comes to light like an a posteriori metamorphosis. In this way, for example, I was able to read Hegel, or Heidegger, in the days that followed their deconstruction, beginning with or following on from that deconstruction, so as to see develop, through a work of *generation – that is, an a posteriori engendering* – if not something like a reconstruction (which would, strictly speaking, be nonsensical in this context), then something like a scar, tugging the skin of the text to distribute its meaning differently, to reveal within it a new organisation, to make possible in the very text different movements and different effects of truth. It is precisely this regenerative force of reading that I call plasticity.

You are going to discover, at work in a single autumn crocus, all sorts of plastic strategies of anticipation that make it difficult to pin down the time of generations. You are going to read the unrecorded history of this flower that speaks the truth of postmodernity.

Cloning

So, how are we to understand 'the autumn crocuses that are like mothers daughters of their daughters'? Lévi-Strauss begins by putting aside those readings of this phrase given by various commentators that prove to be untenable. According to some readers of the poem, 'mothers daughters of their daughters' would mean 'Mothers so outrageously made up that they would be mistaken for their daughters' (Lévi-Strauss 1985a: 211). Or, in yet another reading, the phrase would allude to some botanical peculiarity of the autumn crocus about which 'modern botanical works offer no enlightenment'. These interpretations, Lévi-Strauss says, are 'disarming', first of all because 'the autumn crocus has a discreet, delicate coloring' that would make it impossible to assimilate its tint to an excess of make-up, and then because the autumn crocus indeed has a unique botanical peculiarity that the author of the second interpretation doesn't seem to have taken the time to study.

The anthropologist will put forward three registers for understanding the mystery, thus constituting, as we have already suggested, the structural nucleus of the poem. Three different registers that are nevertheless tightly imbricated, each one in the other two: a botanical register, a theological or mystical register, and a formal symbolic register. We find ourselves, with these three registers, at the very heart of the question of the after that follows, which will reveal itself according to the law of a strange reversal. The daughter, once more, does not follow after the mother; instead, the mother follows after the daughter, is engendered by the daughter. Anteriority and posteriority intermingle in troubling ways. But, seen in another light, this intermingling is not what is truly disruptive. After all, if we understand that an inheritance is always to be regenerated, we can then say that the testator, meaning the author of the testament, is in some way a product of the legatee, and that – to return to the problem of reading – to interpret a text will always, one way or another, require engendering it like a child of whom the reader would properly be the father or the mother. No, what's really troubling is the way Lévi-Strauss shows that the generation of an after to follow is something so complex that it must be understood through several different orders – not merely the order of a reversal. When we investigate these orders, we'll see that the so-called 'structural analysis' developed here, far from being 'classic' or 'as expected', will deconstitute itself, by itself, somehow preventing us from thinking about its succession or about what it might be followed by.

Let's start with the first, botanical register. The phrase 'mothers daughters of their daughters' might first of all be explained by the peculiar way the autumn crocus has of being a kind of vegetal timebomb. We are in fact dealing here with a peculiar plant whose flowers appear before its leaves and whose leaves appear before its seeds: 'the flowers of the colchicum appear in autumn, several months before the leaves and the seeds, which come in the springtime of the following year' (Lévi-Strauss 1985a: 212–13). This time delay would itself be enough, the author continues,

> to explain the epithet 'mothers daughter of their daughters'. Botanists once used the term *Filius-ante-patrem* not only for the colchicum but also for the colt's-foot (*Tussilago*), the butterbur (*Petasites*) [*Encyclopédie Diderot-d'Alembert*, article: 'Fils avant le père'], and the epilobium or willow herb. The term may have been used either because the flowers of all these plants or their stems appear before the leaves, or because their fruit is wholly visible even before their blossoms open. Apollinaire was erudite enough to have encountered and chosen to employ these old terms. And, as I shall show, he had every reason to make them feminine. (1985a: 213)

Here, the inversion of the order of succession would seem obvious. In this botanical phenomenon, the after comes before the before. This confirms the hermeneutic law explored earlier by which a structure would not pre-exist a text but instead would somehow follow after it, as its a posteriori shaping. One single biological, poetic and structuralist fact becomes clear: sometimes, the seed comes last, the seeding [*semence*], a seminal reason, appears *after, follows*.

'That's what I'd call a catastrophe', Derrida confirms in *The Post Card* (1987: 28). Meaning, in the literal sense of the Greek work *catastrophè*, a reversal. There is an 'initiatory catastrophe', an originary reversal: the son comes before the father. Writing precedes speech, Plato comes before Socrates: these flowers had already been saying this, as were poems. A deconstructive drive is at work, everywhere: 'The one in the other, the one in front of the other, the one after the other, the one behind the other [. . .] this catastrophe, right near the beginning, this over-turning that I still cannot succeed in thinking was the condition for everything' (Derrida 1987: 19). It's so strange to *follow up on* a reading of Lévi-Strauss's text by rereading *The Post Card*, to *follow* Apollinaire's poem with Lévi-Strauss and then Derrida. A seed has already been planted, but where and how?

Indeed, how exactly? Because *catastrophic inversion isn't the autumn crocus's only ruse*. Lévi-Strauss writes: 'As we have noted, the flowers of the colchicum appear [. . .] several months before the leaves and seeds [. . .] Yet the seeds seem to play only a circumstantial role in reproduction' (1985a: 212–13). Thus, in the case of the autumn crocus we can't really speak of reproduction through seeds, or through seeding. We learn that the autumn crocus is a *hermaphroditic* flower with the distinctive property of reproducing itself underground through a *doubling of the corm*, a *splitting of its bulb*:

> Every year, the corm that has produced flowers and fruits is exhausted and is destroyed after this period, and replaced by another corm, which has developed right next to it; as a result of this annual renewal of the corms, which always occurs on the same side, the plant moves each year a distance the thickness of its corm. (1985a: 212)

So, there are two orders to be understood in the expression 'mothers daughters of their daughters': a *vertical* order, preceding in inversion – flower before leaf before seed; and a *horizontal* order – an underground doubling, which has nothing to do with inversion but instead proceeds through *reproduction of the identical*. Lévi-Strauss continues:

> [T]he autumn crocus belongs to the large family of *clones*; and we know how difficult, if not impossible, it is to distinguish the mothers and daughters

among several individuals. Certain grasses of the Gramineae family form a clone hundreds of metres long and going back more than a thousand years. In the United States, they have found a clone forest of almost fifty thousand aspens covering a total of nearly two hundred acres; another forest of aspen clones has been estimated to be eight thousand years old. In such cases, the distinction between absolutely or relatively adjacent generations loses all meaning. (1985a: 213, my emphasis)

We should remember that a clone, a word deriving from the Greek *klôn*, meaning 'shoot' or 'sprout', originally signifies the offspring of an individual as produced through vegetative reproduction (apomixis). This suggests that the autumn crocus's mode of reproduction consists in the union, in one single individual, of genealogical generation and generation by cloning (which we have called a vertical and a horizontal order), in such a way that the reversal, or the catastrophe, which makes the daughter precede the mother, is not only the order of inversion but also that of repetition. Wouldn't that mean that we, ourselves part of 'the following generation', would henceforth become beings capable of reproducing themselves in two ways, through 'natural' biological filiation and through cloning?

Lévi-Strauss, in his interpretation of Apollinaire's phrase that explores all of its duplicitousness – the monstrous extent of which, comparable to that of the aspen clones, we are only now beginning to measure – reflects (hence the importance of eyes in the poem) his position of reader and anthropologist. It's as if it were not possible to dissociate the reproductive peculiarity of the autumn crocus from the way in which the flower, somehow, investigates us investigating it. Now this specularity reveals that generating a reading comes back to letting oneself be poisoned by the double aporia of a genealogical inversion and the production of a stereotype. It's as if the poem reminds all those who might believe that they have produced a reading that they have done nothing more than come before the texts that they read, and, what's more, that they can do nothing else but clone those texts, mime them, ape them. Derrida also says this, in his way. The distinguishing feature of a postcard is (to be) always double: first, it is reversible (no front, no back, no father, no son); second, it is reproducible, and there will always be multiple copies of it, perfectly identical ones. But what brings *us* back, comes back *to us*, is the task of producing the reading of this simultaneity, of this contemporaneity of *two types of reproduction in one single subject, in one single biological and symbolic body.*

To come after or to follow would have, speaking literally, no meaning, but two possible directions: the father and the clone. Where, then, might plasticity reside, the plasticity that signifies suppleness, the possibility of receiving but also of giving form? What is a plastic reading, if it can form or reform nothing without marking dates or without cloning?

Autoplasty

Let's turn to the second register of meaning that Lévi-Strauss brings out in the phrase 'mothers daughters of their daughters': the theological or mystical register. The author begins by reminding his reader that in the Christian tradition, the Virgin Mary is simultaneously named 'daughter of God, mother of God'. We can read in pseudo-Augustinian that 'The creator has birthed the creator, the serving-girl has birthed the master, the daughter has birthed father: the daughter, from her divine nature; the mother, from her human nature' (Lévi-Strauss 1985a: 213–14). Lévi-Strauss highlights the phrase's general signification as an eternal auto-generation, evoking the case of the phoenix or certain Eastern gods. The autumn crocus would resemble these divine agencies who regenerate themselves without ageing.

> In a different, though still theological context the figure of speech is ancient: 'The Vedic Indians', notes Georges Dumézil, 'thought about the ability of fire [. . .] to renew itself, to engender itself endlessly'. Also, they called it Tanūnapāt, 'descendent of itself'. (1985a: 214)

The theme of auto-regeneration and auto-engendering appears here. The autumn crocus would somehow find itself invested with the power to be born again from its ashes. By the same token, the poem would become unattainable, unimpregnable, since it would be constantly regenerated, as if it weren't possible to open it, to tear open its fabric, as if reading had no power over it: no power to penetrate, hack into, or hold authority over it. The autoplastic text – since plasticity also designates the capacity of tissues to reform themselves after an injury – would have no need of an alloplastic reading. Here again, but in a different way than we encountered above, there would be neither before nor after. 'Thus, the crocuses figure as the stable and permanent element' – paradoxically, at once immortal and without any lineage – 'and, as such, give the poem its title' (1985a: 216). A poetic element that puts us at the heart of the question of childbirth, the motif of the autumn crocus, through its double generative dimension, paradoxically dismisses the play of life and death; it dismisses family, childhood, descent.

And in fact, having become 'the stable and permanent element', the motif of the autumn crocus finds itself between 'two slopes – the one ascending and the other descending' (1985a: 216): on the one hand, the children – 'children from school come with their commotion' – and, on the other, the cows destined to be poisoned – 'slow moving lowing the cows leave behind them forever this meadow ill flowered by the autumn'. The children (the 'male' element, Lévi-Strauss tells us), who 'will grow up and go away', are indeed – as full as they are of futurity – on the ascending slope. The cows, the female element, who 'are grazing to the slow beat of the anapest and will soon be slaughtered or poisoned', figure descent.[1] The author adds: 'Between these two slopes – the one ascending and the other descending' – and we can clearly see how the orders of anteriority and posterity are mobilised in both cases – 'only the autumn crocuses will remain, on a horizontal level, both literally and figuratively: by being stationary, or almost so, on the surface of the ground (the successive plants being displaced by the thickness of a corm); and by reproducing themselves as identical entities' (1985a: 216). This potential of the autumn crocuses to annul precisely that which they figure by their excess (reproduction, birth and death) drives Lévi-Strauss to tackle the final register of meaning of the phrase 'mothers daughters of their daughters': the formal symbolic register. 'Here, consequently, only the autumn crocuses have full and complete value as a sign' (1985a: 216).

Presence

We have to hear, in this word 'sign', the resonance of the structural understanding of the sign as a reversible entity, through which signified and signifier can invert or reverse themselves in turn. The autumn crocuses do indeed appear, in the light of a structuralist reading, simultaneously as the signifier of the poem (its metaphor, its more eloquent or meaningful element) and as its signified; this reversibility poses the question of descent or lineage, or rather of the impossible possibility of lineage or of following generation(s). From this formal value of reversibility, Lévi-Strauss turns to the mathematician René Thom, who declares:

> In the interaction of signified and signifier [*signifié-signifiant*] it is plain that, swept along by the universal flow, the signified emits, engenders the signifier in an uninterrupted, ramifying wilderness. But the signifier re-engenders the signified every time we interpret the sign. And, as exemplified by biological forms, the signifier (the offspring) can become the signified (the parent); all it takes is a single generation. (Lévi-Strauss 1985a: 216, translation modified)

As we are remarking here, what is truly vertiginous in Lévi-Strauss's analysis and in his reference to René Thom is that the affirmation of the reversibility of the signified and the signifier is already in itself a deconstructive affirmation. Indeed, Derrida ceaselessly affirmed that the signifier is not, as was traditionally thought, the simple double, the simple representative, with no consistency of its own, of the signified; that the signifier's value is not merely that of referring to an idealised presence. Particularly in *Of Grammatology*, Derrida demonstrates how the signifier and signified are at bottom the two – reversible – faces of a single reality. To affirm that the signified and signifier can invert themselves, can take each other's places, is to attack the privileged position of the signifier and to trouble the value of presence assigned to the signifier: '*What broaches the movement of signification is what makes its interruption impossible. The thing itself is a sign*' (Derrida 1997: 49).

Now this is what Lévi-Strauss sees, perfectly, here, and he might see even further by helping us discover that the reversibility of signified and signifier leads us back to the divine, royal motif of infinite regeneration and immortality: *presence*. A presence that is somehow impossible to deconstruct, because it springs from its own deconstruction; a presence always renewed, because it holds the secret and power of its own cloning of itself. Between the children and the cows, the autumn crocuses don't budge, don't die, they remain, immutable horizon of meaning, seemingly capable of reconstituting themselves ad infinitum, death without death [*mort sans mort*]. The profanation of God practised by structuralism and deconstruction here turns on itself to reveal a sacredness hidden in the poem, going by the name of the reversibility of signified and signifier, stitching itself together even as it undoes its weave. And here again, Derrida will himself observe – running ahead of or following after Lévi-Strauss – the text's astonishing power to regenerate itself. In *Dissemination* he declares that the text reconstitutes itself 'as an organism [. . .] There is always a surprise in store for the anatomy or physiology of any criticism that might think it had mastered the game, surveyed all the threads at once' (1981: 63).

Henceforth our starting question – what does 'following after' signify? – receives more and more complex answers that all point towards the complicated problem of a reproductive dualism that seems, through its excess, to bring reproduction to a halt, to arrive at the impassable serenity of a full yet deconstructed presence, a presence full of its own deconstruction. All certitude about the order in which generations succeed each other is impossible. All escape from cloning – hermeneutic or otherwise – is impossible. These two impossibilities, which mark our *generation*, infinitely blur, as we clearly see, the concept of inheritance or heritage which provided us with our departure point. The children will grow up, they will die, cows will be slaughtered, autumn crocuses will remain, semantic venom, symbolic venom that, by its very fragility, its paleness, resists like scotch grass [*un chiendent*], that weed of the neverending. This resistance, another absence of any way out, sets up once more, back-to-back, in yet one more reversibility, the eternity of presence and the profane banality or finitude of the postcard: signified on one side, signifier on the other. Vedic god, Virgin Mary versus floral stock photos on a merry-go-round. Indivisibility of the phoenix, infinite divisibility of the cards that can always be cut. Same difference. Like those eyelids that open and close themselves, 'which flutter like flowers in the mad breeze blown'.

'It is a matter of causing the form that follows presence to arise in works' – that's what I affirmed in my text-manifesto *Plasticity at the Dusk of Writing* (2010: 57, translation modified). But what could such a phrase really mean if it is true that the recall of presence produced when we discover the reversibility of the sign's compositors perhaps *re-engenders* not presence itself but a troubling permanence? In the end, in another aporia, what would it mean to want to think the after, the following of structuralism and deconstruction, if it is true that, as his reading of 'Autumn Crocuses' testifies, Lévi-Strauss reveals himself to be *a few steps ahead of* Derrida? The so-called structuralist reading of Apollinaire's poem is a lecture which, in many respects, inherits its strategies from deconstructive reading, which, nevertheless, follows after it. A place is staked out, in a text, for its off-centre or eccentric centre, and the analysis of this text finds something like its most efficient and most deficient, its most manifest and most hidden point. By fingering the autumn crocuses as what Derrida will name 'supplement', hasn't Lévi-Strauss anticipated those developments (which will be found mainly in *Of Grammatology*) concerning the 'exorbitant' character of all offensive – which is to say, truly critical – readings?

And, for that matter, how could we forget that *Of Grammatology* develops a criticism of Lévi-Strauss according to which he would not have thought of precisely the transcendental anteriority of writing to speech? Doesn't the text we're reading here undo this criticism by going all the way to the very deconstruction of structures of kinship? Aren't we being confronted by a reversibility of structuralism and deconstruction, something that would be like the echo of the reversibility of signified and signifier?

Twinness

In this way, for us to follow after, there would only be two possibilities. The first would be pure and simple rumination, cloning understood in the most primary meaning of faithful copying. We would infinitely return to an assessment made in *Dissemination*:

> To a considerable degree, we have already said all we *meant to say* [. . .] With the exception of this or that supplement, our questions will have nothing more to name but the texture of the text, reading and writing, mastery and play, the paradoxes of supplementarity, and the graphic relations between the living and dead [. . .] Since we have already said everything, the reader must bear with us if we continue on a while. If we extend ourselves by force of play. (Derrida 1981: 65)

Nothing would remain for us but to say how a text is made, how its texture is elaborated, according to the law of a reversal of before and after between structure and arche-writing. What Lévi-Strauss, speaking of the autumn crocuses, calls the 'generative cell' of the poem or text would reveal, as an end result, nothing but a generation of the identical, not leaving very much space for or not giving much of a chance (in the sense of formative possibility) to succeeding or inheriting readers. In fact, we can very well ask ourselves if it's even relevant today for us to try to produce new readings – for us, who follow after thinkers, writers or authors who have all produced so many clones. Consequently, it's clear that to recover the generative cell of a text, its structure or its cornerstone, for all that it is an indispensable move, cannot all by itself produce novelty – it cannot in itself produce posterity.

The second possibility hangs on a change in the way we are looking at things. If it's true that our works are always older than us, if it's true that we mime what we read, if it's true that we chew the cud, if it's true that a text always regenerates itself like a phoenix or like an everyday postcard that always holds one side back, then maybe we cannot escape these aporias – but we might try to sidestep them. It's time to stop thinking of cloning in terms of the pure and simple identical replica. The clone clearly has something of difference in it, and the chief issue of the times to come will be to draw out the proper site of this difference. It suffices to remark that Lévi-Strauss says nothing about the poem's melancholy, which is certainly linked to the amorous suffering being expressed but also to the ineluctable necessity of leaving the autumn crocuses, of leaving behind forever this great meadow ill flowered by the autumn. Which is to say that the duplication leaves us a chance, lets us go. Lets us follow along with our own lives.

Clones (and you shouldn't limit yourself to hearing, in this word, the name given to certain plants; it includes also the possibility of reproductive cloning and its accessories) are certainly conforming copies. But fundamentally, the fact that it's possible to become daughter of your daughter, to be simultaneously older and younger than yourself, to auto-clone yourself in some way, effectively creates a *displacement by the thickness of a corm*; it produces difference not in the sense to which we have become accustomed by good old DNA and other such kinds of code – a difference between individuals – but a difference *between code and message*. What allows us to think about the transfer of the nucleus in cloning is not so much the repetitive and stereotyped character of the results of this transfer, as scientific doxa repeats over and over again, but the fact that the nucleus is, precisely, transferable, displaceable, that birth can follow from a demobilisation, from *a non-disseminatory difference between the nucleus and itself*. The question, consequently, is no longer one of knowing how to differentiate between two individuals who resemble each other but of knowing how to interrogate the way in which the same transfers itself to remain the same in the other. We might not ask ourselves any more if clones are really twins, but instead how the phenomenon of cloning allows us to take twinness as the model of truth. Plasticity, from the perspective of such an investigation, would no longer be linked to the movement of an eternal post-postmodern ruminating rehearsal, but to the eruption of a reversibility between before and after that modernises posterity by giving new forms to atomised, nuclear sameness – whether it be vegetal, logical or ontological. *Following this*, it will be the atoms that split us.

Translated by Simon Porzak

Note

1 *Anapest* (from the Greek *anapaïstos*, 'struck back, reversed') is an ancient term of poetry referring to a metrical foot consisting of two short syllables followed by a long one.

3

Philosophy in Erection: Derrida's Columns

I had thought initially that situating myself between two columns or two erections would be a most pleasurable position, but I discovered that it was not so simple – too many erections transcendentalise erection itself, thus paralysing desire. 'A scandalizing question traverses the text', Derrida writes. 'How can one be the father of two phalli, erected one against the other' (1986: 175a)?[1] This question immediately raises another one: how is it possible to write two texts at the same time? How is it possible to stay here, in the middle, between two phalluses and two texts? Not so simple, as I said, but perhaps even more pleasurable, for that very reason.

I

The question is how to avoid falling, how to prevent the object from falling, and what should we do with what falls down nevertheless? This question is one of desire, how to prevent desire from falling, how to prevent the object of desire from falling, and what we can do with fallen objects of desire? How is it possible to keep desire alive, to preserve it in its full force and energy?

Two sides of *Glas*, its two columns, Hegel and Genet, provide two different answers. Each time, the issue of the *transcendental* is addressed, even (more) where the text seems as far as possible from it.

There seem to be two main ways of preventing something from falling. First, by maintaining the object in connection with other things, so that these other things hold it, secure it, bind it. Such a totality forms a system. Second, by cutting the whole structure into small pieces, like a sheet of paper, so that everything – that is, nothing in particular – falls down. If everything is cut or torn into pieces, then everything, that is, nothing in particular, falls.

Philosophy on the one hand: Hegel and his system. Literature on the other: Genet and his pieces and fragments. Attachment and detachment.

Of course, while reading *Glas*, we constantly find something from the right side sneaking on to the left side and vice versa. As opposed as they may seem in the first place, the two processes – systematisation and fragmentation – are versions of the same problem: *erection*. For the first time in the history of philosophy, with *Glas*, erection appears as a metaphysical and ontological issue, whether the issue of the end of metaphysics or ontology itself.

This problem will be presented through two main moments, each of them being divided in two and each time extended or stretched between Hegel and Genet. Each time the relationship between erection and the transcendental will be examined.

System (Hegel)

Derrida understands *Aufhebung* as the movement of an erection, at once architectural and sexual. We know that, literally, *Aufhebung* means suppressing, preserving and lifting up in the sense of picking up what falls on to the ground in order to secure it by putting it in a higher place. If Derrida chooses the word 'erection' as another translation for *Aufhebung* (the first being, as we know, 'sublation'), it is first because, according to Derrida, dialectical negativity is what accomplishes this lifting up or picking up by building a column, a monument (be it a grave, a crypt or a pyramid) in which the fallen object is firmly maintained or held up as remains connected to the whole, while the whole is raised to a higher ground all together. Dialectics operates, as Derrida himself noted, by raising or erecting that which falls. This movement is at the same time that of desire, a permanent desire, which Derrida understands as a constant phallic erection.

We find here the double meaning of the verb *bander* in French, which is translated in the English version of *Glas* as 'band erect', which means both sexual erection, to have a hard-on, and the act of mummifying or wrapping something in bandages, thus evoking the double operation of desire and preservation.

According to Derrida, in Hegel the double meaning, architectural and sexual, of dialectical erection finds its noetic or philosophical equivalent in the act of interiorising or idealising the object:

> This appropriation that, in order to keep upright, to have constancy, essence, existence, substance, makes it necessary to be raised into its contrary, this appropriation is also an interiorization and an idealization: a magnification, since here the ideal causes growth, enlargement. Negativity erects one in the other. (1986: 13a)

Erection is also spiritual, which divides spirit into a passive and an active side, to the extent that philosophical speculation is spirit's self-penetration (which is different from masturbation): the object has to be interiorised, locked up in a crypt, received in order to be able to be retrieved, reactivated, enlarged.[2]

Phallogocentric idealisation is presented as the possibility for spirit to 'continue to enjoy itself' (1986: 72a). Again, there is a strong link between sexual erection and systematisation, holding of the falling part in a column, a coffin, any rigid tomb or crypt.

Phallic Circulation (Genet)

The Genet side, on the other hand, is about preventing something from falling by tearing off the whole system or structure, so that everything collapses and the isolated part that initially detached itself and fell down becomes indistinguishable from the rest. Derrida therefore insists upon proliferation, dissemination, multiplicity as being central motifs in Genet's work, a work which itself has undergone fragmentation. *Glas* follows the structure of Genet's projected book on Rembrandt called *What Remains of a Rembrandt Torn into Four Equal Pieces and Flushed down the Toilet*. In 1964 Genet was preparing a study on Rembrandt when his young partner, Abdallah Bentaga, committed suicide. Genet was utterly shocked and thought of giving up writing. He consequently destroyed the Rembrandt manuscript, but two fragments that he had already given to a publisher remained. These two fragments were published in *Tel Quel* in 1967. Genet organised them in two columns, one responding to the other. We may also remember that Genet's first novel, *Our Lady of the Flowers*, was written in prison over an extended period, since his manuscripts were constantly confiscated by prison officials. Jean-Paul Sartre writes in *Saint Genet*:

> French prison authorities, convinced that 'work is freedom', give the inmates paper from which they are required to make bags. It was on this brown paper that Genet wrote, in pencil, *Our Lady of the Flowers*. One day, while the prisoners were marching in the yard, a turnkey entered the cell, noticed the manuscript, took it away, and burned it. Genet began again. Why? For whom? There was small chance of his keeping the work until its release, and even less of getting it printed. If, against all likelihood, he succeeded, the book was bound to be banned; it would be confiscated and scrapped. Yet he wrote on, he persisted in writing. Nothing in the world mattered to him except those sheets of brown paper which a match could reduce to ashes. (2012: 9)

Derrida makes several allusions to the Rembrandt book and to its fragmentation:

> 'What Remained of a Rembrandt' develops over its two columns a theory or an event of general equivalence: of subjects – 'every man *is worth* another' – of terms, of contraries exchanged without end, of the '*je m'ec. . .*' ('je m'écoulais,' 'I was flowing' in my body, in the body of the other). (1986: 43b)

Here, in the right-hand column, erection, like writing, becomes a means to maintain torn pieces in their togetherness, to preserve them from dispersion in the paradoxical absence of totality, in the flux, or 'flow'. Everything remains, the whole is a remainder: anti-dialectical relationship to duration and time. What substitutes for the system is substitution itself. Erection is maintained through the continuous change of partners and lovers, all of them substituting for one another ('every man *is worth* another'). Desire's presence circulates through the multiplicity of intercourses:

> The 'inmate', the 'circle of inmates' who stand up straight, resembling one another and substituting for one another in silence like letters on the page, one in place of another, one counting for another, the glob that resounds in cadence off the walls of the grotto like a moiled, guttural, hard and coated *glas.* . . (Derrida 1986: 38b)

Further on:

> But really, like some kind of vermin ready to scamper away: little wheels, little stars, little screws, little worms, little nails, gobs and gobs [. . .] All those little fetuses, penises or clitorises at once living and dead, screws and worms [*vers*], crawling without tail or head, dispensing with tail and head in order to threat their way through your fingers and make their way everywhere, are encased inside one another in trompebelly [*en trompe ventre*]. (1986: 122–3b)

Here, erection is maintained through infinite spacing, punctuating holes made by cuts, amputations, missing limbs, stumps, decapitations. Each time, like the rhythm of all these creatures, the multiplicity of lovers, of the lovers' names, resonate: Darling (Mignon), Divine, First Communion, Mimosa, Our Lady of the Flowers, Milord the Prince, Stilitano, Harcamone.

We cannot help but evoke the fact that *Glas* has been read as a confrontation between heterosexuality and homosexuality: according to its usual representation, heterosexuality means gathering, marriage, children, family (Hegel), while queer means dissemination, multiplicity, detachment, penises then becoming lumps, or amputated members, or cut flowers (in Genet). We propose to read this confrontation as instead a confrontation between two perspectives on the transcendental.

Transcendental Fetishism

We therefore have the two columns, with their respective concepts of erection and their particular relationships to desire, to the fall and to preservation. This seems clear and unambiguous. Each author in his place. Why, then, does Derrida constantly speak of erection as a 'problem'? We find the answer in the very opening of the book. Speaking about the two sides, Derrida declares:

> The first assures, guards, assimilates, interiorizes, idealizes, relieves the fall [*chute*] into the monument. There the fall maintains, embalms, and mummifies itself, monumemorizes and names itself – falls (to the tomb(stone)) [*tombe*]. Therefore, but as a fall, it erects itself there. The other – lets the remain(s) fall. Running the risk of coming down to the same. (1986: 1–2b)

The problem is that the two columns seem to come down to or amount to the same (in French, *revenir au même*) at the very moment when they seem to radically differ or diverge. This problem is also presented as that of a certain contagion between the two sides. Why this risk? Why is there a risk of contagion and of similarity?

Erection is subjected to the very threat that it is supposed to be protected from, or offer protection from. Erection can decrease, fall, the column may collapse, the penis become flaccid. Erection is supposed to prevent something from falling but itself needs to be protected from its own fall. Erection is not something that would remain untouched, unaltered by its own function; instead, it has the same destiny as what it is supposed to guard against, falling. We remember that the word 'phallus' initially designates 'image of the penis' but also what can fall – from the Latin, *fallere*. The armour is vulnerable and susceptible to suffer from the same wound as the one that may affect its inside.

'Can an object comprehend what it is the object of?', Derrida asks (1986: 205b). The answer is negative. The death toll, the *glas*, of erection resonates within erection itself as the threat of its own decline. What does this threat mean? Does it mean the impossibility of detaching anything from the whole if what protects the whole against detachment is itself a part of the whole, that is a detachable part? Is erection doomed to become a metonymy? We would then have a hyper-Genetian element to the issue of desire's preservation. The system is doomed to fail as it necessarily detaches itself from itself. Nevertheless, this hyper-Genetian vision immediately inverts itself in a hyper-Hegelian one. If erection can be detachable from the whole, it becomes at the same time the privileged morsel among them all, since it is supposed, through its own detachment, to protect the system against detachment. Erection then becomes the most significant fragment. The most detachable part. The essential part. A surplus, an excess, that is also what most *systematically* attaches detachment to itself. Here, of course, we think of the psychoanalytic use and understanding of the phallus.

Erection is, then, *at the same time* what disrupts the totality on the one hand, and that which undermines the neutrality of the dissemination on the other. Phallogocentrism is impossible in its very concept.

We are confronted with the monstrous presence of both a metonymic *and* essentialising surplus effect, a monster that Derrida calls the *fetish*. Erection cannot help but become fetishised. Dialectics and perhaps literature itself cannot help but be fetishist. A fetish has a paradoxical and contradictory status: it is both something that can be detached from a series of terms, thus occupying a privileged position, *and* something that can play as a substitute for any other part. A *singular neutral* (a *'singularité quelconque'*, as Jean-Luc Nancy would say). It is an object that can be subtracted from the whole as the distinguished and pre-eminent element to which everything else can be attached or re-attached. The economy of the fetish is that of 'a detachment in chains' – a contradiction in terms (Derrida 1986: 136b).

This helps us to measure the exact distance that separates the penis from the phallus: the phallus is the detachable form of the penis, and is not therefore reserved for men alone. It is the non-anatomical, symbolic, iterable element, particular and essential, *absolute*.

The fetish effect (which perfectly equates to the phallus effect), by which something is both perfectly removable and indispensable, essential, hyper-detachable and hyper-attaching, is what Derrida also calls the *'transcendental effect'* of erection. The fetish is the modern name of the transcendental. Derrida speaks of the transcendental effect that always accompanies taking part, but also asks: 'How can a part take part, be party to?' (1986: 15b).

Glas confronts us with the transcendental value of erection and with erection as the transcendental value. *The problem is that both Hegel and Genet want, precisely, to avoid the fetishist economy of the transcendental.*

For Hegel, the transcendental is by definition the outside or outsider of all systems, what falls down from the system. Against the Kantian vision of a priori given laws and structures of thinking, Hegel affirms that everything may become incorporated into the system. There can be no such thing as a transcendental exteriority or priority to the absolute. Derrida writes:

> the transcendental or the repressed [. . .] the unthought or the excluded [. . .] organizes the ground to which it does not belong.

> What speculative dialectics means (to say) is that the crypt can still be incorporated into the system. The transcendental or the repressed, the unthought or the excluded must be assimilated by the corpus, interiorized as moments, idealized in the very negativity of their labour. (1986: 166a)

Genet, for his part, escapes the transcendental economy by substituting a substitute for the substitute, by replacing a part with another part, by creating a confusion between fetish, pastiche and postiche, for example by calling the erected penis a flower, thus adding a supplementary trope to the trope to occult the 'taking part effect'. Nothing can be placed in a privileged position from the outset.

A strikingly beautiful passage illustrates the redoubling of the fetish by which the fetish is rejected and annulled:

> 'Inside his trousers was pinned [*épinglé*] one of those postiche clusters of thin cellulose grapes stuffed with wadding [. . .] Whenever some queer at the Criolla, excited by the swelling, put his hand on the fly, his horrified fingers would encounter this object, which they feared to be a cluster of his true treasure, the branch on which, comically, too much fruit was hanging.
>
> '[. . .] So, I unhooked the cluster [. . .] but, instead of putting it on the mantelpiece as usual and laughing (for we would burst out [*éclations*] laughing and joke during the operation), I could not restrain myself from keeping it in my cupped hands and laying my cheek against it. Stilitano's face above me turned hideous.
>
> '"Drop it, you bitch!"
>
> 'In order to open the fly, I had squatted on my haunches, but Stilitano's fury, had my usual fervor been insufficient, made me fall to my knees. That was the position which, facing him, I used to take mentally in spite of myself. I didn't budge. Stilitano struck me with his two feet and his one fist. I could have escaped. I remained there.
>
> '"The key's in the door", I thought.' (Derrida 1986: 210–11b)

Violence is done to the fetish. Stilitano is playing with the fetish effect of the postiche grapes, but part of the game consists in forbidding his lover's desire for the fetish. Here, at this specific point, Derrida is doubtful: can we ever drop the fetish? Is it really possible to ban and annul, even in using violence, the fetishising effect of erection? In other terms, can we avoid referring to the transcendental? Derrida goes on: 'Isn't there always an element excluded from the system that assures the system's space of possibility? The transcendental has always been, strictly, a transcategorical, what could be received, formed, terminated in none of the categories intrinsic to the system. The system's vomit' (1986: 162a). Contrary to what Hegel affirms, the system would not have been able to function without the presence of what it rejects, without the transcendental status of the remainder. We are left without choice. Derrida goes on:

> each time a discourse *contra* the transcendental is held, a matrix – the (con)striction here – constrains the discourse to place the non-transcendental, the outside of the transcendental field, the excluded, in the structuring position. The matrix in question constitutes the excluded as transcendental of the transcendental, as imitation transcendental, transcendental contra-band. (1986: 244a)

The fetish should be dialectically sublatable and sublated. As we said, for Hegel there cannot be any inassimilable object or moment in the system: 'If the fetish substitutes itself for the thing itself in its manifest presence, in its truth, there should no longer be any fetish as soon as there is truth, the presentation of the thing itself in its essence' (1986: 209a). Nevertheless, Derrida states the impossibility of avoiding the transcendental effect, even in a philosophy such as the Hegelian one that presents itself as a critique of the transcendental. Such a critique would always negatively fetishise the transcendental in one way or another. Hence the impossibility, for Hegel, of avoiding writing prefaces to his books. Even if his prefaces always thematise the uselessness of all prefaces, they remain what they are a priori: moments in some way or other, or transcendental methodological warnings against the transcendental.

Here, we see that metaphysics and psychoanalysis share broadly the same concept, reading or understanding, to the extent that the transcendental value of the phallus in psychoanalysis is the inverted image of the phallic value of the transcendental within metaphysics. Both work as hermeneutical keys or tools. It is always in prefaces and introductions that Hegel, for example, exposes his key concepts. 'The key is in the lock.' The part becomes the essential part, the essential key to understand the whole, the erected way to penetrate erection itself. In philosophy as in psychoanalysis, it always seems possible to find the key, the essential part. Concerning Lacan's reading of Genet, Derrida writes:

> A note from Jacques Lacan's *Ecrits* [. . .] names this object 'that we could not designate better than by calling it the universal phallus (just as we say: universal key)'.
>
> This transcendental key, the condition of all determined signifiers and the concatenation of the chain, was prescribed and inscribed, but as a piece of an effect in the text, was enchained, entrained in the *Miracle of the Rose*. (1986: 29–30b)

Nevertheless, is it so simple to avoid privileging an element in a chain? Is interpretation possible without this freezing of one word, one motif, one key?

Is not Derrida himself practising a fetishist reading of Genet when he chooses to pick up the image of the flower, for example, as a major figure of the text? By doing so, isn't he erecting a new anti-Hegelian idol, a new statue on the right-hand column of his text? Perfectly aware of such risks, Derrida speaks to us and to himself when he asks:

> Are you going to *fall* precipitously into the trap? And translate The Flower, which signifies (symbolizes, metaphorizes, metonymizes, and so on) the phallus, once caught in the syntax of the cuttable-culpable, signifies death, decapitation, decollation? Anthologos signifying the signifier signifying castration? (1986: 27–8b, my emphasis)

Success?

Obviously, Derrida thinks he can avoid the reductiveness of such a risk. With *Glas*, he is clearly looking for another way of enjoying, loving, having sex, writing, reading – a way of accepting the fall, the dropping of the object. Let the object go! This ecstatic dispossession is still an erection, but this time there is no need to maintain, to retain or to preserve it fully; let's make do with the remainder, the remnant, *le reste*, let's learn how to desire it, to develop a neither attachable nor detachable *jouissance*, a free-floating reading of pleasure. Deconstruction as a meaningless erection: 'Trying to *think* [. . .] a suspended remain(s). Which would not be: not presence, not substance, nor essence. In general, what remains is thought to be permanent, substantial, subsistent. Here the remain(s) would not remain in that sense' (1986: 226a).

This remains would even cease falling: 'the remain(s), it must be added, would not fall' (1986: 226a). On the same page, in the Genet column: 'As soon as the thing itself, in its unveiled truth, is already found engaged, by the very unveiling, in the play of supplementary difference, the fetish no longer has any rigorously decidable status. *Glas* of phallogocentrism' (1986: 226b). The *glas* is, of course, the bell-toll of old hermeneutics. But Derrida also knows that by introducing a signature in Hegel, or a flower in Genet, he perhaps just repeats the traditional reading. Does he then succeed in keeping his desire alive? Does he maintain his erection in dropping meaning, symbols, metaphors, negativity, keys, parts or wholes?

Genet says: 'I do not think they [flowers] symbolize anything', and Derrida echoes this: 'Thus, in (the) place of the flower, the anthographic, marginal and paraphing text: which no longer signifies' (1986: 31b, 30b).

Can we help transcendentalising? Derrida doubts it: 'I am only good for embalming' (1986: 31b). We then gradually understand that *Glas* is a text about failure, the failure to relinquish the transcendental, the failure to deconstruct fetishism, to protect erection from phallogocentrism and symbolism.

Derrida is certain that Genet, for all these reasons perhaps, won't ever read or digest *Glas*: 'he will vomit all that for me, he will not read, will not be able to read. Do I write *for him*? What would I like to do to him? do to his "work"? Ruin it by erecting it perhaps' (1986: 200b). Or:

> I do not know if I have sought to understand him. But if he thought I had understood him, he would not support it, or rather he would like not to support it. What a scene. He would not support what he likes to do himself. He would feel himself already entwined. Like a column, in a cemetery, eaten by an ivy, a parasite that arrived too late. (1986: 203b)

The same reservations might apply to Hegel. Hegel would certainly not have liked *Glas*, which would have appeared to him as the very expression of bad infinity: 'I win and lose, in every case, my prick' (Derrida 1986: 66b).

In the end, we see that situating oneself between two erections and two texts is not as pleasurable a position as one might have first thought. The leading question, which is still mine today, the question which keeps us erect, is the following: has deconstruction succeeded in relinquishing the transcendental? This question will long haunt both philosophy and literature.

Notes

1. Derrida's *Glas* is written in two columns – a left column and a right column. Citations from the left column are indicated with the letter 'a' and citations from the right column are indicated with the letter 'b' – Editor.
2. The division between a passive and an active dimension of spirit echoes Hegel's analysis of feminine and masculine sexuality, as analysed by Derrida (1986: 113a).

4

The Possibility of the Worst: On Faith and Knowledge

There is always *another* possibility. Such is, in the simplest terms, how I would summarise Jacques Derrida's ultimate teaching. This phrase, 'there is always another possibility', is one that we are able to conjugate in every tense. In a certain sense, it is time itself – a sort of transcendental schematism that secretly governs the categories of deconstruction.

There is always another possibility. In the present tense, this means: There is always something other than what is. In the future tense, this means: Another order of things may come to pass, even if one is unable to 'see it coming'. This other possibility is the absolute *arrivant*, which Derrida has also called 'the promise'. A promise can be a promise of good fortune or happiness; it can also be the possibility of the worst, or what Derrida, after Kant, calls radical evil.

There is always another possibility. In the past tense, this means: Our entire history, everything that ever was or has been, could have happened differently. A totally other possibility could have oriented history, which would have brought about another order of things. Other events could have taken place, which would have constituted another tradition. This concept of 'the other possibility' is not equivalent to the traditional concept of 'the possible', which, in the history of philosophy, is coupled with those of necessity and actuality. The other possibility, the totally other possibility, would be that to which no other category could possibly correspond – neither the necessary, nor the actual, not even the impossible.

Derrida tells us that we can do nothing but believe in this other possibility. What are the modalities of such a belief? This is the question to which I would like to respond here. In particular, I would like to examine the motifs of possibility and belief, of faith and the promise, such as they are embedded in Derrida's late texts. Even if it is clearly illegitimate to distinguish between different 'periods' in his oeuvre, it is nevertheless imperative to recognise the different emphases that exist within it. One notices that the immense problematic of the 'messianic', which bears precisely upon both possibility and belief, insists urgently in his last texts and casts new light on that problematic of the trace. Texts such as 'Circumfession' (1993), *Specters of Marx* (2006), 'Khōra' (1995), 'Faith and Knowledge' (2002), 'A Certain Impossibility of Saying the Event' (2007) and 'Marx & Sons' (2008) – to name a few – are the clearest evidence of the privilege bestowed upon 'the crude word' (Derrida 1993: 3).[1]

One of the striking features of these texts is the link Derrida establishes between the *other possibility*, *belief* and *denial* [*denegation*].[2] Let us begin by being more specific about the link that directly connects belief and denial. Believing in something always amounts to considering that something to be undeniable. Conversely, an affirmation of the undeniable always entails an act of faith. The undeniable and the believed-in go hand in glove with the possible. To believe in something is to believe that it is possible. And yet what does it mean to say that a possibility is undeniable? In 'Faith and Knowledge', Derrida answers: 'One can *not* deny it, which means that the most one can do is to deny it' (2002: 94). Which always means, at the same time, that one can *only* deny it. Any affirmation of the undeniable necessarily requires some form of negation in order to be expressed – one can *not* deny it – and therefore always itself constitutes a denial: to say that a possibility is undeniable is 'another way of saying that one cannot avoid denying it: one can only deny it' (Derrida 2008b: 166). Or, put differently, 'There can only be denial of this undeniable' (Derrida 2008b: 155). Are we able to believe in the other possibility? Are we able not to believe in it? These two questions, in a certain sense, amount to the same thing.

This inescapable logic of denial, of course, applies to any determinate belief, to any act of faith, and to religious faith in particular. But every particular case proceeds from what could be called a transcendental condition: to affirm the undeniable character of a possibility and believe in it, whatever it may be, necessarily amounts to postulating that it may happen – not, strictly speaking, in the sense of being fully realised, but in the sense of producing an event. To believe is always to believe in the future; such is the foundation of all messianism. That the totally other may finally, or once again, come to pass: this is the undeniable. Totally other, in this instance, indicates something other than what is, what was, or what could be expected.

The totally other refers not only to the future of expectation, but also to the possibility of a totally other *beginning*. To believe – for this is indeed the transcendental horizon of faith – is always to harbour faith in *another source*: that everything might have been different, that history might have happened

THE POSSIBILITY OF THE WORST

otherwise. The possibility of another tradition. The possibility of what Derrida, in *Athens, Still Remains* (2010), calls 'the other chance'. In this text, the philosopher evokes the death of Socrates:

> The way in which this poor Socrates, between the verdict and the passing of the sails off Cape Sounion, believed that by not fleeing or saving his skin he was saving himself and saving within him, at he same moment, philosophy [...] But as for me, I persist in believing that philosophy might have another chance. (2010: 59)

'I persist in believing that philosophy might have another chance': this is the paradigmatic example of an undeniable affirmation, the classic example of an utterance of belief. Socrates could have escaped – one can believe that, it is undeniable. And one can do so even if Socrates affirms the contrary, even if, in the *Crito*, he declares that it is in conformity with the principle of the good that he stay seated in his prison cell, that *there is no other possibility*. Despite his words, it is always and forever possible to believe that philosophy could have had another chance or another fate. One can believe it; one can only believe it. One cannot, and can only, deny it.

Denial is born in this strange place where the very concept of birth trembles, in the vacillation provoked by the vertiginous question that cannot help but haunt every tradition, every history, every genesis and every sequence of events. The question is the following: *What, then, if something else had occurred, something totally other, something entirely unforeseen and absolutely different from all that has happened?* A question which also, at the same time, opens on to the future: *What, then, if something else – the totally other, the other chance, the other possibility – were possible to happen?* One cannot know. One cannot say, for example, what could have been or will be philosophy's other chance. But neither can one avoid questioning this chance, by looking forward to it, or perhaps back towards it.

Denial is to be found there, at once given and withdrawn, in the way this question necessarily resonates like an irreducible solicitation of thought by thought itself, and in the way this question resonates without ever being able to be asked. The question of the totally other origin, like that of the other destination – be it the best or the worst – insists, hollows out and exceeds the actual event. It is the double of a surplus of possibility that insists by repeating, and by repeating that it cannot be asked. It is an inevitable, impossible and necessary question. Denial, then, names the yes or no at stake in this question.

The other possibility is undeniable, and it is on this basis that one can, indeed must, give it credit. Perhaps it would be this impossibility of exceeding or going further than denial, of saturating or suturing the origin with an instance which, all while making it possible, would never let itself be grasped – perhaps it would be this impossibility of going back to the origin that would liberate, *negatively*, the faith in the totally other origin, in which one can only believe. The secret of the other chance seals the indissoluble alliance between faith and denial.

The new direction of Derrida's examination necessarily leads him, in his final texts, to pursue an explanation by way of what is called 'negative theology'. Does the motif of denial not, then, lead to the elaboration of a new form of 'apophatic' discourse? Indeed, if it is evident that deconstruction

> seems to have recourse in a regular and insistent manner to this rhetoric of negative determination, endlessly multiplying the defences and apophatic warnings: this, which is called X (for example, the text, writing, the trace, différance, the hymen, the supplement, the *pharmakon*, the *parergon*, etc.), 'is' neither this nor that, neither sensible nor intelligible, neither positive nor negative, neither inside nor outside, neither superior nor inferior, neither active nor passive, neither present nor absent, not even neutral (Derrida 2008b: 144)

then it is certainly necessary for Derrida to explain this new proximity to negative theology. However, to avoid being nothing but pure appearance, it must be denounced as masking an irreducible gap.

Derrida the thinker recognises perfectly well that there is a certain necessity for recourse to apophasis – which is to say, a modality of the negative – in order to speak about faith. Moreover, such a recourse is necessary in order to speak at all if it is true that any speech act is only possible by starting from a kind of shared credit, an alliance that unites he who speaks and he who listens. But instead of emphasising the failure of discourse with respect to its referent (the essence, or the hyper-essentiality, of God), this modality of the negative (it is neither this, nor that, and so on), on the contrary, constitutes the unsurpassable horizon of discursivity within the perspective of what the messianic alone is able to herald.

We should, of course, turn to Freud here in order to understand both the logic proper to denial and the novel usage of it employed by Derrida. In the 1925 text entitled 'Negation', Freud confers a specific meaning upon this term. Denial is the act by which a subject refuses to recognise a repressed desire, feeling or object as his own. *The Language of Psychoanalysis* elaborates it as a 'procedure whereby the subject, while formulating one of his wishes, thoughts or feelings which has been repressed hitherto, contrives, by disowning it, to continue to defend himself against it' (Laplanche and Pontalis 2018: 260). The individual says 'no', but this no is a 'yes'.

In a way, therefore, to deny [*denier*] signifies the impossibility of denying, as Freud's famous example shows us. After narrating a dream, the patient says to the analyst, 'You ask who this person in the dream can be. It's *not* my mother' (*SE* XIX: 235).[3] Obviously, the analyst immediately interprets this statement as 'it *is* my mother', being quite certain that the more forceful the patient's denials of his interpretation, the more they betray an actual avowal or affirmation.

According to Freud, this method – which hinges on the logical scandal of transforming a negation into an affirmation – 'is very convenient': '"What", we ask [the patient], "would you consider the most unlikely imaginable thing in that situation? What do you think was furthest from your mind at that time?" If the patient falls into the trap and says what he thinks is most incredible, he almost always makes the right admission' (*SE* XIX: 235). The interpretation, then, consists in systematically assuming the opposite of what the patient says.

Denial, however, is not simply an affirmation of the contrary. If it were nothing more than this, then the analytic cure would be quick and easy. It is certainly true that denial is the converse of affirmation; but it is also something *other* than a mere converse. In fact, it persists as negation despite its manifest dimension of admission. Analysis sees right through the denying subject, and yet he continues to deny, he refuses to admit the obvious. The evidence is deemed inadmissible, and we are confronted with a wall of resistance that will not give way to any truth or reality testing. For, even if the analyst reintroduces the object of denial – in this case, the mother – he does not succeed in rendering it *present* to the subject; he reintroduces it as denied, that is to say, as a pure possible. The analyst says 'it is your mother', but the patient does not accept this, and thus the mother becomes not actual, but probable. 'It is possible', retorts the patient, 'but you are the one who said it.' Neither present, nor absent. Simply *possible* – negatively *possible*. It is forever held in reserve. Indeed, the possible would be precisely that which, having simply been suggested by the other, is held in ontological reserve, without the status of being-there. Freud names this the *repressed* – that which stands at the threshold of being.

The denied object, therefore, is not entirely reduced to the status of non-being, but it is most certainly cast out of being. It is excluded from the register of beings. The repressed, the denied, is expelled from presence. In this sense, it remains forever possible.

Such a possible is not the negation of the actual, nor is it the affirmation of the impossible. Without being reduced to an affirmation, the negative possible is not the expression of any lack or deficit. It bears witness to a power or capacity of the negative which is neither established nor lacking. Therefore,

Freud defines this strange possibility as *the state of that which must not be brought to presence*. The possible, then, corresponds to a prohibition on presence.

Derrida takes up this understanding of the possible, brought into relief by the problematic of denegation, in order to more clearly relate it to the philosophical problem to which it is inextricably bound: *the questioning of the totally other origin*. Denial and its multiple effects, trajectories and modalities would, in this light, be governed by the fundamental motif of the other possibility.

Taken together, Derrida's body of work can be read as the most scrupulous, and at the same time the most audacious, attempt to legitimise the question of the other chance: the power of this question resides in its undeniable character. This theme is clearly present in his earliest texts and is particularly evident in the commentary on Levinas developed in 'Violence and Metaphysics' (1978). Derrida recognises that the Levinasian 'dream' – the dream of a dispossession, a dismantling of the philosophical tradition in the name of the other of the Greek, of the other of the Greek source and its German reappropriation – is undeniable. 'Violence and Metaphysics' characterises this other as an 'ultralogical affect of speech':

> an interpellation of the Greek by the non-Greek at the heart of a silence, an ultralogical affect of speech, a question which can be stated only by being forgotten in the language of the Greeks; and a question which can be stated, as forgotten, only in the language of the Greeks. The strange dialogue of speech and silence. (1978: 133)

And, moreover, 'the question has already begun – we know it has – and this strange certainty about an *other* absolute origin, an other absolute decision that has secured the past of the question, liberates an incomparable instruction: the discipline of the question' (1978: 80).

The later texts emphasise the importance of this 'discipline'. In this sense, a text like 'Faith and Knowledge' gives fundamental importance to the problem of the totally other origin. It makes this problem function as the very origin of faith itself, as the following crucial passage demonstrates:

> But the gap between the opening of this *possibility* (as a *universal structure*) and the *determinate necessity* of this or that religion will always remain irreducible; and sometimes <it operates> within each religion, between on the one hand that which keeps it closest to its 'pure' and proper possibility, and on the other, its own historical determined necessities or authorities. Thus, one can always criticize, reject or combat this or that form of sacredness or belief, even of religious authority, in the name of the most originary possibility. The latter can be *universal* (faith or trustworthiness, 'good faith' as the condition of testimony, of

the social bond and even of the most radical questioning) or already *particular*, for example belief in a specific originary event of revelation, of promise or of injunction, as in the reference to the Tables of Law, to early Christianity, to some fundamental word of scripture, more archaic and more pure than all clerical or theological discourse. But it seems impossible to deny the *possibility* in whose name – thanks to which – the derived *necessity* (the authority or determinate belief) would be put in question, suspended, rejected or criticized, even deconstructed. One can *not* deny it, which means that the most one can do is to deny it. Any discourse that would be opposed to it would, in effect, always succumb to the figure or the logic of denial <*denegation*>. Such would be the place where, before and after all the Enlightenment in the world, reason, critique, science, tele-technoscience, philosophy, thought in general, retain the *same* resource as religion in general. (Derrida 2002: 93–4)

Let us recall the general context of the analysis here: why is the phenomenon of the 'return of the religious', which today is marked by a violent build-up of the religious question – fanaticism, integrism, fundamentalism – so difficult to think and, at the same time, understand and critique?

This is due to the fact that the question of the *return* in Derrida is never simple. There is always more than a return in the return, and every repetition is also divided from itself, or repeats itself. In this sense, to speak of a return of the religious is to recognise that religion returns at least twice – first, in the form of the build-up, and second, in the critique of the build-up. This essentially leads to the return of another religion: not any religious dogma, or some determinate religion, but a certain *faith*, or more precisely, *faith in the totally other chance* (a belief in the fact that the other of the fantasy may come to be), a faith according to which only fantasy may be taken into account and exposed. Thus, one always thinks religion in the name of religion. It would be naïve to think that the return of the religious could be critiqued in the name of reason alone, as if reason were independent of belief, or the classical problem of knowledge were absolutely independent from faith. The last part of the above quotation makes the assertion clear: both thought and religion draw their resources from a single *place*. And it is towards this place – what is it, how to think it? – that Derrida's entire analysis is oriented.

There is 'always more than one source', Derrida says (2002: 100), to reinterpret Bergson's famous title, but also to recall the two etymological sources of the word 'religion' identified by Benveniste (*relegere* and *religare*), and finally to examine the gap established by Kant between 'religion of mere cult' and 'reflecting faith' in *Religion within the Boundaries of Mere Reason*. This reflecting faith, Derrida says, 'does not depend essentially upon any historical revelation and thus agrees with the rationality of purely practical reason' (2002: 49). In radicalising this gap between religion of mere cult and rational faith, Derrida concludes by exploring the way in which Heidegger uproots the thought of the 'being-responsible-guilty-indebted (*Schuldigsein*)' (2002: 51) from every Christian origin and every moral preoccupation, thus envisioning a first attestation that would be more originary than Kantian faith. The word 'religion' here, which indicates the resource of the source, would name both a horizon of faith that would be irreducible to a determinate revelation, as well as the particular religions born of historical revelations.

Derrida asks: 'How then to think – within the limits of reason alone – a religion which, without again becoming "natural religion," would today be effectively universal? And which, for that matter, would no longer be restricted to a paradigm that was Christian or even Abrahamic?' (2002: 53). How to think a religion that would no longer be restricted, in other words, to what has taken place throughout history in the name of religion, given that 'the Testamentary and Koranic revelations are inseparable from a *historicity* of revelation itself' (2002: 48, emphasis added)?

This universal religion is the other name for a faith in *justice* and *democracy*. It is marked by an opening to the coming of the other, an opening that characterises the 'messianic', or 'messianicity without messianism':

> This would be the opening to the future or to the coming of the other as the advent of justice, but without horizon of expectation and without prophetic prefiguration. The coming of the other can only emerge as a singular event when no anticipation sees it coming, when the other and death – and radical evil – can come as a surprise at any moment. (Derrida 2002: 56)

The 'messianic' names a faith without dogma, which 'inhabits every act of language and every address to the other' (Derrida 2002: 56), which is postulated every time I open myself to the other and bear witness to the con*fidence* [con*fiance*] that I have or would like to have in it, in the event of the encounter, or in the future of the community. But – and here I draw nearer to the motif of denial – this faith is, in its very possibility, more originary than every confessional act of faith, every adherence to a historically determined religion. This faith, this credit, is in a certain sense prior to history, arche-originary, for it gestures beyond the historical event of the revelation and towards revealability itself. Derrida examines here, in the figure of this strange faith, an originary surplus or supplement that exceeds the logic of the history that it has nevertheless inaugurated and to which it does not belong. This surplus, which no determinate religion can comprehend, would coincide precisely with the possibility of the totally other chance.

This surplus, therefore, is a place, *the* place – a place that is simultaneously a-topical, which is to say without place, lacking any possible localisation. The pure possibility of the place, which provides a place without itself occupying a space, without taking charge of its own proper space. A place that one can only actually approach through the detour of a certain *via negativa*. This place without emplacement 'ultralogically' affects thought by concealing it, for the totally other origin or the totally other chance did not take place and may, perhaps, never take place. The other origin and other chance make a place, they can give rise to a place, but they themselves do not and will not come into presence. Thus, one can only ever speak of them apophatically, by appealing to the figures of aporia. In 'Faith and Knowledge', Derrida names four such figures: the *island*, the *promised land*, the *desert* and *khōra*.

In a text entitled 'How to Avoid Speaking', there is already an insistence on 'the barren [*désertique*], radically nonhuman and atheological nature of this "place"' (Derrida 2008b: 174). The place of the totally other possibility uproots the very tradition of place, whether this word be understood in the temporal sense (in the tradition of 'taking place', like an event) or the spatial sense (in the tradition of the topic, of the place of discourse and the situation – what takes place happens *there*). The desert, then, is the name of the place of the abstraction of place, the place where place loses its proper trace, according to the paradox which holds that

> the foundation of law – law of the law, institution of the institution, origin of the constitution – is a 'performative' event that cannot belong to the set that it founds, inaugurates or justifies. Such an event is unjustifiable within the logic of what it will have opened. It is the decision of the other in the undecidable. (Derrida 2002: 57)

The desert, or the 'desert in the desert', is thus the paradoxical site of rootedness – the foundation of tradition – where the root is simultaneously torn away from itself, swallowed up by the very source of all radicality. Between the root and the source, then, opens the distance of absolute alterity.

This place is impassable, a place of infinite resistance. Like *khōra* in the *Timaeus*, it is anarchic and anarchivable, 'without age, without history' (Derrida 2002: 58). *Khōra* is nothing, Derrida says, but this nothing is not even presented as 'beyond being'. It is not reappropriable, even by negative theology, for it makes no gesture towards an essence: 'nothing happens through it [*khōra*] and nothing happens to it' (Derrida 2008b: 173). Furthermore, '*khōra*', he says, 'remains absolutely impassable and heterogeneous to all the processes of historical revelation or of anthropo-theological experience, which at the very least suppose its abstraction' (2002: 58). And yet this reserve, this abstraction, which resists as a promise, as an excess of possibility, indeed serves effectively as a source of faith — faith in the totally other chance: 'The chance of this desert in the desert [. . .] is that in uprooting the tradition that bears it, in atheologizing it, this abstraction, without denying faith, liberates a universal rationality and the political democracy that cannot be dissociated from it' (2002: 57).

It is now possible to account for the logic of denial that subtends such a discourse. The place of the totally other possibility, of the totally other chance, is — as demonstrated above — nothing. It resists without being, without time, and without history; it is prior to time, prior to history, with its advance being neither chronologically, logically nor ontologically suitable. It is thus neither a principle, nor an origin, nor an event. It is in no way an instance, but rather is given in the play of an insistence (one can speak here neither of being, nor of appearance) whose force would be drawn from the following fact: it cannot be denied. An insistence on the undeniable, an undeniable insistence. The gap between the opening of the possibility and the necessity of some given religion is *undeniable*. One can *not* deny this possibility. Yet it must be kept in mind that this possibility is not the possibility of *some* undeniable *thing*. As Freud demonstrates, denial does not bear upon the content of the possibility, but rather defines the possibility itself. To be possible, thus, is to be undeniable. To put it otherwise, the possible appears as the possibility of the pure and simple impossibility of being denied. Which is all to say that possibility *is* denial. Possibility is nothing outside of the play of denial, it is only affirmed and posited by pushing denial — and consequently, negation — to the limit; at the very most, one can deny it. And even when one denies it, which one never fails to do, one still believes in it, and one believes in it for the very reason that it is denied.

Denial, or the play of the undeniable, is therefore more originary than the determinate forms of denial that it makes possible, which Derrida enumerates as follows: *putting into question, suspension, rejection, critique* and *deconstruction*. Every offensive discourse, every discourse of refusal, of combat, of struggle, in this case the struggle against some form of religious fanaticism, proceeds from the undeniable — which is to say, from the very possibility of denial. Through combat, one can only ever reach the determinate, and never the arche-originary place or actual resource of that combat.

The discourse that would oppose itself to this, Derrida says, would always give way to the figure or the logic of denial. A first opposition to this discourse could consist in the following affirmation: there is not and there will never be anything other than what there is, nothing other than 'determinate necessity'. Faith in the totally other origin betrays a naïve confidence in a kind of duty to be [*devoir être*], or bad infinity; it is the discourse of the 'beautiful soul', the fraudulent intrusion of an illusory transcendence in the course of historical immanence. In response to this discourse, it could be said that from the very moment one says 'there is only what there is', this enunciation takes part in a faith in the 'there is' and would be impossible without the full faith and credit – opened up by speech – accorded to givenness itself (*il y a, es gibt*). And yet this givenness remains undeniable.

A second objection could show that it is impossible to exceed the horizon of determinate religion: to speak as Derrida does is still to speak from Christianity or Judaism. To this objection, it would be possible to respond that, indeed, Derrida does always speak *from* the testamentary tradition, and that he has never pretended to do anything but that. The gap he seeks to analyse, between possibility and determinate necessity, is not situated beyond religion, but is opened *even within* historically determined religion. There is nothing surprising, then, in already being able to mark out the trace of this or that tradition in his discourse. 'The source is divided at the source.'

A third objection could raise the question of whether what Derrida names faith, tolerance, credit, messianic and so on does indeed stand in relation to faith or religion. The question would be whether or not this constitutes an abuse of language: faith is faith, and not some subtly disguised form of atheism, some cunning of reason, or counterfeit money of faith. Responding to this objection would consist in showing that one can only ever delimit a field of authentic faith by having faith in this authenticity itself, namely, by having faith in faith. And yet this fiduciary reflexivity, the reflexivity of faith, is made possible by an originary act of belief in faith itself, which is not at all to be confused with the object of that faith. This is the gap that is named by possibility, or the decision of the other.

It would, no doubt, be possible to multiply the effects of the denial of denial, which is to say, of the undeniable. They all come up against Derrida's implacable argumentative logic. The undeniable can *only* be denied. Determinate or derivative necessity can only be deconstructed in the name of the undeniable possibility. Thus, metaphysics – as it has been shown, at least since *Of Grammatology*, where writing was considered to be derivative with respect to speech – at one and the same time represses the supplement and, above all, the possibility of the originary supplement and the totally other possibility.

The link that unites possibility and denial is a structural one. The possible – that which must not come into presence – is the very indentation of the future.

To deny always entails an act of faith, which I would define as the faith in another possible beginning, in a totally other source. When I deny something, that is, when I deny the evidence, I postulate, without being able to affirm it, that everything could have been otherwise, that everything could have happened differently. Denial liberates the negative possibility of another history. Negative possibility, the state of that which must not be brought to presence, is the question that cannot be asked and that, at the same time, can only be asked. One is also unable not to maintain this negative possibility as being possible. That which is rejected, that which is excluded – is this not, in one way or another, the vertigo of the totally other origin? That which is most secret – is this not always what I am not, and which bears within itself, fantasmatically, the question of what I could have been? Such is the forbidden question, negatively possible, which lies at the heart of every history, every translation, every genesis. Not what is going to be, but what could have been. This is a question that Hegel misapprehended in the name of actuality, and that nevertheless persists under the name of denial. The question of the totally other origin is a question that is habitually disposed of much too quickly: 'Do not linger on what could have been', 'Stick to what there is', 'One cannot remake history anew', and so on. But despite all of that, are we not always, in one way or another, thinking about the other possibility? About the other of necessity? About that other origin that we maintain as negatively possible? What are we to make of this fringe of non-presence that doubles the present, this negative aura of what could have been that surmounts all actuality, given that it always seems to return?

Negative Hypothesis: This return signifies the implacable hardness of the negative that, as we know, Freud designates by the name of repetition compulsion. What returns, in this case, is the phantom of the possible. In bringing about the return of the scene of the trauma, its denial returns as well, which is to say, the possibility that nothing may have happened. Every question that we level towards the other, be it formulated or not, explicit or not – what if it had not happened, what if something else had taken place? – would be a modality of repetition compulsion. As such, negativity would be but an automatic procedure, a retelling or redoing machine.

Positive Hypothesis: The question of the other possibility, of the totally other version, would not be merely, or even at all, the mark of a backwards-looking, melancholic or pathological attitude, but rather the sign of the coming of another manner of being. A manner of being excluded from the field of traditional ontology. A manner of being that could be said to be one of an *a posteriori possibility*. That which is rejected, excluded and denied is a possibility that is forever on hold.

What is at stake in such a possibility, therefore, is the opening of the history-less within history, what Freud, in *Inhibitions, Symptoms, and Anxiety*, calls 'undoing what has been done' (*SE* XX: 119). In a certain sense, this non-happened, this non-place, this repressed or rejected, bears within itself the possibility of the worst. It is here, without a doubt, that every integrist and fundamentalist endeavour takes root. To try to actualise a presumed fantasmatic origin, to seek control over what could have been and transform it into what must be – this is, indeed, actually the worst. In the attempt to bring into being that which reality has excluded from the outset, one finds the impulse to destroy and the death drive itself.

Let us conclude, then, with the words of 'Faith and Knowledge':

> [T]he *messianic*, or messianicity without messianism. This would be the opening to the future or to the coming of the other [. . .] The coming of the other can only emerge as a singular event when no anticipation *sees it coming*, when the other and death – and radical evil – can come as a surprise at any moment. (Derrida 2002: 56)

Translated by Michael Stanish

Notes

1. These are the first words of the text. [The French here, '*le vocable cru*', plays on the fact that *cru*, in addition to meaning 'crude', is also the past participle of 'to believe'. Thus, 'the crude word' is also 'the believed word' – Translator.]
2. Unless otherwise noted, 'denial' in this text translates the French *dénégation*. This term is also operative in English as 'denegation', but this misses much of the juxtaposition between denial and undeniability in the present text. Denial, in any case, should be read with the force of both terms – Translator.
3. Throughout this book, all of Malabou's citations of Freud appear in parentheses according to the Standard Edition volume and page number – Editor.

5

Before and Above: Spinoza and Symbolic Necessity

In Baruch Spinoza's work, God is without name and without shape. His essence is the very form of the necessity of nature, the infinite regularity, actuality and rationality of what is. And there is no good or bad in this. All representations of God as a legislator, creator or father, endowed with intentions, are merely human projections prompted by an inadequate understanding of what a cause is. A true cause is never separated from its effect but is immanent to it, remaining within it. As cause of himself, that is, of nature, God is nothing but his own effectuation, and, in this sense, he cannot be said to be transcendent – external – to what he produces.

But are the readings of Spinoza that characterise him solely as a thinker of immanence and/or self-regulation entirely fair? Do they do justice to the major issue of the origin of the sacred as developed in the *Theological-Political Treatise*? What is the fount of sacredness for Spinoza? Can it be reduced to sheer error or illusion, a temporary hole in the tissue of immanence, or does it open a specific space in immanence that remains to be explored? What exactly are the relationships between necessity and faith, between truth and its irreducible symbolic dimension? And what does *symbolic* mean for an impersonal God? Following Spinoza's scriptural hermeneutics and discussing it along with thinkers such as Emmanuel Levinas, I develop a new approach to Spinoza's concept of revelation, related to his vision of the sacred as an economy of signs without referent. In so doing, I hope to show that Spinoza's critique of religious dogmatism and fanaticism should not be confused with the dismissal of the sacred; on the contrary, it is propaedeutic to the philosophical delineation of the sacred.

The Space of Revelation

The most famous of all the immanentist readings of Spinoza is undoubtedly that of Gilles Deleuze, who calls Spinoza the 'prince of immanence' (Joughin

1990: 11). Early on in *Expressionism in Philosophy*, Deleuze insists on the difference between *immanere* and *emanare*, showing that Spinoza's God has no eminence, does not hold himself *above* creatures, but is horizontal and *stays* with what he *expresses* (Deleuze 1990a: 41). *Expression* is presented as the logical correlate to *immanence*; that is, it correlates to a specific mode of causation and production of truth – a causation and production that 'produce *while remaining in themselves*' (Deleuze 1990a: 171). Immanent causation implies that the effect remains with the cause with no external help. This type of 'remaining [with] in' is precisely the meaning of *expression*. We must then understand that expression is a mode of exteriorising that never goes outside itself, despite what the prefix *ex* might suggest; it is a modality of production that never separates itself from what it produces, a remnant externality, so to speak. Therefore, *expression* is the logos of immanence, its privileged 'Word' [*parole*], as well as its ontological actuality (Joughin 1990: 406). Deleuze emphasises the 'logical links' that connect immanence and expression on several occasions (Deleuze 1990a: 169).

It goes without saying that Deleuze's reading of Spinoza is one of the most profound. Nevertheless, the main issue raised by Deleuze's understanding and privileging of *expression* is the rigid – dogmatic even – distinction it implies (or creates) between *expression* and *impression*, that is, between rationality and the supposedly other word, other knowledge and other production of meaning at work in Spinoza: *revelation*. According to Deleuze, expression and revelation coexist in Spinoza as two antagonistic and definitely unequal regimes of representation, namely, philosophy and religion. While expression is adequate, revelation is inadequate. Expression, which proceeds '*more geometrico*' and is at work in the *Ethics*, functions as a paradoxical non-linguistic language, whereas revelation is entirely based on signs that *impress* the prophets' souls and consequently also human minds. Expression does not properly signify, while revelation does not properly express. 'Spinoza therefore sets apart two domains which were always confused in earlier traditions: that of expression and of the expressive knowledge which is alone adequate; and that of signs, and of knowledge by signs' (Deleuze 1990a: 181). The difference between these two types of relationships – between 'expression and the expressed' and 'sign and signified' (1990a: 57) – are of very dissimilar sorts. The way in which expression expresses again defines immanent causation. The expressed, as the result or product of expression, is never outside expression; it never separates itself from itself. By contrast, a sign always stands for something other than itself, refers to something external, and that is why knowledge by signs makes us think that

God himself is outside nature, occupying the transcendent position of a reference. Therefore,

> [r]evelation is not an expression, but a cultivation of the inexpressible, a confused and relative knowledge through which we lend God determinations analogous to our own (Understanding, Will), only to rescue God's superiority through his eminence in all genera (the supereminent One, etc.) [. . .] The opposition of expressions and signs is one of the fundamental principles of Spinozism. (Deleuze 1990a: 181–2)

Revelation, then, appears as an inadequate version of immanence, one that humans create.

Why is the distinction between expression and impression problematic? Why can't we adhere to Deleuze's interpretation of a distinction between reason and revelation? Because in reading Spinoza as he does, Deleuze reduces to nothing the *necessity* of revelation, which in principle is not distinct from the necessity developed in the *Ethics* even while it presents itself differently. In reducing revelation to a human mode of understanding, in not questioning revelation at the level of God himself, Deleuze fails to address a question that does not appear in the *Ethics* and that I would like to characterise here as the *origin of the symbolic*, coextensive with the *origin and determination of the sacred*. The way in which God signifies cannot be a pure fantasy of the human mind; rather, it designates a certain regime of ideality by which ideas themselves are symbolically showcased.

To locate the origin of the symbolic (and not that of truth) is the immense task undertaken by the *Theological-Political Treatise* and constitutes an essential dimension of the altogether political, philosophical, ethical nature of Spinoza's biblical hermeneutics. I believe that Spinoza's approach to hermeneutics, as developed in the *Treatise*, opens a space that is precisely neither that of immanence nor of transcendence, and that as such explodes the distinction between impression and expression. What I intend to circumscribe here is just such a space.

To do so, I do not limit myself to a reading of Deleuze but also turn to Levinas with regard to these same questions. According to an apparently contrary perspective, Levinas affirms that Spinoza's approach to revelation, as well as his critical method of interpretation of scripture, *is not immanent enough*.[1] For that very reason, paradoxically, it *misses the true dimension of transcendence* that constitutes the very essence of revelation.

Levinas never understands the role of revelation in Spinoza as limited to inadequate knowledge. Unlike Deleuze, he challenges what he sees as a mistreatment of signs of revelation in Spinoza, a dismissal of signification as such. He reproaches Spinoza for not having gone deep enough in 'what is signified in the signifier [*la signifiance du significant*]' of revelation (Levinas 1994a: 110). (As if there were too few signs in Spinoza's 'knowledge of signs'!) If Spinoza had been consistent with himself, he would have been better able to show that 'knowledge by signs' responds to an essential and necessary dimension of God, not to a weakness of the human mind, and he would have elaborated the accurate hermeneutical method able to bring to light such a necessity. Instead of setting up a method that constantly demonstrates that the Bible *needs help*, he would have discovered in it a principle of hermeneutical self-regulation at work, a self-regulation that constantly both produces and maintains its significative signification. If Spinoza had been a genuine Spinozist, reason and faith, even if fundamentally separated, would nevertheless have been clearly deduced from the same, even if dual, principle, namely, self-regulation – geometrical self-regulation in/as the rational, and hermeneutical self-regulation in/as the religious. For Levinas, as we shall see, the immanent meaning of transcendence is hermeneutical self-regulation.

It is true that there is no hermeneutical self-regulation in Spinoza. Yet, as I intend to demonstrate, such an absence certainly does not prevent him from developing a genuine concept of the symbolic and the significative signification.

Following the logic of the two opposite paths that circle and strangle Spinoza within the bounds of either strict or loose immanence, I shall explain how Spinoza's hermeneutics escapes these bounds by determining the symbolic and, consequently, also situating the sacred as an irreducible dimension of divine necessity. Both Deleuze and Levinas fail to perceive and apprehend this determination. Acknowledgement of such a symbolic space in Spinoza is indispensable to his understanding of both hermeneutics and philosophy.

Revelation and Necessity

In *Expressionism in Philosophy*, Deleuze never presents revelation as what it is first and foremost, that is, a *historical* event or, more precisely, a *necessary historical* event or *fact*. For Spinoza, revelation *absolutely had to happen*.[2]

I find it strange that so few Spinoza readers interrogate the type of necessity that revelation is endowed with, as well as the relationship between such a necessity and the one presented as the nature of God in the *Ethics*. When Deleuze takes revelation as a human 'cultivation', he goes too fast. It is true that revelation is analysed in many passages of the *Treatise* as a way to touch the multitude by other means than reason, which implies a mode of communication that essentially speaks to imagination and fantasy. I shall return to this point below. What I want to suggest at the moment is that the assimilation of revelation to the specific mode of communication that it partly is cannot obliterate what revelation is essentially – that is, ontologically: *a fact.*

In a certain sense, revelation cannot be anything but a fact, and Spinoza's concept of revelation is no exception. In one of the key texts of *Beyond the Verse*, 'Revelation and the Jewish Tradition', Levinas rightly declares: 'I think that [the] fundamental question [. . .] concerns less the content ascribed to revelation than the actual fact – a metaphysical one – called the Revelation. This fact is also the first and most important content revealed in any revelation' (1994b: 129). What revelation reveals first and foremost is revelation itself, that is, its own fact. Revelation reveals its own factuality – a factuality that is both, all at once, historical and ontological. It is unclear how 'the ontological status or regime of the Revelation' (1994b: 131), as Levinas puts it so beautifully, could not have been a question for Spinoza.

Spinoza does acknowledge the factuality of revelation, which is a first reason not to assimilate it to human 'cultivation'. A second major reason why the process of revelation cannot be limited to the inadequate knowledge of humans appears when Spinoza explains in the *Treatise* that the communication between God and the Christ is *rational* and *adequate*. To play with Deleuze's concepts, it is by no means an impression but rather an expression. The fact, as well as the content, of revelation appeared as adequately, that is, entirely rationally understandable to Christ. 'If Moses spoke with God face to face as a man may do with his fellow (that is, through the medium of their two bodies), then Christ communed with God mind to mind' (Spinoza 2001: 14). Further:

> And surely this fact, that God revealed Himself to Christ, or to Christ's mind, directly, and not through words and images as in the case of the prophets, can have only this meaning, that Christ perceived truly, or understood, what was revealed. For it is when a thing is perceived by pure thought, without words or images, that it is understood. (2001: 54)

Revelation and adequate knowledge are then originally and evidently not opposed.

Of course, we must immediately admit that the necessity of revelation, when not seen solely from the point of view of the communication between God and Christ, remains, for the most part, inaccessible to our natural light. Due to the limitations of our nature, we may be forced to perceive the necessity of revelation from the sole pragmatic point of view of its utility. In his remarkable book *Le Dieu de Spinoza*, Victor Brochard, who insists on revelation being a 'historical fact' (2013: 14), assumes that Spinoza identifies the necessity of revelation with its pragmatic function. When Spinoza says: 'I wish to emphasize in express terms [. . .] the importance and necessity of the role I assign to Scripture, or Revelation' (2001: 172), he supposedly understands 'necessity' as *utility*. For Spinoza, the utility of revelation consists in the link it establishes between obedience and salvation, and such a link, as it appears in several passages of the *Treatise*, cannot be rationally deduced, properly speaking. In a sense, its foundation is beyond our philosophical reach. In chapter 15, Spinoza declares: 'I maintain absolutely that this fundamental dogma of theology cannot be investigated by the natural light of reason, or at least that nobody has been successful in proving it, and that therefore it was essential that there should be revelation' (2001: 169–70). The 'necessity' of revelation here only pertains to the 'moral certainty' it confers (2001: 170).

Yet, for Spinoza, the fact that the necessity of revelation remains indemonstrable, that knowledge and faith are totally independent from one another, that moral certainty and philosophical truth are of different natures, and that scripture has no metaphysical meaning (as so powerfully affirmed in chapter 17) cannot erase the ideality of revelation, its originary adequacy once again at the level of God himself and his 'mind to mind' communication with Christ. We may ask, then, what constitutes the threshold between such an ontological divine ideality and the abundance of signs, fictions, images, illusions that accompany revelation for human beings, fashion the prophetic mind, and determine the way in which the multitude immediately receive the concept of God. The determination of such a threshold is precisely the point that Deleuze glides over too quickly.

As we shall see, this threshold, the very in-between of philosophy and revelation, is brought to light with the development of the biblical hermeneutical – historico-critical – method. Spinoza's method of interpretation is the space of negotiation between revelation as divine necessity and revelation as human reception of this necessity.

God's *Adaptation* to the Mind of the Multitude

It is clear to Spinoza that scripture commands obedience and love of one's neighbour in a form that is not that of adequate knowledge or rationality. What is understood adequately by Christ is perceived by the multitude in the inadequate form of a legislator's commandment or law. Adam, the first human, bears witness to this perception:

> Adam perceived this revelation not as an eternal and necessary truth but as a law, that is to say, an enactment from which good or ill consequence would ensue not from the intrinsic nature of the deed performed but only from the will and absolute power of some ruler. Therefore that revelation, solely in relation to Adam and solely because of the limitations of his knowledge, was a law, and God was a kind of lawgiver or ruler. (Spinoza 2001: 53)

It is, then, very easy to conclude that Adam's example – his lack of knowledge of what a law is, his incapacity to mentally access necessity – is paradigmatic of the people in general and hence a statement that the majority of people have a weak mind. Brochard comments:

> The great majority of men are not able to reach true knowledge, their spirit is too weak, the passions that render them dependent upon the rest of nature have too great an influence on their soul to allow them to situate themselves in the correct perspective and perceive the genuine and true chain of natural causes. This implies either abandoning them to their fate or using a detour [*moyen détourné*] to lead them to the correct result. That is why God revealed religion to them. Religion presents the truths that necessarily follow from the essence of God as decrees written by a legislator or king. It replaces intelligence by obedience, love by submission and piety; but in both cases, it is the same truth taught in two different forms. Moral law is the equivalent of natural law, it is natural law expressed in another language, adapted to human weakness, accessible to those who do not have the leisure or means to attain true knowledge. (2013: 19)

It is true that if Christ, who adequately perceived the content of revelation, 'ever proclaimed these things as law, he did so because of the people's ignorance and obstinacy' (Spinoza 2001: 54). Again, the multitude perceives God as a legislator, a king endowed with free will, mystery and power.[3] Moreover:

> For since we cannot perceive by the natural light that simple obedience is a way to salvation, and since only revelation teaches us that this comes about by God's singular grace which we cannot attain by reason, it follows that Scripture has brought very great comfort to mankind. For all men without exception are capable of obedience, while there are only a few – in proportion to the whole of humanity – who acquire a virtuous disposition under the guidance of reason alone. Thus, did we not have the testimony of Scripture, the salvation of nearly all men would be in doubt. (Spinoza 2001: 172)

The threshold we are looking for thus compels us to determine the status of the *accommodation* or *adaptation* of revelation to the opinions of humankind. Where does such an accommodation come from? From God or from humans?

We are touching here on the critical point. Let us examine the two axes of this alternative. 1) We will admit that the 'accommodation' or 'adaptation' is a product of the human mind. Are we to understand then that Spinoza, one of the greatest defenders of democracy and free speech, systematically assigns revelation – understood as a naïve, confused and anthropomorphic mode of transmission – to the multitude, understood as a crowd of ignoramuses and non-rational spirits? 2) If such an 'accommodation' or 'adaptation' pertains instead to the nature of God, are we then to understand that if God has 'adapted' his revelation to human minds, it is because he is *also* a personal God, endowed with free will? Are we to understand that the God of Spinoza is not only the God without a name of the *Ethics* but in some respects also an intentional God? Aren't we forced to acknowledge that he *wanted* to reveal himself?

In reality, such an alternative is a false one and succeeds only in engaging the reading of Spinoza in a series of aporia.

First, Deleuze's reading. Of course, Deleuze never says that the multitude are a bunch of ignorant and weak-minded individuals. Revelation is assigned to the first kind of knowledge and assimilated again with 'a cultivation of the inexpressible'. As Deleuze adds:

> Whatever its sort, knowledge through signs is never expressive, and remains of the first kind. Indication is not an expression, but a confused state of involvement in which an idea remains powerless to explain itself or to express its own cause. An imperative sign is not an expression, but a confused impression which leads us to believe that the true expressions of God, the laws of nature, are so many commandments. (1990a: 181)

Furthermore, the imperative signs of moral laws and religious revelation are 'decisively rejected as inadequate' (1990a: 330).

Such an understanding is highly problematic because once again it fails to explain the necessity of revelation. Revelation is not a prophetic invention but, first and foremost, a divine necessity; otherwise it would not have happened as what it is: an irreducible fact. Inadequate knowledge can, by its essence, be superseded and transformed into superior forms of knowledge, whereas the content of revelation (moral certainty, obedience) is alien to knowledge and cannot be rationalised. The intellectual love of God, as presented in the *Ethics*, is not exactly a *sublation* (Deleuze would have hated the term, but he forces me to use it here) of the religious form of love given and revealed to the common people. If faith and philosophy are separated, then faith is not a form of even inadequate knowledge. In his demonstration, Deleuze conflates two inassimilable levels by identifying revelation with a first kind of knowledge.

It seems then that we can only 1) either dismiss the ontological and epistemological value of revelation by rejecting it 'into the inadequate' as Deleuze does illegitimately, or 2) acknowledge this value but then be forced, at the same time, to admit the intervention of a personal God.

Second, there is Brochard's reading. Brochard arrives at the following conclusion, stating carefully that religion is not an inadequate form of the human mind: 'Men have not invented religion, it is God himself who revealed it to them' (2013: 21). God himself, so to speak, has altered his own truth:

> Humans have not altered the truth out of impotency or impiety; it is God himself who did; or it is possible at least that he adapted and proportioned it to human impotency and weakness. If such is the case, we must admit that this same God that philosophy perceives, is not only the thinking and extended substance that reason conceives. There must be intentions, a benevolent will in him [. . .] In the last instance, the God of Spinoza is a personal God. (2013: 35–6)

It seems that in order to be acknowledged as an originally divine, and not human, phenomenon, the necessity of revelation had to proceed from divine generosity, which, of course, is a problematic reading of Spinozism that introduces a strong Christian dimension to it, along with a philosophical impossibility.

This conclusion leads us to a third aporetic approach to Spinoza. After Deleuze's reading (Spinoza's contempt for the mind of the multitude), after Brochard's reading (Spinoza as a Christian thinker), we must now explore the third: Spinoza as an unfaithful Jew.

Levinas offers us this third reading. The supposed 'Christian' dimension of Spinoza is the reason why Levinas speaks of Spinoza's 'betrayal' of Judaism.

In 'The Spinoza Case', a text written about the rehabilitation of Spinoza in Israel by Ben Gurion in 1953, Levinas states:

> We entirely agree with the opinion of our late lamented and admirable friend Jacob Gordin: Spinoza was guilty of betrayal. Within the history of ideas, he subordinated the truth of Judaism to the revelation of the New Testament. The latter is of course suppressed by the intellectual love of God, but Western being involves the Christian experience, even if it is only a stage [. . .] Our feeling for Christianity is wholehearted, but it remains one of friendship and fraternity. It cannot become paternal. We cannot recognise a child that is not ours. (1997c: 108–9)

We cannot, then, fully recognise Spinoza as one of us, as one of our sons, Levinas says. I shall return later to the argument with regard to Spinoza's supposed Christianisation of Judaism. What I want to insist on at the moment is that, far from dismissing the argument of a personal God in Spinoza, on the contrary, Levinas argues that Spinoza's personal God is not the one it should have been, that is, the God of the Torah, to the extent that he can definitely be identified with the Christian God.

Levinas agrees with Brochard on one point: revelation is conceivable only as a relationship with a personal God. The difficulty is specifying what exactly a personal God means in Judaism. It certainly does not mean that God is a person as it does in Christianity.

Levinas explains the very specific meaning of the 'personal' in Judaism in 'Revelation in the Jewish Tradition'. He follows Spinoza when he affirms that revelation 'from the outset [. . .] is commandment, and piety is obedience to it' (1994b: 137). Nevertheless, the 'message' of revelation does ascertain the immediate, personal presence of God. It 'requires [. . .] a personal God: is a God not personal before all characteristics?' (1994b: 134).

However, 'personal' certainly does not mean what Brochard supposes it does in this instance. A new meaning of personal appears at that point, a non-Christian meaning, a meaning that Spinoza did not acknowledge. Levinas declares: God is personal in the sense that he 'appeals to persons', appeals to each person in their historical uniqueness (1994b: 134). This is the specifically Jewish meaning of *personal*. A personal God does not mean that God is a person but rather that God is met in person, that is, *in* the person, *through* the person: 'Man is the place through which [Revelation] passes' (1994b: 145). In Judaism, each *person* is a reader and an interpreter of the message; each *person* is able to 'extract' the meaning from the letters, as if the letters were 'the folded-back wings of the Spirit' (1994b: 132).

Profoundly missing the authentic spiritual dimension of both the form and content of the Torah, privileging the New over the Old Testament, Spinoza would have remained unaware of this very particular specific meaning of 'personal', and thus failed to understand (was it because he was ill-taught in Jewish studies?)[4] that the 'invitation to seek and decipher, to *Midrach*, already constitutes the reader's participation in the Revelation, in Scripture' (1994b: 133).

We can now clearly formulate what we called earlier the *hermeneutical self-regulation principle* that, for Levinas, lies at the very heart of the Torah, *is the Torah itself*, and escaped Spinoza: each singularity (person) has an immediate (automatic, one might say) access to the universal. Everyone is a reader. Everyone is an interpreter. No need to invoke signs, fantasies, fictions or illusions.

Every approach to the text is just, true, acceptable. The multitude's approach is automatically hermeneutically justified:

> The Revelation as calling to the unique within me is the significance particular to the signifying of the Revelation. It is as if the multiplicity of persons – is not this the very meaning of the personal? – were the condition for the plenitude of 'absolute truth'; as if every person, through his uniqueness, of the revelation of a unique aspect of truth, and some of its points would never have been revealed if some people had been absent from mankind. (1994b: 133)

In 'Spinoza's Background', Levinas writes this beautiful statement: 'Something would remain unrevealed in the Revelation if a single soul in its singularity were to be missing from the exegesis' (1994c: 171).

The authentic ethical mission of Judaism resides in this common/personal participation in the reading and interpretation: 'my very uniqueness lies in the responsibility for the other man' (Levinas 1994b: 142). But in it also lies its democratic (revolutionary even) principle:

> The adventure of the Spirit [. . .] takes place on earth among men. The trauma I experienced as a slave in the land of Egypt constitutes my humanity itself. This immediately brings me closer to all the problems of the damned of the earth, of all those who are persecuted, as if in my suffering as a slave I prayed in a prayer that was not yet oration, and as if this love of the stranger were already the reply given to me through my heart of flesh. (1994b: 142)

Again, there is no need to argue that the people's capacity to interpret the text necessarily proceeds from an inadequate kind of knowledge. The Talmudic scholars are certainly there to guide these interpretations. In essence, such interpretations are nevertheless irreducible to sheer 'subjective impressions'.[5]

The Talmud, which opens the space of an infinite discussion of the Torah, legitimates all readings as long as they are *personal*. When the reading is an authentically personal one, it cannot be arbitrary! The paradox is all but apparent! 'This in no way means that in Jewish spirituality the Revelation is left to the arbitrariness of subjective fantasies [. . .] Fantasy is not the essence of the subjective' (1994b: 134–5).

What, then, is the 'essence of the subjective'? We find a definition of the symbolic at this point. Levinas defines it as what exceeds the strict signification process: 'The aim of the signified by the signifier is not the only way to signify.' 'What is signified in the signifier [*significance*]', and – again – is not reducible to the perfect coincidence between the signified and the signifier, as Deleuze states, is precisely the *symbolic* dimension of signification in general (Levinas 1994a: 110).

If language were only expressive in the Deleuzian sense, if meaning in general were determined by the strict adequacy of signified to the signifier, and of the signifier to the referent, reading and understanding would consist only in silently and objectively receiving such an adequacy. Hermeneutics would not even exist; it would not be necessary. But such is not the case. The subjective solicitation of otherness in the text, the constant alterity of the text to itself, enhanced by its interpretability, forces the reader to intervene. The 'essence of the subjective' is the *extasis* of the identical.

For Levinas, this *extasis* clearly comes from the 'transcendence of the message' of revelation (1994b: 131), the 'rupture of immanence' it provokes (1994b: 144). Paradoxically, this 'rupture' is not antagonistic to the self-regulative hermeneutical principle; on the contrary, it is its very condition of possibility. The transcendence of the message is immanently regulated by the self-engendering movement of the symbolic dimension of the Torah, constituted by the living and constant dynamism of 'personal' interpretations.

Again, Spinoza missed this immanent dimension of transcendence to the extent that he did not credit the Bible with a hermeneutical self-engendering and regulating dimension. In this sense, because of his rejection of transcendence, *there is not enough immanence in Spinoza*. 'Spinoza will not have conferred a role in the production of meaning on the reader of the text, and – if one may put it this way – he will not have given a gift of prophecy to the act of hearing [*à l'oreille*]' (Levinas 1994c: 173). He missed 'a meaning coming from behind the signs that are immediately given: a coming that seeks out a hermeneutic' (1994c: 173). If 'to his credit, Spinoza did reserve for the Word of God a *proper status* outside opinion and "fitting" ideas' – a status that Deleuze does not acknowledge – 'he nevertheless failed to bring to light the hermeneutical inexhaustible treasure of this Word' (Levinas 1997a: 117). We shall see that Spinoza's Christian betrayal is another name for this failure – the failure to acknowledge the symbolic, and consequently also the meaning, of the sacred.

I must now conclude this first movement in my analysis: Deleuze, Brochard, Levinas. However interesting, their three trajectories are unsatisfactory and, again, are aporetic. In them, the specific regime of the necessity of revelation in Spinoza's philosophy is not brought to light carefully enough and is equated with 1) a confused 'cultivation' in which, very strangely, God seems to play no part; 2) the final proof of the personality of God – by which God ceases to be the void and amorphous name of the necessity of nature so as to become a 'benevolent will'; and 3) the evidence of a misunderstanding or misperception of the self-regulative structure and essence of the Bible.

Even if such trajectories aim at making the coherence, cohesion and unity of Spinoza's philosophy manifest (even at the cost of 'betrayal'), paradoxically and inevitably they lead readers to conclude that a major discrepancy, if not a contradiction, exists between the *Ethics* and the *Theological-Political Treatise*.

Spinoza's Scriptural Hermeneutics: Between Immanence and Transcendence

Challenging the above readings, I wish to affirm that another understanding of Spinoza's conception of revelation is possible, one that discloses the symbolic dimension of necessity. In order to do so, I now turn explicitly to Spinoza's hermeneutical method. The interpretation of scripture, in Spinoza, is certainly not a way of bringing some order into the confused and heterogeneous number of 'signs' ('only varying "signs," extrinsic denominations that guarantee some divine commandment', as Deleuze states [1990a: 47]) that would passively and immediately accompany revelation. Nor is it a way to acknowledge the presence of a commanding God (as Brochard states: 'in the end we see that God, in Spinoza, appears to be a will and a power. His predominate contention is that it is necessary to explain everything according to God's power [*puissance divine*]' [2013: 98]). Lastly, it is not a simple artefact aiming at discovering, beyond signs, a '[m]eaning [. . .] from the outset [. . .] already fully itself, reified in the text and almost fitted within it before all historical development and all hermeneutics', as Levinas states (1994c: 172). Again, these interpretations end by obscuring the link between the God of the *Ethics* and the God of the *Treatise*, which is also the link between philosophy and revelation.

Let us put it clearly: for Spinoza, *it is in the nature of God to reveal himself*. Again, we must not ignore the passages in which Spinoza affirms the human incapacity to understand the *natural* possibility of revelation. In chapter 1 of the *Treatise*, for example, he declares:

> As to the particular laws of Nature involved in revelation, I confess my ignorance. I might, indeed, have followed others in saying that it happened through the power of God, but this would be mere quibbling: it would be the same as trying to explain the specific reality of a particular thing by means of some transcendental term. For everything takes place through the power of God. Indeed, since Nature's power is nothing but the power of God, it is beyond doubt that ignorance of natural causes is the measure of our ignorance of the power of God. So it is folly to have recourse to the power of God when we do not know the natural cause of some phenomenon – that is,

when we do not know the power of God. However, there is no need anyway for us now to have an understanding of the cause of prophetic knowledge. As I have already indicated, our enquiry is here confined to the teachings of Scripture, with [a] view to drawing our own conclusions from these, as from data presented by Nature. The causes of these Scriptural teachings are not our concern. (2001: 19–20)

But how exactly are we to understand such a passage? Is Spinoza really stating that we should ignore the origin of revelation (it is 'not our concern')? Or does this passage demand something else, such as trying to grasp the origin of revelation as the very source of the *conflation between the ideal and the symbolic*, that is, between *truth and meaning* within necessity itself?

We should not be too quick to claim that Spinoza's only preoccupation in the *Treatise* is to establish a strict boundary between faith and philosophy *as if they did not share anything at all*. The task of clearly marking the separation between faith and philosophy is certainly the main object of the whole work. It is true that scripture's salient message is not metaphysical but moral and that interpreting scripture does not require philosophical reasoning. 'Therefore all knowledge of Scripture must then be sought from Scripture alone' (Spinoza 2001: 88). We know all this perfectly well. Yet we cannot but be struck by the way in which the hermeneutical, critical method acts as both a barrier and a bridge between rationality and fiction, that is, the reservation of images, signs and fantasies that characterises the reception of revelation. *What if there were some sort of communication between them?* What if philosophy and revelation, the rigour of ideality and prophetic seeing, expression and exaggeration, and, *to a certain extent*, philosophical thinking and superstition originally touched each other?

Such is the risky path I ultimately wish to follow in order to explore the aforementioned space between immanence and transcendence in Spinoza. I shall explore the status of the sacred as it appears through hermeneutical inquiry and as it results from a critical approach to language in general and to Hebrew in particular. This inquiry then leads me to address the central issue of signification.

The Problem of the Hebrew Language

Spinoza's refusal to consider the Hebrews as the elected people is intimately connected with the lack of any hermeneutical self-regulation of scripture, that is, any automatic universal dimension of the singular. By contrast, for Levinas, the universality of Judaism is essentially founded on a singularity: precisely that of election or chosenness. The universal is always given through a particularity. He writes:

> The idea of a chosen people must not be taken as a sign of pride. It does not involve being aware of exceptional rights, but of exceptional duties. It is the prerogative of moral consciousness itself. It knows itself as the centre of the world and for it the world is not homogeneous: for I am always alone in being able to answer the call, I am irreplaceable in my assumption of responsibility. (1997b: 176–7)

The paradox in Levinas is that each person is said to have access to the Books but through election only.

In stark contrast, Spinoza rejects the idea of election and clearly affirms the non-existence of the self-regulating hermeneutical principle according to which, as we saw, each person – should we say each Jew? – has genuine access to the universal meaning of scripture. As a people, the Hebrews do not constitute a privileged singularity. This appears clearly in chapter 3 of the *Treatise*, 'Of the Vocation of the Hebrews, and Whether the Gift of Prophecy Was Peculiar to Them', in which Spinoza affirms:

> We therefore conclude (since God is equally gracious to all and the Hebrews were chosen only with respect to their social organisation and their government) that the individual Jew, considered alone apart from his social organisation and his government, possesses no gift of God above other men, and there is no difference between him and a Gentile [. . .] Therefore at the present time there is nothing whatsoever that the Jews can arrogate to themselves above other nations. (2001: 40–5)

For Spinoza, as we can see, the superiority of the Hebrews only pertains to the stability and efficiency of their political constitution. Such a superiority is, then, purely pragmatic and not spiritual at all.

There is, of course, an intimate link between the theory of the non-election of the Hebrews and that of the absence of privilege of the Hebrew language. For Spinoza, there is no such thing as linguistic election either. Let us recall the fundamental rules of his hermeneutical historical method as developed in chapter 7. A 'history' of scripture consists in treating the Bible as a document and contains an account of the language in which the books of scripture were written, establishing the ordinary use of its terms and possible sources of ambiguity; a thoroughly organised collection of passages on various topics, noting all those that are ambiguous or obscure or seem inconsistent with one another;

and an account of the life and mentality of the author of each book, when and for whom he wrote, how the book was preserved, transmitted and accepted as canonical, and how many variant readings there are. All these rules are necessary to the extent that the text of the Bible is made of partial consistencies, different authors, and a mixture of clear and obscure passages.

Let us go back to the first principle: the knowledge of the language in which the books were written. This implies that the knowledge of Hebrew is necessary in the first place:

> And since all the writers of both the Old and New Testaments were Hebrews, a study of the Hebrew language must undoubtedly be a prime requisite not only for an understanding of the books of the Old Testament, which were written in that language, but also for the New Testament. For although the latter books were published in other languages, their idiom is Hebraic. (Spinoza 2001: 88)

Through the status of Hebrew as both a non-chosen and yet indispensable language, Spinoza presents his concept of signification and, gradually, the sacred.

How should Hebrew be read? The problem with which biblical hermeneutics is immediately confronted is the following: the letter of the Hebrew language is lost. In chapter 7 Spinoza lists all the aspects of this loss:

> Where is [such a knowledge] to be obtained? The men of old who used the Hebrew language have left to posterity no information concerning the basic principles and study of this language. At any rate, we possess nothing at all from them, neither dictionary nor grammar nor textbook on rhetoric [. . .] Nearly all the words for fruits, birds, fishes have perished with the passage of time, together with numerous other words. Then again, the meaning of many nouns and verbs occurring in the Bible are either completely unknown or subject to dispute. (2001: 94)

Spinoza then insists on the ambiguities attached to Hebrew, including the multiple meanings of its words, the difficulty of its grammar, the absence of vowel marks, and the impossibility of identifying with certainty the authors of the books (2001: 94–6).

At this point, Spinoza addresses the question of meaning. We have to suppose that even if the literality of Hebrew is lost, something in the meaning of Hebrew words is incorruptible and has remained legible and understandable. Otherwise, reading scripture would be impossible. We are forced to presuppose such incorruptibility. This integrity is not that of the letter but of the spirit, that is, of the meaning of scripture, which also constitutes its moral content. Spinoza clearly dissociates the semantic content of the message from its literality.

Is this a way to surreptitiously reintroduce the notion of the election of Hebrew? Not at all. The case of Hebrew simply allows Spinoza to develop his conception of signification, which is valid in principle for any other language.

Let us go further in the exploration of what *meaning* means for Spinoza. The striking point is the introduction of a very peculiar distinction between *meaning* and *truth*: 'For the point at issue is merely the meaning of texts', Spinoza declares, 'not their truth' (2001: 88). This implies that *the spirit of the text consists in its meaning, not its truth*. The meaning of words is incorruptible (Spinoza declares: 'it could never have been to anyone's interest to change the meaning of a word') but is not to be confounded with their truth (2001: 93). We must then admit that the semantic content of a word remains stable without this stability constituting any truth.

What, then, is semantic content if different from truth? For Spinoza, the meaning is *neither the signifier* (the letter) *nor the referent* (the truth) – the thing behind, beyond or outside the word. *The meaning pertains to the signified* (what Ferdinand Saussure would call a *concept*).[6] The signified is the stable component of a word. Such a proposition is entirely paradoxical: *how can a signified have any stability by itself, outside of its referent?*

Before answering, let's return to Levinas, as this point is crucial for him. In his view, it is clear that the 'method of procedure taught by Spinoza lacks any appeal to an anticipatory vision of the whole, which spills out over the positivist colligation of texts and is perhaps rooted in an inevitable commitment to a project. Spinoza thinks that a discourse can be understood without the vision of truths enlightening it' and isolates 'the fundamental meanings of an experience while practicing an "epoché" in relation to its truth' (1997a: 113). For Levinas, this 'epoché' of truth forever ruins hermeneutics. What does interpreting mean if truth is suspended? It is at this very moment that we can understand the supposed 'betrayal' of Spinoza.

Levinas demonstrates that in order to sustain the unsustainability of his hermeneutical theory – according to which, as we saw, a signified can exist without truth – Spinoza ultimately has to appeal to a Christian principle. In fact, hermeneutics is not really necessary because God has written the law in the human heart.

> Furthermore, if in accordance with the saying of the Apostle in 2 *Cor.*, chap. 3 v.3 [men] have within themselves the Epistle of God, written not with ink but with the Spirit of God, not on tablets of stone but on the fleshly tablets of

> the heart, let them cease to worship the letter and to show so much concern for it. (Spinoza 2001: 148)

The 'betrayal' lies at the heart of this reference to the Pauline principle of inner writing. To the 'nothing more than paper and ink' of scripture, Spinoza opposes the legibility of the heart (2001: 147).

Spinoza's betrayal cannot consist in the fact that he presents Christianity, and Catholicism in particular, as the universal religion, or in the fact that by scripture he means both the Old and the New Testaments. These positions were perfectly natural and usual at the time, and political and theological censorship left philosophers no other choice anyway. Levinas, of course, knows this. The betrayal pertains more exactly to the distinction between the signified and the truth, which is impossible in and for Judaism. Levinas writes,

> As a man of his time, Spinoza must have ignored the true meaning of the Talmud. Between the interiority of the Divine inscribed in the hearts of men and the interiority of fitting thought, on the one hand, and the exteriority of opinion, on the other, Spinoza would not have recognized, in history, a work of interiorization. (1997a: 117)

In fact, the desacralisation (antisemitism?) that pertains to the signified/truth distinction leads to a 'surreptitious' Christianisation of hermeneutics (Levinas 1997c: 108). The internal inscription infinitely surpasses language, infinitely sublates its own linguistic dimension, infinitely renders hermeneutics ('a work of interiorization') useless. In Spinoza, a preordained inscription substitutes for the self-regulative principle.

Spinoza on the Sacred

Against such a vision, it is now time to expose our reading of the theme of the sacred in Spinoza as linked to the essential symbolic dimension of his hermeneutics. The statement concerning the incorruptibility of signifiers acquires its genuine meaning in chapter 12, where the philosopher exposes his conception of the sacred. The true reason to suppose that signifiers are stable is finally brought to light. The signifier's stability is ascertained by *human usage*, that is, by *convention* only and not according to referents. 'Words acquire a fixed meaning solely from their use' (Spinoza 2001: 146). The incorruptibility of words is, then, not linked with an originary purity or authenticity. It lays its foundation on convention. Truth pertains to the referent and meaning to usage, so that the *true meaning* has definitively separated itself from the *truth of things*.

And why not, after all? A convention may be as long-lasting as a referent. But Spinoza aims at analysing a certain kind of convention, a case of convention within linguistic conventionality itself – a kind of convention that is fragile and unstable in the midst of conventional stability, and that thus contaminates the thesis of incorruptibility itself: *the convention(s) regarding the sacred*.

For Spinoza, what is sacred is neither language nor what language talks about. There are no sacred things per se, and words cannot be sacred in themselves either. The way in which the sacred comes to (its) words is, again, through convention. Sacredness is not eternal and can only be settled through usage. The problem is that, as we just saw, chapter 7 states that the signified is incorruptible thanks to convention and usage. Now, chapter 12 argues that *when it comes to the sacred* the meaning of the signified can vanish. Spinoza writes,

> Words acquire a fixed meaning solely from their use, if in accordance to this usage they are so arranged that readers are moved to devotion, then these words will be sacred, and likewise the book containing this arrangement of words. But if these words at a later time fall into disuse so as to become meaningless, or if the book falls into utter neglect, whether from malice or because men no longer feel the need of it, then both words and book will be without value and without sanctity. Lastly, if these words are arranged differently, or if by custom they acquire a meaning contrary to their original meaning, then both words and book will become impure and profane instead of sacred. (2001: 146–7)

The duet of sacralisation and profanation seems to introduce versatility and changeability into the supposed incorruptibility of words understood as signified. How are we to understand this point? It is not that Spinoza changed his mind, now admitting that which he refused a few chapters earlier – that the signified can be deleted, fall out of use like abandoned conventions, and that the value of sacredness linked to some of them is then also doomed to disappear. We must invert the causal order here. It is when the value of sacredness disappears – because it can disappear and become corrupted – it is when profanation happens that the words that led to devotion can also fall out of use. The sacred introduces a fundamental transience and versatility in the domain of the unchangeable, that is, in this instance, convention. 'A thing is called sacred and divine when its purpose is to foster piety and religion, and it is sacred only for as long as men use it in a religious way; if it is devoted to impious uses, then that which before was sacred will become unclean and profane' (Spinoza 2001: 146). The sacred can become profane because it has no referent and no semantic stability either. In a certain sense, it is a void signified, a *floating signified*, materialised only by transient signifiers: stones (the tablets of the Law), light, fire, a house, a voice, a wind or a breath.

From Hermeneutics to Overinterpretation

What, then, is it that moves the reader to devotion when they read? What confers the value of sacredness – that is, the symbolic dimension – on to words and makes signifiers burn like fires, blow like breath, or kick like stones? What transforms them into *signs*? It is, precisely, fantasy, imagination and all their productions, mysteries, fictions, revelations, *all the propensities of the mind to overinterpret God for want of a stable signified of the sacred.*

In this sense, and such is the thesis I wish to defend, the sacred only comes from an *experience of over-reading* and a certain use of language related to that experience. Spinoza declares: 'Thus it follows that nothing is sacred or profane or impure in an absolute sense apart from the mind [*extra mentem*], but only in relation to the mind' (2001: 147). The 'mind' (and here *mind* means the whole of our faculties) has a *natural tendency to overinterpret – and such is the origin, the very possibility of the sacred.* The sacred is rooted in the capacity of the mind to cope with the absence of any stable referent *and* signified of sacredness itself. Again, nothing (no thing) is sacred per se, not even the supposed sacred language, and no semantic long-lasting content can be conferred on the sacred either. Conventions change so quickly in that domain. Such is also the space of the *symbolic* in Spinoza: the possibility of opening a hole, an empty square, in the network of signs and things for the transience and mutability of the sacred.

This type of opening does not contradict natural necessity. Overinterpretation is not, or not only, the product of a human defect but is something caused by God, a dimension of his manifestation. It is something that appears with the fact of this manifestation, that is, with revelation. Of course, we ignore the 'causes' of revelation, but we can assume that the possibility of over-reading is not alien to rationality or even to expression.

We can, then, suggest that imagination, fantasy and the like are not faulty versions of a not yet rational mind, trapped within the first kind of knowledge. Rather, they are answers to the absence of the signified of the sacred and perhaps *to the absence of the signified for God himself.* After all, the tendency to over-read or overinterpret might be the necessary condition, the very first and primitive one, for the rational acceptance of a God without a name. In that sense, *a new reading of the hierarchy between the three kinds of knowledge in Spinoza is possible* and should be undertaken. It would be a reading that would consider the three forms as intermingled rather than rigidly hierarchised and, in a certain sense, exclusive of one another.

Now, what exactly does it mean to over-read and/or overinterpret? For Spinoza, to over-read or overinterpret means to confer semantic content on a word or phrase by inflating its (absence of) referent. This overinflating is fundamentally both spatial and temporal. Spatial: God is understood as a central power, coming from above, a highness (hence all the superpowers attributed to a God conceived as a legislator: jealousy, arbitrariness, love and others). *Above*, in Spinoza, is the most acute example of the spatial over-reading of the sacred. It implies an overarching and overlooking position proceeding from a hidden and unreachable power. Temporal: in its temporal sense, *above* means 'before'. All prophets have seen, have heard somebody or something that was there before, already, waiting to be seen or heard. *Above* and *before* are the two main structures or patterns of sacralisation (compare to Spinoza 2001: 9–34). In these two structures, we recognise the very economy of *superstition*.

As Emile Benveniste explains in his remarkable article on 'Religion and Superstition': 'The formal structure of the word [*superstitio*] appears to be perfectly clear, but the same cannot be said for the meaning' (1973: 523). In a sense, 'superstition' is also a floating signified. He continues,

> One fails to see how the sense of 'superstition' could emerge from the combination of '*super*' and '*stare*'.
>
> To judge by its form, *superstitio* ought to be the abstract corresponding to *superstes* 'surviving'. But how can these words be connected for their sense? For *superstes* itself does not mean only 'surviving', but in certain well attested uses it denotes 'witness'. The same difficulty arises for *superstitio* in its connection with *superstitiosus*. If we accept that somehow or other *superstitio* came to mean 'superstition', how is it that *superstitiosus* meant not 'superstitious' but 'having prophetic gifts, a seer'? [. . .] How does *superstes*, the adjective from *superstare*, come to mean 'surviving'? This has to do with the sense of *super*, which does not solely or properly mean 'above' but 'beyond' [. . .]; the *supercilium* is not only 'what is above the eyelash', it protects it by overhanging. The very notion of 'superiority' does not denote simply what is 'above' but something more, some measure of progress over what is 'beneath'. Similarly, *superstare* means 'to stand beyond', in fact, beyond an event which has destroyed the rest. Death has come upon a family: the *superstites* exist beyond this event. A man who has passed through danger, or a test, a difficult period, who has survived it, is *superstes* [. . .] This is not the only use of *superstes*: 'to continue existence beyond' implies not only 'to have survived a misfortune, or death' but also 'to have

come through any event whatsoever and to exist *beyond* this event', that is to have been a 'witness' of it [. . .]

We can now see the solution: *superstitiosus* is the one who is 'endowed with the power of *superstitio*', that is, '*qui vera praedicat*', the seer who speaks of past events *as if he had actually been present:* the 'divination' in these examples did not refer to the future but to the past. *Superstitio* is the gift of a second sight which enables a person to know the past as if he or she had been present, *superstes*. This is how *superstitiosus* denotes the gift of second sight, which is attributed to 'seers', that of being a 'witness' of events at which he has not been present. (1973: 523–7)

In this powerfully beautiful analysis, we see how the *above* and *before* are both playing at the heart of superstition. *Superstare* would mean to stand beyond, above [*super*], an event that has destroyed everything and everyone else (the shock of a revelation, for example), thus being a *survivor* of this event that happened *before* and being able to bear witness to it. Or, in a slightly derived sense, it would mean to have a gift of second sight and do and speak as if one has been above or beyond the past event so that one can make it present by seeing it.

I certainly shall not argue that Spinoza is a defender of superstition, but I do think that his acerbic attacks against it seek to dismantle the constitution of superstition as a means of intellectual and political enslavement to authority, rather than condemning it as such. It is when superstition is transformed into dogma, when the floating signifieds are illegitimately filled up, when theology uses it to change obedience into servitude, when political power uses it to install censorship, thus forbidding all freedom of speech, that it has to be deconstructed. What has to be deconstructed, then, is the authority [*auctoritas*] produced by revelation. However, the very basis of superstition, that is, the tendency to over-read, is not bad per se. On the contrary, it marks the origin of the symbolic, and in that sense, it cannot be totally separated from ideality.

Deleuze is, then, not entirely correct when he declares '*Superstition* is everything that keeps us cut off from our power of action and continually diminishes it' or when he identifies revelation with the 'genesis of an illusion' (1990a: 270, 58).

As for Levinas, we may admit that Spinoza perhaps did not insist on hermeneutics and exegesis as he should have, but what he showed is that the origin of interpretation resides in overinterpretation – a dimension that Levinas never takes into account and that he would certainly have confounded only with false prophecy. No need, for Spinoza, to refer to any transcendence in the message. Overinterpretation is, in a certain sense, *immanent* to the message.

Nevertheless, because it introduces some laxity into the tissue of immanence itself, because of the linguistic as well as ontological void lying at the heart of the sacred, as I said earlier, it is better to characterise it as that which opens a space within necessity, a space that is neither a space of immanence nor of transcendence.

Insisting on the importance of such a space, which is neither within truth nor outside it but around it like a void aura, I certainly do not intend to contradict the view of Spinoza as a critic of superstition and religious authorities. I agree with Yirmiyahu Yovel that for Spinoza, 'to clear the mind of transcendent images' is an absolute prerequisite, that 'prior to any positive philosophy of immanence, a critique of [. . .] religions must be undertaken' (1989: 3). I simply aim to demonstrate that Spinoza also acknowledges overinterpretation – the very basis of both superstition and theological dogmatism – as being a necessary *beginning*. Such a beginning should not be conceived of as a first imperfect step on a scale of knowledge but rather as the opening of the symbolic dimension of God, its meaning, whatever its truth.

The hermeneutical critical method, as developed in chapter 7, then appears to be the threshold between reason and over-reading, as well as the threshold between over-reading and superstition when the latter becomes solidified as an ideological/theological alienating power and can foster nothing but fear and hatred. The task of the method is to help reconstitute the *contexts* in which things or words have been considered sacred on every occasion, thus acknowledging that the meaning of the sacred, since it is always contextual, is fundamentally changeable and unstable. This type of instability determines what is clear and what is obscure in the Bible: 'Now here I term a pronouncement obscure or clear according to the degree of difficulty with which the meaning can be elicited from, and not according to the degree of difficulty with which its truth can be perceived by reason' (Spinoza 2001: 88). The methodological mission is to determine on every occasion the part played by over-reading in scripture in order to bring to light the everlasting strict meaning of the Law, its minimal kernel, and to ban any supernatural meaning from it. In return, the method also teaches us that there can be no eternal meaning of the Law, no immediate meaning of the internally written message, without the prior symbolic overdimensioning of all writings and all signs that constitutes our first encounter with the Law, a first encounter without which there would be no Law at all. Over-reading, then, when critically addressed, is not a force of enslavement but instead the opening of truth, its gate.

Conclusion

As we know, Spinoza advocates freedom of opinion, that is, also freedom of overinterpretation. Readers have to be free to see things and words as they want as long as their personal creed concurs with peace, morality and political stability. Therefore, in the *Treatise*, freedom of opinion is founded on the fact that 'every man is bound to adapt [religious] dogma to his own way of thinking, and to interpret them accordingly as he feels' (2001: 188). Freedom of speech is thus essentially linked to the recognition of the legitimacy of every human's natural tendency to overinterpret or over-read and the symbolic dimension of these operations. Everyone is sovereign when it comes to religious matters, and no external authority should ever legislate for them. Such is the foundation of democracy and proof that ordinary people's faith or approach to God is not reducible to a credulous and idiotic act of devotion.

Once again, this does not imply that something like a hermeneutical self-regulative power functions at the heart of overinterpretation and allows superstition to control itself, automatically transforming the exegetical excess into the right understanding of the Law. For Spinoza, the symbolic, as rooted in overinterpretation, is forever engaged in its own contextualisation and has no essence outside of it. By definition, no one is able to know what the next context will be – and it is not for philosophy to decide. Philosophy must remain in its own place – which does not mean that philosophy is not concerned with the symbolic.

This brings me back to Deleuze. Confronting Gottfried Wilhelm Leibniz and Spinoza on expression, Deleuze states that the great difference between them is that Leibniz integrates the symbolic into his concept of expression, whereas Spinoza excludes it. Equivocity, shadows, ambiguity are part of Leibnizian expressionism. With Leibniz, Deleuze says, we have 'a "symbolic" philosophy of expression, in which expression is inseparable from signs of its transformations, and from the obscure areas in which it is plunged' (1990a: 329). This is not the case for Spinoza,

> for what is essential for [him] is to separate the domain of signs, which are always equivocal, from that of expressions, where univocity must be an absolute rule. Thus we have seen how the three types of signs (the indicative signs of natural perception, the imperative signs of the moral law and of religious revelation) were decisively rejected as inadequate. (Deleuze 1990a: 330)

Why the compulsion to castrate Spinoza's expression from its symbols? Why this idolatry of transparency? Against such repressive gestures, I affirm that to acknowledge the symbolic dimension of immanence in no way destroys it. Essentially, it allows it to breathe.

Translated by Carolyn Shread

Notes

1 Levinas wrote three essays on Spinoza: 'The Spinoza Case' (1997), 'Have you Reread Baruch?' (1997) and 'Spinoza's Background' (1994). He also refers to Spinoza sporadically in a number of other texts, but in the present essay I concentrate primarily on his three published essays on Spinoza in the context of his discussions of biblical hermeneutics listed above.
2 Compare to Balibar (1985: 52–6).
3 'Hence it came about that the [one] imagined God as a ruler, lawgiver, king, merciful, just and so forth; whereas these are all merely attributes of human nature, and not at all applicable to the divine nature' (Spinoza 2001: 53). On this point, see also the appendix to book 1 of Spinoza's *Ethics* (1996: 25–30).
4 This hypothesis is repeated twice in Levinas: 'Spinoza, in his Jewish studies, perhaps only had teachers of little calibre' (1997c: 109); and see Levinas (1994c: 169).
5 On the difficult problem of the relationship between learned readings of the Torah [*pardes*] and personal ones, see in particular Levinas (1994a: 101–15).
6 See Saussure (2011).

6

Can We Relinquish the Transcendental?

I borrow the terms of my title's question from Quentin Meillassoux's book *After Finitude*, which I intend to discuss here, a book that has provoked a genuine thunderstorm in the philosophical sky. 'The primary condition to the issue I intend to deal with here', Meillassoux says, 'is "the relinquishing of transcendentalism"' (2009: 27). The French expression is *l'abandon du transcendantal*. I think that 'the relinquishing of the transcendental' is better than 'the relinquishing of transcendentalism'. As for *relinquish*, it implies something softer, gentler, than *abandon*. *Abandonment* means a definite separation, whereas *relinquishing* designates a negotiated rupture, a farewell that maintains a relationship with what it splits from. Whether Meillassoux's *abandon* means 'relinquishing' or 'abandonment' will be examined later. For the moment I wish to insist upon the fact that he proposes that we leave the transcendental, and consequently also Kant, behind. What I intend to question is this very gesture: Can we relinquish the transcendental, and consequently, can we relinquish Kant?

The problem is all the more serious if we admit that Kantianism may be considered the very origin, the very foundation, of European philosophy, that is, of the continental tradition.[1] So the 'we' included in the question 'Can *we* relinquish the transcendental?' addresses all continental philosophers. Its signification then becomes: Can we relinquish the transcendental without relinquishing purely and simply continental philosophy? Without putting at risk continental philosophy's identity? Such is the immense challenge raised by *After Finitude*.

First, I will examine the reasons for such a challenge, which will lead me to expose Meillassoux's main arguments. I will then discuss them.

Transcendental, says Kant in the introduction to the *Critique of Pure Reason*, should be understood both as synonymous with a priori, meaning '*absolutely independently of all experience*' (1998: 137), and as synonymous with the condition of possibility in general: 'The *a priori* possibility of cognition [. . .] can be called transcendental' (1998: 196). The relinquishing of the transcendental, then, implies a break with the a priori, with the idea of the condition of possibility, as well as with their circularity.

Why should we proceed to such a rupture? Because, as Meillassoux argues, this circularity was never able to entirely veil or hide its lack of foundation. There can be no transcendental *deduction* of the transcendental. The a priori is just a presupposition. What Kant calls deduction is only a description, a way to posit simple *facts*. The pure forms of knowledge and thinking – categories, principles, ideas – are just decreed, posited, never deduced or justified. In Kant, Meillassoux argues,

> it is impossible to derive the forms of thought from a principle or system capable of endowing them with absolute necessity. These forms constitute a 'primary fact' which is only susceptible to description, and not to deduction [. . .] And if the realm of the in-itself can be distinguished from the phenomenon, this is precisely because of the facticity of these forms, the fact that they can be only described, for if they were deducible [. . .] theirs would be an unconditional necessity that abolishes the possibility of there being an in itself that could differ from them. (2009: 38)

The transcendental, again, is a fact.

But, one may ask: is this not an old question? How does one not object that the bringing to light of such a facticity has already and often been done? Has not the transcendental already been relinquished, criticised, deconstructed in the name of its defective foundations? Examples of such approaches are numerous; I could, of course, immediately mention Hegel, but we can also consider three examples in twentieth-century philosophy before going back to Meillassoux: Heidegger, Derrida and Foucault.

The vocabulary of the transcendental is evident in *Being and Time*, as well as in *Kant and the Problem of Metaphysics*.[2] The title of *Being and Time*'s first part is 'The Interpretation of Dasein in Terms of Temporality and the Explication of Time as the Transcendental Horizon for the Question of Being'. Originary temporality is defined in both books in terms of 'schemas' ('horizontal schemas of the *extases* of temporality').[3]

Without entering into the detail of Heidegger's philosophical evolution, I will just mention that, after *Being and Time*, in *The Basic Problems of Phenomenology*, for example, and later in the *Contributions to Philosophy*,[4] Heidegger never again uses the term *transcendental*, and assimilates the a priori to an ontic metaphysical principle among others. The signification of the *Turning* in Heidegger may be already considered a relinquishing of the transcendental.

In Derrida's work, we can isolate three main elaborations of the critique of the transcendental – first, the deconstruction of the Husserlian concept of the transcendental *vécu* developed in *Voice and Phenomenon*;[5] second, the critique of the 'transcendental signified' developed in *Of Grammatology* (1997: 20); and third, the dismantling of the notion of system in *Glas*, where Derrida writes: 'Isn't there always an element excluded from the system that assures the system's space of possibility? The transcendental has always been, strictly, a transcategorical, what could be received, formed, terminated in none of the categories intrinsic to the system. The system's vomit' (1986: 163a). What Derrida brings to light here is that the transcendental is in a way arbitrarily imposed upon the system as its form, but remains itself exterior to the system, alien to it, coming from nowhere.

As for Foucault, we know how complex his relationship with the transcendental is. While leaving aside the detail of the crucial analyses in *Archaeology of Knowledge*,[6] as well as those developed in 'What is Enlightenment?', I will just refer to a famous passage from his conversation with Giulio Preti in 1972, 'The Question of Culture':

> In all of my work I strive [. . .] to avoid any reference to this transcendental as a condition of possibility for any knowledge. When I say that I strive to avoid it, I do not mean that I am sure of succeeding. I try to historicize to the utmost to leave as little space as possible to the transcendental. I cannot exclude the possibility that one day I will have to confront an irreducible *residuum* which will be, in fact, the transcendental. (Foucault 1996: 98–9).[7]

We see, from these examples, that the 'break' with the transcendental, to use another of Meillassoux's expressions (2009: 28), is not exactly a new and unexpected gesture; it is inscribed in what already appears to be a tradition.

Nevertheless, to come back to the distinction between *relinquishing* and *abandoning*, I would say, contradicting the translator a little, that Heidegger, Derrida and Foucault *relinquish* the transcendental, whereas Meillassoux *abandons* it. Continental philosophers until now, however violent their reading of Kant, however radical their critique of the transcendental, seem to have always preserved or maintained something of it in the end, calling it 'quasi-transcendental', for example,[8] because even if *transcendental* is too metaphysical a name, it nevertheless circumscribes what may be seen as the minimal creed of continental philosophy. The creed that exists is a set of structures of both theoretical and practical experience that are irreducible to two extremes – to empirical material data, on the one hand, and to purely formal logic entities or procedures, on the other: a set of concepts that allow the real to exist and that could not exist without the real. Foucault, in 'On the Archaeology of the Sciences', gives a helpful definition. The transcendental is said to be 'a play of forms that anticipate all contents insofar as they have already rendered them possible' (1998: 331–2).

So again, the destruction or critique of the transcendental has until now only been a readjustment, never an abandonment of it. What happens today is something way more radical than these destructive-deconstructive-critical re-elaborations. It is something much more abrupt, adamant, dangerous – the idea of an *absolute* abandonment of the transcendental, and of its minimal creed, which we may make even more minimal: the idea of the 'irreducible', the irreducible 'residue'.

Why dangerous? Because if we break the hold of irreducibility, to what shall 'we' be reduced? 'You' will be reduced to what 'you' are, Meillassoux says, that is, 'you' will be identified as subjects, that is, as 'correlationists'. The word *correlationism* at work in *After Finitude* has become infamous. Let us try to understand it specifically in the context of the irreducible, which usually defines the transcendental.

Meillassoux argues that such an irreducibility (also its meaning in phenomenology) is precisely what is non-deductible and purely factual in Kantian philosophy. It is only a decision of thought, an unjustifiable one. This decision pertains to a priori synthesis. What Kant has posited as the irreducible is the originary synthesis, entanglement, correlation between the subject and the object, or the world and the subject as it appears in the passage from Foucault I just quoted. 'The transcendental' is just another name for this conjunction, which again is not explicable in terms of materialism (it is not the product of any empirical genesis) or formal logic.

'By correlation', Meillassoux writes,

> we mean the idea according to which we only have access to the correlation between thinking and being, never to either term considered apart from the other. We will henceforth call correlationism any current of thought which maintains the unsurpassable character of the correlation to be defined [. . .] Correlationism consists in disqualifying the claim that it is possible to consider the realms of subjectivity and objectivity independently of one another. (2009: 5)

Correlation is, of course, another name for synthesis. To relinquish the transcendental implies revising 'decisions often considered as infrangible since Kant' (2009: 26), mainly the decision to confer any priority to the synthesis.

In a sense, as Meillassoux acknowledges, 'we cannot be heirs to Kantianism' (2009: 29). There is no question of denying it; returning to pre-critical philosophy or dogmatism is purely and simply impossible. But what appears as one of the main challenges of our philosophical time is the task of elaborating a genuine post-critical position, non-synthetic, without it pertaining to analytical philosophy either.

In order to explain in a more detailed way the critique of correlationism, I choose two lines of analysis among the most radical. First, this critique coincides with an unprecedented movement of dispossession and expropriation of subjectivity; second, it leads to elaborating a new concept of alterity, an alterity other than that of the utterly other.

I

To relinquish the transcendental implies the neutralisation of the 'proper' and of 'property'. To relinquish the synthesis amounts to admitting that the world is not our world, that the laws of nature are not those of our understanding. That we are not correlated to the world or nature in the first place means that they do not belong to us. The synthesis as Kant defines it is undoubtedly a mark of property; let us recall the beginning of the *Critique of Judgment*, for example, where he distinguishes between a field, a territory and a domain, and affirms that we have to find, in this geography, a place where knowledge is possible for us, as a place of our own:

> Concepts, insofar as they are referred to objects, regardless of whether a cognition of the latter is possible or not, have their field, which is determined merely in accordance with the relation which their object has to our faculty of cognition in general. – The part of this field within which cognition is possible for us is a territory [*territorium*] for these concepts and the requisite faculty of cognition. The part of the territory in which these are legislative is the domain [*ditio*] of these concepts and of the corresponding faculty of cognition. (Kant 2000: 61–2)

The metaphor of the 'land' is very significant here; it conveys the idea of possession, ownership and mastery. Such is the contradiction of Kantianism, that it presents itself as a desubstantialisation of subjectivity; subjectivity, for Kant, is just a form – but it confers on the a priori synthesis the status of an owned space. For Kant, there is nothing prior to our relationship to the world.

The philosophy to come must then restitute the world to itself, and consequently also its anteriority over the a priori itself. The theme of 'ancestrality' is the expression of such an anteriority or precedence: 'I will call "ancestral" any reality anterior to the emergence of the human species – or even anterior to every recognized form of life on earth'; 'a world that is posited as anterior to the emergence of thought and even of life' (Meillassoux 2009: 9–10).

We do not, then, have to fear a return to empiricism or pure logicism. To relinquish the transcendental precisely implies exploring a dimension of speculation that comes prior to any experience as well as to any form of judgement; it implies 'describ[ing] a world where humanity is absent', a 'desert', 'a world crammed with things and events that are not the correlates of any manifestation: a world that is not a correlate of a relation to the world', 'a world anterior to experience' (Meillassoux 2009: 26).

This deserted, neutral, dispossessed world is indifferent to the fact of being thought. This indifference is, for Meillassoux, another name for the absolute, for something radically separated – *absolutus* – from us, 'capable of existing without us [. . .] whose separateness from thought is such that it presents itself to us as non-relative to us, and hence as capable of existing whether we exist or not' (2009: 28). To me, this approach to the absolute indifference of the world is the most radical attempt at dismantling the notion of 'proper', challenging the Heideggerian couple of *Ereignis* and *Enteignis*, or the Derridean deconstruction of the self or of auto-affection, or the Foucauldian concept of *parrhesia*. Playing with the difference between the world and the earth, it appears as the first speculative ecological concept. The earth is a space that is not ours. We have to think of it as it was before colonisation. We have to invent a philosophy without private property.

We reach here the second point of analysis – the other alterity.

II

A world capable of existing without us is, as we just saw, a world that is indifferent to the fact of being thought or judged, and consequently also indifferent to its supposed necessity. Necessity is just one of our categories. In reality, the world is radically contingent. It is this radical contingency that appears as the absolute other.

Let me first explain what contingency means in *After Finitude*. This brings us back to Kant. What is at stake in the Transcendental Deduction is the affirmation that there exists an a priori 'agreement' between pure concepts and the objects of experience. This agreement [*Übereinstimmung*] – another name for correlation or synthesis – guarantees the universal causality and necessity of nature, consequently also the stability and permanence of natural laws: 'For Kant, if our representations of the world were not governed by necessary connections – which he calls the "categories", among which is the principle of causality – the world would be nothing but a disordered mass of confused perceptions, incapable of yielding the experience of a unified consciousness' (Meillassoux 2009: 93). Against Hume and scepticism in general, Kant argues that nature cannot change, that the laws cannot change for no reason.

Again, the a priori synthesis guarantees the universal necessity of the order of things – the order of both nature and the world. The problem, as we already saw, is that such a necessity cannot be deduced but, rather, only described. A priori synthesis is never proved or justified and always appears as purely factual. There is no necessary demonstration of natural necessity. How could it be otherwise, to the extent that the basis of transcendental necessity itself, that is, correlation, does not have any sufficient reason?

It then appears that the correlational structure is itself totally contingent: 'Facticity just consists in not knowing why the correlational structure has to be thus' (Meillassoux 2009: 39). This 'not knowing why' is not the result of a flaw in Kant's argument or reasoning. Contingency is what is. There is only contingency: 'Contingency alone is necessary' (2009: 80). Then why not admit it? Why not call factuality the speculative essence of facticity, that is, the absoluteness of contingency? Why not admit that Kant never solved Hume's problem?

This problem, as we know, 'can be formulated as follows': 'Is it possible to demonstrate that the same effects will always follow from the same causes *ceteris paribus*, i.e. all other things being equal?' (Meillassoux 2009: 85). This question concerns the capacity of physics to demonstrate the necessity of causal connection and consequently the permanent stability of natural laws.

That the world might radically change, that the laws of physics might be totally contingent, is the hypothesis that Kant adamantly rejects. Nevertheless, because of its inability to provide the necessary demonstration of causality, transcendental idealism negatively reveals the very existence of what it disavows. Its deduction is its destruction. Why not, then, open philosophy to its essence, that is, absolute contingency – that is, also, absolute otherness?

'Contingency', Meillassoux writes,

> refers back to the Latin *contingere*, meaning 'to touch, to befall', which is to say, that which happens, but which happens enough to happen *to* us. The contingent, in a word, is something that finally happens – something other, something which, in its irreducibility to all pre-registered possibilities, puts an end to the vanity of a game wherein everything, even the improbable, is predictable. (2009: 108)

A speculative concept of contingency demands that we radically distinguish between contingency and chance, which also means that the contingency of natural laws remains 'inaccessible to aleatory reasoning' (2009: 100).

We have to go beyond Hume to solve Hume's problem because the traditional concept of contingency is linked with the notions of probability and chance. The billiard balls and the rolling of the dice constitute the most famous examples of such a link. Why can't probabilities allow us access to the absolute contingency of natural laws? We touch here an important point. Even if the number of possibilities or probabilities opened by chance is infinite, chance does not and will not ever displace the very concept of possibility itself. Our world might have been different, and it is perhaps just the result of a happy chance. Another world might have been possible. But the concept of possibility itself would remain the same. Chance is not able to modify the meanings of possibility and necessity, because it fundamentally depends upon them: 'The very notion of chance is only conceivable on the condition that there are unalterable physical laws' (Meillassoux 2009: 99). The notion of chance thus requires that one believe in the fact that possibilities, even if innumerable, form a whole and can be totalised as a numerical entity.

Meillassoux then brings to light a non-probabilistic type of reasoning that allows us to access absolute contingency as also 'mathematical in nature'. It is the transfinite. The Cantorian notion of the transfinite corresponds to the impossibility of totalising the possible:

> It is precisely this totalization [of the possibilities] which can *no longer* be guaranteed *a priori*. For we know – indeed we have known it at last since Cantor's revolutionary set-theory – that we have no grounds for maintaining that the conceivable is *necessarily* totalizable. For one of the fundamental components of this revolution was the detotalization of number, a detotalization also known as the transfinite. (2009: 103)

Absolute contingency would thus be associated with the absolute possibility of the non-existence of possibility as such, with the idea of a world in which possibility and necessity would not mean anything, which would for that reason ruin the notion of probability or chance.

Radical contingency has to be conceived as the deprivation of all physical necessity without conferring on this deprivation the status of a possibility. The speculative concept of radical contingency, according to which contingency alone is necessary, brings to light the strong link that binds dispossession, alterity and mathematics together – which is another major challenge. Mathematics, freed from the Copernican revolution, lays bare the ontological principles of a deserted world 'where humanity is absent, a world crammed with things and events that are not the correlates of any manifestation' (Meillassoux 2009: 26).

I totally share Meillassoux's contention that all philosophical attempts at opening philosophy to alterity have until now remained poetic. Let us think of the 'other thinking' in Heidegger (the non-metaphysical thinking), the utterly other in Levinas, or the *arrivant* in Derrida. Let us consider the themes of the unforeseeable, the unanticipatable, the totally unheard of or the absolutely surprising – all these have remained the poetic or literary expressions of a new messianism. What I share with *After Finitude* is that the Other has been said to be absolute out of the absolute impossibility of our reason proving its absoluteness. Meillassoux, then, is right when he affirms: 'By forbidding reason any claim to the absolute, the end of metaphysics has taken the form of an exacerbated return of the religious' (2009: 45).

The attempt to define a new relationship to otherness through mathematical reasoning allows us to elaborate a rational concept of it. Thanks to the transfinite, we can access a speculative notion of absolute otherness, which has nothing to do with a promise, an expectation, an announcement, but, rather, has to do with the otherness of the real itself, the real otherness of the real as it is, that is, according to its contingency. Here is the expression of this radical otherness:

> Everything could actually collapse: from trees to stars, from stars to laws, from physical laws to logical laws; and this not by virtue of some superior law whereby everything is destined to perish, but by virtue of the absence of any superior law capable of preserving anything, no matter what, from perishing. (Meillassoux 2009: 53)

To conclude on this concept, I think that Meillassoux has touched an important point, which is that until now, all gestures of abandonment or relinquishing of the transcendental have induced a separation between philosophy and science, have ignored and despised the scientific deconstructions of the transcendental, and have simply maintained the transcendental in poeticising it. I think that this split between philosophy and science urgently has to come to an end.

Nevertheless, this is what I would briefly like to develop to bring this essay to a close: I am not convinced by the way in which Meillassoux proposes to overcome this split. Let me go back to the previous passage about the meaning of contingency, or *contingere*: 'The contingent, in a word, is something that finally happens – something other, something which, in its irreducibility to all pre-registered possibilities, puts an end to the vanity of a game wherein everything, even the improbable, is predictable' (2009: 108). At this point, we expect an explosion, a surprise. What is this alterity? What does it look like?

What world does it create? What defeat of finitude? What metamorphosis? What is happening?

Well, one is forced to say, nothing. Nothing happens in the end. Even within the transfinite theoretical framework, the world remains what it is. The dice of the world remain what they are.

Here starts the less convincing part of the book, where in the end Meillassoux strives to prove that contingency does not threaten the world's stability. There is no absolute necessity, but there is no Chaos either: 'Our conviction, and here we come to the crux of the matter – is that in order for an entity to be contingent and un-necessary [. . .] *it cannot be anything* whatsoever' (2009: 66). Further, 'to be is necessarily to be a fact, but to be a fact is not just to be anything whatsoever' (2009: 79).

I understand that 'contingency is such that anything might happen, even nothing at all, so that what is, remains as it is' (2009: 63). Nevertheless, I do not understand the rejection of the 'anything' – why alterity, if absolute, could not be anything whatsoever. Why can't contingency be assimilated with the 'anything'?

It seems that we are reconducted here to the old split between authenticity and inauthenticity: there would be the good contingency and the inauthentic one, the 'anything'. Meillassoux in the end says that contingency is only thinkable, mathematically possible, not actual. The contingency of the real is not real. There is no revolution, then, in the end; everything remains as it is. In fact, Kant was right, of course: the cinnabar is always red – and not any red but this red.

It appears that Meillassoux, in the end, wants to consolidate the virtuality of a total change and the constancy and stability of nature. In a very Kantian mode, he preserves the possibility of the world. In a very Kantian mode, he brings to light the conditions of possibility for contingency, that is, its transcendental concept: the transcendental difference between what is contingent and what is or can be just 'anything'.

I will conclude with some questions and a little dialogue:

—Can we relinquish the transcendental? If transcendental means authentic, then not only can we relinquish the transcendental, but we have to. It also means, then, that we have to relinquish the transfinite, which is of an alterity that is only mathematically possible, as this appears as another form of authenticity and irreducibility. We definitely have to relinquish the irreducible.

—Do you mean that nothing is irreducible, authentic or unconditional?

—Yes, this is what I mean.

CAN WE RELINQUISH THE TRANSCENDENTAL?

—Then can we remain continental philosophers if we open the door of the irreducibility to the anything?

—No, if we follow Heidegger, Derrida, . . . or Meillassoux, no. Yes, if we follow . . . if we follow Kant himself.

—Kant himself?

—Yes, Kant himself. The trajectory of the three *Critiques* coincides with the most radical exposure of the transcendental to its own destruction ever. When Kant deals with the living being, in the second part of the *Critique of Judgment*, he deals with the non-transcendental, which is in need of its determination. He then comes to the conclusion that there are two types of necessities, mechanistic and teleological. The Kantian deconstruction of the transcendental pertains to this pluralisation of necessity. What does life do to thought? 'There are so many modifications of the universal transcendental natural concepts left undetermined by the laws given a priori', says Kant in the preface to the third *Critique* (2000: 67). Life is what modifies the transcendental, what relinquishes it by forcing it to transform itself.

—To become plastic, you mean?

—Yes.

—We thus have to negotiate the relinquishing of the transcendental with Kant's own struggle with it.

—How, then?

—Well, in exploring a field that is so often despised by the philosophers – we mentioned it, that of biology.

—In establishing that our categories are reducible to biological concepts, for example?

—Yes, exactly.

—That the transcendental is in the brain?

—Yes, exactly.

—Are you aware of being inauthentically Kantian when you say that?

—I am perfectly aware of it and not certain that Kant would have rejected such an inauthentic approach to his philosophy.

Notes

1 On the relationship between Kantianism and continental philosophy, see Rockmore (2006) and Braver (2007).
2 See in particular sections 21–3, 32–4.
3 *Extases* is the name that Heidegger gives to the three moments of time – present, past and future – to the extent that they are constantly out of themselves (from the Greek *ek-stasis*).

4 See in particular sections 111–12.
5 See chapter VI in particular.
6 See in particular chapter V.
7 See Koopman (2010).
8 *Quasi-transcendental* is a term coined by Jacques Derrida and often used by him, for example, in *Glas* (1986: 163a).

7

Is Science the Subject of Philosophy? Miller, Badiou and Derrida Respond

I

I wish to make you aware of two reading experiences I have had. The first is that of reading Alain Badiou's 1969 text, published in *Cahiers pour l'analyse*, titled 'Mark and Lack', where we can find the affirmation that gave rise to my title: 'Science is the subject of philosophy'.[1] This essay is a response to Jacques-Alain Miller's 'Suture: Elements of the Logic of the Signifier', published a few years prior to Badiou's essay in the same journal. Despite their specific and very dated context – their questions about science had to confront, at that time, both psychoanalysis and Marxism – they contain very important elements for thinking the relations between science and philosophy today, and they have import that, in my opinion, goes well beyond their time.

The second discovery is altogether different. While, for other reasons, I was recently rereading Derrida's 'Passions: An Oblique Offering', I was struck by the coincidence – if not the similarity – of the analyses developed in that book with those developed by Badiou about the *situation* of philosophy. The word 'situation' is being taken here in its proper sense, as venue, place and orientation, all at the same time. This coincidence is more surprising given that the two thinkers have little in common with each other, as is attested to by the extreme difference in the points of departure of their respective discourses. Badiou undertakes the analysis of the relations between philosophy and mathematical logic, while Derrida concerns himself with the relations between philosophy and literature. Despite it all, their conclusions strangely and mutually echo each other.

In both cases, what I will call the law of the fault of philosophy emerges. For both thinkers, philosophy is in need of an answer. It wants to answer for everything, even, which is the problem, for that which does not respond. What does not respond, for Badiou, is science. For Derrida, literature. Examining these two types of non-responses more closely will constitute my subject, which is precisely the question of the subject. There is no subject of science, says Badiou; there is no subject of literature, says Derrida. This double absence of subject constitutes precisely, for them, the subject of philosophy, which is supposed to respond in their place by wrongly characterising this absence as a lack. A lack that is not possible to fill, but is possible at least to make speak.

II

Miller undertakes to show that science, and in particular mathematical logic, proceeds from a denial of lack, and sutures closed all that could leave the place of the other of science (which is to say, the subject function) empty. By definition, science is 'objective' and admits no lacuna or void, no desire nor gap. This constitutes the 'suture' or foreclosure that Miller, with the help of Lacan, intends to deconstruct. To this end, Miller begins with a reading of Frege's *The Foundations of Arithmetic*, where he defends the idea that zero, in mathematics, is precisely not a void or a lack.

In *The Foundations of Arithmetic*, Frege defines number. A number refers to no particular thing. It does, however, have an object. What is the difference between a thing – that empirical X – and an object? The difference between four balls as things and what the number 4 measures? What do things become once they are numbered and numerable, in other words? They become *units*. Because of this, they obey particular syntactic determinations, which are ordered by a fundamental rule or structure, which Frege outlines in the following way: Numbers are extensions of concepts. The number 4, for example, is the extension of the concept 'four'. The two are equinumerical. 'The number which belongs to the concept F', says Frege, 'is the extension of the concept "equinumerical to the concept F"' (1980: 85).

What does 'concept' mean here? 'Concept' signifies self-identity. Saying that a number is an extension of a concept signifies that a number is identical to its concept, that it is identical to itself. In other words, as Miller rightly says, all numbers presuppose 'the concept of identity to a concept' (1965: 42).[2] This rule of identity to a concept is valid for all numbers. 'The concept of identity to a concept' works for every number. This is the rule of unity: being self-identical means to 'be one'. There is thus some 'one' in all numbers. 'This one [that of the singular unit] [. . .] is common to all numbers in so far as they are first constituted as units' (1965: 42).

The object is the thing become one (self-identical), and thus numberable. 'That definition, pivotal to his concept', continues Miller, 'is one that Frege

IS SCIENCE THE SUBJECT OF PHILOSOPHY?

borrows from Leibniz. It is contained in this statement: *eadem sunt quorum unum potest substitui alteri salva veritate*. Those things are identical of which one can be substituted for the other *salva veritate* without loss of truth' (1965: 43). Numbers are substitutable for one another insofar as in them, at any time, the self-identical repeats itself, that is, the 'one' of the unit. We can thus 'pass' from one number to another without losing truth, since identity is preserved.

But the problem then arises of knowing how one 'progresses' from one number to another. How the number can 'pass from the repetition of the 1 of the identical to its ordered succession: 1, 2, 3, 4, 5?' The answer: for that to occur, 'the zero has to appear' (1965: 43). And Miller here makes reference to the very influential Fregean analysis of zero.

Why is the 'engendering of the zero' (1965: 44) necessary for Frege? At this point, we have posited the self-identity of the concept of number, and thus of the number itself. That is to say that 'non-identity with itself is contradictory to the very dimension of truth'. How then to designate non-identity? 'To its concept, we assign the zero', says Miller, reading Frege (1965: 44). Nothing falls under the concept 'non-identical with itself' if not, Miller continues, a void or a gap. Zero is the name of that nothing. Yet Frege nonetheless defines zero as a number, to which he assigns the cardinal 1. This is where the 'suture' comes from, from that eclipse of the zero by the one.

The non-self-identical answers fully, for Frege, to the principle by which, for any object, it must be possible to say under what concept it must be subsumed. Yet zero can be subsumed under the concept of non-self-identity as 'identical to zero'. Thus, zero is identical to its concept, the concept of non-self-identity. Let there be a concept 'identical to zero'. One and only one object, zero, is subsumed under that concept. 'One' is thus by definition the cardinal number that belongs to that concept. Zero is 'one' in the sense of self-identity. Now, in trying to make the number 1 appear, it must be shown that something can immediately follow zero in the series of natural numbers. 'Zero', Miller says, following Frege, 'is the number assigned to the non-self-identical' (1965: 44). This number is 1 [marked zero]. It follows that 1 follows immediately from 0 in the series of natural numbers.[3] From there we can deduce the set of numbers, following the structure of 'following from', with the restriction that no number can follow itself in the natural series of numbers beginning with zero. Inscribing zero as a point of departure for the series of numbers makes it possible that the rule n+1:0 (self-identity of the concept 'not identical to itself') is followed by 1, which itself is followed by 2, then by 3 and so on.

Examining the Fregean argument on the subject of zero, Miller concludes that the zero is at the same time summoned and dismissed. 'That which in the real is pure and simple absence finds itself through the fact of number (through the instance of truth) noted 0 and counted for 1' (1965: 45). The word 'suture' signifies: 1) the uniting, by use of thread, of divided parts after an accident or surgical intervention; 2) the immobile articulation characterised by two jointed surfaces united by fibrous tissue, like those which form the cranium, the apparent line constituting the conjunction of two parts. The suture is thus always at the same time a division and a conjunction. In every case, the seam, the conjunction, remains visible.

What is really sutured in Frege's discourse in particular, and in formal scientific language in particular? Miller responds: the subject-function. 'To designate it I choose the name of suture. Suture names the relation of the subject to the chain of its discourse' (1965: 39). The appearance-disappearance of the zero in the series of numbers figures the appearance-disappearance of the subject in the chain of its discourse.

Frege affirms, however, multiple times, that logic does not follow from a subjective act, which is always, for Frege, psychological. Yet it is precisely this which appears to Miller as a denial. According to Frege, the subject counts for nothing. From this, it follows that suturing the zero can be read as suturing the subject. Indeed, for Miller, only the subject-function can subtend the operations of abstraction, of unification, of progression. There is, therefore, identity only for a subject. The subject that produces the primary unity; it is impossible to think self-identity outside of the subject, since the subject-function *is* the identity-function. We have known since Descartes that a subject is, by definition, a power identical to itself. The subject is the form of identity. At the same time, like the zero, the subject is never self-identical. Like the zero, it receives its identity from a lack, it misses itself. The relationship of the zero to the chain of numbers is the same as the relationship of the subject to the chain of discourse. Like the zero, the subject is both present and absent at once. 'It figures [in the chain] as the element which is lacking, in the form of a stand-in. For, while there lacking, it is not purely and simply absent' (Miller 1965: 39). Lacan shows that, in the same way that the zero is excluded from the beginning from the chain of numbers, the subject is excluded from the field of the Other, which is what comes to bar the subject. The subject displaces this bar on to the A, 'a displacement whose effect is the emergence of signification signified to the subject' (Miller 1965: 47). Yet, 'untouched by the exchange of the bar, this exteriority of the subject to the Other is maintained, which institutes the unconscious' (1965: 48).[4] The 'summation of the subject in the field of the Other calls for its *annulment*' (1965: 49). The subject, in this way, is always alienated from and by the very process of its signification.

Regarding Frege, we have spoken of 1) unity and 2) the role of 0 in succession, its status as number, and finally of its eclipse by the 1. This structure of appearance-disappearance, of suture, would be the point, emergent or derived, of a more originary logic which Miller, with Lacan's help, proposes to name the 'logic of the signifier'. A logic which proposes to 'make itself known as a logic at the origin of logic', which retraces the steps of logic, a 'retroaction', or a repression (Miller 1965: 39). 'What is it that functions in the series of whole natural numbers to which we can assign their progression? And the answer, which I shall give at once before establishing it: in the process of the constitution of the series, in the genesis of progression, the function of the subject, miscognised, is operative' (1965: 40). Zero is the placeholder of the subject, which is itself, insofar as it is sutured, a placeholder.

Analysing more closely the function and erasure of the zero, Miller distinguishes two axes. A vertical axis: the zero marks the bar on truth, separating the non-self-identical from the self-identical; insofar as it is a unit, it delimits a field. At the same time, he finds a horizontal axis: it erases that bar, since it represents itself in this field as 'subsequently cancelling out as meaning in each of the [. . .] numbers which are caught up in the [. . .] chain of successional progression' (1965: 46). In some sense, the zero becomes something like a silent letter present in every number, insofar as they are self-identical but 'non-identical' to other numbers. Miller concludes:

> The impossible object, which the discourse of logic summons as the not-identical with itself and then rejects as the pure negative, which it summons and rejects in order to constitute itself as that which it is, which it summons and rejects wanting to know nothing of it, we name this object, in so far as it functions as the excess which operates in the series of numbers, the subject. (1965: 47)

III

In a gesture the appropriateness of which I will not here question, Badiou assimilates psychoanalysis and philosophy, both being effects, according to him, of 'ideology', or, rather, constituting it. Criticising Miller's argument, he lays into the logic of the signifier, which is to say he lays into the psychoanalytic viewpoint, and slides into philosophy, exaggerating the conclusions of his criticism of the latter with regard to science. This exaggeration makes up the object of section 4 of his article, titled 'The Torment of Philosophy'.

To synopsise the salient points of Badiou's argument, he attempts to show that the concept of lack is profoundly alien to science, that science lacks nothing. It is in this sense that science does not respond, has nothing to answer for itself, does not need to justify any denial, any foreclosure, or any suture. The torment of philosophy, which echoes that of psychoanalysis, comes precisely from the fact that it thinks of itself as the answer to science, as that which gives science its subject – a subject which science has little use for. Here, Badiou is essentially rejecting the concept of alienation. If we identify the zero-function with the subject-function, as Miller does, if we say that the structure of the subject comes from its alienation, which is to say its subjection to the Other, then we make the discourse of logic itself an alienated discourse, thereby giving psychoanalysis priority over logic. Only psychoanalysis would allow one to pass from alienated truth to the truth of alienation, which would account for its superiority over logic.

In 'Mark and Lack', the stakes of which we can now begin to situate, Badiou lashes out at Frege and Miller at once. 'In our view, *both* Frege's ideological representation of his own enterprise *and* the recapture of this representation in the lexicon of signifier, lack and the place of lack, mask the pure productive essence, the positional process through which logic, as machine, lacks nothing it does not produce elsewhere' (1969: 150–1).[5] It is thus necessary to construct something to oppose the discourse of lack.

And here it is: 'To this twofold process (preservation of the true; convocation and marking of lack), we will oppose the stratification of the scientific signifier' (Badiou 1969: 150). Starting from logic, Badiou will later extend his concept of stratification to mathematics and physics. What *is* stratification, here? Badiou elaborates: 'The theory of logic pertains to the modes of production of a division in linear writing' (1969: 151). Logic thus gains its authority from a cut in language between signifying signs – the signs of language – and pure signifiers without signifieds, which are its own marks and conventions.

Logic begins with a stock of graphic marks, the alphabet, a, b, c . . ., which it cuts from their signifying milieu. It thus constitutes a collection of traces. It is this cut that Badiou opposes to the suture, a suture which the zero (or non-self-identity) is meant to introduce in the chain of numbers.[6] As opposed to the suture, which, as we have said, always shows the mark or the scar of what it cuts across, the cut in language effectuated by logic is irrevocable and unambiguous. If logic is inderivable and undecidable, Gödel's theorem shows, it is not because there is a vague zone between normal language and logic, the place of a suture. The cut is perfectly clean, leaving out nothing and no one, which '*presupposes the existence of a dichotomic mechanism that leaves no remainder*', which is to say 'an autonomous order that is indeed closed, which is to say, entirely decidable' (Badiou 1969: 152, 153).

IS SCIENCE THE SUBJECT OF PHILOSOPHY?

Logic is a system of traces, closed in upon itself. Consequently, any concept of a tear or of a suture can be nothing more than a 'psychical' effect of this closure; *it takes shape only in ideology* (which is to say in psychoanalysis and philosophy). The suture is an a posteriori effect, 'the inevitable price of that closure' for the disciplines or discourses that suffer it, whereas such a suffering is alien to science. 'What must be said, instead, is that the existence of an infallible closed mechanism conditions the existence of a mechanism that can be said to be unclosable, and therefore internally limited. The exhibition of a suture presupposes the existence of a foreclosure' (1969: 153). The relations are inverted now. By revealing lack as the original truth, psychoanalysis and philosophy deduce or derive it, aiming to trace their own lack of closure and independence on to science.

Badiou is playing with the word 'foreclosure' – the foreclosure of science is not a psychotic foreclosure; only ideology would propose such an interpretation, by struggling to characterise the scientific discourse as a discourse alienated from the fact of its presupposed lack of subject. Badiou continues, 'Gödel's theorem is not the site of separation's failure, but of its greatest efficacy' (1969: 155). In the same way, 'The zero is not the mark of lack in a system, but the sign that abbreviates the lack of a mark' (1969: 155). If there is lack, it does not even appear; it puts an end to itself, immediately compensated for by a substitution. The signs used in logic are mutually substitutable; they can replace each other according to the rules of their closed system. And there we find the 'identity of the signifying order with itself' (1969: 156). 'The logico-mathematical signifier is sutured only to itself – it is indefinitely stratified' (1969: 156). There is no substantial self-identity. Here, identity is that of marks, traces, by definition without external model or referent, which can replace each other, which are interchangeable, all without creating holes in presence.

At this point in the analysis, we see the expansion of this stratification to sciences other than mathematical logic: 'Moreover, it is science as a whole that takes self-identity to be a predicate of marks rather than of the object. The rule certainly holds for the facts of writing proper to mathematics. But it also holds for the inscriptions of energy proper to physics' (1969: 157).

If we define self-identity by substitutability – if, in other words, we move from essence to sign – then, because nothing is not substitutable for itself, there is no longer any 'non-self-identical'. And, in any case, the non-identical is nonetheless substitutable, which is proven by the substitution of the 0 by the 1. What is not thinkable for mathematics is that which cannot be substituted for itself. But this 'unthinkable' does not constitute an 'unthought'. Science does not have an unthought, and this is what makes philosophy and psychoanalysis suffer. We could just as well say that this is a radical unthought, if we understand by this that it is not part of the order of scientific thought: 'What is not substitutable-for-itself is something radically unthought, of which the logical mechanism bears no trace. It is impossible to turn it into an evanescence [. . .] What is not substitutable-for-itself is foreclosed without appeal or mark' (1969: 157).

Subsequently, scientific writing is a 'play of appearances and disappearances between successive signifying orders; never exposed to the convocation of a lack, whether in the object or the thing' (1969: 160). Later, Badiou continues:

> On this side of the signifying chain, if the latter is scientific, there are nothing but other chains. If the signifier is sutured, it is only to itself. It is only itself that it lacks at each of its levels: it regulates its lacks without taking leave of itself. The scientific signifier is neither sutured nor split, but stratified. (1969: 161)

We must remember that for Miller, the suture is a 'placeholder' for the subject. Now, according to Badiou, because there is no suture in the signifying chains of logic, *there is no subject of science.*

'Must we therefore renounce [*annuler*] the concept of suture?', asks Badiou (1969: 161). Must we therefore renounce the subject-function? No. It is rather a matter of 'assigning to it its proper domain' (1969: 161). Its domain is ideology, and Badiou now slides from psychoanalysis into philosophy, which makes this state of affairs perfectly obvious: 'We will call "philosophy,"' he says, 'the ideological region specializing in science' (1969: 163). Philosophy is 'charged with effacing the break by displaying the scientific signifier as a regional paradigm of the signifier-in-itself: this is Plato's relation to Eudoxus, Leibniz's relation to Leibniz, Kant's relation to Newton, Husserl's relation to Bolzano and Frege, and perhaps Lacan's relation to mathematical logic' (1969: 163). The specificity of the philosophical gesture, vis-à-vis science, which is its most intimate other, would consist, then, in designating its signifiers (those of science) as belonging to a specific region of ideality – but only to one such region – which would call for its replacement in and by a philosophical ideality. That is the expression of its lack, which only philosophy would be able to suture. A scientific idea cannot be characterised as an 'idea' except by means of a philosophical determination of that ideality. It would be philosophy's task alone to define the idea. Thus the traditional auto-positioning of philosophy as region of all regions, arch-region, arch-discourse. In this manner, philosophy assigns lack to science, denying that it makes a clean cut in order to renew science's dependence on philosophy (which is certainly clear in the Platonic figures of the divided line and the cave).

Philosophy, Badiou continues, thus constructs a properly philosophical concept of science, but the problem is that science 'cannot receive this mark' (1969: 163). Further, Badiou writes,

> that which, in philosophy, declares itself science, is invariably the lack of science. That which philosophy lacks, and that to which it is sutured, is its very object (science), which is nevertheless marked within the former by the place it will never come to occupy. We can claim in all rigour that science is the subject of philosophy, and this precisely because there is no subject of science. (1969: 163)

In this way, philosophy alienates itself in lending its own subject to science.

In the language that I have chosen to adopt here, which is that of the response, we can thus say that philosophy is that discourse which attempts to respond for science, which is to say, that attempts to be ontologically responsible for it. It is a discourse that undertakes to make science respond by constituting itself as a placeholder for a response that science does not give. Hegel says it well, in the Preface to the *Phenomenology of Spirit*, that mathematics is dead, that it does not respond. Only a speculative grasp of mathematics can reanimate it, make it speak. But such a response, we could object, is the problem, as it is destined in principle to never be scientific.

IV

I do not plan to critique Badiou's argument here, nor to show how he has changed his position and point of view in his later works. I choose instead to end on the strange resonance that I have detected between his remarks and the admirable analysis of the question of a response made by Derrida in 'Passions: An Oblique Offering'.

V

Derrida asks himself what it means to respond, playing at the outset with his situation as an invitee to a colloquium, asking what it means to respond to an invitation. Quickly, the question grows and gets deeper. It is a question of seeing how responding always leaves open the possibility of not responding, and how the 'not responding', which is what concerns me here, cannot be interpreted in terms of lack. Not responding, writes Derrida, 'would have nothing to do with a shortcoming, a lapse in logical or demonstrative rigor, quite the contrary' (1995b: 11).

The non-response would be inscribed in every response as its characteristic secret, not as a lack. If it is in principle entirely possible to detect the non-response in the philosophical response itself, it is nonetheless necessary to leave the realm of philosophy in order to demonstrate it. It is thus not to philosophy that Derrida turns, nor is it, incidentally, to science, but to literature. If it is 'impossible to respond', says Derrida, such an impossibility is not of the order of knowledge. But philosophy is linked to knowledge. Nor can that impossibility be of the order of science. That which does not respond, either in philosophy or in science, is not the unconscious, either. The non-response is what Derrida calls the secret. Once again, this secret belongs neither to psychoanalysis, nor to philosophy, nor to science.

The space of the secret, of the non-response, is literature. 'Not that I want to reduce everything to it [literature]', says Derrida, 'especially not philosophy' (1995b: 27). He continues, 'but if, without liking literature in general and for its own sake, I like something *about it*, which above all cannot be reduced to some aesthetic quality, to some source of formal pleasure [*jouissance*], this would be *in place of the secret*. In place of an absolute secret' (1995b: 28).

By literature, one must not understand 'belles-lettres or poetry', but that 'modern invention' that has mixed itself up with the '*right to say everything*'. 'Literature thus ties its destiny to a certain non-censure, to the space of democratic freedom' (1995b: 28). However, Derrida continues, 'this authorization to say everything paradoxically makes the author an author who is not responsible to anyone, not even to himself [. . .] This authorization to say everything acknowledges a right to absolute nonresponse' (1995b: 28–9). Later, Derrida continues, 'there is, in the exemplary secret of literature, a chance of saying everything without touching upon the secret' (1995b: 29).

It seems to me that at a certain moment, two extremes meet – that the foreclosure, the absolute closure in which Badiou encloses the scientific signifier, can immediately invert itself into the absolute openness in which Derrida situates literature. Beginning with an enclosed whole or with an open whole, the signifier, in either case, does not respond. That is its secret. A secret that is not something hidden, which would be possible to detect, a secret that, maybe, does not even exist, or is nothing other than what it is: a non-response without lack.

There is something secret. But it does not conceal itself. Heterogeneous to the hidden, to the obscure, to the nocturnal, to the invisible, to what can be dissimulated and indeed to what is nonmanifest in general, it cannot be unveiled. It remains inviolable even when one thinks one has revealed it. (Derrida 1995b: 26)[7]

There would then be, at the heart of the process of truth, a non-response, an indifference to response, a special space, separated but without suture, in which psychoanalysis and philosophy would certainly have their place, like all discourses, but which could not be subjected to them, precisely because that space, immensely open and immensely closed, is absolutely alien to the subject. The secret is 'not of consciousness, nor of the subject, nor of Dasein' (Derrida 1995b: 30).

VI

For a long time, Althusserian Marxist discourse defined truth as a 'process without subject'. Badiou's essay 'Mark and Lack' undeniably belongs to that history. Even if the times have changed, later premises 'without subject' have a point in common with such a discourse. Derrida's position, and more recently that of Quentin Meillassoux in his work *After Finitude*, put forward the idea of an *absolute* non-response of the real, which is another way of saying the critique or deposing of the subject. Even if their perspectives are very different, even sometimes opposed to each other, it is a matter of, in each case, circumscribing the space of a void that is neither a lack nor a flaw, but that of science (Badiou), of the secret (Derrida), or of the real (Meillassoux). In *After Finitude*, it is the real that is said to not respond, in the form of those fossils that do without us, of that being of a non-correlated world, indifferent to human presence, indifferent to any subject.

There, too, philosophy seems like a forced response, a determination to answer for, to make respond, or to respond in the place of. Philosophy would then indeed move closer to psychoanalysis, which, as Foucault affirmed, has as its function extracting confessions and revealing secrets. Philosophy would be, like psychoanalysis, a glutton for the subject [*une acharnée du sujet*].

Must we and can we today content ourselves with such a vision of philosophy? Who can say if the 'secret' or the 'non-response', the 'non-lack' or the 'non-correlated' is not the subjective portion of reality? A subjectivity that would not be external to the real, correlated to it, but a subjectivity of the real itself, its autonomous support structure? The subject must always answer for the fact that it is at the same time substance, which is to say, absolutely independent of any 'subject'. Dialectical negativity, then, is not the expression of a lack, but the voice of the real insofar as it reflects itself as ego-less subjectivity of the connection of things. Lacan was perhaps saying that when he wrote that the individual subject is always excluded from the real subject.

Translated by William Samson

Notes

1 *Cahiers pour l'Analyse* published ten issues in France between 1966 and 1969. All of the essays can be found in a bilingual French-English edition on the website created by CRMEP at the University of Kingston, titled *Concept and Form: The* Cahiers pour l'Analyse *and Contemporary French Thought*, with indications of the original pagination. PDFs of the original version of each article are also available on the site. Alain Badiou's essay 'Marque et manque, à propos du zéro' appeared in *Cahiers pour l'analyse* vol. 10, *La Formalisation*, 1969, 150–73.
2 Citations for Miller's essay refer to the original 1965 French edition, but the translation follows that by Jacqueline Rose, which first appeared in volume 18.4 of *Screen* in 1977.
3 From there, he can deduce the other numbers by positing the proposition: 'There is a concept F and an object x that falls under it, such that the number that corresponds to the concept F is n and the number that corresponds to the concept "falls under F but is not equal to x" is m.' Which means the same as 'n follows in the series of natural numbers directly after m' (Frege 1980: 89).
4 'The signifier [is] that which represents the subject for another signifier' (Miller 1965: 48).
5 Citations for Badiou's essay refer to the original 1969 French edition, but the translation follows that by Zachary Luke Fraser and Ray Brassier.
6 The cut, Badiou says, takes place in language. By the three mechanisms of 'concatenation', 'formation' and 'derivation', logic establishes the 'series', which is to say the chain (1969: 151).
7 In *The Post Card*, Derrida already affirms that lack is a metaphysical term, which has no meaning except in reference to presence. 'The difference which interests me here', he says, 'is that – a formula to be understood as one will – the lack does not have its place in dissemination' (1987: 441).

Part Two

Masks

8

The Crowd:
Figuring the Democracy to Come

> The crowd, suddenly where there was nothing before, is a mysterious and universal phenomenon. A few people may have been standing together – five, ten or twelve, not more; nothing has been announced, nothing is expected. Suddenly everything is swarming with people [*Soudain tout est noir de monde*] and more come streaming from all asides as though streets had only one direction. Most of them do not know what has happened and, if questioned, have no answer; but they hurry to be there where most other people are. There is a determination in their movement that is quite different from the expression of ordinary curiosity. It seems as if the movement of some of them transmits itself to the others. But that is not all; they have a goal, which is there before they can find words for it. The goal is the most intense darkness where the most people are gathered. (Canetti 1984: 16)

These sentences, taken from the very first pages of Elias Canetti's *Crowds and Power*,[1] describe rather well how I hear 'Democracy to Come' [*La démocratie à venir*], the title of our colloquium.[2] I understand this title quite literally as 'the crowd will come' [*la foule va arriver*], the people are going to flood in: in a minute from now, five minutes, an hour, in x amount of time, the greatest number will come, 'the most intense darkness', the gathering, the mass. And I foresee this real and fantasised moment when this assertion – both banal and full of meaning – can be made: 'Suddenly everything is swarming with people.'

I have long dreamed of having Canetti and Derrida walk together, at least for a moment. Their meeting has always seemed, to me, necessary. The time has come, and it is Baudelaire whom I ask to introduce them to each other. I remember Derrida reading Baudelaire's poem 'Crowds' in a seminar:

> It is not given to every man to take a bath of multitude: enjoying a crowd is an art; and only he can relish a debauch of vitality at the expense of the human species, on whom, in his cradle, a fairy bestowed the love of masks

and masquerading [*du travestissement et du masque*], the hatred of home and the passion for roaming. (Baudelaire 1974: 20)

It is to this taste for masks and masquerading and to this nomadic secrecy that I will devote the greater part of my talk.

To what end? With Canetti and Derrida, I would like to explore the fragile space of play that opens up between the crowd and the mass, on the one hand (I purposely employ the one term for the other since both have been proposed as translations of the German *Masse*) and democracy, on the other; so as to show precisely, as Baudelaire invites us to think, that democracy is the *aristocratic* secret of the mass – 'It is not given to every man to take a bath of multitude' – a secret that ensures, within the greatest number of people, the possibility of a separation that alone can grant democracy its power.

But why begin with the crowd? The crowd allows Canetti to avoid democracy's *genesis*. Such a genesis is, in fact, impossible. One finds in *Crowds and Power* neither a theory of the contractualist type nor, consequently, any theory of representation. The mass is not representable. As a result, contrary to the assertions of modern political philosophy, democracy is not defined as what can be represented by the mass or the crowd – namely the people – but, rather, as what, in the crowd, is the most invisible, the least delegatable or assignable to an identity, particularly to a national one. Upon opening *Crowds and Power*, one cannot but be struck by the *worldwide* character of the investigation it carries out. In 1928, the year in which he began his work, Canetti wrote: 'I sought crowds in history, in the histories of *all* civilizations' (1990: 490). Thus, *Crowds and Power* takes us everywhere – to China, the Middle East, Australia, Mongolia, South America, Europe. This world tour, however, conforms to no philosophy of history. Rather, its apparently disorganised, dense and a-theoretical character tends to dissociate, precisely, the motif of the mass from any strictly national-spiritual attachment. There are *some* masses organised, to be sure, according to certain structures, but organised without the latter constituting a universal. There can be no transcendental philosophy of the mass.

What is the most salient feature of these structures? Canetti and Freud agree on this point: relief from the phobia of touch [*la levée de la phobie du toucher*]. In the mass, in the crowd, the individual is freed from the 'contact phobia' that usually regulates his or her relations with others.

> It is only in *a crowd* that man can become free of this fear of being touched [. . .] The crowd he needs is the *compact* crowd, in which body is pressed to body; a crowd, too, whose psychical constitution is also dense, or compact, so

that he no longer notices who it is that presses against him. As soon as a man has surrendered himself to this crowd, he ceases to fear its touch. Ideally, all are equal there; no distinctions count, not even that of sex. The man pressed against him is the same as himself. He feels him as he feels himself. Suddenly it is as though everything were happening *in one and the same body*. (Canetti 1984: 15–16)

As we know, the distinction between Canetti and Freud is profound. For while both analyse the very particular touch of the crowd – *massive* touch, we might say – their point of departure is not the same. Canetti writes *Crowds and Power* explicitly to denounce the inadequacies of Freudian analysis, which inscribes the problem of the crowd within the limits of a psychology whose starting point is necessarily the individual psyche. The fiction of the original horde leaves no doubt on this point. Freud fundamentally overlooked the phenomenon of the mass. In one of his autobiographical writings, 'The Torch in My Ear', Canetti confides the aversion he felt, when still very young, 'from the very first word' of *Group Psychology and the Analysis of the Ego* (1990: 406–7). 'I saw crowds around me', Canetti continues, 'but I also saw crowds within me [. . .] What I missed most in Freud's discussion was recognition of the phenomenon' (1990: 407).

The phenomenon that must be recognised and further developed is indeed the particular connection that the mass maintains with touch. The mass relieves [*lève*] and reverses contact phobia, but, and it is in this sense that I orient my interpretation, this relief [*levée*] and reversal produce not a pure and simple fusion as one might expect – a sort of uninhibited and assumed collective touching – but, rather, *another* avoidance of touch, one that is not phobic but *political*. There is a disparity of touching within touching that only occurs in the mass, a split about which the individual psyche consequently has no idea. Readers of Canetti have never, to my knowledge, insisted on this disparity; instead they see in the concept of the mass a sort of formless swarming that the English call a 'mob', a conglomerate without organisation. In an issue of the journal *Multitudes*, Toni Negri rightly opposes the multitude to the 'mob' and to the mass as Canetti is presumed to define it:

> We must put [the multitude] in contrast with the masses and the plebs. Masses and plebs have often been terms used to name an irrational and passive social force, violent and dangerous precisely by virtue of its being easily manipulated. On the contrary, the multitude is [. . .] *something organised*. (Negri 2008: 117)

It seems to me, on the contrary, that nothing is more organised than the mass that Canetti describes and that it is indeed a certain *relation of distance* in the very heart of the mass – the distance of the mass from itself – that paradoxically assures its organisation. This relation of distance inscribes the possibility of *democracy* within the mass.

I am aware, here, that I am making Canetti's book talk and perhaps making it say more than it would on its own. For, in starting from the mass, the author never clearly formulates the question of democracy. Yet this excessive reading – which, in my opinion, illuminates a text that remains obscure if we confine it to a simple morphological description of crowds – is authorised, precisely, by a confrontation with Derrida's thought.

Derrida has shown in *On Touching: Jean-Luc Nancy* that a pure and simple abolition of the phobia of touch is impossible under any circumstances. We can deduce from this that what takes place within the mass is no exception to the rule, that the mass is subjected to what Derrida calls *the law of tact*: a 'tact that would know how to touch without touching, a contact without contact' (2005: 68). Now, this contact without contact is undoubtedly at work in collective touch; this contact is at the root of the democratic possibility. Democracy is the mass's tact.

How can we understand this? One must, in order to respond to this question, go straight to the heart of the originary phenomenon of the mass, right to its founding event or what Canetti calls its founding 'instant'. According to him, this phenomenon is the *Wandlung* – a word that translators render sometimes as 'change', sometimes as 'transformation' or 'modification', just as we see in this excerpt: 'What happens to you when you are in a mass is a drastic and enigmatic modification of consciousness' (Canetti 1990: 353). And Canetti admits that the mystery of this *Wandlung* pursued him 'for the better part of [his] life'. In fact, when Canetti declares, 'What happens to you [. . .] is a drastic and enigmatic modification', he means to say that what happens to you *is* drastic and enigmatic modification. The mass is the very possibility of change. Solitude, isolation: for Canetti, these mean the paralysis of the metabolic, the inability to transform. With the mass comes transformation. And democracy itself arises from an occurrence of this general transformation, from a certain metabolism of this *metabolē*.[3]

What is it that links this transformation *within* transformation to the emergence of democratic tact? The link depends on a specific modality of transformation: *metamorphosis* or *Verwandlung*. There is metamorphosis (*Verwandlung*) in transformation (*Wandlung*), and it is indeed this metamorphic possibility upon which the democratic possibility depends. Democracy has to do with a certain metamorphosis of the mass, which is to say, a certain metamorphosis of the transformable, a certain mutability of the mutable.

This change in the mass is equalisation — the fact that all *feel* equal is precisely what relieves contact phobia.

> *Within the crowd there is equality.* This is absolute and indisputable and never questioned by the crowd itself. It is of fundamental importance and one might even define a crowd as a state of absolute equality. A head is a head, an arm is an arm, and the differences between individual heads and arms is irrelevant. It is for the sake of this equality that people become a crowd and they tend to overlook anything which might detract from it. All demands for justice and all theories of equality ultimately derive their energy from the actual experience of equality familiar to anyone who has been part of a crowd. (Canetti 1984: 29)

Now, democracy arises from the transformation of this massive equality — which still ignores its proper aphoristic capacity — into a detached equality [*égalité distante*]. Between the one and the other, the space of metamorphosis unfolds. Paradoxically, distance only results from the shifting identification with others, from the possibility of being everyone without being anyone in particular. Baudelaire defines this possibility as the very place of poetry. 'The poet enjoys the incomparable privilege of being able to be himself or some one else. Like those wandering souls who go looking for a body, he enters as he likes into each man's personality. For him alone everything is vacant' (Baudelaire 1974: 20). It is precisely this vacancy in the identification with the other, this non-attachment [*non-adhesion*] in belonging to the people, that can permit the regulation of distance in the democratic space between each one, everyone and each other, self and other.

I propose therefore to explore the irreducible link between the motifs of metamorphosis, on the one hand, and the social-democratic, on the other. The confrontation between Canetti and Derrida on the subject of this link will unfold in three movements respectively entitled 'Mask and Power', 'Secret and Transformation' and 'Flight and Melancholy'.

Mask and Power

Contrary to what one might think when opening Canetti's book, there is no 'crowd' *and* 'power' in the sense of two separate entities. There is power only in relation to the mass, for and in the mass, power at once submitted to and produced by it. For Canetti, power has no essence; in this sense it 'is' not but instead consists of the different figures of its actualisation. Hence the fact that Canetti, far from seeking a universal definition of power, offers a *morphological* analysis of it. This morphological logic is obviously not foreign to the thematic of metamorphosis. Power appears as a kind of reign of figures sculpted in the mass – by it, against it, on its level.

Canetti postulates a difference between power and force [*entre puissance et pouvoir*] that he demonstrates in a very straightforward way.

> The word 'force' suggests something close and immediate in its effect, something more directly compelling than power [. . .] The distinction between force and power can be illustrated very simply by the relationship between cat and mouse.
>
> The cat uses force to catch the mouse, to seize it, hold it in its claws and ultimately kill it. But while it is *playing* with it another factor is present. It lets it go, allows it to run about a little and even turns its back; and, during this time, the mouse is no longer subjugated to force. But it is still within *the power* of the cat and can be caught again. If it gets right away it escapes from the cat's sphere of power; but, up to the point at which it can no longer be reached, it is still within it. The space which the cat dominates, the moments of hope it allows the mouse, while continuing however to watch it closely all the time and never relaxing its interests and intention to destroy it – all this together, space, hope, watchfulness and destructive intent, can be called the actual body of power, or, more simply, power itself. (1984: 281, emphasis added)

Power is, therefore, force that takes its time.

It does not seem wrong, as a result, to characterise power as the spacing and temporalisation of force, which is to say, as the spacing and temporalisation of the final grasping and sentencing, of the decisive instant. There is no force without power, without the opening, in the heart of force itself, of a certain horizon of expectation or a ground of play. A horizon that allows the emergence of all sorts of *figures* that are precisely postures of power and that stage, in the strong sense, relations of domination. Now, it is in the mass that this economy of power, this originary violence of the force–power structure, lends itself most clearly to experience. Indeed, the relief from contact phobia corresponds to the transformation of force into power. Force is direct contact, the grasp, the muzzle that opens and closes. Every living being has this phobia. The horror of touch is thus explained in Canetti by way of the apprehension induced by the possibility of capture, of fatal seizure. Yet as soon as a mass forms, force is deferred, for there can be no immediate capture of a mass; and it is in this way that power appears as both the limit and supreme condition of force. The mass then appears to be the very body of the *différance* of force, a space of play that opens within force itself. Inasmuch as it is confronted by power – whether its own or that embodied in another essentially changes nothing – the mass keeps contact with contact, but it is a matter of a contact with contact's distance, the distance between the mouse and the cat's muzzle. The play of contact at a distance. When all the people in the mass touch, they do not fuse; they instead enjoy the gap of power; they are all reciprocally cat and mouse to each other. This is the change that takes place, fundamentally, with the mass and in it.

As I have said, the possibility of metamorphosis is lodged in the distance between force and power. And, consequently, the possibility of democracy. More precisely, democracy supposes not only a metamorphosis of change but also a metamorphosis *of* metamorphosis. For all power implies metamorphosis. There is no hunt [*chasse*], no capture of an animal by another, without metamorphosis. For example, Canetti writes, 'The transformations which link man with the animals he eats are as strong as chains. Without transforming himself into animals he would never have learnt to eat them' (1984: 357). There is a double play of transformation between dominating and dominated: the victim seeks to enter into a metamorphic cycle of flight, transforming itself into a tree, a wall, another animal. The executioner or the pursuer seeks by play to mimic its prey.[4] Imitation and dissimulation are evidently fundamental conditions of power.

These games of imitation and dissimulation, at work in nature or in the most primitive forms of metamorphosis, reveal another crucial element of my analysis. The fact that there are metamorphic relations between hunter and prey, that they exchange roles for a moment, that they render themselves assimilable or compatible, one might say – all of this is nothing new. Indeed, it is well known. However, more interesting in Canetti's analysis is his highlighting of another process within this very same one: at the heart of the exchange of identity a defence is created, however fragile, obsolete and derisory, against identifying with the other. Metamorphosis is at once mimicry of the other and ban on this very mimicry, the creation of a gap, of a limit to identification and to contact. It is thus that, for Canetti, all metamorphosis constitutes a mask. Any animal, in this sense, is always its own totem; at the moment it is going to die, at the moment it will be eaten, it wears the mask of its own inedibility, of its rigorously unassailable [*imprenable*] character. This is the mask that is seen in its death throes. Thus, the process of mutual metamorphosis that takes place between hunter and prey can be read in two opposed and inextricably linked senses. It is both a process of imitation, on the one hand, and a process of infinite distancing, on the other, with the mask authorising both senses.

> The working of the mask is mainly outwards; it creates a *figure*. The mask is inviolable and sets a distance between itself and the spectator. It may come

nearer to him, as sometimes in a dance, but he must always stay where he is. The rigidity of form brings about distance: its immutability produces its *fascination* [. . .] Charged with a menace that must not be precisely known – one element of which, indeed, is the fact that it *cannot* be known – it comes close to the spectator, but in spite of this proximity, remains clearly separated from him. It threatens him with the secret amassed behind it. (Canetti 1984: 375–6)

We have seen that contact phobia was lifted in the mass but that this release simultaneously produced a new distance. This distance results, here again, in a constitution of masks. The mass is the place of a mutual metamorphosis – all its members identifying with each other – and of a masked separation by which those members make themselves unrecognisable.

Canetti shows that the mask is at once visible and audible in the mass. *The visible mask*: In the mass, the mask is the appearance that each puts on, the appearance that I will define as the 'appearance of being together', the face you put on with others whom you do not know, an all-purpose appearance, the mask of universal resemblance. *The audible mask*: Canetti recounts, in the previously cited (and suggestively titled) 'The Torch in My Ear', how he had noticed, when living next to an asylum, a similarity between the cries of the insane and the cries of the crowd in a stadium, particularly at football matches. The acoustic mask is that which separates, precisely, cry from cry. The cry of the insane and the cry of fans are cries that say something other than the cry, which is to say, something other than nothing: they express something like a foreign language within the same language.

In the mass, then, individuals are metamorphosed in the sense that they all wear a mask that allows them simultaneously to make themselves identical and not identical to all the others, a mask at once visible and audible, speaking and not speaking the same language, a foreignness within the same. Starting from there, several types of political organisations are possible according to Canetti. The most violent organisation, which Canetti calls dictatorship or potentate, aims to *unmask* individuals in one way or another, tending in that way to annihilate power in order to reduce it to force.

A ruler wages continuous warfare against spontaneous and uncontrolled metamorphosis. The weapon he uses in this fight is the process of *unmasking*, the exact opposite of metamorphosis, which one could call *enantiomorphosis*.[5] It is a process the reader has already met; Menelaus unmasked Proteus, the old man of the sea, when he refused to be frightened by any of the forms he adopted to escape, and held him fast until he became Proteus again. (Canetti 1984: 378)

Another potentate is the caste system, which Canetti defines as a system of 'prohibited metamorphosis':

> The division into classes is most rigid in a caste system. As in India, membership of a caste absolutely precludes social transformation of any kind. There is meticulous separation both from what is above and what is below [. . .] so that it is not even possible to achieve transformation through the kind of work one does [. . .] (1984: 381)

In contrast to this type of organisation, we could thus call *democracy* the mask-form taken by the being-together that defines itself by resistance to every will to return that form to some 'true' face or some natural identity – resistance, by the same token, to every kind of ban on transformation. Democratic metamorphosis is a particular figure of power that tolerates neither its de-figuration nor its rigidification.

Secret and Transformation

Democratic liberty thus appears to be fundamentally linked to the possibility of metamorphosis. It is in this sense that it is *poetic*. On this point we find once again Baudelaire and Derrida. Baudelaire defines poetry as the art of metamorphosis that allows you to take a walk in the crowd while being both yourself and another. But how can we not think here of *Demeure*? Derrida writes:

> There is no essence or substance of literature: literature is not. It does not exist. It does not remain at home, *abidingly* [*à demeure*] in the identity of a nature or even of a historical being identical with itself. [*I pause here to ask Jacques whether or not the mask is precisely the mode of being for this non-identity.*] It does not maintain itself abidingly [*à demeure*], at least if 'abode [*demeure*]' designates the essential stability of a place; it only remains [*demeure*] *where* and *if* 'to be abidingly [*être à demeure*]' in some 'abiding order [*mis en demeure*]' means something else. (2000: 28)

Democracy and literature, both dedicated to a common metamorphic destiny, would then essentially share the same secret: never to unmask, never to be unmasked. Literature, which 'can say anything, accept anything, receive anything, suffer anything and simulate anything' (Derrida 2000: 29), can do so if only it shelters the secret of this mutability within itself. If it were to 'become proof, information, certainty, or archive, it would lose its function' (2000: 29–30). If it became an attempt to unmask or if it lost these masks itself, it would self-destruct.

Derrida constantly speaks of the mass. Not, admittedly, as the crowd that takes over streets or stadiums, but, rather, under the title of proliferation, dissemination or that which he calls, once more in *Demeure*, 'embastardisation'. We have known this since *The Post Card*: 'As soon as, in the first second, the first stroke of a letter divides itself, and must indeed support partition in order to identify itself, there are nothing but post cards, anonymous morsels without fixed domicile, without legitimate addressee' (1987: 53, translation modified). The post card: what is it if not democratised address and writing, the letter essentially in pieces, *which goes from anywhere to anywhere?* And Derrida has tirelessly shown that these pieces are at the same time secrets, are simultaneously masks, 'open letters, but like crypts' (1987: 53).

The community of literature and democracy – which, moreover, Blanchot so often highlighted – derives from this way of wearing the mask of any being while being together, of touching without touching, of having people touch while maintaining, between them and in them, their unknown secret, their mask, their post card. This, according to what Derrida calls an 'impossible' injunction: 'to remain secret [*demeurer secret*]' in the very heart of what is manifest and public (2000: 30). Democracy's poetics, democracy's art, is therefore based on this way of wearing the secret in the open, of engaging it as publicly as possible in order to hide better.

'I am sighing', Derrida writes, 'to know until when I will be going round myself in this way, phantom or prophet charged with a mission, heavily charged with a secret unknown to him' (1993: 257). And we know, since *Specters of Marx*, that the 'phantom', the spectral, never comes alone but always in a crowd, *en masse*.

> [Men] are present for each other only in a ghostly fashion, as specters. Humanity is but a collection or series of ghosts [. . .] Marx only feigns to count them, he pretends to enumerate for he knows that one cannot count here [. . .] One can neither classify nor count the ghost, it is number itself, it is numerous, innumerable as number, one can neither count on it nor with it [. . .] It proliferates, one can no longer count its offspring or interests, its supplements or surplus values. (Derrida 2006: 173)

Consequently, when Derrida describes himself as a phantom, he describes himself as a crowd, a mass, a proliferation, and what pushes him from behind is the injunction to wear all the masks at once, in all their secrecy, without favouring one of them. The phantom is the mask, the masked mass, the mass of mask, without exception.

Without exception? Let us remember that, for Baudelaire, the art of wearing the mask is not given to everyone: 'It is not given to every man to take a bath of multitude.' According to the poet, it is not everyone's lot to be at the level of the multitude. Here we must address the formidable problem of the relation between privilege and democracy. We read in *Specters of Marx*: 'If the ghost is disseminated everywhere, the question becomes a distressing one: where does one begin to count the progeniture? It is again a question of the head. Who is to be put at the head of all those whom one gets in one's head?' (Derrida 2006: 172). Here, the question of the sovereign appears. Both Canetti and Derrida show how sovereignty is linked, precisely, to the secret, and in two contradictory senses. In democracy, every individual is sovereign because every individual is masked, wears his or her secret. The secret, in this sense, is the very secretion of the mass. At the same time, the art of the secret is not given to all; it is given to a solitary few, to a few sovereign exceptions. The secret, in this sense, is the mass's absolute limit, its negation. The one who possesses the art of the secret – the poet or the politician – penetrates the identity of others and wears all the masks. But what of his mask, who can wear it? Who can penetrate it or reach him?

Flight and Melancholy

'Secrecy', writes Canetti, 'lies at the very core of power. The act of lying in wait for prey is essentially secret. Hiding, or taking on the color of its surroundings and betraying itself by no movement, the lurking creature disappears entirely, covering itself with secrecy as with a second skin' (1984: 290). The poet, the philosopher and the politician are exceptional precisely because they know, so well, how to envelop themselves in the secret of others – to the point of becoming secret from themselves. Canetti continues:

> [The Sovereign] has secrets even from himself. They lose their conscious and active character and merge into that other, more passive form, transacted in the dark cavities of one's body, hidden safe where they can never be known, and forgotten even by oneself.
>
> 'It is the privilege of kings to keep their secrets from father, mother, brothers, wives and friends.' Thus it is written in the Arab *Book of the Crown*, which records many of the old traditions of the Sassanid kings of Persia. (1984: 293)

This is the paradox: he who wears the secret to the point of swallowing it, of forgetting it, who brings the art of metamorphosis to perfection, ends up no longer being able to transform himself. He is threatened by silence, by the rupture of the mask. Canetti declares: 'Silence isolates. A man who remains silent is more alone than those who talk. Thus the power of self-sufficiency is attributed to him. He is the guardian of a treasure and the treasure is within himself' (1984: 294). I continue reading:

> Silence inhibits metamorphosis. A man who will not speak can dissemble, but only in a rigid way; he can wear a mask, but he has to keep a firm hold of it. The *fluidity* of metamorphosis is denied him; its result is too uncertain; he cannot know where it would take him if he surrendered to it. People become silent when they fear metamorphosis. Silence prevents them from responding to occasions for metamorphosis. (1984: 294)

We can then ask if the poet, the politician, the philosopher or the smuggler (the one Lévi-Strauss calls the *trickster*) are not constantly threatened with *becoming what they are*; if they do not always end up adhering to the self-vacancy of which Baudelaire speaks; if this vacancy does not end up composing a rigid mask, the mask of the powerful or even of the tyrant – the one who hates the crowd. Essentially, how are we to think *solitude* within democracy? How are we to think solitude and democracy together? How can one want to isolate oneself while at the same time not wanting it? (I think back to the Isle of Capri, birthplace of 'faith and knowledge'.)[6] How to keep the secret from forsaking the common space?

In fact, the metamorphic capacity – equality's sole guarantor – is always likely to turn against itself. That is to say, he who knows how to wear all the masks is always likely to end up changing back into himself, to confuse himself with his own mask. This is the shared torment of the writer and the politician. Canetti shows that this torment is a form of melancholy, the melancholy of being selfsame, of no longer being able to transform oneself. Poetic power thereby becomes force again. Metamorphosis, Proust would say, becomes simple pastiche. Canetti writes:

> Melancholia begins when flight-transformations are abandoned because they are all felt to be useless. A person in a state of melancholia feels that pursuit is over and he has already been captured. He cannot escape; he cannot find fresh metamorphoses. Everything he attempted has been in vain; he is resigned to his fate and sees himself as prey [. . .] (1984: 347)

Flight is no longer possible.

A politically depressive affect then emerges: the melancholy of the self in the crowd, the failure of fluidity and of slipping away. Détienne and

Vernant, in their celebrated book *Cunning Intelligence in Greek Culture and Society*, also analyse the failure of metamorphosis in terms of *Stimmung*, or attunement, as a pathological phenomenon of power. Metamorphosis, the authors explain, is the only possible mode of being in the face of fluid, mobile and polymorphic realities. Waves, tentacles, the crowd. It is thus that there are gods of metamorphosis, who impose their power by means of their transformations, becoming more fluid than fluidity itself. Be that as it may, these gods always end up, in their fights, exhausting their metamorphic potential. When the cycle is finished, they become themselves again. Détienne and Vernant write:

> The series of transformations cannot continue indefinitely. They constitute a cycle of shapes, which, once exhausted, returns to its point of departure. If the monster's enemy has been able not to lose his grip, at the end of the cycle the polymorphic god must resume his normal appearance and his original shape and thereafter retain them. So Chiron warns Peleus that whether Thetis turns herself into fire, water, or a savage beast, the hero must not lose his hold until he sees her resume her first form, her *archaia morphē*. (1978: 112–13)[7]

The melancholy of being oneself is the limit of 'becoming like everyone else', the limit of the 'becoming imperceptible' of which Deleuze speaks. Suddenly everything is swarming with people. Will we be able to take part in this world, to become like everyone, to dissolve in *différance*, to give the slip in the gap [*donner le change dans l'écart*]? Or will we freeze in a state of melancholic exception? Derrida continually asks these questions, letting run through all of his texts an infinite series of metamorphoses, even to the point of confiding his childhood love for silkworms.[8] Transformations, changes, masks and disguised secrets are everywhere in his work. The ancient messenger, for example: 'I resemble a messenger from antiquity, an errand boy, a runner [. . .] and I run, I run to bring them news which must remain secret' (Derrida 1987: 8). Derrida quotes the same figure, the courier from Marathon, in Sartre: 'We say that the courier from Marathon was dead an hour before arriving in Athens. He was dead and he still ran; he ran dead and he announced Greece's victory dead' (1996: 22). There is also the marrano, there is Artaud, there is, of course, the animal. *The Animal That Therefore I Am*: 'my animal figures multiply, gain in insistence and visibility, become active, swarm, mobilise and get motivated, move and become moved all the more as my texts become more explicitly autobiographical, are more often uttered in the first person' (2008a: 35). At the same time, Derrida never stops saying that this first person solidifies and annuls the power of its own plasticity, immuring itself, withdrawing from the crowd, paralysing itself. Paralysis: is this not precisely the definitive mask that inscribes the figure's absence on the face?

> I seem to have seen myself near to losing my face, incapable of looking in the mirror at the fright of truth, the dissymmetry of a life in caricature, left eye no longer blinking and stares at you, insensitive, without the respite of *Augenblick*, the mouth speaks the truth sideways, defying the diagnostics or prognostics, the disfiguration reminds you that you do not inhabit your face because you have too many places, you take place in more places than you should, and transgression itself always violates a place, an uncrossable line, it seizes itself, punishes, paralyzes immediately, topology here both being and not being a figure, and if it is a disfiguration, that's the trope I've just been hit right in the face with for having violated the places, all of them, the sacred places, the places of worship, the places of the dead, the places of rhetoric, the places of habitation, everything I venerate [. . .] (Derrida 1993: 123–4)

There is no democratic compulsion – every place is violated, all locks broken – without punishment. Paralysis is the crowd's punishment against its own gap. In the space of this strange reflexivity dwells the possibility of another approach to the social bond.

Which one? The one that consists of thinking democracy-to-come in terms of figuration and not in terms of representability or representativity. Perhaps it is a morphological ontology that opens up here. Between its two extreme shores of metamorphic fluidity and paralysis, it is surely *hospitality* that gives itself to be thought. With all its validity and all its melancholy. With this very figural presentation, more schematic, in the strong sense, than thematic, I have attempted to highlight, with Canetti and Derrida, a new impetus of political thought, one that works to show that the mass has no foundation outside itself, that being-together, what Derrida also calls 'being-huddled-together [*être serré*]' (2008a: 10), must inevitably schematise itself.

By insisting on fluidity as the limit of political metamorphosis, I have attempted to show that social cohesion, on the one hand, and the snags and ruptures of metamorphoses, on the other, have the same origin; that those solitary by exception and those solitary by exclusion or by 'disaffiliation', to borrow a word from Robert Castel, are the two opposed faces of the same reality. In his appropriately titled book, *Métamorphoses de la question sociale*, Castel writes:

> It is impossible to draw a distinct hermetic line between those who withdraw from the game and those who fall, and this is for a very basic reason: it is not simply a matter of 'ins' and 'outs' but a continuum of positions that exist in a

collectivity and that 'contaminate' one another [. . .] No one is really outside of society, but there are a set of positions whose relationship to the center are more and more attenuated. (2003: 414)

Suddenly everything is swarming with people. Worldwide crowds: three million people in Rome after the [2001] G8 summit in Genoa. Great social waves: the [2002] World Cup in South Korea. At the darkest heart of this world, where there is neither inside nor outside but holes even within crystals of density,[9] there comes the promise of democracy, the promise, that I will call, in a final word, *la figurante*.[10]

Translated by Dashiell Wasserman

Notes

1 Carol Stewart's English translation of *Masse und Macht* renders the German *Masse* as 'crowd', while Malabou uses 'la masse' to retain its Germanic inflection – Translator.
2 This essay was originally delivered as an address during a ten-day conference held at Cerisy-la Salle, Normandy, in 2002. The conference's theme, *La démocratie à venir* [Democracy to Come], explored the political significance of Derrida's work. Malabou's essay was published in the acts of the conference: *La démocratie à venir*, edited by Marie-Louise Mallet (2004).
3 Though *metabolē* can broadly refer to any change – from medical pathology to musical pitch – Malabou refers to the rhetorical device of using related but morphologically distinct terms such as the similar German words *Wandlung* (transformation) and *Verwandlung* (metamorphosis) – Translator.
4 '[The hunter] knows [the prey's] manner of flight, he knows its shape and knows how and when it can be seized. The moment of transformation throws him into confusion; he has to think of a new manner of hunting to match the change in his quarry; he has to transform himself' (Canetti 1984: 342).
5 Enantiomorphosis, from *enantiomer*, meaning mirror image: a distinction viewed from an outside perspective. This concept refers to an intervention in metamorphic movement by outside involvement. Deleuze and Guattari elaborate: 'This is the sense in which Canetti speaks of "enantiomorphosis": a regime that involves a hieratic and immutable Master who at every movement legislates by constant, prohibiting or strictly limiting metamorphoses, giving figures clear and stable contours, setting forms in opposition two by two and requiring subjects to die in order to pass from one form to the other' (1987: 107) – Translator.
6 See 'Faith and Knowledge' (Derrida 2002) – Translator.
7 From another perspective, one can think back to Alain Ehrenberg's very interesting book, *The Weariness of the Self: Diagnosing the History of Depression in the Contemporary Age*. The author writes, 'If melancholia was the domain of the exceptional human being, then depression is the manifestation of the *democratization of the exceptional*' (2010: 218).
8 See 'A Silkworm of One's Own' (Derrida 2001) – Translator.
9 Canetti writes: 'Crowd crystals are the small groups of men, strictly delimited and of great constancy, which serve to precipitate crowds. Their structure is such that they can

be comprehended and taken in at a glance. Their unity is more important than their size. Their rôle must be familiar; people must know what they are there for. Doubt about their function would render them meaningless. They should preferably always appear the same and it should be impossible to confound one with another; a uniform or a definite sphere of operation serves to promote this' (1984: 73) – Translator.

10 *La figurante* is a feminisation of the French word for 'extra' or 'walk-on', which bears connotations of the sudden participant in a flash mob as well as the dynamic, plastic capacity of the mob to form or 'figure' itself suddenly – Translator.

9

Life and Prison

The Prison of Language

In his inaugural lecture for the establishment of the Chair of Semiology at the Collège de France in Paris on 7 January 1977, Roland Barthes made a very strange and striking statement: 'language [. . .] is quite simply fascist'.

> Language is legislation, speech is its code. We do not see the power which is in speech because we forget that all speech is a classification, and that all classifications are oppressive [. . .] Jakobson has shown that a speech-system is defined less by what it permits us to say than by what it compels us to say. In French (I shall take obvious examples) I am obliged to posit myself first as subject before stating the action which will henceforth be no more than my attribute: what I do is merely the consequence and consecution of what I am. In the same way, I must always choose between masculine and feminine, for the neuter and the dual are forbidden me [. . .] Thus, by its very structure my language implies an inevitable relation of alienation. To speak, and, with even greater reason, to utter a discourse is not, as is too often repeated, to communicate; it is to subjugate: the whole language is a generalized *rection* [. . .]
> But language – the performance of a language system – is neither reactionary nor progressive; it is quite simply fascist; for fascism does not prevent speech, it compels speech. (Barthes 1979: 5)

The problem, of course, is that there is no way to escape language; there is no way out. 'Unfortunately, human language has no exterior: there is no exit' (Barthes 1979: 6). We are then in the prison-house of language, as Jameson says (1972).

The Prison of Philosophical Concepts

The capture of language is even more conspicuous when it comes to philosophical concepts. Let's look at the etymology of the word *concept*, at least in French and in English. It comes from *concipere*, which itself comes from *capere cum*, to grasp together. The term *concept* thus has the same origin as *capture, captivity*:

> captive (adj.)
> late 14c., 'made prisoner, enslaved,' from Latin *captivus* 'caught, taken prisoner,' from *captus*, past participle of *capere* 'to take, hold, seize' (from PIE root ★kap- 'to grasp').
> captive (n.)
> 'one who is taken and kept in confinement; one who is completely in the power of another,' c. 1400, from noun use of Latin *captivus*. An Old English noun was *hæftling*, from *hæft* 'taken, seized,' which is from the same root. (Harper 2021)

The term *prison* also derives from the act of seizing, *prendre* in French, from the Latin *pre(n)siōnem*, acc. de ★*pre(n)siō*, contraction of *prehensiō*, 'the action of apprehending the body', becomes *preison*, then *prison*, with the core inflation of *pris*, past participle of *prendre*, 'to take' (CNRTL 2012). In German, the verb *greifen*, in which we hear *Begriff* (concept), means to capture someone. It seems that philosophy is doomed to redouble the fascism of language.

I want to link these preliminary remarks with the fact that the most important and profound contemporary philosophical texts devoted to the issue of life almost always comprise, in their very core, a reflection on the prison, on what it is to live in prison. As if life were the privileged victim of philosophical concepts *as well as* the privileged victim of language, of language's fascism. Some of the important texts that provide us with a reflection on concept, language, captivity and life include *Carnets de captivité* by Emmanuel Levinas (2009), *Marx* by Michel Henry (1983), *Discipline and Punish* by Michel Foucault (1977) and *Homo Sacer* by Giorgio Agamben (1998).

I will start by referring to Michel Hardt's article 'Prison Time' (1997), which is devoted to Jean Genet, to expose, on the one hand, how philosophers generally account for the relationship between life and imprisonment, and, on the other hand, how they explore the possibility of a way out from within language. I will then question how African American thinkers such as Martin Luther King, Jr and Frank Wilderson have challenged the traditional philosophical approach to both language and captivity.

Prison and Writing

In 'Prison Time', Hardt develops a metaphorical connection between actual prison and the prison of language. Through Genet's life, he is able to draw parallels between the fact of being in jail and being trapped within language. As Hardt writes, 'Inmates live prison as an exile from life, or, rather, from the time of life' (1997: 65–6). They think, 'The first thing I'll do when I get out is. . . Then I'll really be living' (1997: 66).

Captivity produces the fantasy of an outside: authentic life is outside. Outside walls – we might add outside concepts and outside language. But Hardt shows that this fantasy disappears when one discovers that there is no outside, that the outside of prison does not liberate life from its capture.

> Those who are free, outside of prison looking in, might imagine their own freedom defined and reinforced in opposition to prison time. When you get close to prison, however, you realize that it is not really a site of exclusion, separate from society, but rather a focal point, the site of the highest concentration of a logic of power that is generally diffused throughout the world. Prison is our society in its most realized form. That is why, when you come into contact with the existential questions and ontological preoccupations of inmates, you cannot but doubt the quality of your own existence. If I am living that elsewhere of full being that inmates dream of, is my time really so full? Is my life really not wasted? My life too is structured through disciplinary regimes, my days move on with a mechanical repetitiveness – work, commute, tv, sleep [. . .] I live prison time in our free society, exiled from living. (1997: 66–7)

In a certain sense, life in prison just reveals life as prison. My life outside is a prison; my life as a free subject is a prison. Because I speak. Because I am a speaking subject. Being a speaking subject in the prison of language paradoxically brings me close to those who don't speak, to animals, animals in captivity, when they develop what is called stereotypic behaviours, made up of repetition and routine.[1]

When Hardt says that prison is everywhere, that our lives are always already captured by power, he describes the series of stereotypes in which we are always already locked, these repetitions, habits, routines and manifestations of meaninglessness that first appear in language and are redoubled by philosophy.

Prison as a Condition for Liberation

Barthes also characterises the originary entanglement of power and language as what gives way to the production of stereotypes:

> The sign is a follower, gregarious; in each sign sleeps that monster: a stereotype. I can speak only by picking up what *loiters* around in speech. Once I speak,

these two categories unite in me; I am both master and slave. I am not content to repeat what has been said, to settle comfortably in the servitude of signs: I speak, I affirm, I assert tellingly what I repeat.

In speech, then, servility and power are inescapably intermingled. (1979: 5–6)

Philosophy usually radicalises such a situation by affirming that captivity is not a specific state or mode of being among others, but constitutes the very form of being in the world. This means that power would not only be the external force that subdues life and captures it, but also what exploits a virtuality of life itself, something immanent to life itself. Stereotypic behaviours would then reveal a potentiality of life, something that is always already present in life.

The specific task of traditional philosophy is to affirm that, instead of trying to escape the closure of concepts, we first have to accept it and to acknowledge the essential complicity between the closure of concepts and the captivity of life. It is the task of philosophy to understand captivity as internal to life. Philosophy, as Plato so powerfully demonstrates in the allegory of the cave, starts in prison.

Philosophy wants us to think that something exists within life that constitutes its own tendency to imprison itself. Heidegger, in *Phenomenological Interpretations of Aristotle* (2001), which was written at a time when he still talked about life and not yet of existence, brings to light the category of *Abriegelung*, 'blocking-off' in English, or *verrouillage* in French. *Riegel* in German means 'lock'. 'Blocking-off' is the prefiguration of what will later be called, in *Being and Time*, the 'taking care', the inauthentic version of 'care'. It is a form of closure, of *Benommenheit*. Life necessarily imprisons itself; the lock is an essential structure of life.

Abriegelung comes from the fact that life has a tendency to 'miss' itself, to remain blind about its ontological determination. It encloses itself in stereotypes because it does not see what it really is. 'Life does its utmost to mistake itself for something else', Heidegger writes.

> For example, life tends to 'miss' the fact that it is finite. It misses that fact like a shot misses its target [. . .] Life blinds itself, puts out its own eyes. In the *Abriegelung* (sequestration), life leaves itself out [. . .] Factical life leaves itself out precisely in defending itself explicitly and positively against itself. (2001: 80)

Why does 'life' need to 'defend itself against itself'? The lock, the *Riegl*, coincides with life's immediate understanding of itself. It is a misunderstanding because of the language used to describe such an understanding: life appears as something that is ahead of me, as a free space. In stating this, it precisely locks itself out. It misses the authentic opening, which is the opening towards death. Life is imprisoned because it disavows its own death.

In the philosophical tradition, the concept of alienation has long been used to designate this originary captivity of life. Michel Henry's *Marx* contains an interesting analysis of what he calls 'subjective alienation', as distinct from objective alienation. Henry's thesis is that Marx's main concern is life, understood in its most material, empirical determination. In Hegel, Henry explains, alienation characterises a becoming-object. For example, if I say that my life is alienated, this means in Hegelese that my life has become a thing. It is true that labour, for Marx, is what transforms life into a commodity, a thing. The problem with this is that the worker's life is inseparable from them, so what they alienate is something subjective, something that they cannot depart from without dying. Labour is subjective alienation, the selling of something that cannot become an object.

> If alienating oneself does not mean to objectify oneself any longer, to posit oneself in front of oneself as something which is there, alienation then occurs within the very sphere of subjectivity, it is a modality of life and it belongs to it [. . .] Alienation is 'a specific tonality of life, when life means suffering, sacrifice' [. . .] What is the most proper becomes the most alien. (Henry 2009: 608)²

For Henry, too, social alienation comes from an immanent tendency of life. Life is always already alienated, imprisoned, because it cannot speak of its own alienation. It does not have the words. Here again, the first prison is language. The ambiguity of philosophy is that it roots alienation, or *Abriegelung*, within life itself.

Prison and Disalienation

Philosophers have also thought how to disalienate life, which amounts to elucidating the issue of the outside where there is no outside. Hardt affirms that Genet succeeded in carving out a space of freedom within captivity. He was able to build an outside from inside the prison, an outside which that was not an elsewhere.

> The fullness of being in Genet begins with the fact that he never seeks an essence elsewhere – being resides only and immediately in our existence [. . .] Exposure to the world is not the search for an essence elsewhere, but the full dwelling in this world, the belief in this world. (Hardt 1997: 67–8)

Hardt explains that prison is still a world, and being captive a modality of exposure to the world. And it is from the experience of prison, when we learn how to dwell in prison, that we can get out of it: 'When we expose ourselves to the force of things we realize this ontological condition, the immanence of being in existence. We merge with the destiny we are living and are swept along in its powerful flux' (1997: 68).

The important term here is 'immanence', which means 'inside'. There is a possible transcendence in immanence. Through writing, Genet is at one with the bodies of the prisoners, their living bodies: 'In this exposure the bodies are fully realized and they shine in all their gestures' (Hardt 1997: 68). This gain in intensity inside is what Hardt calls the saintly, divine, sublime passivity of being in prison. Writing, or, as Heidegger would say, thinking: a certain use of language that emancipates the writing or thinking subject from stereotypes.

Hardt uses a Spinozist, Nietzschean and Deleuzian vocabulary to characterise how Genet increases his power of acting, how life becomes joy, affirmation, creation, in the 'energy of erotic exposure' of captive life (1997: 70). This transcendence in immanence is not only an artistic or erotic gesture; it is a revolutionary one. Hardt even begins his article by writing that 'Lenin liked to think of prison as a university for revolutionaries' (1997: 64). But '[e]xposure itself [. . .] is not enough for Genet' (1997: 70). Exposure has to transmute itself into the revolutionary event. Instead of getting out, into the outside, the externality comes from a reversion from within. Writing is an enduring movement that inverts directions.

> Revolution is defined by the continuous movement of a constituent power [. . .] Revolutionary time finally marks our escape from prison time into a full mode of living, unforeseeable, exposed, open to desire. This mode of living is at all times constituent of our new, revolutionary time. (1997: 78)

The redemption of prison space first has to happen within prison itself. According to the thesis defended by Hardt and Negri in *Multitude* (2004), prison time characterises the situation of the global proletariat, the carceral mode of living imposed upon it by globalisation. We find here again the point made by Henry about subjective alienation and the cutting of life in two by the capitalist exploitation of labour. The revolution to come appears first as a revolution of language in language. Barthes again:

> But for us, who are neither knights of faith nor supermen, the only remaining alternative is, if I may say so, to cheat with speech, to cheat speech. This salutary trickery, this evasion, this grand imposture which allows us to understand

speech *outside the bounds of power*, in the splendor of a permanent revolution of language, I for one call *literature*. (1979: 6)

Revolution starts with an upheaval of language, an event that keeps language 'alive'. Such an operation coincides with Hardt and Negri's 'liberation of living labor' (2000: 61), the counterpower to Empire seen as 'a mere apparatus of capture that lives only off the vitality of the multitude' (2000: 62).

Life, through revolution, does not lose its capacity to be captured, its essential relationship to exile, closure and separation. Revolution itself can always exploit and subject the originary passivity of life. Therefore, there is no clear and univocal meaning of the way out.

What does the outside look like? This question is very difficult, and to answer it requires taking a different direction. The outside of prison though revolution consists mostly in the transformation of the social jail into the emancipated community, the building and fashioning of the commune, of networks of interrelationality. Through this network, life returns to itself, is restituted to itself. But, in turn, this interrelationality can be considered a new prison. As Martin Luther King, Jr affirms in his 'Letter from Birmingham Jail':

> I am cognizant of the interrelatedness of all communities and states. I cannot sit idly by in Atlanta and not be concerned about what happens in Birmingham. Injustice anywhere is a threat to justice everywhere. We are caught in an inescapable network of mutuality, tied in a single garment of destiny. Whatever affects one directly, affects all indirectly. (2000: 87)

King reiterated this interrelationality and mutuality during a commencement address at Oberlin College in 1965, two years after his Birmingham letter:

> All I'm saying is simply this: that all mankind is tied together; all life is interrelated, and we are all caught in an inescapable network of mutuality, tied in a single garment of destiny. Whatever affects one directly, affects all indirectly. For some strange reason I can never be what I ought to be until you are what you ought to be. And you can never be what you ought to be until I am what I ought to be – this is the interrelated structure of reality. (1965)

Black Death and the End of Prison Idealism

King's words describe something like the universal condition of life, what all people share, caught as they are in the same net. The 'inescapable network' may be considered the origin of freedom, in the same way that Sartre said that men are doomed or destined to be free. However, they can also be read as announcing a new mode of being locked in, within the community and the revolutionary act itself. The network formed by humanity, even if interrelated, is a mechanism of exclusion.

In his book *Red, White and Black: Cinema and the Structure of U.S. Antagonisms* (2010), Frank B. Wilderson III proposes an interpretation of Hardt's text from the point of view of Afro-pessimism. For Wilderson, Hardt's analysis acts like a lock and a new modality of separation. His discourse on revolution 'assumes a universal grammar of suffering' that does not exist (2010: 276–7). There is no universal grammar of prison or concept of imprisonment. The very concept of life, Wilderson states, necessarily precludes Blackness: 'Black time is the moment of no time at all on the map of no place at all' (2010: 279). The duality inside/outside cannot apply to Blackness.

The slave, who for Wilderson is the fundamental identity of Blackness, is not a prisoner, but a slave – that is, a non-being, a life that is not one. Marxist ontology 'either take[s] for granted or insist[s] on . . . the a priori nature of the subject's capacity to be alienated and exploited' (2010: 279). Revolution itself is a concept, is a capture. 'One cannot think loss and redemption through Blackness, as one can think them through the proletarian multitude or the female body, because Blackness recalls nothing prior to the devastation that defines it' (2010: 281). Furthermore, Wilderson states, 'Blackness exists on a lateral plane where "it [is] possible to rank human with animal"' (2010: 298). The Black subject is therefore exiled from the human relation, which is predicated on social recognition, volition, subjecthood and the valuation of life itself. For Wilderson, Black existence is marked as an ontological absence posited as sentient object and devoid of any positive relationality, in contradistinction to the presence of the human subject. White life is constructed upon Black death, whereas Black lives are Black deaths.

Philosophy and literature never take into account lives that are excluded by the concept or the immanent passion of the word. Wilderson affirms that Blackness is ranked with animal life insofar as animal life is itself excluded from the concept, and that Black lives and animal lives are both reduced to pure stereotypes.

Black Lives Matter, the international activist movement created in July 2013, has evoked many reactions. Its perception in the United States varies considerably. The phrase 'All Lives Matter' sprang up as a response to the Black Lives Matter movement. However, 'All Lives Matter' has been criticised for dismissing or misunderstanding the message of Black Lives Matter. And following the shooting of two police officers in Ferguson in 2014, the hashtag 'Blue Lives Matter' was created by supporters of the police.

We can see through this example that life, whatever its definition, always seems to fall back into ghetto, prison, separation and fragmentation. Blackness is the most obvious case of the impossibility of opening a space of freedom within life, because Black life is deprived of any inside; it is always already emptied by non-Black concepts of non-Black lives.

In conclusion, literature and philosophy, as Barthes, Hardt and Genet define them, are other ways of reintroducing a form of almost religious transcendence within the analysis of life as closure and the fascist essence of language. Revolution remains idealised as a way of finding one's own salvation from within the prison of reality. What kind of language has to be found, then, that would not re-imprison Black lives? Does it still belong to philosophy? Does it still belong to literature? For sure, this issue requires the opening of a yet unheard of space. Afro-pessimism might be its name. A name born in prison.

Notes

1 'Stereotypic behaviour is an abnormal behaviour frequently seen in laboratory primates. It is considered an indication of poor psychological well-being in these animals. It is seen in captive animals but not in wild animals [. . .] Stereotypic behaviour has been defined as a repetitive, invariant behaviour pattern with no obvious goal or function. A wide range of animals, from canaries to polar bears to humans can exhibit stereotypes. Many different kinds of stereotyped behaviours have been defined and examined. Examples include crib-biting and wind-sucking in horses, eye-rolling in veal calves, sham-chewing in pigs, and jumping in bank voles. Stereotypes may be oral or involve bizarre postures or prolonged locomotion.

   A good example of stereotyped behaviour is pacing. This term is used to describe an animal walking in a distinct, unchanging pattern within its cage [. . .] The locomotion may be combined with other actions, such as a head toss at the corners of the cage, or the animal rearing onto its hind feet at some point in the circuit' (Philbin n.d.: 1).

2 Kathleen McLaughlin's 1983 translation, *Marx: A Philosophy of Human Reality*, includes only parts of Henry's two-volume study, *Marx* (reprinted in a single volume by Gallimard in 2009). Here, Malabou provides her own translation of a passage from the French edition not included in McLaughlin's translation – Editor.

10

Odysseus's Changed Soul: A Contemporary Reading of the Myth of Er

Preamble

In April 2014, while I was in residence at the Townsend University Center at UC Berkeley, I taught a four-week graduate seminar entitled 'Animation/ Reanimation: New Starts in Eternal Recurrence', and, in relation to that seminar, I delivered publicly the Una's Lecture, entitled 'Odysseus's Changed Soul: A Contemporary Reading of Plato's Myth of Er'. Two years later, in April 2015, I revised this lecture in preparation for publication in the present volume,[1] and delivered it as a new talk at UC San Diego. The title of the lecture this time was 'Plato, Reader of Agamben, from *Homo Sacer* to the Myth of Er'. In both versions, I referred to Giorgio Agamben's *Homo Sacer: Sovereign Power and Bare Life*, and this for four main reasons. First, because Er, as Plato describes him, immediately appeared to me as a possible figure of the *homo sacer*. Second, because the myth addresses the issue of the choice (αἵρεσις) of lives by the souls of the dead before their reincarnation, and because 'life' here is to be understood as ζωή and βιός at the same time. Third, because the myth proposes in its own terms a reflection on sovereignty, and fosters what seems to be the first critique of it, thus already articulating a distinction between βασίλεια and the pure principle of exception, that is, the very specific combination of injustice and violence that Plato calls tyranny. Fourth, and in this case inverting the direction of analysis from that of Agamben's, because Plato's argument may be read as an anticipated response to Agamben's insistence on 'impotentiality' as a possible deconstitution of sovereignty. Socrates, as I argue, is the anti-Bartleby *par excellence*, and incarnates quite another version of such a deconstitution. I am then reading Plato through Agamben, and Agamben against himself through Plato.

I then sent my paper to Jacob Greenstine, who helpfully informed me of the recent publication in English translation of Agamben's *The Use of Bodies*, the final volume in the *Homo Sacer* project, which contains a short chapter titled 'The Myth of Er'. I had not yet bought the book, and at first felt upset by such a coincidence. Would this chapter challenge, or worse obviate, both my approach to Plato and my use of *Homo Sacer I*? Reading the chapter, I was relieved to discover that Agamben's and my interpretations differed on all points, except perhaps when it comes to the insistence on the importance of the choice of lives and the meaning of the soul as a site of both differentiation and imbrication of ζωή and βίος. Apart from this, he and I do not focus on the same parts of the myth, and Agamben does not say anything about what is for me the most important point, that is, Odysseus's choice of life, which is in no way comparable to others. My interpretation of the part played by Odysseus allows me to read the interaction between the three characters Er, Odysseus and Socrates as a fluid process of identity exchange which underlies the reflections on justice developed in the myth, an exchange that is not considered by Agamben.

I then decided, in agreement with Jacob, to publish my text as it was, with just a few added references to *The Use of Bodies* when they appeared necessary.

The Myth of Er forms the conclusion of Plato's *Republic*. Socrates introduces the tale by explaining to Glaucon that the choices we make and the character we develop in this life will have consequences after death. He narrates this myth in order to give an account of the reward and punishment that the just and the unjust person, respectively, receive after death. The story begins as a man named Er, the son of Armenias of Pamphylia, is given a chance to witness what occurs in Hades and is brought back to life to tell what he has seen.

Er is supposed to have died in battle, but when the bodies are collected, ten days afterwards, Er remains undecomposed. Two days later he revives on his funeral pyre. When he wakes up, he tells others of his journey in the afterlife. His destiny is, then, one of a messenger. When Er's soul arrives in Hades, as Socrates tells, the judges there 'said that he was to be a messenger to human beings to tell them about the things happening there, and they told him to listen to and look at everything in the place' (*Republic* 614d).

What Does Er See in Hades, and What Can He Tell Us About the Afterlife?

We can distinguish three main moments in the myth.

First, we are told that the souls of those judged to have lived justly are sent upwards to heaven to enjoy a beautiful sojourn for a thousand years. The souls of those judged to have been unjust, by contrast, go under the earth to be punished. The souls of those who committed serious crimes (tyrants, mostly) receive especially severe punishment and are finally thrown into Tartarus. In a thousand years all the souls, except those eternally damned, join from up above and from down below, and travel to the centre of the Universe, which is a meadow reigned over by Necessity.

In a second moment, the souls come before Lachesis, one of the three Fates, and are told to choose the lives they are going to live for the coming reincarnation. Samples or models of lives (τὰ τῶν βίων παραδείγματα) are displayed, and the souls are each to pick one from among them in turn. The order in which they choose has been decided by a lottery. After making the choice, each soul elects its own guardian (δαίμων), and is insolubly bound to the chosen life. A 'sort of spokesman' declares: 'your daimon will not be assigned to you by lot; you will choose him. The one who has the first lot will be the first to choose a life to which he will be bound by necessity' (*Republic* 617d–e).

In a third and last moment, the souls drink from the river Lethe and forget everything. They are then born again to this world. Of course, Er is not judged, does not choose any life sample and does not drink from the river – he comes back as the man he used to be to tell the living what he has seen. He opens his eyes to find himself lying on the funeral pyre, early in the morning, and able to recall his journey through the underworld.

I will focus here on a specific moment of the myth, that of the choice of lives. A puzzling problem appears at this point. In most cases, the souls pick the same kind of life as the one they are used to. Plato writes: 'Er said it was a sight worth seeing how the various souls chose their lives, since seeing it caused pity, ridicule, and surprise. For the most part, their choice reflected the character of their former life' (*Republic* 619e–620a). There is a major exception to such a repetition, though. The myth exposes a case of someone who does not select the same sample, but chooses, on the contrary, a new kind of life, a life that is not the same as his former one. This case is that of Odysseus, who is the last to choose. Socrates tells us that Er reported:

> Now it is chanced that Odysseus' soul drew the last lot of all, and came to make its choice. Remembering its former sufferings, it rejected love of honor, and went around for a long time looking for the life of a private individual who did his own work, and with difficulty it found one lying off somewhere neglected by the others. When it saw it, it said that it would have done the same even if it had drawn the first-place lot, and chose it gladly. (*Republic* 620c–d)

Odysseus chooses a different soul, a different life. He chooses to become 'a private individual who did his own work', βίον ἀνδρὸς ἰδιώτου ἀπράγμονος, translated by Allan Bloom as 'the life of a private man who minds his own business' (2016: 303).

This choice is highly perplexing. What could have motivated it? Of course, it might be related to what Socrates said a little bit earlier, regarding the best kind of choice. The just, Socrates declared, 'will know to choose the middle life in such circumstances, and avoid either of the extremes, both in this life, so far as possible, and in the whole of the life to come. For this is how a human being becomes happiest' (*Republic* 619a–b).

We can then understand Odysseus's decision as being commanded by such an imperative. At the same time, the extremes which Socrates speaks of are 'wealth and other evils' and 'tyranny or other similar practice' (*Republic* 619a–b). None of these 'irreparable evils' were committed by Odysseus. So what is Odysseus trying to avoid in choosing this middle life? Again, the text claims: 'remembering his sufferings'. But is such a reason sufficient for him to choose to stop being the hero that he is?

Commentators do not generally pay much attention to this puzzling case. To my knowledge, the only genuinely profound analysis of Odysseus's choice is that of Patrick Deneen, in his beautiful book *The Odyssey of Political Theory: The Politics of Departure and Return*. He writes:

> Many commentators on the Myth of Er do not pause to reflect on the grounds or rationale for admiring the particular life that the soul of Odysseus chooses. Those few that have reflected on the grounds for Odysseus' soul's specific choice agree that it is noteworthy, but disagree on the grounds. (2003: 106)

What they generally disagree on is whether Odysseus, when choosing to become a private man who minds his own business, chooses (without saying it) the life of Socrates. Allan Bloom, for example, declares: 'The wise voyager Odysseus gains higher status [in the myth]. All he needed was to be cured of love of honor (a form of spiritedness), and he could live the obscure but happy life of Socrates' (2016: 436). According to Seth Benardete, on the contrary: 'Socrates himself seems never to have been Odysseus. His *daimonion*, he said, was probably unique' (1992: 229).

The complexity of Odysseus's gesture seems to add to the general difficulty of interpreting the myth, underscored by many readers. Stephen Halliwell, for example, affirms: 'Given the *Republic*'s wavering images of the afterlife, Er's story appears out of nowhere, professing to carry an eschatological authority that the *Republic* had not previously envisaged' (2007: 460). Or: 'In a visionary mode whose complexity tests the limits of understanding [. . .] the narrative raises more questions than it can answer' (2007: 460). Julia Annas, for her part, claims that the myth of Er is 'a painful shock', offering a 'lame and messy ending' to 'a powerful and otherwise impressively unified book' (1981: 349, 353). Odysseus's choice seems only to confirm this shocking ending! What about this uninteresting, neutral and banal model of life, that of a private bourgeois minding his own business? The conclusive part of the *Republic* definitely seems to disappoint.

Let's try to propose another reading of this passage. It must be noticed first that the myth stages a strange interplay between the three characters – Er, Odysseus and Socrates – which reveals a complex structure of identity and difference. Each of them, in a way, might exchange his part with the two others. First, the myth of Er has striking resemblances with Odysseus's journey in Hades as related in book XI of the *Odyssey*. Second, Er's voice is, in fact, that of Socrates, to the extent that Socrates is the one who speaks and tells us what Er has seen. Third, Socrates himself shares common characteristics with both Odysseus and Er. It seems that Er, Odysseus and Socrates exchange names in a loose or fluid identification process. Nevertheless, Odysseus's new life – the life of 'a private man who minds his own business' or 'does his own work' – does not match any of these three characters. As Deneen notices:

> Odysseus seems to choose exactly the life that most opposes his past history and seemingly his own disposition. In the pages of the *Odyssey*, neither is Odysseus a private man (*idiotēs*) – after all he is king of Ithaca, even when he is absent from his island – nor does he 'mind his own business'. Indeed, minding one's own business requires one to avoid 'being a busybody' (*polupragmonein*) or literally avoid 'doing many things' (cf. 433d). Odysseus – he of 'many ways' (*polutropos*) – is the supreme example of the human who does many things [. . .] The man who is neither private nor avoids 'doing many things' is said to choose the seemingly opposite life when his soul is given the choice of all possible lives after death. (2003: 107)

Socrates is a private man in the sense that he does not seek public office, but he nevertheless does many things and certainly does not mind his own business. His life is neither obscure nor happy. As for Er, he is a soldier, an occupation which by definition is not a private one, and as a witness, he precisely does not mind his own business. So the exchangeability of these three characters contrasts with the unappealing style or mode of Odysseus's chosen second life. Again, we do not see exactly what motivates this choice, and why it appears to be the best one.

Unless – unless we imagine a reincarnation of the myth of Er itself, a return of the myth in the twenty-first century, a new life, a rebirth of the narrative in a new framework or new 'life paradigm'. Would this help us to interpret Odysseus's choice differently?

I imagine the myth of Er coming back today to help us propose a solution to one of the major political and philosophical issues of our time: that of thinking beyond, or after, sovereignty. More precisely, I imagine Plato coming back on the scene today to discuss Giorgio Agamben's statement in *Homo Sacer* according to which it has become necessary to think 'beyond the principle of sovereignty', beyond the 'sovereign ban', and to 'have moved out of the paradox of sovereignty' (1998: 47–8, 59).

Is not this myth a very profound example of what deconstructing sovereignty might mean? In choosing to become a private man who minds his own business, in renouncing being the king of Ithaca, Odysseus would dismiss or relinquish his sovereignty.

According to Agamben, the paradox of sovereignty consists in the fact that everything which sovereignty includes as an essential part of its definition is at the same time excluded by this definition itself. In reverse, what sovereignty excludes from its concept is at the same time essentially included in it. This strange situation, which constitutes the very foundation of sovereignty, its fundamental logic, follows from the fact, as Agamben subtly shows, that the concept of sovereignty coincides with the concept of exception: exception is the rule. Sovereignty, Agamben argues, implies 'the state of exception as a permanent structure' (1998: 38). If supreme power is founded on exception, then there is no way in which we can rigorously distinguish between the exceptional and the regular. Agamben again: 'The paradox of sovereignty consists in the fact the sovereign is, at the same time, outside and inside' (1998: 15). Outside and inside the juridical order, outside and inside nature, outside and inside violence, outside and inside the law. The book establishes no less than fifteen 'zones of indistinction' between the outside and the inside.

What allows the paradoxical structure of a zone of indistinction to exist is a certain type of relation: the relation of the self with itself. Sovereignty is by definition and precisely the very form of this being-in-relation with itself. This erases the difference between normality and excess, the allowed and the forbidden, between the inside and the outside. The sovereign is everything – the same and the other – all at once. Agamben:

> It has often been observed that the juridico-political order has the structure of an inclusion of what is simultaneously pushed outside [. . .] Confronted with an excess, the system interiorizes what exceeds it through an interdiction and

in this way 'designates itself as exterior to itself' [. . .] We shall give the name *relation of exception* to the extreme form of relation by which something is included solely through its exclusion. (1998: 18)

Deconstructing sovereignty thus implies the interruption of self-foundation, of self-sufficiency, of, again, the relation of the sovereign's self to itself defined as the origin of all limits or boundaries, as that which decides on the interior and the exterior, the inclusion and the exclusion, the rule and the exception.

It is possible to see Earth and Hades as Greek versions of the inside/outside dichotomy. This is what Heidegger, in *Parmenides*, demonstrates when commenting on the myth of Er. He shows how in ancient Greece the relationship between interiority and exteriority, the inside and the outside, are thought in terms of relationships between the earth, or the above, and the underground. We know that from the beginning of the *Republic*, Plato's reflections on power, sovereignty (βασιλεία) and justice are constantly sustained by a determination of the relationship between this world and the other world underneath. The myth of Er teaches us that if nothing changes in Hades, in the world underground, if the unjust chooses the same model of life again, then tyranny and abuse of sovereignty in general will never end and justice will never reign. Which is another way of saying that if sovereignty cannot renounce being both the interior and the exterior, the legal and the illegal, life and death, the sub- and the super-terrestrial, then the Republic cannot actualise itself as the achievement and accomplishment of the philosophical ideal of justice. Again, something has to change, to be interrupted. It is at this point that Odysseus's choice appears and situates itself.

In order to sustain such an interpretation, I have to go further in the reading of the interplay between Er, Socrates and Odysseus. Er exactly coincides with the definition of the *homo sacer*, even if the first identifiable figure of the *homo sacer* is, according to Agamben, Roman and not Greek. For him the first concrete emergence of *homo sacer* as a political category is the *devotus*, a man who is devoted by the consul, the dictator or the praetor 'in order to save the city from a grave danger' (1998: 96–7). The *devotus* is the symbol of the sovereign, to the extent that the *devotus* is exposed to death in his place. Armed on horseback and plunged into the thick of his enemies, the *devotus* wears a special cloak and appears openly before both armies. 'What is the status of the living body that seems no longer to belong to the world of the living?' (1998: 97). The *devotus*, Agamben continues, either dies – and the ritual of devotion is thus accomplished – or he survives. What 'happens to the surviving devotee? [. . .] The surviving devotee is a paradoxical being, who, while seeming to lead a normal life, in fact exists on a threshold that belongs neither to the world of the living nor to the world of the dead: he is a living dead man' (1998: 98–9). Er is precisely a surviving *devotus*, a living dead.

Following Agamben's characterisation, we might see Er as the very symbol of the most extreme effect of sovereign power. Er is 'the living pledge to his subjection to a power of death'; he has 'entered into an intimate symbiosis with death without, nevertheless, belonging to the world of the deceased' (1998: 99–100). Moreover:

> The surviving devotee, *homo sacer* [. . .] is [. . .] a bare life that has been separated from its context and that, so to speak surviving its death, is for this very reason incompatible with the human world. In every case, sacred life cannot dwell in the city of men [. . .] we are confronted with a residual and irreducible bare life, which must be excluded and exposed to a death that no rite and no sacrifice can redeem [. . .] [A] life that may be killed but not sacrificed. (1998: 100)

We remember the distinction made earlier in the book by Agamben between the two Greek works for life, ζωή and βίος (transliterated in Agamben's work to *zōē* and *bios*). As we know, ζωή means bare life, that is, natural life. It expresses 'the simple fact of living common to all living beings (animals, men, or gods)' (1998: 1). βίος means qualified life, the way of life, the choice of a life in general; it indicates 'the form or way of living proper to an individual or a group' (1998: 1). The life of the *homo sacer* is bare, stripped from its quality. A life that can only be killed.

Moving away from sovereignty, interrupting the sovereign's relationship to itself, implies for Agamben that bare life itself becomes a form of life rather than being a murderous ontological result. We have to invent creative and affirmative ways of erasing the borders between bare and qualified life, so that the very notions of inside and outside, inclusion and exclusion, themselves disappear. Emancipation from sovereignty necessitates 'a constitution and installation of a form of life that is wholly exhausted in bare life and a *bios* that is only its own *zōē*' (1998: 188), that is, a unity between symbolic and biological life. Such a constitution would prevent any violent dissociation between them. The problem is how to conceive such a unity, the indifference or non-difference between βίος and ζωή. Odysseus helps us to address this specific problem.

From Er to Odysseus

We just saw that Er was, as a living dead, a life 'separated from its context' (Agamben 1998: 100). In both his κατάβασις, his descent, his journey through Hades, and his ἀνάβασις, his ascent and awakening on the pyre, Er does not have a form of life, a βιός, what Plato names a model of life – βιός παράδειγμα – any longer. While travelling through the underground, he is no longer a soldier but instead a nobody, a witness with no qualities. He does not choose a new life like the other souls. He is not simply a soul itself: he is still embodied. He survives as a living being in the realm of death.² We do not know anything about the life he will lead when he returns as a surviving *devotus* among the living. How will Er return to life? How will he give a βιός to his ζωή? Odysseus shows him the way.

We should remember that the sight of the souls choosing their lives 'caused pity, ridicule, and surprise' (*Republic* 620a). One reason for the grotesquerie of this scene is the fact that all the models of lives mix bare life and qualified life, each is a βιός and a ζωή at the same time. Some human souls choose to be reborn as animal souls, for example a swan, a lion, an ape or an eagle. Even great and famous human beings are taken in those exchanges. Er saw

> the soul that once belonged to Orpheus, he said, choosing a swan's life: he hated the female sex because of his death at their hands, and so was unwilling to be conceived in a woman and born. He saw the soul of Thamyris choosing a nightingale's life, a swan changing to the choice of a human life, and other music animals doing the same. The twentieth soul chose the life of a lion [. . .] Similarly, souls went from the other animals into human beings, or into one another. (*Republic* 620a–d)

There are no strict frontiers, in these models, between natural and social life, human and animal existences. Even if the soul's choices are motivated by past experiences, most of the time their results are very similar to the previous ones, as noted above. It is clear that Plato is looking for a way to save this absence of a boundary from either chaos or sheer repetition. Socrates reports that there is a sort of 'exchange of evils and goods for most of the souls' (*Republic* 619d). Those who were formerly rewarded chose poorly while those recently punished are patient with their choices: but this remains a single transaction, not a transvaluation proper. Whatever the mythological dignity of the personages (Orpheus, Ajax, Agamemnon, Atlanta, etc.), whatever the kinds involved (human, animal, man or woman, gentle or fierce beast, athlete or craftswoman, etc.), whatever the transformation (exchanging a qualified life for a ζωή or a ζωή for a qualified life, or a qualified life for a qualified life, or a ζωή for another ζωή), this metempsychosis does not open a new future, it does not resolve the problem of justice, and it does not deconstruct the threat of tyranny immanent to sovereignty. The task is to discern the right measure of the fusion and communication between the two dimensions of life.

Odysseus's choice – a case which certainly is not a simple exchange – allows us to consider a new way of joining or bringing together ζωή and βίος, a way that does not suggest any abuse of power or tyrannical sovereignty. The model of life he chooses implies a neutralisation of the distinction between βίος and ζωή. Odysseus chooses the life of a man whose qualification is that of having none. The myth does not specify what kind of occupation he has. In what sense is such a choice genuinely different from the others? What is the political meaning of Odysseus's gesture? Socrates shows us the way.

From Odysseus to Socrates

According to Deneen, Odysseus's choice is not only exemplary for Er, it also represents a philosophical answer to one of the main concerns in the *Republic*. Odysseus's choice is a veiled answer to a problem with the famous image of the cave: how does one who has exited the cave return? 'In the *Republic*', Deneen writes, 'Odysseus' choice of souls in Book 10 has significant implications for the philosopher's choice whether to redescend to the cave in Book 7' (2003: 112). We will see that this second orientation is not separated from the first one: the question of the philosopher's re-descent involves also the status of philosophical life as an indiscernible state between βίος and ζωή.

As we know, with the allegory of the cave Socrates depicts our condition as chained within a cave such that we cannot recognise the truth, describes the ascent of the philosopher out of this condition, and then posits the possibility of his re-descending. 'The Cave allegory describes the macabre death-like existence in the cave, the true life afforded by ascent, and the unwilling return to the underworld' (Deneen 2003: 113). This situation is strikingly similar to the one described in the myth of Er, except that in the myth the return is a return to this life. Yet the question is the same in both cases: how are we to return?

There is, apparently, no doubt that Socrates urges the philosopher to descend into the cave again. 'If the philosopher refuses to descend', Deneen writes, 'the solution of the philosopher-king to the problem of justice proves impossible' (2003: 113). Socrates is adamant about this point: it is not permitted 'to stay there [above ground] and refuse to go down again to the prisoners in the cave and share their labors and honors, whether the inferior ones or the more excellent ones' (*Republic* 519d).

Of course, as Socrates admits in the course of his analysis, re-entering the cave involves the risk for the philosopher of being put to death at the hands of the crowd. Thus Glaucon raises the crucial question: 'You mean that we are to treat them unjustly, making them live a worse life when they could live a better one?' (*Republic* 519d).

The question of whether the philosopher, having reached the bright land of truth above the cave, would choose to re-descend to the subterranean region and try to rule has been a source of much controversy for readers of the allegory of the cave. 'Would the philosopher seek to rule the inhabitants of the Cave at the risk of his own life?' (Deneen 2003: 116).[3] Deneen reminds us that 'the thesis that the philosopher would refuse to redescend was primarily established by Leo Strauss [in *The City and Man*] and popularized by Allan Bloom in his "Interpretive Essay" appended to his translation [of the *Republic*]' (2003: 126). Elsewhere Bloom declares:

> It is true [. . .] that the potential philosophers must be compelled to leave the cave as well as return to it. But once out, they recognize how good it is to be out. They never see a reason to go back, and compelling them to go back is said to be good for the city, not the philosophers. If they thought it good to go back, they would not be good rulers. It is only by going out that they became aware that the kallipolis is a cave, nay Hades, and to be in it is as to be a shade. (qtd. in Deneen 2003: 113).

Again, Socrates admits that there is significant danger in the philosopher's re-descent. He asks about the returned philosopher:

> Now, if he had to compete once again with perpetual prisoners in recognizing the shadows, while his sight was still dim and before his eyes had recovered, and if the time required for readjustment was not short, wouldn't he provoke ridicule? Wouldn't it be said of him that he had returned from his upward journey with his eyes ruined, and that it is now worthwhile even to travel upward? And as for anyone who tried to free the prisoners and lead them upward, if they could somehow get their hands on him, wouldn't they kill him? (*Republic* 516e–517a)

Odysseus's choice offers an answer to precisely this dilemma: if the wise individuals are to return, they must not reveal themselves as who they really are. They have to return in disguise. We may thus understand that the model of life chosen by Odysseus is a mask. Nevertheless, the kind of disguise that Plato here proposes is other than the one Odysseus chose in the *Odyssey*, namely his disguise as a beggar, which he wears after he returns to Ithaca from his long journey away. Odysseus dresses this way so that he can accustom himself to the new political situation in Ithaca before he appears as what he really is: the king. In the myth of Er, Odysseus's new life does not coincide with this earlier impoverished transvestment. Dressed as a poor man, Odysseus prepares the moment of his violent revenge. Eventually he reveals himself, starts fighting the suitors, and seeks revenge on the new political order of Ithaca which has been established in his absence. What results from this violence is the threat of permanent wars of revenge, and Odysseus cannot resolve this threat by himself. He has to implore the help of Athena to put an end to the chaos he himself instigated.

Hiding oneself might be necessary. But most of the time, wearing a mask is not an interruption of tyranny, just a new ruse. In the myth of Er, Plato raises the question of how to disguise oneself not as a temporary ruse, a prelude to violence, but on the contrary as a means to neutralise tyranny. Such a mask is designed to produce a permanent ontological disruption of absolute power. For example, it might be the mask of a private mind minding his own business.

Socrates again indirectly intervenes at this point, helping us to determine what wearing a mask might mean in the case of politics. A striking fact in the myth is that among the various models of lives, τὰ τῶν βίων παραδείγματα, available to choose, the life of a philosopher was nowhere to be found. Strangely, the philosophical does not constitute a sample life. We thus have to guess, by reflecting on Odysseus's choice of disguise, what a Socratic life paradigm might be.

If the philosopher is to become a king without being a sovereign, does this mean that he must renounce all power? Let us turn again to Agamben. He contends that in order to move away from the sovereign exceptions we have to figure out the existence of a power which is at the same time a non-power. Something that would correspond to the Greek word ἀδυναμία, 'impotentiality', 'incapacity'. This power would be a specific mode of δύναμις: a potentiality that never actualises itself, that never comes to any form of ἐνέργεια, but instead remains a pure virtuality. The model of life corresponding to this kind of power is not just another mask of violence. It is not about being a beggar outside and a king inside. Instead it is about being nobody; it is about being a life whose only quality is barrenness. This is the life paradigm of a non-person. For Agamben, the model of life of such an impotent, ἀδύνατος soul is certainly not that of Odysseus (who of course appears most of the time as the accomplished energetic figure, the ἐνέργεια *par excellence*), but that of Melville's Bartleby. Bartleby is the perfect example of a life which is indiscernible, a ζωή and a βίος:

In modern thought, there are rare but significant attempts to conceive of being beyond the principle of sovereignty [. . .] But the strongest objection against the principle of sovereignty is contained in Melville's Bartleby, the scrivener who, with his 'I would prefer not to', resists every possibility of deciding between potentiality and the potentiality not to. (Agamben 1998: 48)

In challenging Odysseus's sovereignty, does Plato anticipate Melville and suggest that Odysseus has to renounce his ενεργεια and become a proto-Bartleby? Is Bartleby the correct philosophical equivalent of a private man who minds his own business? Is Bartleby truly the modern reincarnation of Odysseus, and consequently also that of Socrates? Is impotentiality – or the potentiality of the 'not to' – the response to the deconstruction of sovereign power? Is it in this way that the philosopher must descend in the cave again, saying: 'I am going, but I would prefer not to'? Deprived of any determined identity? Anonymous? Must the privation of sovereignty entail impotency?

This, of course, is not Plato's answer. We know that Socrates' demon intervenes to discourage him from doing certain things. Yet Socrates would never have uttered a phrase like 'I would prefer not to'. His paradigm is not that of impotentiality or non-potentiality, but, on the contrary, that of a free and affirmed living being. If there cannot be a model of life for the philosopher, it is because such a thing would be in contradiction with itself; it would stabilise, solidify, the being of a soul whose character is to be essentially in motion. Plato has a name for this specific philosophical mobility and dynamism. It is φρόνησις, often translated as 'practical virtue'. In reality, φρόνησις is not a virtue, but the virtue of all virtues, which allows each virtue to be what it is. An essential point here is that φρόνησις situates itself right at the crossing between the biological and the spiritual or noetic components of the soul. It occupies the exact middle, between ζωή and βιός. It is strange that Agamben, in *The Use of Bodies*, does not mention φρόνησις when he affirms that the 'soul is not (only) *zōē*, natural life, or (only) *bios*, politically qualified life: it is, *in them and between them*, that which, while not coinciding with them, keeps them united and inseparable and, at the same time, prevents them from coinciding with each other' (2015: 261).

I do not think that the soul, ψυχή, can be defined as being 'in between' ζωή and βιός, as if it, in a certain sense, transcends them. Because Agamben does not address the issue of what a philosophical model of life might be, he transfers on to soul in general what pertains to the activity of philosophy. It is philosophy, in the form of φρόνησις, that works to both hold together and separate these two kinds of lives, and thus constitutes a self-discipline of the soul, because ψυχή is nothing outside the interplay of these two lives.

Φρόνησις is what transforms a purely biological life into a psychic life, a source of animation into an autonomous centre of movement and action. Φρόνησις is thus what both displays and suppresses the difference between βιός and ζωή. As Plato says, the philosopher is, in a certain sense, always already dead; but this strange state constitutes the proper strength of the soul. It is a task, an ἔργον, not an impotentiality. It is a force which never results in violence; it is the very ἐνέργεια of justice. As we know, after Plato, Aristotle gives a profound analysis of φρόνησις understood as prudence, such that φρόνησις is a way to expose and protect oneself at the same time. If the philosophers have to descend into the cave again, they will have to be cautious, prudent by being able to play with the plasticity of their life, sometimes appearing as pure ζωή, bare life without qualities, sometimes, on the contrary, as philosopher-kings-and-queens, thinkers, wise rulers. Philosophers must let their lives appear in their disappearance, wearing a mask in between.

The paradigm of the philosopher appears at the very crossing point between humanity and animality, the beauty and splendour of Odysseus and the banality of a private individual. Socrates is very often compared to an animal, a ray or a gadfly, for his specific mobility is in between the species. Socrates does not pass from the human to the animal, or from the animal to the human, as ordinary souls do. The plasticity of his soul is the very site of φρόνησις. Therefore, he can be said to be, as Heidegger notices, uncanny: 'The uncanny [. . .] has nothing to do with the monstrous or the alarming. The uncanny is the simple, the insignificant, ungraspable by the fangs of the will' (1992: 101). The uncanny is always masked. Yet these masks are not artefacts or ruses. Instead they are the necessary detours or differences in the eternal return of the same.

Return is the central problem of the myth of Er. This problem, in its turn, must be understood through a host of questions: how is it possible to make a non-violent use of one's force and power when lost in the crowd, when alone in tyranny, when possibly exposed to murder? How is it possible to remain sovereign while going beyond sovereignty? Can return be anything other than a lost cause? What model or sample of life should be chosen for such a return? Odysseus's return to Ithaca? The philosopher's return to the depths of the cave? Er's return to the earth and life? Plato does not tell us what use Er makes of all that he learned in Hades. Does he return masked, as a beggar, as a private man, or as a φρόνιμος? Does he become an ungraspable, uncanny character? And are all of these possible returns and becomings different types of *homini sacri*, or do they present an alternative to the very meaning of the *homo sacer*?

To transform Plato into a contemporary theorist of some of the most urgent political issues (such as those of biopolitics, life, and the difference between sacrifice and killing) is not a new gesture. Yet the enigmatic myth of Er has often been overlooked and underestimated. It now appears that this concluding part of the *Republic* is not a disappointment or a weak ending at all. On the contrary, through a series of enlightening dissimulations it addresses the capacity to distinguish between force and violence, between kingship and sovereignty, without defending impotency and exalting the absence of decision.

There are three myths of judgement after death in Plato: in the *Gorgias*, *Phaedo* and the *Republic*. As Julia Annas rightly analyses, the myth of the *Gorgias* is relatively simple:

> there is a judgement after death; the good are rewarded and the bad punished [. . .] The *Gorgias* myth, then, expresses a kind of optimism: we should not be depressed by the fact that around us we plainly see the good suffering and the wicked flourishing, for this is not the end of the matter; ultimately there will be a judgement where everyone gets what they deserve. (1982: 122–3)

Metempsychosis, or reincarnation, appears in the myth of the *Phaedo*. In the first place, 'the *Phaedo* myth appears to be giving basically the same judgement story as the *Gorgias*', but in fact there are 'several shifts of emphasis which together downgrade the role of the judging' (Annas 1982: 125). As it happens, 'reincarnation [. . .] appears as a punishment for a bad life, and the highest kind of virtue is said to belong to the philosopher, who by refusing to identify with the body's concerns renders his soul at death "pure", unattracted by the body and presumably not liable to reincarnation' (1982: 126–7). According to Annas, though, 'reincarnation and the final judgement myth have not been successfully combined' (1982: 127), and the myth ends up confused, and confusing as a whole.

The myth of Er for its part 'is more complex than the *Gorgias* myth, without being confused and eccentric like the *Phaedo* myth' (Annas 1982: 129). Why, then, has it been considered as disappointing, or at times even repellent? Because 'there is no longer any suggestion that [the judgement] is a *final* judgement' (Annas 1982: 131). The cycles of reincarnation are endless, which means that

> there is no way in which justice gets to predominate [. . .] The afterlife judgement, then, can no longer serve as a moral rectification to individuals, a guarantee that in the end just people do get their due reward. In the Myth of Er the cosmos is horrifyingly indifferent to individuals' moral achievements, and presents no guarantee at all that those achievements will 'in the end' get their due reward and not have been thrown away. (Annas 1982: 135)

As Agamben notices in *The Use of Bodies*, this cosmic indifference pertains to the intermingling of necessity (ἀνάγκη), which sets the conditions of choices, and contingency (τύχη), with its lottery and arbitrariness (2015: 251). Of course, 'the myth seems to explain the irreparable union of each soul with a certain form of life in terms that are moral and, in some way, even juridical: there has been a "choice", and there is therefore a responsibility and a fault (*aitia*)' (2015: 251). At the same time, however, all justice is 'impossible', because both necessity and choice are 'blind' (2015: 256).

A strange conclusion for a dialogue devoted to justice: that justice might not, in the end, triumph. That there is perhaps no reward at all for a life of virtue. To 'mind one's own business', then, means that we should not expect anything from the gods. The mythical 'spokesman' of beyond is clear when he tells the souls: 'Virtue has no masters: as he honors or dishonors it, so shall each of you have more or less of it. Responsibility lies with the chooser; the god is blameless' (*Republic* 617e). The life of virtue is worth possessing, because it is precisely detached from all hope for gratification or benefit. It does not depend on anyone, and does not wait for any reward. Such is, perhaps, the ultimate significance of kingship: indifference to gratifications. Desire of justice for itself. From Er to Odysseus to Socrates, the voices of the living dead still resonate to tell us that such a desire, in its utmost fragility, is what will, eternally, return and survive.

Notes

1 The volume to which Malabou refers is *Contemporary Encounters with Ancient Metaphysics* (2017) – Editor.
2 On this point, see the powerful study by Claudia Baracchi, *Of Myth, Life, and War in Plato's Republic* (2002).
3 Deneen attributes this question to Dale Hall's 'The *Republic* and the "Limits of Politics"' (1977).

11

Epigenesis of the Text: New Paths in Biology and Hermeneutics

Let me start by making four points before explaining what relates them in an essential way. At stake is the possibility of sketching new crossings between contemporary biology and philosophical and textual practices.[1]

First, a definition of epigenesis. The term comes from the Greek *epi*, which means 'above', and *genesis*, 'genesis' or 'constitution'. 'Epigenesis' refers to a mode of embryonic development through the successive addition of parts that form and are born from one another. Aristotle uses the term *epigenesis* for the first time in *Generation of Animals* to refer to the formation of the living individual.[2] Modern usage of the term begins in 1650 with William Harvey who, in his book *Exercises on the Generation of Animals*, presents epigenesis as characteristic of an organism in which 'all parts are not fashioned simultaneously, but emerge in their due succession and order' (Harvey 1847: 336). Later, in the early eighteenth century, Maupertuis and Buffon argued for the superiority of epigenetism over preformationism, thereby instigating the conflict that became central to the mid-century.[3] The theory of growth through epigenesis – embryonic formation by progressive complexification – is opposed to the preformationist theory that claims that the embryo is a fully constituted being, a miniature individual whose growth, which is solely quantitative, consists in the unveiling of organs and already formed parts.

Secondly, in §27 of the *Critique of Pure Reason*, Kant makes use of the expression 'system of the *epigenesis* of pure reason' (1998: 265). §27 is part of the Transcendental Deduction, where Kant exposes the question of the origin of the necessity of the agreement (*Übereinstimmung*) that connects the categories to the objects of experience a priori. Kant claims that this agreement cannot be innate. If such were the case, we would have to consider that categories are 'implanted [*eingepflanzte*] in us along with our existence' (1998: 265). But nor can the agreement come from experience and derive from an empirical source. We must therefore opt for another approach: a pure production of the categories. This is the point where Kant has recourse to an analogy: the analogy of the biological process of epigenesis. Kant declares that, if correctly understood, the a priori agreement between the categories and experience opens what amounts to 'as it were a system of *epigenesis* of pure reason [*gleichsam ein System der Epigenesis der reinen Vernunft*]' (1998: 265).

Clearly, Kant is referring to the epigenetism-versus-preformation conflict, taking the side of the epigenetic conception of the 'agreement'. Indeed, he contrasts epigenesis with 'a kind of *preformation-system* of pure reason', which assumes the existence of a 'pre-established harmony' between our cognitive structures and their objects and defines categories as innate 'subjective predispositions' (1998: 265). Countering this view, Kant claims that the relation of the categories to objects develops through self-differentiation, as do all embryos. Epigenesis, the concept that finally achieved widespread favour at the end of the eighteenth century, then becomes the privileged biological figure of the spontaneity of understanding: there is then a *transcendental formation* of the elements of thinking. A pure epigenesis.

Thirdly, 'epigenetics' is a neologism created in 1940 by the British biologist Conrad Waddington that derives from epigenesis. The noun 'epigenetics' refers to the branch of molecular biology that studies the relations between genes and the individual features they produce, that is, the relation between genotype and phenotype. Reflecting with hindsight on the creation of this term, Waddington commented:

> Some years ago, I introduced the word 'epigenetics', derived from the Aristotelian word 'epigenesis', which had more or less passed into disuse, as a suitable name for the branch of biology which studies the causal interactions between genes and their products which bring the phenotype into being. (Waddington 1968: 9–10)

The adjective 'epigenetic' refers, then, to everything to do with this interaction and is concerned with the mechanisms of expression and transcription of the genetic code. These mechanisms are largely determinant for the activation or inhibition of genes in the process of constituting the phenotype. Take, for example, cellular differentiation. In 1935, in his acceptance speech for the Nobel Prize, Thomas Morgan was already asking: 'if the characters of the individual are determined by the genes, then why are not all the cells of the body exactly alike?' (Morgan 2018: 323). How can the difference between a neuron and a hepatic cell, for example, be explained, given that their starting point is one and the same, since all the cells of a single organism share an identical genetic heritage? Differentiated cellular development depends on selective use via the activation and silencing of certain genes. Epigenetic mechanisms structure the auto-differentiation of the living.

One essential aspect of the meaning of 'traditional' epigenesis is thus found also in contemporary 'epigenetics'. It is still a matter of defining individual development as an autonomous, self-formed and formative growth, which is also called 'epigenetic history'. Epigenetics is currently becoming a prominent field, which might even supplant the importance of genetics. We will see in a moment that the development of the brain, for example, is for the most part an epigenesis, and is certainly not reducible to genetic determinism.

Fourthly, Ricoeur's concept of epigenesis is highly important to the extent that, first, very few philosophers are making use of the concept of epigenesis and, second, he is the only one to make use of it in the context of hermeneutics. Ricoeur views epigenesis as both an exegetical tool and as a structure that allows us to question meaning in a very specific way. According to him, epigenesis is even capable of founding a theory of reading. What is epigenesis in the hermeneutical context? Ricoeur provides us first of all with a negative definition: an epigenesis is not a genesis. In *The Conflicts of Interpretations*, he asks: 'Is meaning in genesis or in epigenesis?' (1974: 146). Where should we look for it? Does it lie in 'the return [. . .] or in the rectification of the old by the new?' (1974: 146–7).[4] This distinction between 'return' and 'rectification of the old by the new' helps explain the difference between genesis and epigenesis. Genesis always brings the new back to the old, while epigenesis marks the current meeting point between the old and the new, the space where they reciprocally interfere and transform one another – the embryo of a specific temporality.

Starting from a common point, a name, epigenesis, we then have: a biological phenomenon, a transcendental structure, epigenetics and a hermeneutical instrument. How can we unify these different points? How can we exhibit the theoretical space that opens at the crossing of these tracks? And how are we to determine such a space in order that it appears as one of the most important in the contemporary theoretical scene?

Let's come back to the etymology of 'epigenesis'. We recall that the prefix *epi* means 'above'. 'Epigenesis' therefore literally means 'above genesis', 'over' it. This literal meaning is very difficult to understand initially. What can this 'over genesis' mean? To clarify, we often transform the 'above' into an 'after'. Isn't epigenesis just a development that follows a first genesis, a first source, one that takes off from it? The embryo does form starting from the seed, *after* it. Epigenesis thus appears commonly as a second genesis, one that takes place after engendering. According to an order of priority that is both logical and ontological, the 'above' therefore paradoxically appears to situate it *below* genesis.

Let us, however, examine this 'above' a little more closely. The *geological* meaning of the prefix *epi* is very illuminating and comes to our rescue. It helps us understand the above not as an extension that comes 'over' something else, but as a *surface effect*. In geology, the 'epicentre' is the point of projection of the 'hypocentre', the underground site where an upheaval emerges, on the surface of the earth. The hypocentre is the underground focus of an earthquake, while the epicentre is its surface event. The epicentre lies exactly on the vertical line of the underground focus.[5] The work of determining the position of the epicentre, the place where destruction is the greatest, is called 'localisation'. All epigenesis also necessarily comes to light starting from a focus corresponding to a hypocentre. The question then becomes that of knowing how to read epigenesis. Should it be related systematically to its focus, explained by its before, its 'underground', which would then be viewed as its foundation? Does recognising epigenesis mean penetrating its underground? If so, the problem is that the reading is a genetic reading and is no longer strictly epigenetic.

Ricoeur is right: *epigenesis is not genesis*. To own up to its own logic, it is necessary to remain on the surface in some way, and this does not mean being superficial, but rather working where *it occurs*, at the contact point between the underground and the ground. We have to be able to *locate* the epicentre and remain at the point of impact. In this way, of course, it would be possible to look below later on, but only *after* and without this changing anything that occurred. In the case of an earthquake, in many ways the epicentre becomes primary with regard to the hypocentre. If we follow the epicentric logic, as we must, then we conclude that the seat of the 'system of the epigenesis of pure reason' should not be sought *below*. This is the first essential common characteristic to the different points: they all work at the surface, that is they never refer to a hidden ground. They convey the idea of a *founding at the point of contact and not by the root or focus*. Kant was already very clear on this point: reason is a ground [*Boden*] whose solidity must be ensured without digging. Thus, when he speaks about morals in the Transcendental Dialectic, he says:

> we now concern ourselves with a labour less spectacular but nevertheless not unrewarding: that of making the terrain for these majestic moral edifices level and firm enough to be built upon; for under this ground there are all sorts of passageways, such as moles might have dug, left over from reason's vain but confident treasure hunting, that make every building insecure. (Kant 1998: 398)

The challenge is, then, to understand how a surface can be foundational and to what extent epigenesis can prove to be more fruitful than genesis. For this, I will go back to Ricoeur. As we just saw, epigenesis situates itself in the middle, at the contact point, and is in the process of bringing to fruition the fusion of times. Epigenesis is then both spatial and temporal. In order to make this clearer, let me resituate the specific context in which Ricoeur makes use of epigenesis. In both *The Conflict of Interpretations* and *Freud and Philosophy*, it is a matter of bringing to light an 'epigenesis of religious feeling' (Ricoeur 1970: 534): the intermediary between the Freudian approach of the primordial event of the killing of the father – which, in as much as it repeats itself without alteration through time, authorises no evolution, but instead 'sempiternal treading' (Ricoeur 1970: 534) – and the Hegelian vision of a constant dialectical transformation of meaning that renders religion nothing but a simple moment of the mind. The unconscious and consciousness pull meaning in two opposing directions. Ricoeur sets out to show that there is actually no 'antinomy' between the two, and that archaeology and teleology share solidarity: all archaeology is a wait, and all teleology proceeds from the archaeological traces of the past.

Epigenesis then appears as the *intersection of the archaic and the teleological* (Ricoeur 1970: 534). Meaning therefore lies in the medium point between pure repetition of the archaic and dissolution of the archaic in a constant dialectical sublation of the past. Epigenetic reading defines itself as a prospecting tension towards the future which rectifies after the fact the primitive or 'archaic' dispositions that made it possible. It situates itself between two versions of what we will call the program, the pre-determined set of rules or constraints implied in the notion of the archaic, and the systematic sublation of these rules in absolute knowing. In fact, epigenetic reading is a way of making the epigenesis of a text appear, of finding the precise point of contact between times in a text, of exhibiting a surface which is not pre-programmed – a surface contact from which a form has to emerge; in other words, a synapse.

We have seen that biological epigenesis includes the dual dimension of regression and progression, since the embryo gradually becomes more complex through the addition of new parts that complete pre-existing parts. The epigenetic economy and the hermeneutic economy thus concur, with both of them combining repetition and exploration, recapitulation and invention. It might be objected that all genesis also involves this dual dimension. This is true, but in the case of epigenesis, these dimensions are but one; they fuse together at the point of their shared impact, the synaptic point. Admittedly, the context in which Ricœur develops his idea of interpretative epigenesis is very different from Kant's Transcendental Deduction. But this difference is not enough to proscribe the comparison with the epigenesis of reason. Critical philosophy is organised entirely by the dual prospective and retrospective movement of epigenesis. In the *Critique of Pure Reason*, Kant situates transcendental epigenesis as the development that occurs *upon contact* between the categories and experience. To wish to go back to the source of this contact, as far too many commentators do, is thus not coherent with the Kantian process, which takes place precisely at the meeting point. Once again, the transcendental ground hides no treasure, and this allows me to view the transcendental as a 'synaptic point'. Kant, before Ricoeur, already warns us against this view: the originary validity of the transcendental is not to be sought in its genesis, but rather in its epigenesis. The transcendental is subject to epigenesis, not to foundation.

Let us now turn to epigenetics. The prefix *epi* is illuminated in an entirely remarkable manner at this point, since epigenetics studies the mechanisms that modify the function of genes by activating or deactivating them. *Insofar as these modifications never alter the DNA sequence itself, epigenetics is said to work on the 'surface' (epi–) of the molecule.* This meaning of 'surface' is not excluded from the semantics of epigenesis. Indeed, contemporary epigenetics actually studies the transformation mechanisms at work *on the surface of* DNA molecules during their transcription. While epigenetics has a wide field of action, it does not have any impact on the code. It is striking that the complex relation between the genetic and the epigenetic, a relation that is one of the fundamental questions of contemporary biology, is a renewed version of the debate between preformationism and epigenesis, which has given rise to so many polemics. In the second half of the twentieth century, the concept of 'program' dominated genetics. It was often described as the symptom of a 'resurgence of preformationism'.[6] But the idea of a program is exactly what is in question today as a result of the importance of epigenetic factors in debates on heredity.

This new orientation in the 'logic of life' derives largely from the results of the sequencing of the human genome. On 15 February 2001, the American scientific journal *Nature* published the virtually complete sequence of the three billion bases of this genome. The result was surprising: the human genome is made up of only 30,000 genes; in other words, just 13,000 more than drosophila or fruit flies. Furthermore, it appears that genes only make up 5 per cent of the genome. Assembled in bunches and clusters, they are separated by vast expanses of so-called 'gene deserts', made up of DNA called 'junk' or 'repetitive', that is, non-coding. According to studies, this 'non-coding' DNA accounts for a quarter or a third of the totality of the genome.

This means that within chromosomes there are long DNA sequences which, according to current understanding, do not appear to match the genes and cannot be given any particular function.[7] The sequencing of the genome did not, therefore, offer the expected revelations. Nor did the sequencing of the genome show the all-powerful effect of genetic determinism; instead, it indicated its weakening. In his book, eloquently entitled *La Fin du "tout génétique"?*, Henri Atlan notes the challenge to the 'genetic paradigm'. He writes: 'The idea that "everything is genetic" is starting to be seriously unsettled' (1999: 16). More recently, he wrote:

> During the last forty or fifty years, the classical ideal that seeks to explain very complex observations by reducing them to laws or simple mechanisms appeared to have been attained in biology thanks to the discovery of the genetic code and its universality. This was truly an extraordinary discovery that ought to have led to the invariable law underlying all biological processes. As such, a genetic reductionism crowned with success appeared to be in sight and the achievement of the sequencing of the human genome was assumed to meet this expectation. In fact, the completion of this project showed that everything was not written in DNA sequences, even at the molecular and cellular level. (Atlan 2009)

And again:

> the idea that the totality or essential aspects of the development and functioning of living organisms is determined by a genetic program tends to be gradually replaced by a more complex model that is based on notions of interaction, reciprocal effects between the genetic, whose central role is not denied, and the epigenetic, whose importance we are gradually discovering. (Atlan 1999: 16)[8]

We have thus entered the biological 'post-genomic' era.[9]

Epigenetic modifications depend on two types of causes: *internal* and *structural* on the one hand, *environmental* on the other. First, it is a matter of physical and chemical mechanisms (RNA, nucleosome, methylation). Secondly, epigenetics also supplies genetic material with a means of reacting to the evolution of environmental conditions. For example, while plants do not have a nervous system, they have the ability to memorise seasonal changes at the cellular level.[10] Among animals, reactions to environmental conditions are even greater. Many geneticists now think that the behaviour of genes can thus be modified by life experiences.[11] An important element in epigenetic factors in fact derives from the environment, the outside and, as we shall see with brain epigenesis, learning, the environment, habit – in a word, experience. The definition of phenotypical malleability proposed by the American biologist Mary Jane West-Eberhard is eloquent in this respect. She says that it is a matter of the 'ability of an organism to react to an environmental input with a change in form, state, movement, or rate of activity' (2003: 34). The example of brain epigenesis appears to confirm these conclusions once and for all. Let us return to synaptic epigenesis. During the life of the foetus, most of the 100 billion neurons at work in the brain as well as the innumerable synaptic connections that link them are formed. Under the influence of experiences lived *in utero* and later on during the first years of life, many of these so-called 'irrelevant' or redundant connections are eliminated while others are consolidated. This is the work of epigenesis. This process does not only take place during the 'critical' periods of development: throughout life, the brain undergoes synaptic modifications imposed on it by experience. In fact, brain development continues long after birth and depends to a large extent on environmental and cultural factors. As Changeux (1985) constantly reminds us, the theory of epigenesis by synaptic stabilisation is thus the *opposite of innatism*. This results in a widened definition of epigenesis: epigenesis now concerns everything 'that is not preformed'. Our brain, then, is like a text. A text that would not be exactly written though, but shaped, fashioned, by the constant interaction between genetic determinations and epigenetic modification. Each time unique, the plastic configurations of our neural connections (that is, of our synapses) are the forms of our identity. Plasticity, then, is the transcendental structure of our existential experience.

Setting aside the genetic paradigm (and here I am playing with both the hermeneutic and scientific meanings of the word 'genetic') involves considering the structure of an internal growth process which, moving by self-differentiation, plays with the forces *of its own outside*, starting with its creative, formative and transformative resources. The idea of such a process is at once transcendental, biological and hermeneutical. One of the main tasks for critical theory and continental philosophy today is, I believe, to inscribe within their own fields the resources provided by current cellular, molecular and neuro-biology. We are witnessing the birth of the epigenetic paradigm, which, again, is not pregnant only in biology but is also an invaluable resource for the humanities.

The phrase 'epigenetic paradigm' echoes the phrase 'genetic paradigm' coined by Henri Atlan who, as we have seen, now criticises it as being obsolete. The term 'paradigm', borrowed initially from Kuhn (1962), is adopted freely by Atlan to designate, in a general manner, 'a set of ideas, concepts that form a framework in which to [. . .] imagine, plan experiments, interpret results, develop theories' (1999: 11–12). Understood in this way, a paradigm is not only the set of principles and methods shared by a scientific community; it also acts as a reading and interpreting tool that dominates various theoretical and disciplinary fields at any given moment. Today, the genetic paradigm is under reconsideration. We have seen that some scientists would prefer no longer to use the notion of program. The increasing importance of epigenetics prompts us to propose that an epigenetic paradigm is in the process of constituting itself. There is reason to believe that in the future it will also become one of the structuring tracks of current rationality. A new transcendental.

Epigenesis takes place at the moving contact point between origin and the present state of affairs, until their difference disappears right into their contact – tensed origin, retrospective present, future in the making. What an epigenesis shows, says Ricoeur – and this is a particularly important point – is that it 'has meaning only in later figures, since the meaning of a given figure is deferred until the appearance of a new figure' (1974: 113). This new figure is neither a pure product from outside, nor the revelation of a preformed meaning. The logic of epigenesis, its own dynamic, requires that we seek out and show this place where a structure, be it a brain, a text or a transcendental framework, is 'both archaic in origin and susceptible of an indefinite creation of meaning' (Ricoeur 1970: 548). And, if it really is impossible to differentiate between the transcendental, the biological and the hermeneutical, we may affirm that what emerges today is a new form not only of development, but also, and consequently, of history.

Notes

1. Though previously unpublished as it currently stands, in this chapter Malabou presents an early version of what would later become, after revision, a closing chapter in her book *Before Tomorrow: Epigenesis and Rationality* (2016) – Editor.
2. See Chapter 1 of Book II of Aristotle's *Generation of Animals* – Editor.
3. Buffon develops the theory of the 'inner mold', which is a reformulation of Harvey's 'formative faculty' (Buffon 1830: 7–8). See also Maupertuis (1754).
4. See also *Freud and Philosophy*, especially the chapter entitled 'Dialectic: Archeology and Teleology' (Ricoeur 1970: 459–93). Ricœur draws a very clear distinction between genesis and epigenesis. On this point, see in particular *The Conflict of Interpretations* (1974: 109ff.). See also the very fine work of Øystein Brekke (2013: 73–82).
5. Seismic waves follow the shortest route to reach the surface of the earth. In this way, they lose very little energy because they travel through fewer rocks. As they have more energy at the epicentre, the destruction caused at this spot is greater than elsewhere.
6. See Ludwig and Pradeu (2008: 120). See also Henri Atlan: 'We are witnessing a return of extreme preformationism, in the form of a new avatar, in which everything is contained in the genes' (1999: 58). [All translations of Atlan's work are Malabou's own – Editor.]

7 See 'Le génome humain cache de "vastes deserts"', *Le Monde*, 13 February 2001.
8 See also *La Recherche*, no. 463, 'Épigénétique: L'hérédité au-delà des gènes' (2012: 38–54).
9 'Post-genomic' biology assumes an interdisciplinary approach that expands the field of molecular biology in order to study element systems (DNA, proteins, supramolecular structures, small molecules) interacting with each other.
10 Research on certain types of cress have, for example, made it possible to show that being exposed to cold during the winter led to structural changes in the chromatin, which silenced the flowering genes. These genes are reactivated in the spring when the longer and warmer days become suitable for reproduction. The environment may also provoke changes that will have effects on future generations.
11 See Ho (2003) and 'Epigenetic Inheritance' (2009).

12

Reading Lázló Földényi's 'Dostoyevsky Reads Hegel in Siberia and Bursts into Tears'

'Dostoyevsky Reads Hegel in Siberia and Bursts into Tears' is a short text written in 2003 by László Földényi, a Hungarian cultural critic and professor of Theatre, Film and Television at the University of Budapest.[1] I discovered this little masterpiece in a bookshop in Paris, quite a long time ago, in 2008, when it came out in French with Actes Sud.

This text opens a multiplicity of interpretations. The one I choose to follow here is Földényi's profound meditation on the relationship between philosophy and literature. In an article published in the *New Yorker* in May 2020, James Wood asks of *Dostoyevsky Reads Hegel in Siberia and Bursts into Tears*: 'Who could resist the title?' The title is for sure irresistible. It is so, I think, because it is at once and indistinctly philosophical and literary. It announces a narrative and sounds like the title of a novel or short story. At the same time, Hegel's readers immediately understand what is philosophically at stake in it: Hegel's supposed indifference to suffering, Hegel's indifference to Siberia, Hegel's indifference to exile, Hegel's indifference to literature. Or, more exactly, to what literature has to say that definitely escapes the realm of the concept, that is also of world history.

I will examine three aspects of this literary-philosophical intertwining.

I

First intertwining: the intermingling of fiction and reality. The fiction is that of Dostoyevsky reading Hegel's *Lectures on the Philosophy of History* in his Siberian exile. This fiction is undoubtedly based on factual truths, though. What are they? It is important to resituate the context. Before he was sent to Siberia, Dostoyevsky had participated in a radical intellectual discussion group called the Petrashevsky Circle. The group was suspected of subversive activities, which led to Dostoyevsky's arrest in 1849 and his sentencing to death.

On 22 December 1849, Dostoyevsky was led before the firing squad but received a last-minute reprieve and was sent to a Siberian labour camp in Omsk, where he worked for four years. On his release, in the spring of 1854, he was sent to Semipalatinsk, in southern Siberia, where he began several years of military service. A military service that was in fact an exile, a consignment to a place unnoticed and forgotten, a desert far from 'European' Russia. This is where Földényi's narrative/philosophical essay takes place.

> In the spring of 1854, after four years of forced labor, Dostoyevsky was sent as a conscript soldier to Semipalatinsk, in the southern part of Siberia. The town, somewhat larger than a village, had a population of between 5,000 and 6,000, half of whom were nomad Kasakhs, for the most part living in yurts. The local residents hardly felt anything in common with the so-called European Russians; they referred to them as 'mainlanders', observing all of them with suspicion. Their number, however, only grew: between 1825 and 1846, the number of exiles sent to Siberia increased to 159,000.
>
> The town was surrounded by a barren sandy desert; there was not even a tree or a bush in sight, only sand and thistles [. . .]
>
> This is where Dostoyevsky lived, in a spacious but low-ceilinged room, in which were set a bed, a table, and a trunk; on the wall hung a tiny framed mirror. And here he made friends with the local public prosecutor, Aleksander Yegorovich Vrangel, twenty years old at the time, who ended up selflessly supporting the writer for more than ten years from the date of their initial acquaintance. Dostoyevsky related his narrative plans to Vrangel; at times he recited his favorite poems from Pushkin and crooned his favorite operatic arias [. . .] And in the meantime he worked and worked on the manuscript of *Memoirs from the House of the Dead*, allowing Vrangel a glimpse every now and then. In return, the public prosecutor got hold of some books for him. And shortly thereafter they began to study together, assiduously, day after day. (Földényi 2020: 19–20)

We know from Joseph Frank, Dostoyevsky's American biographer, that Dostoyevsky wrote to his brother in St Petersburg in 1854 to ask him to send Kant, Vico, Ranke and the Church Fathers, and 'to slip Hegel in without fail, *especially Hegel's History of Philosophy*. My entire future is tied up with that' (Frank 1987: 169). What we do not know is whether Dostoyevsky actually read Hegel's *Lectures* in Siberia.

Földényi's fiction starts with this hypothesis: What if he did? What if he did read the *Lectures* while in Semipalatinsk?

> In his memoirs, Vrangel does not give away the title of the textbook they were studying from. He does, however, mention the name of a single author: Hegel.

The titles of the books that Vrangel might have been ordering from Germany are unknown to us, but he also subscribed to the *Ausburger Allgemeine Zeitung*. As there is some room for hypothesis, let us assume that he ordered Hegel's lectures on the philosophy of world history, presented between the fall of 1822 and the spring of 1831 at the University of Berlin – occurring in parallel with the tens of thousands of exiles continually arriving in Siberia. The lectures were published in book form for the first time in 1837, with a revised edition issued in 1840. Perhaps this was the book that Vrangel would have ordered, after having leafed through a few pages. It is possible; in his lectures Hegel makes mention of Siberia. Only briefly, it is true. And these few words, it appears, he held in reserve only so that he could justify the reason for his general lack of knowledge about Siberia. His discussion of Asia, in other words, begins with this remark: 'We must first of all eliminate Siberia, the northern slope of Asia. For it lies outside the scope of our enquiry. The whole character of Siberia rules it out as a setting for historical culture and prevents it from attaining a distinct form in the world-historical process.' (Földényi 2020: 20–1)

II

Second intertwining: Dostoyevsky's fictive reaction to these words and Földényi's first philosophical analyses of it.

We can well imagine Dostoyevsky's consternation as he came upon these lines while sitting next to the tallow candle. And we can easily imagine his despair as well, as he was obliged to confront the fact that 'over there', in Europe – for whose ideals he had been sentenced to death but then sent into exile – no significance whatsoever was attributed to his many sufferings. For his sufferings had followed him into Siberia, into that world which was not a part of history. As seen from the European point of view, none of this could ever been redeemed. Dostoyevsky might have felt – and justifiably so – that he had not only been exiled to Siberia, he had been expelled into nonexistence itself. And from here only a miracle could redeem him, a miracle whose possibility was precluded not only by Hegel but by the entirety of the contemporary European intellectual mind as well [. . .]

It is very possible that it was exactly at that moment – when Dostoyevsky became aware that he had been torn away from the history for which he had nonetheless assumed every vilification – that the conviction was born in him that there are dimensions to life which cannot be compartmentalized into history, and the criteria of existence within history cannot be the only proof of existence. If someone truly feels and experiences the weight of his own existence, then he is, so to speak, torn out of history, and that same weight – one that is beyond history – weighs upon him in Semipalatinsk as it does in Berlin. (Földényi 2020: 21–2)

Földényi will now mingle his account of Dostoyevsky's reaction and despair with an interpretation of Hegel's concept of world history. He writes:

> This is the foundation [of Hegel's argument].
> 'Whoever looks at the world rationally will find that it in turn assumes a rational aspect, the two exist in a reciprocal relationship.' Or he doesn't even bother to look, Dostoyevsky could have answered, glancing into his small framed mirror hanging on the wall of his room. Nobody *looks* back at us from a mirror. We can try to bravely face ourselves: our gaze is engrossed in the eyeballs of a *stranger*, who stares fixedly into nothingness. Not only does this stranger not look outward, he does not even look inward. He is dead, numb – if we pay long attention – even haunting. (Földényi 2020: 25)

The Hegelian concept of history would be the product of the making, the fabrication of a specular self-gaze – Földényi's interpretation of the speculative – that in reality sees nothing, or, more precisely, sees only what it can see: itself, that is, Spirit. The spiritual self-gaze only mirrors nations that belong to world history, nations that are precisely able to reflect on themselves with what Földényi also calls 'fulfillment, fortune, and fame' (2020: 29). What the self-gaze cannot see is the 'suffering of the vanquished' (2020: 30), the suffering of the unsuccessful, the victims, the exiles. Against Hegel, Földényi argues that perhaps history reveals itself not to rational people but '*to those whom it has cast out of itself*' (2020: 230). 'Földényi regards Hegel', James Wood declares, 'and by extension the eighteenth- and early-nineteenth-century Enlightenment project, as a vast, disenchanting bulldozer, crushing God and mystery under the machinery of its rationality' (2020).

Földényi's text, when it touches on the issue of God, definitely looks both like a Dostoyevskian novel and a philosophical reflection, as it confronts two figures of the divine: the 'God of reason' and the 'God of transcendence' – a transcendence that is absent from Hegel's system. The God of reason, Földényi argues, is in reality a dead God. 'In the Hegelian interpretation of history, everything designated "divine" is subordinated to something under the supervision of human beings' (2020: 31). Enlightenment rationalism proceeded '[i]n the name of God, but lacking all divine spirit' (2020: 31). Behind Hegel's dismissal of Siberia 'lies his secret wish to assassinate God' (2020: 36). Therefore, 'God, subjected to rationality, is not the God of freedom, but of politics, conquest, and colonization. *This* is the secular religion of the God of the modern age. And history – looking at it from a Hegelian point of view – is the history of secularization' (2020: 33). And Siberia had no part to play in it. 'Hegel had so few words to say about Siberia. The reason for this is simple: the philosopher, right before turning to Siberia, discusses the continent of Africa, which, in his view, similarly falls outside history' (2020: 33). Dostoyevsky's God, on the contrary, is the Saviour. 'It could be seen as a divine ruse that it was precisely in Siberia – this no-man's-land supposedly excluded from God's providence – where Dostoyevsky became convinced of the existence of God and the indispensability of transcendence' (2020: 38). The Siberian experience turned out to be a regenerative one.

> He once told Vladimir Solovyov, the brother of the philosopher Vsevolod Solovyov, 'Oh, it was a great happiness for me: Siberia and the forced labor! [. . .] I only had a happy, healthy life there, I understood myself there [. . .] I understood Christ.' [. . .] This is the redemption that Raskolnikov will experience in Siberia: his life there 'is the story of a gradual renewal of a man, of his gradual regeneration, of his slow progress from one world to another, of how he learned to know a hitherto undreamed-of reality,' as Dostoyevsky writes at the end of *Crime and Punishment*. (2020: 41–2)

This clash of Titans, God versus God, Hegel versus Dostoyevsky, definitely entangles the philosophical and the literary, an account of dialectics with the imaginary portrait of a 'cursed' writer finding redemption in his solitude and banishment from dialectics itself.

III

Third intertwining, and the most gripping one: the use of ventriloquism. More precisely, of different ventriloquisms echoing each other. Földényi first gives a voice to Dostoyevsky, makes him speak. This voice is his own. Of course, he could not have read Hegel's dismissal of Siberia and Africa in the *Lectures* without thinking of his own situation as a Hungarian intellectual. Who among us knows anything about contemporary Hungarian philosophers, thinkers, artists? We do not have to travel as far as Siberia to discover deserts. They exist at the heart of Europe. Is not Hungary one of them, devastated by fascism, a solitary island within 'democratic' nations? In order to make such an isolation resonate, Földényi chooses to animate Dostoyevsky, to speak through him, for him; and, at the same time, he lets Dostoyevsky haunt him, ventriloquise him in return, thus appearing in disappearance, thus redoubling banishment, oblivion and exile.

Also, both Földényi and Dostoyevsky ventriloquise Hegel. The few passages that appear from his work are never explained from his point of view; they are always filtered by Dostoyevsky's and Földényi's grief.

This astonishing textual phenomenon raises a fundamental question: can a philosopher have something like a voice without immediately borrowing it from literature? By 'voice', I mean something like a singular individual soul, a singular affective tonality. Is this voice possible without immediately disappearing as a philosopher? Can a philosopher ever weep without immediately being exiled from philosophy?

We here touch on the most interesting aspect of the literature–philosophy intertwining, which is Földényi's invention, through Dostoyevsky, of Hegel's voice – that is, first of all, of Hegel's subjectivity. Hegel, Földényi says, would have written what he wrote about Africa, or Siberia, in order to escape, inhibit or foreclose his own subjectivity, to the extent that being a particular subject would be, in his eyes, incompatible with systematic philosophical thinking. By dismissing Siberia and Africa, Hegel would effectively dismiss himself. That is, himself also as a Siberian, as an African. Himself also as a writer.

> In his repudiation of Africa and Siberia, [Hegel] is only denying something perceptible relevant to his own inner self. And here he does not simply exploit his own feelings but repudiates his own shadow self – all that monstrosity, horror, and heinousness; he would not have had to deny them so vehemently had he not discovered the roots of these qualities in his own heart. The passion with which he depicts the alleged untrammelled course of atrocities taking place in Africa, describing indefatigably ever newer instances, anecdotes, horrifying stories without ever discovering the least cause for joy, beauty, or something worthy of amazement – this tells us that Hegel was not afraid of Africa (for he certainly had reason to feel quite safe in Berlin) but was at war with his own instincts. The frail philosopher, now light-years distant from any genuine experience of freedom, then cobbled together, for reasons of self-therapy, his own history of philosophy and explanation of existence. Perhaps, however, in the depths of his heart he desired nothing more than to be able to say – as both Rimbaud and Genet were to say later on – I am a Negro. (Földényi 2020: 34)

So we see how Földényi voices Hegel negatively by thematising his absence of voice and his absence of self.

Hegel, as we know, never speaks in the first person. In his system, death is never 'my' death. Hegel shuts down any 'mineness', as Heidegger would say, of existence.

This leads me to the issue of suffering, a word that I have used several times so far without pausing on it. Hegel, as an individual, certainly was not alien to suffering. Among other difficulties, he had to wait a long time before being recognised as a philosopher and before becoming a professor. While Schelling's career was thriving, Hegel had to be a journalist, then a head of school in a gymnasium. Marie, his wife, often wrote to their friends about his sadness and depressive mood. A few years after, at long last, he was appointed professor in Berlin, he contracted cholera and died in great pain at only fifty-nine years old. Karl Rosenkranz has a beautiful chapter on Hegel's death in his *Hegel's Leben* (1844).[2] The epidemic was raging, he says, and Marie obtained at the last moment permission to organise a decent funeral, allowing Hegel's students and colleagues to attend and to accompany him to the small Dorotheenstadt cemetery, where he was buried between Fichte and Schiller – a spot that Hegel had himself chosen.

Of course, Hegel's dramas are not comparable to Dostoyevsky's. However, one cannot help interrogate Hegel's silence on his individual life, on individual life in general. Kierkegaard relentlessly asked this question. Who was the subject Hegel?

In paragraphs 23 and 24 of the *Encyclopaedia Logic*, Hegel talks about the 'I' and declares,

> When I say 'I', I mean myself as this singular, quite determinate person. But when I say 'I', I do not in fact express anything particular about myself. Anyone else is also 'I', and although in calling myself 'I', I certainly mean me, this single [person], what I say is still something completely universal.
>
> 'I' is pure being-for-itself, in which everything particular is negated and sublated – consciousness as ultimate, simple, and pure [. . .] 'I' is this void, this receptacle for anything and everything, that for which everything is and which preserves everything within itself. Everyone is a whole world of representations, which are buried in the night of the 'I'. (Hegel 1991b: 57)

Because everyone is an 'I', then every 'I' is similar to any other. Such is the universal character of the particular. So, what about suffering? What about individual suffering? When Hegel talks about 'the seriousness, the suffering, the patience and the labour of the negative' in the *Phenomenology of Spirit* (1977: 10), how does he understand 'suffering'?

In *Civilization and Its Discontents*, Freud declares, 'in the last analysis, all suffering is nothing else than sensation; it only exists in so far as we feel it, and we only feel it in consequence of certain ways in which our organism is regulated' (*SE* XXI: 78). Which means that all suffering is reducible 'in the last analysis' to physical pain and thus to the body, to this or that body. By inventing Hegel's subjectivity, Földényi also invents Hegel's corporeal existence through Dostoyevsky's tears.

IV

I could continue to show how the writing, the very weaving of Földényi's text does something unique, something that many critiques of Hegel lack: the identification of Hegel's dismissal of individual suffering with his dismissal of entire civilisations or countries. I don't intend to argue against Földényi and try to redeem Hegel from his severe and merciless condemnation. His text is strong and beautiful, and so it has to stay. So, why argue?

I would just like to introduce another voice, that of Heidegger, and let him ventriloquise Hegel and provide something – not as an answer but as a question. Heidegger strongly disagrees with Freud and argues that neither suffering nor pain are reducible to sensations. Which does not mean that suffering and pain have no relation to the body, but that all suffering and pain also necessarily bear an impersonal dimension. Let me refer to two texts. The first is a passage from a seminar held in 1942 and published in volume 68 of the *Gesammtausgabe*, called *Hegel*. The volume contains two studies, and my passage appears in the second one, called 'Elucidation of the "Introduction" to Hegel's *Phenomenology of Spirit*' (Heidegger 2015: 51–111). In this text, Heidegger characterises the experience of consciousness, the very notion of dialectical experience as 'transcendental pain [*tranzendentaler Schmerz*]'.

> The course of experience is a 'path of despair,' and therefore experience is essentially a 'painful experience.' Hegel always conceives of 'pain' metaphysically, i.e., as a type of 'consciousness,' the consciousness of being-other, of the tearing, of negativity [. . .] The experience is the transcendental pain of consciousness. Insofar as the experience of consciousness is 'pain' it is at the same time a going through in the sense of an elaboration [*Herausarbeiten*] of the essential shapes of appearing self-consciousness. To say that experience is the 'labor of the concept' means that it is the self-elaboration of consciousness into the unconditioned totality of the truth of its self-comprehension [. . .] Experience is the transcendental labor of consciousness. (2015: 79–80)

The notion of a 'transcendental pain' is, of course, apparently contradictory. If Freud is right, how is it possible to talk about a transcendental pain, irreducible to physical pain? Isn't this, precisely, what makes Dostoyevsky weep, the idea that something monstrous – like a transcendental pain – can exist?

How could there be an a priori pain? Yet as I said, for Heidegger, there is always something impersonal in pain, prior to any 'self' as an entity. A 'there is' pain before the 'I feel pain', a 'there is suffering' before the 'I suffer'. As if pain and suffering make the existence of a subject possible, as if pain and suffering are the *form of the subject*. 'Experience' is not only, then, the consciousness of pain but the production of consciousness as pain. To speak of a 'transcendental pain' would amount to considering it, in Kantian terms, as a condition of possibility.

In a text titled 'Hegel versus Heidegger', Slavoj Žižek proposes a very interesting critique of Heidegger's reading of Hegel that, at the same time, makes Heidegger's reading even more interesting.

> What Heidegger misses in his description of the Hegelian 'experience' as the path of despair [*Verzweiflung*] is the proper abyss of this process: it is not only the natural consciousness that is shattered, but also the transcendental standard, measure, or framing ground against which natural consciousness experiences its inadequacy and failure – as Hegel put it, if what we thought to be true fails the measure of truth, this measure itself has to be abandoned. This is why Heidegger misses the vertiginous abyss of the dialectical process: there is no standard of truth gradually approached through painful experiences; this standard itself is caught in the process, undermined again and again. (Žižek 2012)

This means that transcendental pain is also the pain of the transcendental itself, its inadequacy to the phenomena it regulates. What Žižek very rightly points out is that, for Hegel, logic also can suffer. Which does not mean that *only* logic can suffer.

In *On the Question of Being*, Heidegger seems to have anticipated Žižek's remarks. In this passage, Heidegger is in dialogue with Ernst Jünger, author of the treatise *On Pain*. Heidegger:

> This would be the place to go into your treatise *On Pain* and to bring to light the intrinsic connection between 'work' and 'pain' [. . .] [T]he Greek word for pain, namely, ἄλγος, would first come to speak for us. Presumably ἄλγος is related to ἀλέγω, which as the *intensivum* of λέγω means intimate gathering. In that case, pain would be that which gathers most intimately. (1998: 305–6)

This passage enables us to understand that pain maintains an intimate tie with the logos, with gathering, or even co-belonging [*Zugehörigkeit*]: 'Pain would be that which gathers most intimately.'

Heidegger is not saying that there exists a logical pain, but that gathering is common to logos and pain. Such a gathering is prior to any 'having'. Just as Dasein does not 'possess' logos, neither does it 'have' pain. Rather, and conversely, logos and pain are what constitute Dasein as such. And this is because logos is in pain. Such a pain is the origin of language. We speak because there is 'logoalgia'. If we follow Heidegger, it is perhaps possible to see something else in the Hegelian system and the anonymous painful labour of the negative, something else than the crushing of all individuality.

The problem, Földényi would say, is what to do with the kinds of pain and suffering that escape logos, gathering and synthesis. Exile, in Földényi's text, is also a metaphor for experiences that are not registered in the *Phenomenology of Spirit*, and forms that are not concepts. Pains that are not necessarily reducible to sensations either, but trigger only tears. Once again, is not literature, the non-logical language, the only possible way to give those pains and sufferings a voice?

V

One of the biggest challenges for continental philosophers of the second half of the twentieth century has been, on the one hand, to acknowledge Hegel's affirmation of the originary bond between logic and pain, and thus also the existence of an impersonal pain; and, on the other hand, to struggle against what Hegel excludes from the transcendental realm of pain, that is, all the Siberias and Africas clearly excluded from the system. This double gesture, of acceptance and rejection of Hegel, has profoundly transformed philosophical writing, maintaining it on the verge of literature. It seems that, for Földényi, this effort has been and still is a lost cause. Philosophy is a lost cause. Philosophy can only be Hegelian because it is still and will always be unable to suffer or to cry.

I do not want to decide. I prefer to leave the question entirely open and let Földényi have the last word. At the end of his text, he says that both Hegel and Dostoyevsky had a vision of hell. Two very different, incompatible visions of hell: the European hell and the Siberian hell.

> The *colourful* Siberian hell stands in opposition to the *grey* European hell – the hell which appears in the twentieth century in the works of Kafka and Beckett, in Tarkovsky's *Stalker*, an impersonalised – because mechanised – destruction, and in self-oblivion, brought about by technology, and to all appearances definitive. (Földényi 2020: 45)

Here are the last words of the text:

> Really existing hell [. . .] is never as colourful as in fairy tales. Instead, it appears to be natural, sober, self-evident. It is something like the world of Hegel, the world to which Dostoyevsky returned after his Siberian exile. It was the only place he could go. A place bereft of every enchantment. When the entirety of existence, the cosmic whole, is reduced to a world that can be technically manipulated – this is hell. It requires no devils, no tongues of flame leaping

into the heights or lakes filled with boiling tar. All that is needed is oblivion and the illusion that the confines of humanity is not constituted by the divine but by the tangible, and that the nourishment of the human spirit is not the impossible but the possible – monotonous beyond all measure, and rational. (Földényi 2020: 49)

What is the most hellish dimension of hell? Is it this duality or the frightening gap that opens between them?

Notes

1 *Dostoyevsky Reads Hegel in Siberia and Bursts into Tears* has become the general title of a collection of Földényi's essays written between the years 1990 and 2015. The collection was published in English translation in 2020.
2 Specifically, Book III, Chapter 21.

13

Philosophy and the Outside: Foucault and Decolonial Thinking

The title 'Philosophy and the Outside' has to be understood as a name given to a confrontation.[1] A confrontation between two outsides, two concepts of the outside, as well as two different philosophies and two different concepts of philosophy. All of them issue from the same problem, namely that 'the outside' can only become a philosophical issue if it points to a possible outside of philosophy itself. The first concept of 'outside' that I examine here comes from the inside of Western philosophy and gestures towards a new space of thinking that cannot continue to be called philosophy. The second I borrow from some prominent Latin-American thinkers and writers; it appears as the outside of the Western philosophical attempt at producing its own outside. It then opens an outside of the outside. The two approaches to the outside share many traits, but rapidly part ways.

The first concept is to be found in Foucault's text, *Maurice Blanchot: The Thought from Outside*. Foucault analyses the shift that gave birth, in the middle of the twentieth century, to what he calls 'modern literature'. Modern literature defines a specific kind of writing that situates itself in a space where truth and falsity are deactivated and have lost their meaning. This writing does not write about anything else but the very act of writing. Its only justification is this simple statement: 'I speak.' 'I speak' are the first words of Foucault's piece. '"I speak"', he says, 'puts the whole modern fiction to the test' (1987: 9). He contrasts the 'I speak' with the 'I lie' of the Cretan thinker Epimenides, famous for having exposed a paradox.

> Epimenides the Cretan says 'that all the Cretans are liars,' but Epimenides is himself a Cretan; therefore he is himself a liar. But if he be a liar, what he says is untrue, and consequently the Cretans are veracious; but Epimenides is a Cretan, and therefore what he says is true; hence the Cretans are liars, Epimenides is himself a liar, and what he says is untrue. Thus we may go on alternately proving that Epimenides and the Cretans are truthful and untruthful. (Fowler 1869: 163)

Such a paradox is unsolvable.

Nevertheless, Foucault persists. When I say 'I lie', I implicitly refer to the pre-eminence and pre-existence of truth. It is because truth exists, or pre-exists, that I can say something like 'I lie.' Epimenides would not have been able to develop his paradox without presupposing an established difference between the true and the untrue. When, on the contrary, I say 'I speak', I cannot refer to the pre-eminence or pre-existence of language, because language as such does not precede the act of speaking. Language has no essence, and does not constitute a substantial presence from which particular speech acts or utterances would detach themselves, as accidents are detached from a subject. Language, in a sense, does not exist. Behind the 'I speak', there is only an 'it speaks', an anonymous murmur. It is in that sense that language can be said to be beyond truth and non-truth. When we reflect on language, when we try to refer the 'I speak' to its supposed origin, we are projected outside, it means that we have to speak. '"I speak" refers to a supporting discourse that provides it with an object. That discourse, however, is missing' (Foucault 1987: 10). The supporting discourse on language cannot support itself, it is a 'desert', an 'an unfolding of pure exteriority' (1987: 11). If this experience of the outside and this inessentiality of language are said to put 'the whole of modern fiction to the test' (1987: 9), it is because modern literature has recently and definitely ceased trying to hide this anonymity behind a narrative. Literature has precisely ceased to lie. It just lets the outside speak for itself, as an impersonal voice deprived of origin. Literature has thus become the fiction, or fictionalisation, of itself. 'This neutral space is what characterizes contemporary Western fiction', Foucault adds (1987: 12).

With Blanchot,

> language escapes the mode of being of discourse [. . .] and literary speech develops from itself, forming a network in which each point is distinct, distant from even its closest neighbours, and has a position in relation to every other point in a space that simultaneously holds and separates them all. Literature is not language approaching itself until it reaches the point of its fiery manifestation; it is rather language getting as far away from itself as possible [. . .] [I]n this setting 'outside of itself', it unveils its own being. (Foucault 1987: 12)

The 'I speak', then, puts philosophy itself to the test. Are Blanchot's writings philosophical, critical, literary? Impossible question. Blanchot's writings are outside philosophy, as well as outside traditional 'literature', outside any 'genre'; they make the specificity of both genres explode in neutrality.

Because it challenges the concept of truth, such a writing, of course, also and precisely challenges philosophy. If the 'I speak' has no ideal or essential ground, if it is just surrounded by the anonymous ocean of language, then this means that speech is deprived of reflexivity at the very moment when it speaks about itself. When the speaking subject turns back on itself, it cannot grasp anything. The supposed consciousness of the ego is dismantled: '"I speak" runs counter to "I think." "I think" led to the indubitable certainty of the "I" and its existence; "I speak," on the other hand, distances, disperses, effaces that existence and lets only its empty emplacement appear' (Foucault 1987: 13). Such affirmations contradict the whole philosophical tradition and the privilege it has always conferred on interiority, subjectivity and reflexivity. The 'I speak', then, puts philosophy to the test. It estranges it. It threatens its mastery.

Can we go so far as to suggest that it decolonises it? How not to think here of the critique of Descartes developed by Enrique Dussel, the Argentinian-Mexican philosopher who has assimilated the Cartesian *ego cogito* of 'I think, therefore I am' with the imperial *ego conquiro* of 'I conquer, therefore I am'? As Ramón Grosfoguel rightly states,

> We should recall that Descartes formulated his philosophy in Amsterdam at precisely the moment in the mid-17th century at which Holland came to be the core of the world-system. What Dussel is telling us with this is that the political, economic, cultural, and social conditions of possibility for a subject who assumes the arrogance of speaking as though it were the eye of God is a subject whose geopolitical location is determined by its existence as a colonizer/conqueror, that is, as Imperial Being. (2012: 89)

In his book *Philosophy of Liberation*, Dussel develops a strong and beautiful concept of the outside. He opposes what he calls the 'philosophers of the centre' to those of the 'periphery'. He writes,

> Distant thinkers, those who had a perspective of the centre from the periphery, those who had to define themselves in the presence of an already established image of the human person and in the presence of uncivilized fellow humans, the newcomers, the ones who hope because they are always outside, these are the ones who have a clear mind for pondering reality. They have nothing to hide. (1985: 4)

This passage seems to echo Foucault's analysis. The challenging of Western philosophical imperialism is also centred on the sovereignty and centrality of the 'I think' that has generated a certain vision of language revolving around 'the sovereignty of the signifier', or the 'imperialism of the phoneme', 'the illusion of an autonomous discourse' (Blanchot 1987: 74, 80). An illusion that has for so long justified 'reason, exclusion, repression' of the outside (Blanchot 1987: 80), or, precisely, the 'periphery'. It then seems quite possible to identify Foucault's analysis once again with a form of decolonisation of language and of writing.

There is a second resonance between *The Thought from Outside* and Dussel's decolonial discourse. For Foucault, the outside of philosophy does not lead to an abandonment of philosophy proper. As an outside of traditional metaphysics, it does not nevertheless *transcend* it, properly speaking, as if the radical otherness of metaphysics could be reached beyond metaphysics itself. The outside undermines the tradition from within. It operates in another space than that of the usual duality between the inside and the outside, and it transgresses the strict opposition between the internal and the external. Therefore, Foucault explains, the outside has to be understood as the outside of the outside, the outside of the traditional concept of the outside.

Derrida also characterises deconstruction as an outside from within, so to speak. In *Of Grammatology*, he declares, 'The movements of deconstruction do not destroy structures from the outside. They are not possible and effective, nor can they take accurate aim, except by inhabiting those structures. Inhabiting them *in a certain way*, because one always inhabits, and all the more when one does not suspect it' (1997: 24).

Dussel affirms that the periphery is not beyond the centre, that it does not constitute an utterly other exteriority, a sacred or divine dimension of language. There can be no 'absolute outside to this system' (Grosfoguel 2011: 25). The outside appears as a frontier, on the frontier, not, once again, as an unreachable promised land. Decolonial thinking inhabits 'exterior spaces not fully colonized by the European modernity' but still coexisting with the colonised ones (2011: 28). Other occurrences of this topography are Gloria Anzaldúa's image of 'the "borderlands" between two people, between people and non-people, between the non-people themselves' (Maldonado-Torres 2006: 9); Grosfoguel's 'border thinking', which he uses as 'a critical response to both hegemonic and marginal fundamentalisms' (2011: 4); and Maldonado-Torres's 'border, archipelago and the sea', which are like 'the cracks of the continent, in borders, in the global south' (2006: 5, 8).

Is this to say that the critique or deconstruction of Western metaphysics and the critique or deconstruction of theoretical colonialism speak the same language? In many respects, and at many levels, the vocabulary of critique, deconstruction and decolonisation, or rather decoloniality, seems to coincide, as it points at holes, even if tiny and imperceptible, in all systems in general.

If we admit that deconstruction and decoloniality speak the same language, we also have to take for granted that the philosopher, whoever she is, whatever culture she belongs to, can travel from one country to another, from one continent to another, and talk about the outside of philosophy, and the philosophy of the outside, without encountering major difficulties of comprehension or of translation between incompatible thinking paradigms. Aren't we now living in the age of what Dussel calls 'transmodernity' or 'transmodernism', an era that comes after postmodernity, a kind of post-postmodernity, not restricted to Europe and open to the whole world? 'Dussel's transmodernity would be equivalent to "diversality as a universal project" which is a result of "critical border thinking," "critical diasporic thinking" or "critical thinking from the margins" as an epistemic intervention from the diverse subaltern locations' (Grosfoguel 2011: 27). In a certain sense, Blanchot's writings also open a subaltern location. *The Space of Literature* can be read as such.[2]

Is it from such 'geopolitics of knowledge', another concept of Dussel's, that 'critical decolonial thinking' should aim at figuring out a 'pluriversal transmodern world of multiple and diverse ethico-political projects in which a real horizontal dialogue and communication could exist between all peoples of the world' (Grosfoguel 2011: 28)? It would no doubt be possible to show how Foucauldian critique, Blanchotian writing and Derridean deconstruction also designed the limits of the hegemony of the West and dealt with subaltern concepts repressed or ignored by the traditional philosophical heritage.

And yet such a proximity between Western and decolonial thinkers is itself full of 'cracks and fractures'. The two outsides remain foreign to each other. However critical of the French colonial system that shapes the French language and its 'I speak', however critical and deconstructive of traditional metaphysics, it is still the case that Foucault, Derrida and all other contemporary European continental philosophers belong to a tradition that is theirs, their own. Their deconstructive gestures encounter no issues of legitimacy. They are heirs of the most classical philosophical bequest, with its Greek roots, its German crossings and its French institutionalisation.

Of course, one will say that the French academic system has been strongly rejected by Foucault and Derrida, to continue with the same examples. In *Michel Foucault As I Imagine Him*, Blanchot writes,

> What seems to me the difficult – and privileged – position of Foucault might be the following: do we know who he is, since he doesn't call himself (he is on a perpetual slalom course between traditional philosophy and the abandonment of any pretension to seriousness) either a sociologist or a historian or a structuralist or a thinker or a metaphysician? (1987: 93)

This multifaceted identity, which Foucault identified with his transformability, was of course the reason for his rejection from the French academic institution.

He was never able to get a full professorship in a French university. The same applies to Derrida, who was never recognised by French academe or appointed to the philosophy department of any university. Very often, French thinking comes from outside, outside of France (as was already Descartes' case, as people too easily tend to forget). Nevertheless, however painful and unjust such an exile can be, it will never coincide with a definitive exile from the inside of the philosophical European canon, with its good and pure origin, its Greek-German-French nobility. Studying philosophy in France or in Europe is, of course, always violent because it is always a form of spiritual colonisation. Neither continental nor analytic philosophies can be separated from the cultural normativity they represent, the type of language they request from the students, and the gender bias that accompanies it.

That being said, European philosophy always remains a mother tongue for the exiled philosopher. This point is missing in Foucault's beautiful analysis in *The Thought from Outside*. When the 'I speak' turns back on itself, it is not forced to silence; the outside of language is still a language. Foucault still speaks the language of truth when he criticises the language of truth, because his concept of the anonymity of language is fundamentally Western and thus remains attached to the logos. The 'I speak', in Foucault's case, is always 'I speak philosophically of the outside of philosophy' – 'I speak philosophy' as one would say 'I speak French' or 'I speak Spanish.' The experience of the outside may well be an experience of the outside of philosophy, but it is made possible only through the filter of philosophy. The authors quoted in *The Thought from Outside* are Nietzsche, Bataille, Klossowski, Descartes, Kant and Hegel. We thus see that the anonymity of language is already culturally bounded, shaped, produced from the inside of a culture. Such a situation is very different, incompatible maybe, with that of countries that certainly have their own philosophers and their own philosophical traditions, but whose philosophers and traditions are not considered canonical, or are little known in Europe, even if this situation is slightly and fortunately changing today. It is as if these non-European philosophers and traditions remained outside, outside the outside, and, if we want to play a bit more, outside the outside of the outside. The colonisation of literature.

The relationship to language, the being of language, as Foucault calls it, is of course very different in countries where philosophical language was initially brought from outside, that is, from Europe. I would like to quote a few lines from 'En qué lengua se habla hispanoamérica?', a beautiful text by Patricio Marchant:

> Thus, we ask, in what language does Hispano-America speak? Reduced to two of its moments in Chile, the problem of space and others, this question

implies asking: a) if philosophy currently exists in Chile; b) if it has ever existed in Chile; and c) if philosophy can exist – and in what mode, with what form – in the Hispano-American language. This question must work, must let itself be worked, through the relation between a particular Language, the Hispano-American language, and this other Language, philosophy. (1987: 307)[3]

Two 'concepts' of philosophy operate in the mother tongue and in translation.

The 'universality of spirit', Marchant continues, is a 'theoretical imperialism' (1987: 309). Marchant is doubtful about the possibility of translating European philosophy into Castellano because, in Latin America, there is a necessity to translate European philosophy into European Spanish first, and then from European Spanish into what he calls a 'future Hispano-American language' (1987: 317). And it is at the same time necessary for this 'future Hispano-American language' to fight against European Spanish.

The conclusion Marchant draws from this is particularly striking; it signals the scission between the two approaches of the outside.

> In this way, in the *necessary* Hispano-American struggle against the Spanish-European [*el español-europeo*], there is the need to be, to be a *name, reparation for the violation as a 'new' language*, the need for a so-called 'proper name', of a so-called 'cultural identity', of a so-called 'proper history', that is, a Language in which absolutely no philosophers are absent – Suarez wrote and thought in Latin – or a Language reduced to 'words' (means of communication) and not a Language of *names*. There is the need of a double task: to convert, that is, to translate, Spanish words into *names*, and to dress the Spanish-European's words with the Hispano-American experiences or discoveries. Thus, Gabriela Mistral took the word *desolación* to mean the discovery or imposition [. . .] of an other writing; thus Neruda and the name; thus Vallejo and Borges and all the great Chilean poetry. (1987: 317)

This passage is symptomatic of the difference I am trying to bring to light. First, because Marchant is calling for names, which precisely contradicts the anonymity of language. Hispano-America needs new names, that is, irreducible singularities. The names of singular ancestors. Second, because these names are names of poets. Poetry provides for the names. Names as substitutes for the missing philosophers. Poetry is the ancient Greece of Latin America. Marchant mentions Neruda's *Alturas de Macchu Picchu*, for example, as a sort of temple. Brian Henry (2010) insists on the difficulty of translating Neruda:

> The themes of *Alturas de Macchu Picchu*, with its blending of indigenous and Christian values, make the poem particularly difficult to render in English

because this mixture of heritages points to the paradox of identity in Latin America. The language transfer is only part of the challenge. An entire value system must be absorbed in Spanish and delivered in English for the poem to work in English.

Outside and outside. What travels are possible between them? Between the names of the poets and the anonymity of writing, between languages without philosophemes and languages that are only made of concepts? Has the 'I speak' actually deconstructed the 'I lie' when, after all, both can mean the same thing, when it becomes clear that the 'I speak' may only be able to speak to itself, while leaving the other . . . outside?

Notes

1 Malabou originally wrote the text of this chapter for delivery as a lecture at Andres Bello University in Santiago, Chile in August 2018. It came as a conclusion to a seminar she had taught on 'Philosophy and the Postcolonial'. She remarks on the work of this seminar in the following reflections: 'Of course, the discussion on the outside developed in the talk could have included many more examples, borrowed from many more countries and cultures. The seminar did not focus only on Latin America, but also on Africa, India, French West Indies and Jamaica. I wish I also had time (and the space necessary) to speak about those writers and thinkers who have no countries, and have lived all their lives in exile, without being able to refer to any home philosophers or poets' – Editor.
2 Transmodernity cannot be understood as a new concept of the universal but as designating a polycentric world or a 'pluriversal horizon' (Mignolo 2011: 109). As Ramón Grosfoguel puts it: 'Subaltern epistemologies could provide, following Walter Mignolo's redefinition of Caribbean thinker Édouard Glissant's concept, a "diversality" of responses to the problems of modernity leading to "transmodernity." Liberation philosophy for Dussel can only come from the critical thinkers of each culture in dialogue with other cultures' (Grosfoguel 2011: 27).
3 Many thanks to D. J. S. Cross for his assistance with the translation of Marchant's text from Spanish into English. All translations of Marchant's text here and in the rest of the chapter are by Cross. – Editor.

Part Three

Psyches, Brains, Cells

14

The Brain of History, or, The Mentality of the Anthropocene

I

This essay is a response to the highly challenging topic on which Ian Baucom and Matthew Omelsky asked me to elaborate: 'For your contribution', they wrote, 'we would be particularly interested in an essay that investigates the intersection of philosophy and neuroscience as it relates to climate change' (10 October 2015). After some time, I decided to explore the link between the current constitution of the brain as the new subject of history and the type of awareness demanded by the Anthropocene.

An immediate answer to Baucom and Omelsky's challenge would have been an exploration of the relationship between the brain and the 'environment'. It is, of course, a widespread idea in global change literature that 'the Anthropocene idea abolishes the break between nature and culture, between human history and the history of life and Earth', as well as between 'environment and society' (Bonneuil and Fressoz 2016: 19, 37). The blurring of these frontiers, of course, necessitates a study of the profound interaction between the sociological and the ecological, understanding them as part of the same metabolism. I believe that this notion of 'interaction' requires closer analysis, though, and renders necessary a preliminary study of the specific concept of history in which it currently takes place.

If the Anthropocene acquires the status of a true geological epoch, it is obvious that such an epoch will determine the historical representation as well as the social and political meaning of the events occurring in it. In other words, this new geological era will not and cannot have the neutrality and a-subjectivity characteristic of geological eras in general. The Anthropocene situates the human being itself between nature and history. On the one hand, it is still the subject of its own history, responsible and conscious. Consciousness of history, or 'historicity', is not separable from history itself. It entails memory, capacity to change and, precisely, responsibility. On the other hand, the human of the Anthropocene, defined as a geological force, must be seen as neutral and indifferent, as a geological reality itself. The two sides of this new identity cannot mirror each other, causing a break in reflexivity.

The awareness of the Anthropocene, then, originates through an interruption of consciousness. Such is the problem. I intend to ask whether such an interruption opens the space for a substitution of the brain for consciousness. I proceed to a confrontation between two different points of view on this question. According to the first, the Anthropocene forces us to consider the human as a *geological* agent pure and simple. Such is Dipesh Chakrabarty's position. I refer to his two now-famous articles (Chakrabarty 2009, 2012). According to the second, understanding the Anthropocene necessarily privileges the role of the brain and thus biology. This is the approach Daniel Lord Smail takes in his *On Deep History and the Brain* (2008). I show how their two approaches may be seen as complementing each other, and introduce into the debate, as a medium term and under a new form, some important and unjustly forgotten elements brought to light by some prominent French historians from the École des Annales – such as 'mentality' and 'slow' or 'long-term' temporality.

Chakrabarty denies any metaphorical understanding of the 'geological'. If the human has become a geological form, there has to exist somewhere, at a certain level, an isomorphy, or structural sameness, between humanity and geology. This isomorphy is what emerges – at least in the form of a question – when consciousness, precisely, gets interrupted by this very fact. Human subjectivity, as geologised, so to speak, is broken into at least two parts, revealing the split between an agent endowed with free will and the capacity to self-reflect, and a neutral inorganic power, which paralyses the energy of the former. Once again, we are not facing the dichotomy between the historical and the biological; we are not dealing with the relationship between man understood as a living being and man understood as a subject.

Man cannot *appear* to itself as a geological force, because being a geological force is a mode of disappearance. Therefore, the becoming force of the human is beyond any phenomenology and has no ontological status. Human subjectivity is in a sense reduced to atoms without any atomic intention and has become structurally alien, by want of reflexivity, to its own apocalypse.

A major common point between Chakrabarty and Smail is the necessity to consider that history does not start with recorded history, but has to be envisaged as deep history. As Chakrabarty suggests, 'Species thinking [. . .] is connected to the enterprise of deep history' (2009: 213). Let us recall the definition of *deep history* proposed by Edward Wilson, to whom both Chakrabarty and Smail refer: 'Human behaviour is seen as the product not just of recorded history, ten thousand years recent, but of deep history, the combined genetic and cultural changes that created humanity over hundreds of [thousands of] years' (Wilson 1996: ix–x).

According to Chakrabarty, however, the biological 'deep past' is certainly not deep enough. In that sense, therefore, a 'neurohistorical' approach to the Anthropocene remains insufficient. Neurocentrism is just another version of anthropocentrism. Focusing on the biological only, Smail would miss the geological dimension of the human:

> Smail's book pursues possible connections between biology and culture – between the history of the human brain and cultural history, in particular – while being always sensitive to the limits of biological reasoning. But it is the history of human biology and not any recent theses about the newly acquired geological agency of humans that concerns Smail. (Chakrabarty 2009: 206)

The human's recent status as geological agent paradoxically draws the historian back to a very ancient past, a time when the human itself did not exist – a time that thus exceeds 'prehistory'.

One will immediately argue that Smail, in his book, is precisely undertaking a deconstruction of the concept of prehistory. Clearly, the notion of deep history represents for him the result of such a deconstruction. Deep history, then, substitutes itself for prehistory. According to the usual view, history starts with the rise of civilisation and departs from a 'buffer zone' between biological evolution and history proper – such a buffer zone is what precisely is called prehistory. If history must be understood, as Wilson suggests, as the originary intimate interaction between the genetic and the cultural, it starts with the beginning of hominisation and does not require the 'pre' (Smail 2008).

Smail's approach is clearly an epigenetic one, which forbids the assimilation of 'hominisation' with the history of consciousness. Epigenetics is a branch of molecular biology that studies the mechanisms that modify the functions of genes by activating or deactivating them without altering the DNA sequence in the formation of the phenotype. Epigenetic modifications depend on two types of causes: *internal* and *structural*, on the one hand, and *environmental*, on the other. In the first case, it is a matter of the physical and chemical mechanisms (RNA, nucleosome, methylation). In the second, epigenetics supplies genetic material with a means of reacting to the evolution of environmental conditions. The definition of phenotypical malleability proposed by American biologist Mary Jane West-Eberhard is eloquent in this respect: it is a matter of the 'ability of an organism to react to an environmental input with a change in form, state, movement, or rate of activity'

(2003: 34). Contemporary epigenetics reintroduces the development of the individual into the heart of evolution, opening a new theoretical space called 'evolutionary developmental biology', or 'evo-devo'.

Lambros Malafouris, in his book *How Things Shape the Mind: A Theory of Material Engagement*, shows how epigenetics has modified the usual view of cognitive development, thus constituting cognitive archaeology as a major field in historical studies. 'Cognitive development', he writes,

> is explained as the emergent product [...] of these constraints [from genes and the individual cell to the physical and social environment]. In this context, the view of brain and cognitive development known as *probabilistic epigenesis* [...] which emphasizes the interactions between experience and gene expression [...] is of special interest. The unidirectional formula (prevalent in molecular biology) by which genes drive and determine behaviour is replaced with a new scheme that explicitly recognizes the bidirectionality of influences between the genetic, behavioural, environmental, and socio-cultural levels of analysis. (2013: 40)

This new scheme requires, as Malafouris brilliantly shows, a materialist approach to the interaction between the biological and the cultural. Hence the subtitle of the book: *A Theory of Material Engagement*. The epigenetic crossing and interaction in question take place *through things*, *through matter*, which is also to say, *through the inorganic*. It is a 'non-representative' vision of interaction, which requires no subject–object relationship, no mind seeing in advance what has to be made or fabricated. Mind, brain, behaviour and the created object happen together; all are part of the same process. 'The cognitive life of things is not exhausted by their possible causal role in shaping some aspect of human intelligent behaviour; the cognitive life of things also embodies a cruel enactive and constitutive role' (Malafouris 2013: 44). Therefore, to explore the relationships between the brain and its 'environment' is a much wider and deeper task than to study the role of the 'human' in its 'milieu', precisely because it has its foundation, for an essential part, in a non-human materiality and cannot be limited to a biological form of inquiry. In that sense, ecology to come acquires a new meaning:

> This new ecology cannot be reduced to any of its constitutive elements (biological or artificial) and thus cannot be accounted for by looking at the isolated properties of persons or things. The challenge for archaeology, in this respect, is to reveal and articulate the variety of forms that cognitive extension can take and the diversity of feedback relationships between objects and the embodied brain as they become realized in different periods and cultural settings. (Malafouris 2013: 82)

Malafouris then argues that this ecology should be understood as a result of the 'embedment' of the human brain. 'The term "embedment"', Malafouris writes, 'derives from the fusion of the terms "embodiment" – referring to the intrinsic relationship between brain and body – and "embeddedness" – describing the intrinsic relationship between brain/body and environment' (2010: 52).

To conclude on this point and go back to our initial discussion, we can see that Smail's and Malafouris's approaches to the brain/environment relationship are not 'strictly' biological but include, as a central element, the inorganic materiality of things. As Smail declares:

> The great historical disciplines, including geology, evolutionary biology and ethology, archaeology, historical linguistics, and cosmology, all rely on evidence that has been extracted from things. Lumps of rocks, fossils, mitochondrial DNA, isotopes, behavioral patterns, potsherds, phonemes: all these things encode information about the past. (2008: 48)

'History is something', he continues, 'that *happens* to people, things, organisms, and is not *made* by them' (2008: 57).

Deep history, conjoined with archaeology of the mind or 'neuroarchaeology', would then extend the limits of the 'brain' well beyond reflexivity and consciousness, well beyond 'historicity' as well. As archaeological, the brain/environment relationship is already also geological. It remains clear, though, that Chakrabarty would not be entirely convinced by such an argument. Even if non-anthropocentric, even if thing- and inorganic-matter-oriented, even if including at its core a neutral, a-reflexive, non-representative type of interaction as well as cognitive assemblages, the conjoined point of view of deep history and archaeology of the mind still takes the 'human' as a point of departure. The process of hominisation is, of course, inseparable from an evolutionary perspective. Chakrabarty's perspective is very close to that of French philosopher Quentin Meillassoux in his book *After Finitude*. Meillassoux argues for a 'non-correlationist' approach to the 'real', which would not lay foundations on the subject–object relationship at all and would totally elude the presence of the human on earth as a point of departure. There exists a mode of exploration of the deep past (of the extremely deep past) that does not even consider the emergence of life in general as a 'beginning'. Deep past, then, becomes an 'ancestrality' devoid of any 'ancestors': 'I will call "ancestral"', Meillassoux writes, 'any reality anterior to the emergence of the human species – or even anterior to every recognized form of life on earth' (2009: 10). The archive, here, is not the object, not even the thing, not even the fossil, but what Meillassoux calls the *arche-fossil*:

> I will call 'arche-fossil' or 'fossil-matter' not just materials indicating the traces of past life, according to the familiar sense of the term 'fossil', but materials indicating the existence of an ancestral reality or event; one that is anterior to terrestrial life. An arche-fossil thus designates the material support on the basis of which the experiments that yield estimates of ancestral phenomena proceed – for example, an isotope whose rate of radioactive decay we know, or the luminous emission of a star that informs us of the date of its formation. (2009: 10)

For Meillassoux, the earth is entirely indifferent to our existence, anterior to any form of human presence – be it neural, be it neutral.

Again, these affirmations resonate with Chakrabarty's claim that the notion of the 'geological', in the term *geological agent*, forever remains outside human experience. 'How does a social historian go about writing a *human* history of an uninhabited and uninhabitable vast expanse of snow and ice?', he asks when talking about the Antarctic (Chakrabarty 2012: 11). A decorrelated subject cannot access itself as decorrelated. 'We cannot ever experience ourselves as a geophysical force – though we now *know* that this is one of the modes of our collective existence' (2012: 12). Chakrabarty's analysis adds an important element to Meillassoux's thesis when it takes into account the experience of the impossibility of experiencing decorrelationism. We can conceptualise it but not experience it.

> Who is the we? We humans never experience ourselves as a species. We can only intellectually comprehend or infer the existence of the human species but never experience it as such. There could be no phenomenology of us as a species. Even if we were to emotionally identify with a word like *mankind*, we would not know what being a species is, for, in species history, humans are only an instance of the concept species as indeed would be any other life form. But one never experiences being a concept. (Chakrabarty 2009: 220)

At this point, a major issue appears, relaunching the discussion and a return to Smail's analysis. First, we do not see what a species can be outside the biological point of view. Why keep that term? Second, I do not understand why the fact of becoming a geological form would have to remain entirely conceptual, without producing a kind of *mental phenomenon*.

> Climate scientists' history reminds us [. . .] that we now also have a mode of existence in which *we* – collectively and as a geophysical force and in ways we cannot experience ourselves – are 'indifferent' or 'neutral' (*I do not mean these*

as mental or experienced states) to questions of intrahuman justice. (Chakrabarty 2012: 14, emphasis added)

Before coming to the political consequences of such a statement, I would like to ask why precisely we could not be susceptible to experiencing mentally and psychically the indifference and neutrality that have become part of our nature. Deprived of any empirical, mental or psychic effects, the assumption of the human as a geological force remains a pure abstract argument, and, in that sense, it appears as an ontological or metaphysical structure. Just like Meillassoux, Chakrabarty ends up failing to empiricise the very structure that is supposed to detranscendentalise, so to speak, the empirical. Why should there be any intermediary locus of experience between consciousness and the suspension of consciousness?

This is where the brain demands recognition! Is not the brain, on which Chakrabarty remains silent, an essential intermediary between the historical, the biological and the geological? That site of experience we are looking for?

II

This brings us back to Smail and to one of the most important and interesting aspects of his analysis, the *theory of addiction*. Smail insists that the constant interaction between the brain and the environment is essentially based on brain–body alterations. The brain maintains itself in its changing environment by becoming addicted to it, understanding 'addiction' in the proper sense as a 'psychotropy', a significant transformation or alteration of the psyche. These altering effects result from the action of neurotransmitters 'such as testosterone and other androgens, estrogen, serotonin, dopamine, endorphins, oxytocin, prolactin, vasopressin, epinephrine and so on. Produced in glands and synapses throughout the body, these chemicals facilitate or block the signals passing along neural pathways' (Smail 2008: 113). Such chemicals, which determine emotions, feelings and affects in general, can be modulated according to the demands of the behavioural adaptation they make possible. Adaptation, here, is two-sided. It is, of course, adaptation to the external world, but it is also the adaptation of the brain to its own modifications.

All important changes in deep history, like the passage of one age to another, have always produced new addictive processes and chemical bodily state modulations:

> A neurohistorical model offers an equally grand explanatory paradigm, proposing that some of the direction we detect in recent history has been created

> by ongoing experiments with new psychotropic mechanisms that themselves evolved against the evolutionary backdrop of human neurophysiology. The Neolithic revolution between 10,000 and 5,000 years ago transformed human ecology and led to fundamental and irreversible changes in demographics, politics, society, and economies. In this changing ecology, new mechanisms for modulating body states emerged through processes of undirected cultural evolution. (Smail 2008: 187)

We have to understand that

> the expansion in calories available for human consumption, the domestication of animals useful as sources of energy, the practice of sedentism, the growing density of human settlements – such were the changes characteristic of the Neolithic revolution in all parts of the world where agriculture was independently invented: Mesopotamia, Africa, China, Mesoamerica, and other sites. All these changes created, in effect, a new neurophysiological ecosystem, a field of evolutionary adaptation in which the sorts of customs and habits that generate new neural configurations or alter brain–body states could evolve in unpredictable ways. (Smail 2008: 155)

From this, Smail concludes, 'Civilization did not bring an end to biology' (2008: 155). Again, deep history reveals the profound interaction of nature and history through the mediation of the brain as both a biological and cultural adaptor. Human practices alter or affect brain–body chemistry, and, in return, brain–body chemistry alters or affects human practices. Brain epigenetic power acts as a medium between its deep past and the environment.

'The mood-altering practices, behaviours, and institutions generated by human culture are what I refer to, collectively, as *psychotropic mechanisms*', Smail explains. '*Psychotropic* is a strong word but not wholly inapt, for these mechanisms had neurochemical effects that are not all that dissimilar from those produced by the drugs normally called psychotropic or psychoactive' (2008: 161). Further, 'Psychotropy comes in different forms: things we do that shape the moods of others; things we do to ourselves; things we ingest' (2008: 164).

We can distinguish here between autotropic and allotropic psychotropy, that is, addictive substances and practices acting on the self, and addictive practices acting on other political addictive practices. Among the former are 'coffee, sugar, chocolate, and tobacco', which first began circulating in Europe in the seventeenth and eighteenth centuries. 'All of these products have mildly addictive or mood-altering properties' (Smail 2008: 179). To these alcohol and drugs would later be added.

Smail recalls that the current meaning of the term *addiction* emerged in the late seventeenth century. 'Earlier, the word had implied the state of being bound or indebted to a person – to a lord, for example, or perhaps to the devil' (2008: 183). This old meaning helps us understand what constitutes allotropy. Psychotropic addictive chemical mechanisms can also be induced in subjects as a result of power excess and abuse of domination. Stress and more general affective states of dependence, what Baruch Spinoza calls 'sad passions', are essential aspects of psychotropy, caused in contexts of dominance. The crossing point between modularity and change coincides precisely with the crossing point between biology and politics: 'Humans possess relatively plastic or manipulable neural states and brain–body chemistries', such that 'moods, emotions, and predispositions inherited from the ancestral past' can be 'violated, manipulated, or modulated' (Smail 2008: 117).

According to Smail, autotropic and allotropic addictive processes automatically mark the point of indiscernibility between biology (chemical substances and mechanisms) and culture (being-in-the-world). We find again the idea that the brain is the mediator between the two dimensions of (deep) history: the natural and the historical.

How can we extend these remarks to the current situation? First, they lead us to admit that only new addictions will help us to lessen the effects of climate change (eating differently, travelling differently, dressing differently, etc.). Addictive processes have in large part caused the Anthropocene, and only new addictions will be able to partly counter them. Second, they force us to elaborate a renewed concept of the addicted subject, of suspended consciousness and intermittent freedom. Third, they allow us to argue that the neutrality Chakrabarty speaks of is not conceivable outside of a new psychotropy, a mental and psychic experience of the disaffection of experience. Such a psychotropy would precisely fill the gap between the transcendental structure of the geological dimension of the human and the practical disaffection of historical reflexivity. The subject of the Anthropocene cannot but become addicted to its own indifference – addicted to the concept it has become. And that happens in the brain.

The motif of a narcolepsy of consciousness, as both cause and effect of the technological destruction of nature, had already been interestingly and importantly suggested by Marshall McLuhan. His analysis seems to fit the framework of the current ecological crisis perfectly. Technological development coincides for him with an extension of the nervous system to the very limits of the world: 'After three thousand years of explosion, by means of fragmentary and mechanical technologies', he writes, 'the Western world is imploding. During the mechanical ages we had extended our bodies in space. Today, after more than a century of electric technology, we have extended our central nervous system itself in a global embrace, abolishing both space and time as far as our planet is concerned' (McLuhan 1990: 52). The extension of the nervous system to the world has a double contradictory effect, acting as a painkiller (a 'counter-irritant') to the extent that it suppresses all alterity and, at the same time and for the same reason, acting as a destructive power. Such is the structure of our 'narcotic culture'. Every technological device is a prolongation of the brain and the organism, and McLuhan characterises this prolongation as a process of 'auto-amputation' that helps lower the pressure and creates anxiety, thus putting at work an economy of pleasure as 'numbness'.

One might argue that the world about which McLuhan talks, the world to which the nervous system extends its frontiers, is an image, a reflecting surface, whereas the split Chakrabarty analyses as the separation between the human as a historical agent and the human as a geological force confronts two heterogeneous entities that cannot reflect each other at all. Nevertheless, if we look closely at what McLuhan says about mirroring, narcissism and the projection of one's own image, we see that reflection is for him immediately suspended by a spontaneous petrification, a geologisation of both the gaze and the image. On the myth of Narcissus, McLuhan writes: 'As counter-irritant, the image produces a generalised numbness or shock that declines recognition. Self-amputation forbids self-recognition' (1990: 53). Indifference and neutrality, once again, can be mental phenomena, even when their manifestations may seem totally alien to any mental or internalising structure. Again, I do not think that the neutralisation of consciousness due to its 'geologisation' can happen without the intermediary of brain processes resulting from its interaction with the world. Indeed, I have tried to show elsewhere that indifference has become the current global *Stimmung*, that is, atonement or affect (Malabou 2012).

Such an indifference, this interruption of consciousness or awareness, directly challenges the concept of responsibility, which is of course central to our debate. How can we feel genuinely responsible for what we have done to the earth if such a deed is the result of an addicted and addictive slumber of responsibility itself? It seems impossible to produce a genuine awareness of addiction (awareness of addiction is always an addicted form of awareness). Only the setting of new addictions can help in breaking old ones. Ecology has to become a new libidinal economy.

These are some of the issues that political discourses on climate change, as demonstrated at conferences such as the recent twenty-first session of the Conference of the Parties (COP21) to the United Nations Framework Convention on Climate Change in Paris, do not genuinely take into account. Most of the time, the official ecological discourse is still only a discourse on awareness and responsibility. That does not mean, of course, that the human is not responsible for global warming. Nevertheless, the type of responsibility required by the Anthropocene is extremely paradoxical and difficult to the extent that it implies the acknowledgement of an essential paralysis of responsibility.

Chakrabarty would no doubt argue that these last developments remain caught in the correlationist frame. They would still be human, all too human. Do they not leave aside the issue of nature as such only to take into account humanity's technoscientific power and its psychotropic causes and consequences?

The traditional concept of history, Chakrabarty writes, implies a disavowal of the fact that nature can have a history. It presupposes a strict border between pure contingent facts (natural ones) and events understood as acts of agents. Benedetto Croce, for example, claims that 'there is no world but the human world' (Chakrabarty 2009: 203). French historian Fernand Braudel, in his book *The Mediterranean and the Ancient World*, rebelled against such a vision by taking into account the specific temporality of the Mediterranean natural environment, the soil, the biosphere, and so on. Nevertheless, this time of nature is still seen as purely repetitive and mechanical, deprived of any agency or eventual power; it 'is a history of constant repetition, ever-recurring cycles' (Chakrabarty 2009: 204). Such a contention is no longer sustainable, because the age of the Anthropocene teaches something already widespread in the 'literature of global warming': 'The overall environment can sometimes reach a tipping point at which this slow and apparently timeless backdrop for human actions transforms itself with a speed that can only spell disaster for human beings' (Chakrabarty 2009: 205).

III

How do we respond to this? It is obvious that Braudel has not thematised or even perceived the historicity of nature, its mutability and ability to transform itself. In *The Mediterranean and the Ancient World*, the analysis of climate is poor, as Braudel does not say a word, or at least nothing significant, about ecology. In that sense, Chakrabarty is right to challenge the cyclical vision of natural time that governs Braudel's notion of nature's time and space. It seems to me, though, that Chakrabarty does not see how helpful Braudel nevertheless can be for our discussion. It is true that what Braudel calls 'geohistorical time', the archaic natural time, does not change. The 'very long-term' time, made up of thousands of years, geological time proper, seems to be deprived of any capacity to transform itself. But it is striking to note that the two other levels Braudel distinguishes, that of economic and social time (middle-term duration) and that of the event (short-term temporality), are also contaminated by the first level's immobility. And here is the interesting point. Braudel has perhaps failed to take into account the historical force of nature, but he certainly very early and accurately perceived the irrevocable naturalisation of human history, that is, of economic, political and social time. He described better than anyone else the narcolepsy of historical temporality, to such a point that he was accused of depoliticising it.

Deconstructing the privilege of the event, Braudel showed that a geological principle, that of a blind slowing force, was operating at all layers of time. In that sense, he anticipated something from the current situation, to the extent that he announced that historical consciousness had to acknowledge its own naturalisation of that suspension by entering the reign of immobility. In that sense, what Chakrabarty sees as a consequence (the human transformed into a geological force because of climate change and the entry into the Anthropocene), Braudel saw as a beginning (history has always already slowed down, thus preparing itself for its own neutralisation by nature). What Braudel said about capitalism is extremely interesting in this respect. He argued that material life progresses by means of 'slow evolutions'. Advances occur 'very slowly over long periods by the initiative of groups of men, not individuals [. . .] and in countless varied and obscure ways' (1973: 258). Great technical revolutions infiltrate society 'slowly and with difficulty [. . .] [T]o speak of revolution here is to use a figure of speech. Nothing took place at break-neck speed' (1973: 442).

One might object again that long-term temporality presupposes an essential passivity and unchangeability of nature, that it cannot account for a sudden constitution of nature itself as a historical acting agent, like the one we are currently witnessing with the Anthropocene. That is true. But the problem, as we have seen all along, is that approaching the historical force of nature paradoxically leads us to slow down, to face the suspension of consciousness, the numbness and slumber of our responsibility. It is in a certain sense like exchanging roles, nature becoming historical and the Anthropos becoming natural. This exchange constitutes a new form of human experience, and this Braudel helps us to conceptualise.

The third generation of the Annales School in France – Marc Ferro, Jacques Le Goff and Emmanuel Le Roy Ladurie – increased the part played by very long-term temporality. As one of them declares: 'Time is fully human, and yet it is as motionless as geographic evolution' (Aries 1981, qtd in Dosse 1987:

165).[1] Braudel's work found itself extended and prolonged by the introduction of an important concept that emerged at that time in historical science, that of 'mentality', closer to the psychological than to the intellectual. The acknowledgement of slow time, or long-term time, gave way to a 'history of mentalities [*histoire des mentalités*]'. Based on 'material culture', that is, on the similarities between the mind's rhythms and natural cycles, the history of mentalities provided its readers with descriptions and analyses of uses, repetitions, habits and representations. Philippe Aries declared that the history of mentalities situated itself 'at the crossing point between the biological and the social' (qtd in Dosse 1987: 198).

As we already noted, this crossing point between the biological and the social does not mean that the biological must be taken as a point of departure, nor that the human as a living being should become the origin of historical research. The history of mentalities also includes, as one of its essential dimensions, the materiality of inorganic nature, the soil, the rocks, the mountains, the rivers, the earth. A mentality is a hybrid concept that comprehends not only the psychic and the social but also the originary likeness of the mind and the fossil, the inscription of naturality in thought and behaviour. Mentality, in that sense, is rooted in the brain and not in consciousness. 'The human reduced to its "mental" is the object rather than the subject of its own history [*L'homme réduit à son mental est objet de son histoire plutôt que sujet*]' (Dosse 1987: 206). Jean Delumeau, author of the important *Sin and Fear: The Emergence of a Western Guilt Culture, Thirteenth to Eighteenth Centuries*, writes, while playing with the multiple sense of the term *natural*: 'Fear is natural' (qtd in Dosse 1987: 206). As a consequence of all previous analyses, we may consider the history of mentalities to be the first form of environmental studies in France. Could it be that new histories of mentalities, which would bring together the geological, biological and cultural current dimensions of historical (non-)awareness, might open a new chapter of Anthropocenic study?

IV

What seems to be challengeable in Chakrabarty's work is the claim of the impossibility of phenomenalising the geological becoming of the human. This 'species', the human, remains a pure void concept until it can be filled with intuition, that is, with empirical and sensuous content, if not with awareness. A renewed and re-elaborated concept of mentality might precisely help to provide the missing content of this form. There necessarily exists a mental effect of numbness and paralysis of consciousness, a mental effect of the new narcoleptic structure of humanity's (impossible) reflection on itself. We have seen, with Smail and McLuhan, that this mental effect was a neural one in the first place. Again, it is not a matter of thinking the brain 'in' its environment; it is a matter of seeing the brain *as* an environment, *as* a metabolic place. Therefore, I prefer to use the term *mental* rather than *neural*, because *mental* immediately evokes the merging and mingling of different registers of materialities. In that sense, getting accustomed to the new condition of the human as a geological agent will require a new mentality, that is, new addictions, new bodily adaptations to an inorganic and earthly corporeity, a new natural history. A history, still, nevertheless.

Reading Braudel and his followers helps us perceive that the narcolepsy of consciousness constitutes an irreducible dimension of history. Long-term temporality, immobility and very slow evolution show that deep history has always been inscribed at the heart of history, as this numbness of time and action that submits cultural evolution to a geophysical rhythm. Braudel is perhaps not a thinker of climate change, but he is a great theoretician of a new form of Marxism that binds the critique of capital to a study of the irreducible naturality, neutrality and passivity of time. The critique addressed to the historians of long-term duration and mentalities was the same as the one currently addressed to Chakrabarty, pointing, in both cases, at a supposed depoliticisation of history. François Dosse wrote that with the École des Annales, in the end 'history ha[d] negated itself' (1987: 258). He wished that 'the event' might come back in order to wake up time from its geological slumber. He could not foresee that with the Anthropocene, long-term temporality would precisely acquire the status of an event – which would free the attempt to think ecology and politics differently.

Note

1 Unless otherwise indicated, all translations are Malabou's own – Editor.

15

Whither Materialism? Althusser/Darwin

I

Whither materialism? This title echoes another one, 'Whither Marxism?', that of a conference held in 1993 in California where Derrida presented an oral version of *Specters of Marx*. With regard to this ambiguous title, Derrida proposed that 'one may hear beneath the question "Where is Marxism going?" another question: "Is Marxism dying?"' (2006: xiii).

The same ambiguity will be at work throughout this chapter.[1] Where is materialism currently going? Is materialism currently dying? These two questions will, of course, allow me to address the problem of Marxism proper but from the point of view of what Marxism has repressed, that is, materialism itself. This strange approach to Marxism, according to which, in all Marx's work, an official materialism would be repressing a more secret one, is defended by the late Althusser in a fascinating text from 1982: 'The Underground Current of the Materialism of the Encounter' (2006: 163–207).

In this text, Althusser brings to light

> the existence of an almost completely unknown materialist tradition in the history of philosophy [. . .] a materialism of the encounter, and therefore of the aleatory and of contingency. This materialism is opposed, as a wholly different mode of thought, to the various materialisms of record, including that widely ascribed to Marx, Engels and Lenin, which, like every materialism in the rationalist tradition, is a materialism of necessity and teleology; that is to say, a transformed, disguised form of idealism. (2006: 167, 168)

Such a repressed materialism is the one I intend to interrogate here: a materialism that threatens necessity, order, causality, meaning, a 'dangerous' materialism, as Althusser characterises it (2006: 168), a materialism – this is the central idea of this essay – 'which starts out from nothing' (2006: 189). I will constantly ask: What does 'starting out from nothing' mean, and is it possible?

I quote Althusser again: 'to free the materialism of the encounter from this repression; to discover, if possible, its implications for both philosophy and materialism; and to ascertain its hidden effects wherever they are silently at work – such is the task that I have set for myself here' (2006: 168).

This task is clearly an answer to the first question: Whither materialism? Where is it going? At the same time, the second question immediately appears. Althusser asks: Is this materialism of the encounter still a materialism? Is not the revelation of the repressed always the end of what is revealed? Will materialism wither in its contingent form, in the nothingness it presupposes? Will it open new paths, or will it die?

Again, I intend to show that these two questions are of particular philosophical and political relevance and have urgency for our time.

Now, why Darwin? The list of authors Althusser considers representative of the new materialism includes Epicurus, Machiavelli, Spinoza, Hobbes, Rousseau, Nietzsche, Heidegger, Derrida, Deleuze, a certain Marx and Darwin. Why Darwin? Is it an arbitrary choice? It is in a way. It has to be. Contingency alone can adequately respond to contingency. So, why not Darwin? And it is not, of course. The encounter between Althusser and Darwin I am risking here helps to situate the specific problem raised by the notion of the encounter itself. Both share the same vision of this strange ontological point of departure: nothingness, nothing, the same critique of teleology, the same concept of selection – thus the same materialism.

Darwin? A materialist? Yes, indeed, according to Althusser, Darwin is a materialist of the encounter.

Let me propose some definitions before I start the demonstration. Materialism is the name for the non-transcendental status of form in general. Matter is what forms itself in producing the conditions of possibility of the formation itself. Any transcendental instance necessarily finds itself in a position of exteriority in relation to that which it organises. By its nature, the condition of possibility is other than what it makes possible. Materialism affirms the opposite: the absence of any outside of the process of formation. Matter's self-formation and self-information is then systematically non-transcendental.

There are, then, two possibilities for explaining and understanding the origin of this immanent dynamic. Dialectical teleology is the first well-known one. The formation of forms – forms of life, forms of thought, forms of society – is governed by an internal tension towards a telos, which necessarily orients and determines every self-development. This teleological vision of materialism, which has long been predominant, is precisely the one Althusser rejects here. Such a materialism presupposes that 'everything is accomplished in advance; the structure precedes its elements and reproduces them in order to reproduce the structure' (Althusser 2006: 200). It amounts in reality to a transcendental analytics, which is why Althusser may identify it with idealism.

Materialism of the encounter, on the contrary, doesn't presuppose any telos, reason or cause – such a materialism claims, against any transcendental structure, 'the non-anteriority of Meaning' (Althusser 2006: 169). From this second point of view, forms are encounters that have taken form. Althusser constantly insists on such a 'form taking' or 'crystallization': 'The crystallization of the elements with one another (in the sense in which the ice crystallizes)' (2006: 170). Here, the formation of form has to be sought in what 'gives form' to the effects of the encounter. The encounter has to 'take form' and 'take hold' in order to last and become necessary.

It is while explaining this very specific type of plasticity – the crystallisation and taking of form out of nothing – that Althusser turns towards Darwin.

> Instead of thinking contingency as a modality of necessity [. . .] we must think necessity as the becoming-necessary of the encounter of contingencies. Thus we see that not only the world of life (the biologists, who have known their Darwin, have recently become aware of this), but the world of history, too, gels at certain felicitous moments, with the taking hold of elements combined in an encounter that is apt to trace such-and-such a figure: such-and-such a species, individual, or people. (2006: 194)

It is precisely the passage between a species, an individual and a people that I will examine here. Are these forms equivalent? Can we transpose what happens at the level of nature to that of the political and of history?

I first ask to what extent social selection is assimilable to natural selection as Darwin elaborates it. I will then examine the difference between a natural encounter and a social and political one. Here I ask where in society is the void, the nothingness, the point zero from which a form can emerge? In conclusion, I attempt to situate Althusser's new critique of capitalism, its impact on our philosophical time, and the current emergence of new materialisms.

II

My use of the word 'plasticity' a moment ago to describe the crystallisation of form in the materialism of the encounter was not entirely my decision. An attentive reading of *On the Origin of Species* reveals that plasticity constitutes one of the central motifs of Darwin's thought. Indeed, plasticity situates itself effectively at the heart of the theory of evolution. How does a 'form' take form according to Darwin?

The concept of plasticity allows the articulation – as Darwin indicates at the beginning of his book – of a fundamental connection between the *variability* of individuals within the same species and the *natural selection* between these same individuals.

Variability first: There is no species without it. To refer to Althusser's terminology, variability is the 'void' or 'empty point' or 'nothingness' from which forms can emerge. The most important characteristic of a species is its mutability; the great number of potential morphological transformations observable in the structure of the organism is a function of its aptitude to change forms. Contrary to a widespread misreading of Darwin, a species is never rigid or fixed. Filiation reveals the high degree of a species' plasticity. Considering descent, one has the impression that 'the whole organisation seems to have become plastic' (Darwin 2008: 13). At the beginning of chapter 5, Darwin writes, 'the reproductive system is eminently susceptible to changes in the conditions of life; and to this system being functionally disturbed in the parents, I chiefly attribute the varying or plastic condition of the offspring' (2008: 101). Characteristic of variability, plasticity designates the quasi-infinite possibility of changes of structure authorised by the living structure itself. This quasi-infinity constitutes precisely the openness or the absence of predetermination that makes an encounter possible.

The form 'takes' when variability encounters natural selection. Natural selection transforms the contingency of the former into a necessity. 'I am convinced that the accumulative action of Selection [. . .] is by far the predominate Power' in the economy of mutability and variability (Darwin 2008: 36).

One must therefore understand that selection guides variability and that it regulates the formation of forms. Selection allows the taking of *oriented* form, which obeys the natural exigency of the viability, consistency and autonomy of individuals. The plastic condition – otherwise called the motor of evolution itself – therefore hinges on plasticity, understood as the fluidity of structures on the one hand and the selection of viable, durable forms likely to constitute a legacy or lineage on the other. The materialism of the encounter thus pertains to a natural process that assures the permanent selection and crystallisation of variations.

The relation between variation and selection raises the fundamental philosophical question I would like to address here to Althusser. In nature, the relation between variation and selection is not, properly speaking, planned. Paradoxically, natural selection appears in Darwin as a mechanism deprived of all selective intention. The best is the fittest, but aptitude is here independent of all value judgements or any actual teleology.

Natural selection is a-teleological, without intention. It is, again, an encounter. Insofar as it is no more than a mechanism – a term that, by definition, evokes blind movement, the opposite or reverse of freedom – natural selection is paradoxically non-anticipatable, a promise of forms never chosen in advance, of differences to come.

However, this is again the central problem; it seems that this natural formation of forms cannot have, without disguise or misrepresentation, a social destiny. We know the errors of 'social Darwinism', which is everything but a philosophy of plasticity to the degree that it reduces to a simple theory the struggle of strong against the weak. For many years, particularly in France, natural selection came to be understood as simply a process of eliminating the weakest and of life as a merciless struggle for power in all its forms. We may also have confused Darwinism and Malthusianism, despite the precise precautions taken regarding this subject in *On the Origin of Species*, taking natural selection as a simple quantitative dynamic governed by the ratio of the number of individuals in a population and the availability of resources.[2] This interpretation is absolutely not Darwinian and, again, is a misunderstanding.

If such a misunderstanding is possible, though, is it not because a materialism of the encounter seems to be socially and politically unsustainable because it can work only at the level of atoms or of forms of life, never when it comes to individuals and peoples? The automaticity and non-teleological character of natural selection seems definitively lost in social selection. Why – in the logic of exams, in competitions, or in professional selection in general, the discrimination of candidates regarding aptitude functions, competencies, or specific technical capacities – does selection seem to lack plasticity; that is, fluidity on the one hand and the absence of any predetermined selective intention on the other? Why, most of the time, does social selection give the feeling of being an expected or agreed-upon process, a simple logic of conformity and reproduction, whereas natural selection is incalculably open to possibility?

Is not the materialism of the encounter always doomed to be repressed by teleology, anteriority of meaning, presuppositions, predeterminations?

The plastic condition Darwin describes calls for a particular articulation of identity and difference. Identity, because individuals selected are able to reproduce and therefore to inscribe themselves into the stability of an identifiable type. Difference, because this identity is not rigid and is obtained precisely from variability. Specific identity is an identity produced by the differentiation of structures and types. However, in nature, there is an automatic and blind equilibrium between identity and difference, while it seems that, in the social order, there is always a predominance of identity over difference and that the natural grace of the balance is interrupted. The idea of choice, according to an apparent paradox, is again entirely absent from natural selection. In nature, selection is unconscious. As soon as selection becomes an intention of selection, which presupposes predefined criteria, certainly programmed this time – as soon as there is no more naturality or spontaneity in the promotion, the plastic condition is menaced or even non-existent. A materialism, again, is repressing another.

In nature, the fittest is never the one that accidentally falls upon a favourable environment for its survival. It is a matter of simply 'adjust[ing] a response' to the environment, to restate it in François Jacob's terms (1973: 8). Adaptation, the agreement between the environment and variation, can of course be unpredictable. There is no better 'in itself'. Certainly, Darwin described natural selection as a work of perfecting or as an 'improvement', but these notions of 'better' remain without intention. Darwin was very reticent to speak of 'progress'; he himself never wanted to understand his theory as a theory of 'evolution', a term that could risk suggesting a linear progress comparable to the Lamarckian law of complexification. The improvement of which Darwin speaks is not subordinated to a finalism. The form of survivors, its permanence over time, is in a certain way sculpted by the disappearance of the disadvantaged, by the return of eliminated living forms to the inorganic. In the words of Canguilhem, 'death is a blind sculptor of living forms' (1994: 212). The inanimate therefore becomes, negatively, the condition of sense or the project of the living.

Could we, then, consider that Darwinism stops itself at the threshold of society and culture and that all social destiny betrays it, which is to say, precisely alters it? Selection would then be nothing other than a reproductive process of the identical.

Can we not envision, in spite of everything, a plasticity of social conditions and recover the wealth of variations and deviations of structure at the heart of culture? Is it not possible to think a social and political equilibrium in the relation between variation and selection? Where are we today with Darwin on this point?

And where are we with Althusser? According to him, the same plasticity as the biological one should prevail in the social and political order. This is the profound meaning of his new materialism. Let us go back to individuals and peoples.

Althusser comes to the 'taking form' of the individual when he talks about Machiavelli's *Prince*. Here is the political version of the materialism of the encounter at the level of the individual: 'Machiavelli [. . .] moves on to the idea that unification will be achieved if there emerges some nameless man

[. . .] Thus the dice are tossed on the gaming table, which is itself empty' (2006: 172).

So we have here this void, this absence of meaning, telos or predetermination. Form will emerge out of the encounter between fortune – that is, contingency – and the prince's virtue – that is, his ability to select the best possibilities that fortune offers, yet a selection made with no intention to do so. As if there were a naturally plastic balance between the lion and the fox, fortune and *virtù*.

> Consequently, the Prince is governed, internally, by the variations of this other aleatory encounter, that of the fox on the one hand and the lion and man on the other. This encounter *may not take place*, but it may also take place. It has to last long enough for the figure of the Prince to 'take hold' among the people – to 'take hold', that is, *to take form*, so that, institutionally, he instils the fear of himself as good; and, if possible, so that he ultimately is good, but on the absolute condition that he never forget how to be evil if need be. (Althusser 2006: 173)

But how can there exist, in the social, such a nameless man, able to begin from nothing, from such a nameless place, from such a non-teleological formation of forms?

The problem becomes all the more urgent when Althusser comes to the people or community via Rousseau. The specific political issue Rousseau raises is the following: to the extent that men have been 'forced to have encounters' (Althusser 2006: 185) when they were in the state of nature, forced into the social, is it possible to transform this imposed and illegitimate state of things into a legitimate one? That is, is it possible to recreate the conditions for a contingent and non-teleological form of encounter once the encounter has already taken place? To plasticise it retrospectively in some way? 'To rectif[y] an illegitimate (the prevailing) form, transforming it into a legitimate form?' (Althusser 2006: 187). Such is, according to Althusser, the leading question of *The Social Contract*.

> The most profound thing in Rousseau is doubtless disclosed and covered back up [*découvert et recouvert*] here, in this vision of any possible theory of history, which thinks the contingency of necessity as an effect of the necessity of contingency, an unsettling pair of concepts that must nevertheless be taken into account. (2006: 187)

Again, where is the void, the empty square from where we can start to undertake such a shift? 'It is in the political *void* that the encounter must come about', Althusser writes (2006: 173). But where is it and what can it be?

III

There seems to be no void in our societies. Let's have a look at the process of social selection – understood, for example, as the sorting and choosing of capacities or special aptitudes within the framework of examinations, contests or recruitment interviews – which immediately appears as the antonym to the plastic condition that presides over the economy of natural selection and its non-signifying sense.

The catalogue of tasks, the outline of jobs, the protocol of exams always precedes the real encounter with the variability and diversity of candidates, thus preventing differences from emerging by themselves. Such selection cannot, in fact, consist in the production of differences but, instead, only in the perpetuation of the criteria through which one chooses them. It is not the best that are selected or even those who exhibit an astonishing capacity for adaptation, but those who are the most conformable. Agreement takes precedence over value. Ensuring the perpetuation and renewability of the identical, social selection therefore ensures the return of sociological heaviness, never the emergence of singularities out of nothing.

Marx, particularly in his *Critique of Hegel's Philosophy of Right*, was the first thinker to denounce the conservative characteristic of the social selection of aptitudes. Taking the example of 'functionaries', Marx shows that one expects of them no special competence beyond that which consists in perpetuating the established order (1977: 21ff.). Hegel writes in his *Elements of the Philosophy of Right* that these 'individuals are not destined by birth or personal nature to hold a particular office, for there is no natural or immediate link between the two. The objective movement of their vocation is knowledge and proof of ability' (1991a: 332). However, these capabilities, says Marx, are not capabilities; no 'technique' is necessary to become a functionary, no specific expertise except for the talent of obedience, of respect for the state, and therefore of conformism.

Another critique of social selection would be conducted in the work of Pierre Bourdieu, notably in the famous text *The Inheritors*, which he co-authored with Jean-Claude Passeron in 1964 and which concerns the class trajectory of students. Selection norms, always defined in advance, constitute a veritable program and coincide, again, with pure and simple values of conformity, those of the dominant class, that fix the criteria of 'cultural legitimacy'. The principal characteristic of this legitimacy is to be a dissimulated cultural authority. This is the function of the social reproduction of cultural reproduction, founded upon 'privilege' – by definition the most predetermined selective criterion ever.

Social selection has the goal of reproducing order, privilege or the dominant ideology. One never selects an aptitude for action or political struggle, for example, but always aptitudes that respect order. Who among us has never been shocked by the injustice of this sorting, this triage, which retains only those individuals most compliant, never the most singular, and which, finally, elects so many mediocre, incompetent and narrow minds? Who has never had the feeling that social selection was, in effect, a program and never a promise, and that the morphological transformations of society were, deep down, only agents of conservatism?

The question that arises then is whether the destiny of social selection is a fantasy, or if selection could, in the political realm, join in any way the natural plastic condition. How can we ensure, within the realm of community and culture, the equilibrium between variation and selection, the future of difference, the promise of unexpected forms?

IV

Althusser is in reality perfectly aware of these difficulties, of the discrepancy between the encounter in the ontological or natural order and the encounter in the political realm. There could only be one solution to this: to know that criteria do not pre-exist selection itself. In society, such would be the recovered plastic condition. The whole problem always concerns knowing how not to identify the difference in advance, since selection in the order is always an act that confers value and therefore creates hierarchies and norms. How might one think at once the evaluating character inevitable to all social selection and its possible indetermination or liberty?

The only philosopher to have clearly posed this question is Nietzsche, and that is why Althusser refers to him after dealing with Machiavelli and Rousseau. It is certainly not for him to condemn selection, for the latter is inevitable, and it has an ontological foundation: becoming is itself nothing other than selection. Do not forget the following saying of Heraclitus: 'For even the best of them choose one thing above all others, immortal glory among mortals, while most of them are glutted like beasts' (Fragment 29). Becoming is so rich in differences that it can occur only upon the mode of choice. The task of philosophy is essentially selective since it chooses the differences opened by the flux of life, sorts them, and interprets them. In *On the Genealogy of Morals*, Nietzsche asks, 'What is it, fundamentally, that allows us to recognize *who has turned out well?*' (1989: 224). Which could be translated as 'who has taken form'.

In *Difference and Repetition*, Deleuze, to whom Althusser also refers, shows that selection produces its own criteria *as* it operates (1984: 300). It therefore becomes sensitive to the validity and viability of differences. The difference will be selected, as it unfolds, demonstrating its aptitude for return, which is to say the possibility of engendering a heritage or tradition. Thereby 'good' music, for example, engenders a tradition of interpretation, a great text engenders a lineage of readers. Selection should therefore happen *after* the emergence or springing of difference in the same manner that variability precedes natural selection.

Althusser knows perfectly well that the 'political void' in which the 'encounter must come about' (2006: 172), this political void which is also, as he says, 'a philosophical void' (2006: 174), may not exist; if we could be certain of its existence, if we were able to know in advance, the encounter would never take place, and we would fall back into teleology again. The determination of this void of nothingness, of this point of possibility that opens all promise of justice, equality, legitimacy, cannot be presupposed and cannot be as blindly and automatically regulated as in nature either. It has to be made possible. This is the philosophical task that appears with the end of the repressed materialism.

Machiavelli's Prince is, Althusser says, 'a man of nothing who has started out of nothing starting out from an unassignable place' (2006: 172). To find and give form to this unassignable place is what we have to do. 'Unassignable' is the translation of the French *inassignable*, but I am not sure that the word has the same meaning in both languages. In French, it means indeterminate and infinite. In English, it means incapable of being repudiated or transferred to another: inalienable. But I also found unassigned: not allocated or set aside for a specific purpose. The English is, then, much more interesting because it opens a space within the idea of a proper, something that cannot be attributed to someone else, that cannot be denied without destroying the subject, that belongs to no one and has no destination. We can call this place, the unassignable place, the *properly anonymous*. Without qualities, without privilege, without legacies, without tradition. People of nothing, people of valour. From there and there only can new forms emerge – singular, unpredictable, unseen, regenerating – as Althusser also says.

Before I ask a few questions about this 'place', let me evoke the changes caused by this new materialism in Althusser's reading of Marx and, consequently, in his critique of capitalism. In the light of this new materialism, Althusser writes, Marx 'was constrained to think within a horizon torn between the aleatory of the Encounter and the necessity of Revolution' (2006: 187). Hence, all his disavowals, debarments and philosophical betrayals. Very briefly:

WHITHER MATERIALISM?

> In innumerable passages, Marx [. . .] explains that the capitalist mode of production arose from the 'encounter' between the 'owners of money' and the proletarian stripped of everything but his labour-power. It so happens that this encounter took place, and 'took hold,' which means that it [. . .] lasted, and became an accomplished fact [. . .] inducing stable relationships and laws [. . .] the laws of development of the capitalist mode of production. (2006: 197)

So, initially, Marx analyses the constitution of capitalism as an encounter starting from the plastic void, the nothingness of the proletariat – its fundamental dispossession. But instead of remaining faithful to this vision, to the vision of a mode of production as a form taking form out of nothing, aggregating different elements and becoming gradually necessary, Marx and Engels inverted the process. They eventually affirmed that the different elements constitutive of the encounter 'were from all eternity destined to enter into combination, harmonize with one another, and reciprocally produce each other as their own ends, conditions and or complements' (Althusser 2006: 200). They substitute an analysis of the reproduction of the proletariat for its production.

> When Marx and Engels say that the proletariat is 'the product of big industry', they utter a very great piece of nonsense, positioning themselves within *the logic of the accomplished fact of the reproduction of the proletariat on an extended scale*, not the aleatory logic of the 'encounter' which produces (rather than reproduces), as the proletariat, this mass of impoverished, expropriated human beings as one of the elements making up the mode of production. In the process, Marx and Engels shift from the first conception of the mode of production, an historico-aleatory conception, to a second, which is essentialistic and philosophical. (Althusser 2006: 198)

So, again, the task is to free the repressed philosophical status of impoverishment, expropriation, dispossession, nothingness as the origin of any formative process. Poverty, dispossession, exploitation are the points of departure of philosophical thinking not because they would constitute objects or topics for philosophers, but because practice and theory both owe their energy, the power of their dynamism, to their originary absence of determinate being. The same originary 'virgin forest', Althusser says (2006: 191).

'The Underground Current of the Materialism of the Encounter' is no doubt a surprisingly anticipative text. The attempt to clear a point of void, nothingness and dispossession is at the heart of the most important current philosophical trends, which define themselves as materialisms. Speculative realism, for example, in its search for a non-correlationist mode of thinking, elaborates a notion of an absolute which would be not 'ours', which would remain indifferent to us.

Opening the unassignable place in a global world, where every place is assigned, has become the most urgent ethical and political task. The problem is to succeed in not constituting it as a transcendental structure. This is what I am struggling with myself, trying to disengage my plasticity from any symbolic grip and attempting to empty it constantly of its own sovereignty.

All this is extremely fragile; the waves are constantly, repeatedly, covering up the 'open fields' (Althusser 2006: 191) of singularity, surprise, non-anticipatable selection, recognition of aptitudes, the capacity to welcome new forms without expecting them. The waves of ownership, appropriation, reproduction are constantly and repeatedly covering up the originary deprivation of ontological wealth.

Whither materialism? The question won't ever lose its ambiguity. But, as Darwin says, when considering the changing nature of species, one at times has the impression that the 'whole organisation seems to have become plastic' (2008: 13). Let's live for those times.

Notes

1 This chapter was first given as a presentation under the auspices of the Centre for Research in Modern European Philosophy (CRMEP) and the London Graduate School of Kingston University London in May 2013.
2 On the relationship with Malthus, see the conclusion to Darwin's *On the Origin of Species* (2008: 338–60).

16

Philosophy and Anarchism: Alternative or Dilemma?

I

To explore the relationships between philosophy and anarchism amounts to deciphering a long and complex process of disavowal. If many philosophers have overtly proclaimed their involvement in Marxism, or their sympathy for it, none of them, at least in the continental tradition, have ever declared themselves anarchists.[1] None of them ever produced a detailed and patient analysis of anarchist texts. Decisive readings of Proudhon, Kropotkin, Bakunin, Malatesta, Goldman, Bookchin or others are nowhere to be found. Anarchism has always been and still is almost unanimously condemned for being naïve, uncritical and mostly impracticable or unworkable. Alain Badiou, for example, declares that anarchism 'has never been anything else than the vain critique, or the double, or the shadow, of the communist parties, just as the black flag is only the double or the shadow of the red flag' (qtd. in Noys 2008). And this, because it 'sets up a simple-minded opposition between power and resistance' (Noys 2008: 109). Anarchism would, then, be a simple and immature 'anti-' movement deprived of any dialectical elaboration or sophistication.

However, philosophers' contempt for anarchism remains ambiguous. More than a pure and simple rejection of it, this contempt appears to be a disavowal, a type of negation that is a veiled or repressed affirmation.

Why this claim? It is striking to see how some prominent twentieth-century philosophers, while strongly rejecting political anarchism, have at the same time developed strong concepts of anarchy. Such is the case for Schürmann, Levinas, Derrida, Foucault, Deleuze, Agamben and Rancière, mainly. The conspicuous contradiction that exists between their distancing from anarchism and their promotion of ontological anarchy is the reason why I use the term disavowal. This disavowal becomes even more visible when one notices the fact that these philosophers are currently considered to be the new voices of contemporary anarchism, that is, of 'post-anarchism'.

Such is the paradox of an anarchy without anarchism, of a metaphysical but non-political, ontological but non-practical anarchism. Why has it become important to analyse these twisted, convoluted structures today? Why has it become urgent to think anew the relationships between philosophy, anarchy and anarchism?

Anarchy comes from the Greek *an-arkhia*, which literally means without an *arkhè* – that is, without a principle, which in turn means both inception and commandment. The core trend of all anarchist movements, regardless of their diversity, pertains to the radical and uncompromised rejection of domination. Domination is not to be mistaken for mastery, authority or power. These last terms are ambivalent. They all possess a positive and a negative value. Power, for example, can designate a force, in the sense of a talent or a capacity. The same applies to mastery or authority: 'I see nothing wrong in the practice of a person who, knowing more than others in a specific game of truth, tells those others what to do, teaches them, and transmits knowledge and techniques to them', Foucault declares (2003a: 40). The concept of 'domination' clearly lacks such an ambivalence, and thus blurs the distinction between the use and abuse of power. Domination is synonymous with subjugation, subordination and alienation. This is the reason why Max Weber, for example, stopped using 'domination [*Herrschaft*]' to designate the political constitution, in the Greek sense of *politeia*, and preferred 'power' instead, thus reserving the word 'domination' for abusive and violent economies of power.[2]

The anarchist critique of domination immediately echoes the critique of representation. Traditional anarchists claim that whoever is mandated to represent someone else, be it society as a whole, a group or a person, if not quickly replaced, is inevitably led to subdue, alienate and dominate the represented. The critiques of domination and representation converge, thus challenging the idea of a necessary partition between those who are meant to govern and those who are meant to be governed. This idea has never been philosophically critiqued, and this perhaps because all philosophers agree, without always saying it explicitly, that human beings fundamentally need masters.

To insist upon domination does not amount to denying economic exploitation, as Marxists often argue against anarchists. It is not to dismiss the critique of capitalism – a critique that anarchism never abandoned. It is to recognise that there exists a specific problem of power, a problem that exists on its own. The problem of power is domination, the problem of power is abuse of power. It is not only economic, not only political, it is also institutional, academic, or psychic or domestic.

It is clear that anarchism is not only an anti-statist movement; the destruction of the state is perhaps no longer even its primary goal. Anarchism is first and foremost a question of the mechanisms of domination that raise political issues far beyond the political. These mechanisms work at both the collective and individual levels. The great anarchist activist Emma Goldman complained that most radicals, radical feminists in particular, paid attention only to the 'external tyrannies', while the 'internal tyrants', operating in small circles, even in one-to-one relationships, remained unexamined and undefeated. In 'The Tragedy of Woman's Emancipation', she declared:

> The explanation of such inconsistency on the part of many advanced women is to be found in the fact that they never truly understood the meaning of emancipation. They thought that all that was needed was independence from external tyrannies; the internal tyrants, far more harmful to life and growth – ethical and social conventions – were left to take care of themselves; and they have taken care of themselves. They seem to get along as beautifully in the heads and hearts of the most active exponents of woman's emancipation, as in the heads and hearts of our grandmothers. (Goldman 1917: 227)

In a 2006 interview with Charlie Rose, David Graeber develops the same idea about the existence of domination in everyday life: 'In academia there is a hierarchy', he says, 'and you're supposed to be scared [. . .] If you give people complete impunity and power over others, it creates a psychological dynamic which is almost sadomasochistic' (Graeber 2006: 17:30–17:47). Rose responds by asking, 'To be an anarchist is not to respect authority?' 'No', Graeber answers,

> I think that to be an anarchist is to be critical of authority and to always examine [. . .] if it's legitimate. And I think there are forms of authority that are legitimate, but you don't worship authority as a thing in itself. For example [. . .] I like the notion of self-subverting authority. I think that there are forms of authority that undermine their own basis, and I think those are very good – like a teacher. If you're a teacher and you teach someone very well, they know what you used to know, so there's no further basis for your authority [. . .] The relationship subverts its basis. If you are a doctor and you cure someone, you no longer have any reason to have authority on that person. (Graeber 2006: 18:04–19:00)

Domination or illegitimate authority happens, he adds, when one person is constantly subordinated to and by another and becomes a prisoner of such a situation.

The notion of self-subverting authority, of self-subverting domination, is of course central. It is a significant claim of anarchist thinking that domination can be challenged, fought against, overthrown even, by external forces, but that it also possesses at its core an internal line of fracture, a crack that allows for its self-subversion.

But where is and what is the limit between legitimate and illegitimate authority? Between power and domination? When exactly is the frontier transgressed?

It is the task of philosophy to answer these questions. The anarchist way of dealing with them should not be ignored by philosophers. Yet such an ignorance is at work. How is it possible to explain this fact? As I mentioned earlier, I certainly wouldn't have addressed the problem of the relationship between philosophy and anarchy if the concept of anarchy had not paradoxically constituted a leading thread of deconstructionist and poststructuralist thinking. Some of the most important European continental philosophers, starting with Heidegger, have determined the task of philosophy as a process of *Abbau*, or deconstruction, of what one might call the archic paradigm, that is, the supremacy of the *arkhè* in all theoretical and practical domains. Three main trends of such a deconstruction can be distinguished: the deconstruction of the archic paradigm in metaphysics (Schürmann, Derrida), the deconstruction of the archic paradigm in ethics (Levinas) and the deconstruction the archic paradigm in political philosophy (Foucault, Rancière). Let me expose only three of them here: Schürmann, Levinas and Foucault.

II

In his famous book *Heidegger On Being and Acting: From Principles to Anarchy*, Reiner Schürmann characterises the Heideggerian gesture of *Abbau*, or deconstruction, as liberating an anarchic, yet unheard of, mode not only of thinking, but also of acting. The metaphysical tradition was governed all along, Schürmann explains, by an essential subordination of practical philosophy to theoretical philosophy via the primacy of the *arkhè*. 'The prime schema which practical philosophy has traditionally borrowed from first philosophy is the reference to an *arkhè*' (Schürmann 1987: 5). For Aristotle, inventor of the philosophical meaning of *arkhè*, politics borrows its central conceptual schema from ontology and the derivative order it establishes between the individual and the universal: individual actions and ends are articulated to those of the city, just as accidents refer to the substance, or predicates to the subject as their chief. The archic paradigm, then, consists in the solidarity between *arkhè* and *telos*. *Telos*, as Schürmann suggests, is not only 'the complementary notion of *arkhè*', it is synonymous with *arkhè* (1987: 107). In his *Metaphysics*, Aristotle declares, 'Everything that comes to be moves toward an arkhè, that is, a telos: in fact, that for the sake of which a thing is, is its arkhè, and becoming is for the sake of its telos' (qtd. in Schürmann 1987: 103). Schürmann coins the term 'teleocracy' to characterise the primacy of the metaphysical unity between inception and domination. Teleocracy secures the order of things from arbitrariness and chaos by imposing a normative matrix upon being. Anything *adynaton* – impotent, chaotic, anarchic – is excluded from it.

The Heideggerian *Abbau* tends, on the contrary, to let 'the an-archic, anti-teleocratic element' freely appear, and liberates its force of dislocation and fragmentation (Schürmann 1987: 29). The an-archic thinking is visible in Heidegger through the motifs of the 'without why', 'without a goal', 'without reason' (Schürmann 1987: 236). The dismantling of teleocracy determines a conception of politics that goes beyond what is usually identified with political philosophy or political theory, which is generally fed by the 'principial' economy. Following Heidegger up to a certain point, but abandoning him also (Heidegger never made use of the term 'anarchy'), Schürmann radicalises deconstruction and announces the coming of a 'post-hegemonic, non-principial, and an-archic understanding of the political' (Villalobos-Ruminot 2017).

The disavowal happens when Schürmann strictly differentiates anarchy from anarchism, almost in a gesture of decontamination. He writes,

> Needless to say, here it will not be a question of anarchy in the sense of Proudhon, Bakunin, and their disciples. What these masters sought was to displace the origin, to substitute the 'rational' power, principium, for the power of authority, princeps – as metaphysical an operation as has ever been. They sought to replace one focal point with another. The anarchy that will be at issue here is the name of a history affecting the ground or foundation of action, a history where the bedrock yields, and where it becomes obvious that the principle of cohesion, be it authoritarian or 'rational', is no longer anything more than a blank space deprived of legislative, normative, power. Anarchy expresses a destiny of decline, the decay of the standards to which Westerners since Plato have related their acts and deeds in order to anchor them there and to withdraw them from change and doubt. It is the rational production of that anchorage – the most serious task traditionally assigned to philosophers – that becomes impossible with Heidegger. (Schürmann 1987: 7)

Being accused of simply substituting one principle for another, traditional political anarchism is supposedly still governed by the archic, teleocratic paradigm, and thus stands behind deconstruction. Such is a usual leitmotiv of the critique of anarchism: it is still obeying a principle, albeit the principle of having no principle.

Schürmann would not have been able to elaborate the concept of ontological anarchy without Proudhon, who was the first to transform – that is, to subvert – the initial meaning of 'anarchy' as chaos and disorder. Only with Proudhon was anarchism able to designate something different from disorder. 'Society finds its highest perfection', Proudhon writes, 'in the union of order with anarchy' (2011: 138). *Organised disorder.* So why this rejection of Proudhon's anarchism at the very moment when one borrows his positive, affirmative concept of anarchy?

III

The theoretical framework of Levinas's thinking is different, but the disavowal is the same. Levinas constantly worked at dismantling the archic ethical paradigm that governed the whole Western philosophical tradition, by bringing to light the concept of 'anarchic responsibility'. This concept appears early in his work, in texts such as *Humanism of the Other*, which has a chapter called 'Humanism and An-archy' (Levinas 2003: 45–57). However, it is in *Otherwise Than Being, Or, Beyond Essence* that anarchy finds itself most strongly elaborated (Levinas 1998: 257). The challenging of the archic paradigm is even more radical in Levinas than in Heidegger, to the extent that it operates on Heidegger's philosophy itself. An-archic, Levinas explains, designates what comes before all ontology. Being, in the traditional and Heideggerian senses, cannot be said to resist the archic paradigm. On the contrary, it is at one with it. Domination, for Levinas, pertains to the power of totality, and ontology is the very structure of totality. Anarchy, for Levinas, lies 'beyond essence': a space that does not obey any principle, whose economy does not derive from a pre-existing being, the space of the utterly other, alien to any command, any beginning. Anarchy starts with the Other, from the Other, which means that it does not start. 'An-archy [is] more ancient than the beginning and freedom' (Levinas 1998: 257).

It is clear that Levinas also 'refuses a purely political conception of anarchy', as Miguel Abensour rightly says (2011: 123–4). Political anarchism is analysed here again as a simple attempt to replace the principle of authority with the principle of reason. Abensour declares that, for Levinas, 'anarchy reaches a realm that is more profound, one that is pre-political, or rather one that is beyond the political and the ontological' (2011: 124). Levinas is very explicit on this point: 'It would be self-contradictory to set it [anarchy] up as a principle (in the sense that the anarchists understand it). Anarchy cannot be sovereign, like an *archè*' (qtd. in Abensour 2011: 124).

However, there certainly is a critique of state power in Levinas: 'Anarchy can only cause turmoil – but in a radical way – making possible moments of negation without any affirmation. The State then cannot set itself up as a whole' (1998: 194). One wonders about this radical turmoil that does not subvert what it targets. What is it? The answer is contained in the title of Levinas's *New Talmudic Readings*: 'Beyond the State in the State' (1999a: 79–107). The critique of the empirical political state is sustained by the idea of the messianic state; the anarchic future of the state of Caesar is the state of David. Anarchism is what carves out a dimension of transcendence within the immanence of the political, an immanence in which traditional anarchism would remain trapped. The space beyond the state remains a state because only a state that is also a government can guarantee the existence of justice. Anarchy in Levinas is like a closed opening, more exactly a foreclosure, and here is the denial, something that is at the same time opened and shut down.

Levinas's concept of 'substitution', which sustains his ethical view of anarchy, is politically strong, however. Remarking on Levinas's writings on the 1968 rebellions in Paris, Mitchell Verter states: 'The radicals of '68, and indeed all revolutionaries "who best merit the name revolutionary," are characterized by their capacity to substitute ethically their selves for the suffering of other people' (Verter 2010: 80). Substitution is the ethical expression of mutuality, the end of 'allergy', as Levinas often says. Substitution opens an ontological and political space and an economy that cannot be gathered under or subdued to a centralised control.[3] There is 'an anarchy essential to multiplicity', Levinas goes on (1969: 294), and this anarchy, far from being a chaos, appears as an economy of mutual aid and responsibility for the Other.

Nevertheless, Levinas never refers to Kropotkin, who also argues, against Hobbes, that mutual aid and substitution are more fundamental than competition. A reader of Darwin, Kropotkin affirms that natural selection is not the only evolutionary law. Animals do not only compete; they also help each other. Protection against enemies, the necessity of survival, unity and mutual support for the sake of the community are the reasons for mutual aid. In the first part of his book, *Mutual Aid: A Factor of Evolution* (1902), Kropotkin analyses the behaviour of ants and bees, the mutual protection systems among birds, cranes, parrots. In the second part, Kropotkin moves to political communities and affirms the need to recreate mutual aid and altruism where the biological trend to cooperation has been lost through evolution. Such a recreation is the major challenge and orientation of his anarchism.

Yet Levinas never mentions him. He certainly would not have admitted the existence of a biological basis to ethics. We may wonder, though, if his concept of substitution would not have been strengthened by a confrontation with something like the anarchist tendency of life. . .

IV

Let us now examine Foucault's position. As we know, after having focused his attention on the critique of sovereignty, he started to develop the concept of 'governmentality', which became central in his work. 'Governmentality' refers to the multiple sets of techniques that aim at normalising subjects and populations.

There have been quite a number of attempts to demonstrate that Foucault, because of this double critique of sovereignty and governmentality, was a thinker of anarchism, and perhaps even an anarchist himself. Such is, for example, Derek C. Barnett's main argument in his remarkable doctoral dissertation, 'The Primacy of Resistance: Anarchism, Foucault, and the Art of Not Being Governed' (2016). Barnett mentions three reasons that sustain such a view. First, Foucault's definition of critique as 'the art of not being governed' – even if Barnett forgets a little too quickly that Foucault adds, 'not being governed quite so much [. . .] like that and at this price' (2003c: 265). Second, the characterisation of the archaeology of governmentality as an 'anarchaeology' in *On the Government of the Living*. In the 30 January 1980 session, Foucault affirms that 'power has no intrinsic legitimacy' (2014: 77). Power is always contingent in its origin, and Foucault has always proclaimed 'the non-necessity of all power of any kind' (2014: 78), to such a point that this non-necessity becomes a principle of intelligibility of politics. Foucault provides a very interesting follow-up that clarifies his relationship with anarchism:

> You will tell me: there you are, this is anarchy; it's anarchism. To which I shall reply: I don't quite see why the words 'anarchy' or 'anarchism' are so pejorative that the mere fact of employing them counts as a triumphant critical discourse. And second, I think there is even so a certain difference. If we define, very roughly – and I would be quite prepared moreover to discuss or come back to these definitions, which I know are very approximate – in any case, if we define anarchy by two things – first, the thesis that power is essentially bad, and second, the project of a society in which every relation of power is to be abolished, nullified – you can see that what I am proposing and talking about is clearly different. First, it is not a question of having in view, at the end of a project, a society without power relations. It is rather a matter of putting non-power or the non-acceptability of power, not at the end of the enterprise, but rather at

the beginning of the work, in the form of a questioning of all the ways in which power is in actual fact accepted. Second, it is not a question of saying all power is bad, but of starting from the point that no power whatsoever is acceptable by right and absolutely and definitively inevitable. You can see therefore that there is certainly some kind of relation between what is roughly called anarchy or anarchism and the methods I employ, but that the differences are equally clear. In other words, the position I adopt does not absolutely exclude anarchy – and after all, once again, why would anarchy be so condemnable? Maybe it is automatically condemned only by those who assume that there must always, inevitably, essentially be something like acceptable power [. . .] [I]nstead of employing the word 'anarchy' or 'anarchism', which would not be appropriate [. . .] I will say that what I am proposing is rather a sort of anarcheology. (Foucault 2014: 78–9)

We understand, then, that 'anarchaeology' does not begin with the thesis that all power is condemnable per se, but that it is always contingent in its origin and structure. In other words, no *arkhè* is stable enough to guarantee any firm and definitive necessity and legitimacy to power, whatever its form, including the democratic form.

Third: the fact that Foucault always made clear that resistance was prior to power. In his seminar *Society Must Be Defended* (2003), Foucault analyses power relations through antagonisms and strategies that resist it. These lectures were given a few months before *The History of Sexuality*, and the two texts are often read together as support for Foucault's major thesis 'that resistance is never in a position of exteriority in relation to power' (1990: 95). Power is productive and not only repressive. In *Society Must Be Defended*, Foucault provides an unorthodox reading of Hobbes, in which he develops the idea that the state of nature is in reality a state of civil war. As Barnett declares,

> The question of 'civil war' as set forth in *Society Must Be Defended* is [. . .] a paradigm of the general form resistance takes within [an] alternative conception of politics [. . .] Foucault reads Hobbes as revealing a way in which the political concept of civil war can be redefined as a paradigm of resistance. In Foucault, then, the concept of civil war at once designates an alternative political paradigm in which the history of the political can be understood agonistically – that is, as a theory of permanent struggle and conflict – as well as how this conception of the political necessarily turns upon the politics of resistance as its defining characteristic. (Barnett 2016: 348)

Some other of Foucault's declarations definitely support Barnett's thesis about the existence of an anarchic trend in Foucauldian thinking:

> There must be a moment when, breaking all the bonds of obedience, the population will really have the right, not in juridical terms, but in terms of

essential and fundamental rights, to break any bonds of obedience it has with the state and, rising up against it, to say: My law [. . .] must replace the rule of obedience. Consequently, there is an eschatology that will take the form of the absolute right to revolt, to insurrection, and to breaking all the bonds of obedience: the right to revolution itself. (Foucault 2007: 356)

However, there are also several passages in which Foucault clearly distances himself from anarchism. The main argument is that classical anarchism has conceived of the relationships between power and resistance as two clearly opposed entities. Generally speaking, the anarchist vision of power tends to determine power as a substantial unity of forces commanding from above and to be resisted from the outside, rather than seeing it as a multiple, fragmented and creative force. 'It should be said that I am not an anarchist', Foucault says, 'to the extent that I don't admit this entirely negative conception of power' (2001: 1510).[4]

In her reading of Foucault's 'What is Critique?', Judith Butler, commenting on the 'art of not being governed', writes, 'He does make clear, however, that he is not posing the possibility of radical anarchy, and that the question is not how to become radically ungovernable' (2002: 218).

V

In each of these three positions – Schürmann's, Levinas's, Foucault's – a strange configuration is at work, that of a *dissociation*, proceeding from a too quickly analysed separation between anarchy and anarchism. My two initial issues – philosophy's disavowal of anarchism in the name of anarchy and the need for a refreshed, rejuvenated critique of domination – appear as closely intertwined. Exploring one amounts to bringing an answer to the other. It seems that the critique of the archic paradigm has only been only possible until now – at the cost of a repression, the repression of the deconstructive force of anarchism itself. As if philosophy wanted to keep its own anarchist drive at bay. From what is philosophy protecting itself?

Of course, several answers are possible. To utter 'I am an anarchist' publicly is difficult. It immediately resonates with terrorism and violence. It remains a highly subversive position. At the same time, the philosophers I have mentioned were never afraid to express some other very radical positions. Is it because of the verb to be? I *am* an anarchist. Being and anarchy might seem incompatible, as 'being', understood in an ordinary way, connotes fixity. Nevertheless, philosophers never use the word 'being' in an ordinary way. I think that there is something else at work.

Let's repeat the question: What is philosophy afraid of? Why does it hinder its own power of subversion? What secret attachment to domination does it maintain that bans it from radically subverting domination?

My contention is that there exists a strategy of avoidance of anarchism within the philosophical discourse on anarchy. Derrida, who is not exempt from such a strategy, has reminded us of the impossibility of hiding or excluding totally what one wants to preclude. All strategies of avoidance are doomed to fail. In *The Post Card*, he declares: 'The avoidance never avoids the inevitable in whose grasp it already is' (1987: 263).

How not to think then here of Freud's *Verneinung*? 'The manner in which our patients bring forward their associations during the work of analysis gives us an opportunity for making some interesting observations', Freud writes.

> 'Now you'll think I mean to say something insulting, but really I've no such intention.' We realise that this is a rejection, by projection, of an idea that has just come up. Or: 'You ask who this person in the dream can be. It's not my mother.' We emend this to: 'So it was his mother.' In our interpretation, we take the liberty of disregarding the negation. (*SE* XIX: 235)

Further:

> There is a very convenient method by which we can sometimes obtain a piece of information we want about unconscious repressed material. 'What,' we ask, 'would you consider the most unlikely imaginable thing in that situation? What do you think was furthest from your mind at that time?' If the patient falls into the trap and says what he thinks is most incredible, he almost always makes the right admission [. . .] What he is repudiating, on grounds picked up from his treatment, is, of course, the correct meaning of the obsessive idea. Thus the content of a repressed image or idea can make its way into consciousness, on condition that it is negated. (*SE* XIX: 235)

We can then easily imagine how Freud would have interpreted the sentence, 'I am not an anarchist. . .'

Notes

1 Jean-Paul Sartre is one of the very few exceptions.
2 On these points, see Arendt (1970).
3 See Levinas (1998), particularly chapter IV, section 1: 'Principle and Anarchy'.
4 Foucault's statement occurred during the Q&A session following his lecture. This discussion session does not appear in the available English editions of this text, so the quotation cited here is Malabou's own translation – Editor.

17

One Life Only: Biological Resistance, Political Resistance

That a resistance to what is known today as biopower – the control, regulation, exploitation and instrumentalisation of the living being – might emerge from possibilities written into the structure of the living being itself, not from the philosophical concepts that tower over it; that there might be a biological resistance to the biopolitical; that the bio- might be viewed as a complex and contradictory authority, opposed to itself and referring to both the ideological vehicle of modern sovereignty and to that which holds it in check: this, apparently, has never been thought.

Philosophy's Anti-biological Bias

What am I saying? It's a fact that in our time we have witnessed the definitive erasure of the limit between the political subject and the living subject that for centuries was believed to be secure. Michel Foucault illuminated magnificently the erasure of this limit, an erasure that marked the birth of the biopolitical and that acts as the characteristic trait of modern sovereignty: 'For millennia, man remained what he was for Aristotle: a living animal with the additional capacity for a political existence; modern man is an animal whose politics places his existence as a living being in question' (1990: 143).

These celebrated remarks define biopower as the means by which life is introduced 'into political techniques'. On the threshold of modernity, power was exercised over 'life processes and undertook to control and modify them' (Foucault 1990: 142). In *Homo Sacer*, Giorgio Agamben returns to the analysis of this undifferentiated zone between biological life and political life that has defined the space of community. In the eighteenth century, the living being entered politics once and for all.

And yet we have to admit that this 'entry' is unilateral, non-dialectical, unreciprocated. The 'double and crisscrossing politicization of life and the biologization of politics' take place without tension because the biological is deprived of the right to respond and appears to flow simply into the mould of power (Esposito 2013: 71). It's as if, since its birth in the eighteenth century, biology were preparing itself for its political investiture by offering renegade categories to power. Indeed, according to Foucault, all 'biological concepts' have a 'comprehensive, transferable character' by which they exceed their technical significance and take on a normative meaning (1994: 35). Yet the political becoming of biological concepts moves in only one direction: the control and regulation of both individuals and populations. Apparently, there cannot be any *bio*political resistance to the bio*political*.

Taking this point to the extreme, Agamben does not hesitate to say that Nazism did not even have to adapt genetic concepts to its ends; they sat, as it were, ready for use:

> It is important to observe that Nazism, contrary to a common prejudice, did not limit itself to using and twisting scientific concepts for its own ends. The relationship between National Socialist ideology and the social and biological sciences of the time – in particular, genetics – is more intimate and complex and, at the same time, more disturbing. (1998: 145–6)

In the same vein, Roberto Esposito does not hesitate to write that Nazism 'is actually *biology* realized' (2013: 80).

This way of thinking clearly leaves aside everything in biology that is not related to the training of bodies or the regulating of conduct and instead reveals the reserve of possibilities inscribed in the living being itself. It is a dimension confirmed by the revolutionary discoveries of molecular and cellular biology today. These discoveries, which are largely ignored by philosophers, are the very ones able to renew the political question. This can be demonstrated via two central categories. The first is the epigenetic. The second is cloning, with its two fields of operation: asexual reproduction and regeneration (or self-healing).

I am well aware that I am dealing with explosive notions here, notions that more often than not function as the privileged tools of contemporary biopolitics and its industrial, biologist and eugenicist offshoots. Nonetheless, it is my contention that these categories allow us to reconsider the anti-biological bias of philosophy.

What bias? Contemporary philosophy bears the marks of a *primacy of symbolic life over biological life that has been neither criticised nor deconstructed.* Symbolic life is that which exceeds biological life, conferring meaning upon it. It refers to spiritual life, life as a 'work of art', life as care of the self and the shaping of being, peeling our presence in the world away from its solely obscure, natural dimension.

Foucault's concept of body and Agamben's concept of bare life bear witness to this unquestioned splitting of the concept of life. Paradoxically, they expel the biological that is supposed to constitute their core – and it thereby becomes their unshakable residue.

Let's go back to the phrase in *The History of Sexuality*: 'modern man is an animal whose politics places his existence as a living being in question'. Foucault is swift to equate 'existence as a living being' with the *body*: 'The purpose of the present study is in fact to show how deployments of power are directly connected to the body' (1990: 151). The body acts as a hyphen connecting 'anatomy, the biological, the functional' and is the lowest common denominator in the various determinants that supposedly describe the specificity of the 'living being': the 'fact of living'; 'to be a living species in a living world'; having conditions of existence; life probabilities; and individual and collective health (1990: 151, 142).

Yet it is immediately clear in fact that the body is 1) all and part of a list in which the biological is defined diffusely – 'bodies, functions, physiological processes, sensations, and pleasures' – or as 'organs, somatic localizations, functions, anatomo-physiological systems, sensations, and pleasures'; and 2) that it both is and is not reducible to the biological. The biological is said to be 'what is most material and most vital' in bodies (Foucault 1990: 152–3). How should we understand this? That in the body there is something more and less vital, more and less material? If so, the 'less vital' and 'less material' is that which is incorporated in the body: the spiritual or the symbolic.

The same problem arises for the bare life that Agamben borrows from Walter Benjamin (*bloss Leben*), which constitutes a central category in his analysis of the biopolitical. In many respects, bare life seems to merge with biological life. It relates to the 'simple fact of living' and refers to 'natural life' (for which there is neither good nor evil but only 'the pleasant and the painful') – 'biological life as such' (Agamben 1998: 1, 3). Bare life is often described as 'pure' or 'simple': 'simple fact of living', 'simple natural life' (1998: 182, 3). But it is also synonymous with the body: 'simple living body', docile body ('power penetrates subjects' very bodies') (1998: 3, 5). But here we find the same confusion. As Agamben writes, 'Bare life [. . .] now dwells in the biological body of every living being' (1998: 140). Once again, therefore, there is space for something other than bare life in the biological body. In what, then, does that which is *not* the bare life of this body consist? More precisely, we come to see that bare life is that which lives in the biological body without being reducible to it – its symbol.

It must be said that biologists are of little help with this problem. Not one has deemed it necessary to respond to these philosophers or to efface the assimilation of biology to biologism. It seems inconceivable that biologists do not know Foucault, that they have never encountered the word *biopolitical*. Rather, fixated on the two poles of ethics and evolutionism, they do not think through the way the science of living being could – and from this point on should – unsettle the equation between biological determination and political normalisation. The ethical shield that surrounds biological discourse today does not suffice to define the space of a theoretical defence against accusations of complicity between the science of the living being, capitalism and the technological manipulation of life.

The Gap between the Living Being and Itself

To lay out the foundations of this discussion would require asking of contemporary biology 'permission' – to use Georges Canguilhem's phrase – to identify its 'fundamental philosophical concepts' (2008: 59). Epigenetics and cloning are some of these fundamental concepts, linked by a set of complex relations that position the living being as the centre of interactions.

In the first instance (epigenetics), interactions occur between two systems of transmission of hereditary information, as much at the level of individual development (ontogenetic development) as at the level of the perpetuation of the characteristics of the species (phylogenetic heredity). In the second instance (cloning), exchanges take place between two regimes of reproduction: procreation and the transfer of the nucleus. Each of these cases reveals the living being as an open structure in which the plural regimes of transmission of memory and inheritance intersect.

'What is most material and most vital in bodies' must be thought as an interactive space, a formative and transformative dynamic of organic identity that operates *within* the economy of the living being itself, not outside it. The gap that is opened between the living being and itself through the double interface of regimes of transmission and regimes of reproduction is a paradoxical memory gap in that it reveals the now fundamental shifting between the *irreversibility and reversibility of difference*.

Epigenetics

First and foremost, epigenetics allows us to question the definition of the living being as a set of functions; secondly, it makes it possible to question the definition of the living being as a program; and, thirdly, it blurs the dividing line between the fact of living and the elaboration of a mode of being. The word *epigenetic* comes from the noun *epigenesis* (from the Greek, *epi*, 'above, next to', and *genesis*; *epigenesis* thus literally means 'above or next to genesis'), which appeared in the seventeenth century in reference to a biological theory that claimed that the embryo develops through gradual differentiation of parts, and thereby opposed preformationism. By contrast, preformationism assumes that the living organism is wholly constituted in advance, in miniature, in the seed.

Something of *epigenesis* remains in contemporary *epigenetics*, as this is a science that does indeed have a certain type of gradual and differentiated development as its object. The term was used for the first time by Conrad Waddington in 1941 to refer to the area of biology that deals with relations between genes and the phenotype, that is, the set of observable characteristics of an individual for which genes are responsible.[1] The study of the hereditary and reversible changes in the function of genes that take place without altering their sequence is thus called epigenetics. Since the 1970s, epigenetics has been concerned with the set of mechanisms that control genetic expression via transcription through RNA and that modify the action of genes without modifying the DNA sequence. Known primarily for its role as a messenger transferring the genetic information of DNA to the manufacturing sites of proteins situated outside the cell nucleus, RNA is increasingly recognised as a key actor in epigenetic history. But what is it that we call epigenetic history?

First, epigenetic history concerns an essential dimension of ontogenetic development. Thomas Morgan already articulated the need for recourse to epigenetic phenomena to understand individual development in 1934 when he asked: 'If the characters of the individual are determined by the genes, then why are not all the cells of that body exactly alike?' (2018: 323). Since each cell of a single organism has the same genetic heritage, we must presume the existence of differential gene expression. Epigenetic mechanisms are this expression, which is concerned essentially with cellular differentiation and the methylation of DNA via RNA, which either favours or weakens the transcription of code.

The notion of epigenetic history also refers to a type of heredity, that is, once again, a specific mode of transmission of information from one generation to the next; hence the importance of its phylogenetic dimension. In *Evolution in Four Dimensions*, Eva Jablonka and Marion Lamb, who go so far as to speak of the 'epigenetic turn' of our era, emphasise the fact that genetic transmission is not the sole mode of hereditary transmission: 'The idea that DNA alone is responsible for all the hereditary differences between individuals is now so firmly fixed in people's minds that it is difficult to rid them of it'; the idea that 'information transmitted through nongenetic inheritance systems is of real importance for understanding heredity and evolution' is not yet accepted (Jablonka and Lamb 2014: 107).

And yet epigenetic heredity is indisputable today. Epigenetic modifications in fact have the particular quality of being heritable from one generation of cell to the next, which renders the idea of evolution more complex and reveals its multiple dimensions.[2]

Lastly, the notion of epigenetic history relates to the way in which modifications of the master of the genes depend not only on internal and structural factors, like those mentioned above, but also on environmental factors. So the epigenetic also provides genetic material with a means of reacting to the evolution of environmental conditions. Although plants have neither nervous systems nor brains, their cells do have the ability to memorise seasonal change. Reactions to environmental conditions are even greater among animals. Laboratory studies of consanguine mice have recently shown that a change in food regime can influence their offspring. The young have brown, yellow or dappled fur depending on this change. When females in gestation receive a certain food, their offspring develop mainly brown fur. Most of the young born to control mice (which did not receive the additional food) had yellow or dappled fur. There is therefore a transmissible memory of changes due to environment.

Thomas Jenuwein, director of the Department of Immunobiology at the Max Planck Institute, suggests that:

> The difference between genetics and epigenetics can probably be compared to the difference between writing and reading a book. Once a book is written, the text (the genes of DNA: stored information) will be the same in all the copies distributed to the interested audience. However, each individual reader of a given book may interpret the story differently, with varying emotions and projections as they continue to unfold the chapters. In a very similar manner, epigenetics would allow different interpretations of a fixed template (the book or genetic code) and result in different readings, dependent upon the variable conditions under which the template is interrogated. (qtd in McVittie 2006)

The living being does not simply perform a program. If the structure of the living being is an intersection between a given and a construction, it becomes difficult to establish a strict order between natural necessity and self-invention.

Cloning

Let us turn now to cloning. In order to approach cloning as a new conceptual category posed by contemporary biology, it is important to return to the problem above regarding the interplay between the reversibility and irreversibility of difference – an interplay that 'definitively shakes up our conceptions about the irreversible nature of processes of cellular differentiation' (Nau 1999).

The first research on cloning was initially designed to study the mechanisms of cellular differentiation. But it was logical that the question of a possible de-differentiation of cells should soon present itself. As Nicole Le Douarin writes:

> The goal of pioneering experiments on cloning sought to explain one of the great questions of life: how are multicellular organisms in which the division of labour between cells is the rule built? The curiosity of biologists obviously led them to ask a general question about this phenomenon. Are the nuclei of differentiated cells of higher level organisms such as mammals capable, like those of amphibians, of being reprogrammed in order to reclaim the particular and unique state of the nucleus of the egg? (2007: 160)

In other words, is it possible to reach the primary state of the cell at the embryonic stage, when the cells are not yet specialised? Le Douarin's response is as follows:

> The experimental methods that would have made it possible to answer this question were not available in the 1960s. It was only later that the growing of the mammal egg and embryo became possible, thereby opening up very interesting research fields. It enabled the arrival of biotechnologies that led to human assisted reproductive technologies (ART), the production of embryonic stem cells from 1981, the cloning of Dolly the sheep in 1996, and that of many other species of mammals since then. (2007: 160)

Let us try to take stock of this list by emphasising two biotechnological operations made on the cell: first, the production of embryonic stem cells as the basis for a first type of cloning known as therapeutic cloning; second, the cloning of mammals, known as reproductive cloning. These two operations prove the possibility of a reversibility of cellular differentiation and thereby upset a dogma that, until then, was viewed as definitive.

The challenge that cloning makes to the category of difference is not related primarily to the copy, to the threat of an eternal return of the same, for the clone will never be a faithful and perfect copy:

> *Epigenesis* is a powerful determinant in development [. . .] insofar as it regulates gene functions and the establishment of neuronal networks. It is even more

significant for the development of the singularity, aspirations and talents of each individual. The environment in which the becoming human lives plays a considerable role in this field. (Le Douarin 2007: 334)

If, therefore, the possibility of reproduction via cloning presents the problem of difference, this is not to be sought initially in the economy of the replica. Rather, the site of the problem, within the dialectical relation between epigenetics and cloning, is that of the unidirectional and definitive nature of cellular differentiation, the program and the trace. In other words, the stakes are tied to the possibility of going back to a time *before difference*.

Indeed, the radical novelty of the concept of the living being elaborated today by biology is paradoxically related to the return of cellular potentials, present among primitive animals and thought to have disappeared, or at least weakened, among so-called higher order animals. These potentials are precisely asexual reproduction and regeneration, both of which represent ancient forms of life realised by the state-of-the-art technologies of therapeutic and reproductive cloning. Biotechnological innovation – far from being a mere instrumentalisation, manipulation or mutilation – thereby realises a memory, that of the living beings erased within us. The posthuman is thus also the prehuman. On this dimension of the *return to nature* of the technology no philosopher has ever spoken a word.

Repairing, Regenerating: The Interplay of Possibilities

In the course of evolution, regeneration – the possibility of naturally repairing all or part of the body – has largely been lost among mammals. This is why the discovery of stem cells – able to repair, reform and regenerate organs and damaged tissue – forces us to look two ways at once, both to the future and to the past: to the future, that is, towards the perfecting of technology destined for the medical use of these cells; and to the past, to regeneration as very ancient property connected to primitive animals, such as hydra, planarians and starfish.

In many ways, advances in biology are bringing back, or renewing, a period that was believed to be past. Jean-Claude Ameisen interprets this interplay of return as a play of possibilities that must be 'drawn from their slumber': we 'could try to renew ourselves and to become perpetual starting from our own stem cells, starting from the spores that sleep in our body' (Ameisen 1999: 322). And he adds:

> The innumerable innovations of the living are built [. . .] on the basis of the – temporary – repression of most of their potentialities. And the wealth of these potentialities that sleep in the depths of our body no doubt surpass by far anything that we can yet imagine. (1999: 323)

At the heart of contemporary biological research lies the reactivation of phylogenetic remains that we believed to be forever lost.

And how might the return of these possibilities offer a power of resistance? The resistance of biology to biopolitics? It would take the development of a new materialism to answer these questions, a new materialism that asserts the coincidence of the symbolic and the biological. There is but one life, one life only.

Biological potentials reveal unprecedented modes of transformation: reprogramming genomes without modifying the genetic program; replacing all or part of the body without a transplant or prosthesis; a conception of the self as a source of reproduction. These operations achieve a veritable deconstruction of program, family and identity that threatens to fracture the presumed unity of the political subject, to reveal the impregnable nature of its 'biological life' due to its plurality. The articulation of political discourse on bodies is always partial, for it cannot absorb everything that the structure of the living being is able to burst open by showing the possibilities of a reversal in the order of generations, a complexification in the notion of heritage, a calling into question of filiation, a new relation to death and the irreversibility of time, through which emerges a new experience of finitude.

Translated by Carolyn Shread

Notes

1 See Waddington (1968: 1–32).
2 This occurs during mitosis – or even over several generations of organisms during meiosis – even if the cause has disappeared.

18

Philosophers, Biologists: Some More Effort if You Wish to Become Revolutionaries!

Cultural barriers are almost of the same nature as biological barriers: the cultural barriers prefigure the biological barriers all the more as all cultures leave their mark on the human body. (Lévi-Strauss 1985b: 16)

To live, to err, to fall, to triumph, to recreate life out of life. (Joyce 2007: 150)[1]

Norman MacLeod's (2016) response to my essay 'One Life Only: Biological Resistance, Political Resistance' is extremely helpful because it allows for a long-awaited discussion, that is, for a new type of exchange among biologists and philosophers. The problem is that this discussion is not the one imagined by MacLeod. Rather, it is generated, in a certain sense, by the holes in his response and argument.

When I speak of a 'new type of exchange among biologists and philosophers', I mean a discussion that goes beyond the classical, well-known ethical debate on the one hand (which questions what should be the ethical limits of biotechnologies), and the no-less-famous assimilation of biology to biopolitics on the other (which demonstrates how biological science always necessarily ends up being an ideological servant of biopower). In both cases, philosophers – such as Monique Canto-Sperber in France, Martha Nussbaum in the United States, as representatives of the first debate, or Michel Foucault, Giorgio Agamben and Roberto Esposito, as representatives of the second – have always tried to elaborate a strategy of resistance to the political hazards and threats potentially and actually contained in biological scientific practices. The exchange I am talking about is clearly not the only 'bio-ethico-techno-politico-scientific' one.

In my essay, I challenge the critical skills of current biology – molecular biology in particular – namely, its assertion of itself not only as a research field but also as an autonomous sphere of discourse. I state that biologists have never reacted to the meaning conferred by Foucault to the prefix *bio* in the concept of biopolitics – which is that of a pure vehicle of power. I suggest that biologists have never affirmed the capacity of both biology and life itself to resist biopolitical hegemony. My claim that 'the biological operator in the transition [from sovereignty to modern biopolitics, as Foucault analyses it] has been entirely passive' nonetheless calls for further clarification (qtd. in MacLeod 2016: 193).

MacLeod very rightly and accurately recalls that biology fought against itself when it came to some crucial issues such as eugenics. It has shown a self-critical capacity to resist its ideological, fatal drive towards totalitarian, purificationist and racist ideologies. 'Many prominent biologists (such as Franz Boas, J. B. S. Haldane, R. A. Fischer)', MacLeod writes,

> opposed the biopolitical doctrine of enforced sterilization of 'undesirables' in order to remove their characteristics from the normative population not only on the basis of moral repugnance but also because scientific evidence [. . .] showed quite clearly that such a program would not produce the effects on human populations claimed by the eugenists. (2016: 193)

He says the same thing about the supposed evidence of 'hierarchical ranking of the innate capabilities of human races' (2016: 193). On such urgent issues, biologists have evidently proven their genuine capacity for opposition and have shown no need to have philosophers come to their rescue. MacLeod is thereby right when he affirms that, 'contrary to Malabou's implication [. . .] biology has not simply rolled over and provided scientific justification for the exercise of biopower. Rather, many of its practitioners have been consistent and effective forces for controlling the expression of biopower' (2016: 194).

Yet, my notion of 'biological resistance' does not exactly refer to the capacity of biology to go against its own political and ideological drift. No, it is something else. Among the different 'levels' at which MacLeod situates this resistance, one is still lacking. It is upon this level that I insisted in my essay, and I continue to insist upon it here. It is the *symbolic*.

MacLeod reproaches my category of the symbolic as an appeal 'to a somewhat vague metaphysics' (2016: 194). I want to argue that this 'vague' and apparently indeterminate concept is, nevertheless and surreptitiously, the locus for the new discussion. Again, this locus is not biopolitics. It is the one that allows a new discussion to begin where MacLeod paradoxically wants it to end. It pertains to the following question: *Are we facing a revolution in contemporary biology with the postgenomic era and the shift from the genetic to the epigenetic paradigm?*

My essay advocates for such a revolutionary turn. The central issue, to reiterate, is not to determine whether epigenetic mechanisms and cloning techniques are manipulated towards obvious biopolitical instrumentalisations and normalisations. Beyond this, and in a much more radical way, the challenge that epigenetics and cloning offer pertains to the emergence of new conceptual categories. *How is a revolution in biology to be recognised?* Such is the question that we are now challenged to address.

The answer to such a question engages not only the realm of scientific discovery, not only the philosophical gaze, not only epistemological scrutiny, but also the originary region where all three interfere with each other. Such a region is precisely the space of the symbolic. Is the symbolic a vague, metaphysical term? No. My category of the symbolic refers to Claude Lévi-Strauss's law of exchange that pertains to four domains: the psychic, social, linguistic and biological. For Lévi-Strauss, the law of exchange (that is, the possibility of exchanging one thing for another, which is the meaning of *symbolism*) is indissociable from the law of reproduction. Exchange implies not only communication or trade but also exogamy, filiation and inheritance. It is clear, then, that the symbolic designates at once an indissoluble crossing point between the natural and the cultural, sexuality and language. Roughly defined, the symbolic is the way in which, literally, *life makes sense*.

A biological revolution can thus be defined as a phenomenon or an event that necessarily provokes a shift within the symbolic order. The symbolic, conceived of as the articulation point among different systems of exchange, is transformable, mutable and historically plastic. It is at once synchronic and diachronic, structural and mutable. The ways in which the interactions among the psychic, social, linguistic and biological are assembled and displayed are therefore different each time, different at each of their historical occurrences. To determine how exchanges, reproduction, filiation and so on are regulated and controlled by this state is one question. It is an entirely different question to examine whether exchanges, reproduction, filiation and so on are both conceptually and empirically entering a new epoch and knowing a new destiny. It seems that the constant focus on biopolitics is hiding the revolutionary turn that is currently happening to the bio itself. Biopolitics today functions as a form of disavowal of the present for both philosophers and biologists.

Before developing this point, I want to emphasise that structuralism has been far too quickly dismissed. The great accomplishments of Lévi-Strauss's concept of the symbolic – the careful definitions of where the biological meets the social, of how they both depart from each other and are at one with each other, and of how to 'spell out [a] [. . .] coherent set of biological, archaeological, linguistic [. . .] data' – have been too hastily and contradictorily assimilated with either a pure idealism or a sheer positivism (Lévi-Strauss 1985b: 16). After Lévi-Strauss, after Jacques Lacan (the relationship between the psychic and the symbolic), after Pierre Bourdieu (the relationship between the social and the symbolic), after Tzvetan Todorov (the relationship between the linguistic and the symbolic), after François Jacob (the relationship between genetics and hermeneutics), no one has ever returned to the essential problem raised by the symbolic function. *There is only one life.* The symbolic is the name of the differentiated games life plays with itself without ever fragmenting or dividing itself.

In their haste to criticise or deconstruct Lévi-Strauss and jump into post-structuralism, philosophers such as Foucault, Deleuze and Derrida have reintroduced a gap between all the dimensions aforementioned, and particularly between symbolic and biological life. Foucault's concept of the body paradoxically bears witness to this fact. Most of the time, symbolic life (the fashioning of the self, ascetic existence, the economy of pleasures) remains for him apart from empirical biological life. Body and organism still diverge, and the latter remains subordinated to the former, as a slave to his or her master. For his part, Deleuze affirms that the symbolic body is without organs. Derrida claims that zoology does not know what an animal is.[2] At the very moment when biology has been said to occupy a central political and philosophical space (as is the case with the notion of biopolitics), the old divide between the biological and the symbolic body, or life, has been secretly reintroduced.

We know how deeply biologists, geneticists in particular, got involved in the structuralist debate. Through explicit exchanges with Lévi-Strauss, geneticists such as Jacob (1973), for example, developed some powerful analyses of the DNA code as a text that advances the notion of a genetic program. Richard Lewontin agreed that the symbolic and the biological are always, as shown by the image of the triple helix, emerging from each other, shaping each other, and exchanging their mutual terminations. Humberto Maturana and Francisco Varela (1991) elaborated the concept of organic autopoiesis.[3] Duplication, reproduction, filiation (sexually or asexually produced, by cloning) are what make the symbolic and the biological merge, fuse and render the difference between the natural and the cultural improbable. Exchange, the very concept of exchange, has no proper sense in one *or* the other but in both at the same time. The symbolic dimension of biology pertains to the impossibility of limiting the definition of life to a mere aggregate of molecules, and the biological dimension of the symbolic pertains to the fact that this excess itself can never be exceeded, that is, extended beyond the biological realm towards any kind of spiritual transcendence. As Lévi-Strauss declares, 'genetic recombination plays a part comparable to that of cultural recombination' (1985b: 18). They are two faces of the same reality.

SOME MORE EFFORT IF YOU WISH TO BECOME REVOLUTIONARIES!

Where are biologists now on these issues? Have they not themselves abandoned, along with the structuralist debate, their reflections on the intricacy of matter and meaning?

Let us now come to the epigenetic debate. When I ask if we are currently witnessing a revolution in biology, I ask to what extent epigenetics is revealing something like a new epoch in the symbolic order.

Contesting the positive answer that I attempt to bring to these issues in my essay, MacLeod declares,

> far from being a revolutionary development in molecular biology that changes the way in which we think about inheritance, evolution, and/or the ability of information to be passed between generations in any fundamental manner, this new information represents, at present, a rather limited, minor, and still controversial footnote to our understanding of mechanics of inheritance in complex organisms whose significance is, at best, not well understood. (2016: 196)

I will not here remind the reader of the current definition of epigenetics, which is made sufficiently clear in my essay as well as MacLeod's response. Is or is not epigenetics a revolutionary tool? MacLeod insists on the fact that I am not a biologist and that I cannot provide an objective answer to this question. I, of course, don't contest this point. But in his refusal to agree with me he also, by the same token, is in disagreement with a great majority of his fellow scientists. Do I have to summon the names of Henri Atlan (1999), Eva Jablonka and Marion J. Lamb (2014) and Jean-Pierre Changeux (1985, 2012), to mention only a few researchers who affirm that we are currently facing a dramatic shift in both biology and culture with the passage from the genetic to the epigenetic paradigm? They affirm that our ideas about heredity and evolution are undergoing a revolutionary change, that there are four 'dimensions' in evolution – four inheritance systems that play a role in evolution: genetic, epigenetic (or non-DNA cellular transmission of traits), behavioural and symbolic (transmission through language and other forms of symbolic communication). Whether or not we share these views, it remains extremely difficult, impossible even, to contest that something is happening in the realm of current molecular biology. Evelyn Fox Keller (2000), as we know, is devoting herself to the analyses of these changes.

My precise (or specific) intervention consists in what I am perceiving about this current change at the level of the symbolic. The images of the musical score and its interpreters used by Jablonka and Lamb and that of the book and its readers used by Thomas Jenuwein in order to characterise the relationships between the genotype and the phenotype as determined by epigenetic mechanisms show sufficiently and clearly that with epigenetics we are starting a new adventure, a new version of the exchange between life and itself, that is, between the biological and the symbolic. Revolutions in biology and in the symbolic (in all its dimensions) happen every time reproduction, filiation, lineage and inheritance are both *experienced* and *interpreted* differently – when exchange exchanges with itself.

I am not nostalgic for the glorious days of structuralism. I worry, however, about the demise of the notion of the symbolic. In my opinion, it has to be revisited and re-elaborated because it is the sharpest instrument of analysis of the interaction of social context and biology. Such a re-elaboration might help us to conceive epigenetics as both an objective, empirical and material series of mechanisms, and as a moving, fluid, imaginary functioning across social and theoretical spheres. I am grateful to MacLeod for giving me the opportunity to express these ideas in a more radical way and most of all for allowing the biology/philosophy debate to sublate its dead biopolitical form.

Notes

1 J. Craig Venter and his team have inscribed this line into a synthetic genome using DNA coding.
2 Compare Deleuze's *Proust and Signs* (2000) and volume 1 of Derrida's *The Beast and the Sovereign* (2009).
3 We can think of the multiple dimensions of the work of someone like Gregory Bateson as well. See Bateson's *Steps to an Ecology of Mind* (2000).

19

How is Subjectivity Undergoing Deconstruction Today? Philosophy, Auto-Hetero-Affection and Neurobiological Emotion

Contemporary neurobiological research is engaged in a deep redefinition of emotional life: the brain, far from being a non-sensuous organ, one devoted only to logical and cognitive processes, now appears on the contrary to be the centre of what we might call a new *libidinal economy*. A new conception of *affect* is undoubtedly emerging.

The general issue I would like to address here[1] is the following: does the neurobiological approach to affect accomplish a material and radical deconstruction of subjectivity? I mean: does neuroscience engage in a more material and radical deconstruction of subjectivity than the one led by deconstruction itself? Does this approach help us to think of affects outside the classical conception of auto-affection, of affects that would not proceed from a primary auto affection of the subject? Does the study of the emotional brain challenge the vision of a self-affecting subjectivity in favour of a *hetero-affected* one?

I borrow the concepts of auto- and hetero-affection from Derrida, the concept of affects from Deleuze, and the concept of the emotional brain from Damasio, the famous neurobiologist and author of *Descartes' Error*, *Looking for Spinoza* and *The Feeling of What Happens*. Intertwining these notions will help me set the stage for a confrontation between the three authors, as well as between continental philosophy and neuroscience. I will start with some definitions.

Affects, Auto- and Hetero-Affection and the Emotional Brain

First, *affects*. This generic term includes emotions, feelings and passions and characterises a *modification*. To be affected means to be modified or altered by somebody or something. In his 24 January 1978 lecture on Spinoza, Deleuze refers to *The Ethics*, Book III, Definition III, where Spinoza says, 'By affect (*affectus*) I understand the affections of the body by which the body's power of activity is increased or diminished, assisted or checked, together with the ideas of these affections.' Deleuze then declares: 'I would say that for Spinoza there is a continuous variation – and this is what it means to exist – of the force of existing or of the power of acting [. . .] An affect is a continuous variation of the force of existing, insofar as this variation is determined by the ideas one has' (Deleuze 1978).

An affect is thus always related to the feeling of existence that is produced through the modification of our power of acting, of what we are able to do: in Spinoza, all the affects that follow from joy increase our power of acting, while, on the contrary, all those that follow from sorrow diminish this power. The difference between these different kinds of states gives the subject the feeling of being alive. 'Affect' can then be used as a generic term that not only comprises Spinoza's definition but also characterises every kind of *modification or difference that generates the feeling of existence*.

What is the feeling of existence, though? Does it coincide purely and simply with the feeling of oneself? When I feel myself existing, do I feel existence or just myself? These issues lead to the problem of auto-affection. Is every kind of affect, to the extent that it is related to the feeling of existence, the expression of a self-affection, of an affection of the self by itself? The term auto-affection was coined by Heidegger in *Kant and the Problem of Metaphysics*. Kant, as we know, distinguishes between two forms of subjectivity that coexist in the same subject: the transcendental form of apperception, and the empirical form of the inner sense. The 'I' cannot know itself as a thinking substance, since it can only appear to itself by affecting the inner sense. This is auto-affection. Heidegger shows that the affection of the subject by itself, which he understands as temporality, is the origin of many particular kinds of affects: passions, emotions or feelings. Auto-affection would then be the condition of possibility for every other kind of affect. Love, hatred, envy, jealousy would be possible because the core of our self is auto-affected in the first place.

There is no such thing as 'pure' auto-affection, Derrida objects. The 'I' who feels or affects itself is not the dominant and pregnant structure of all affects. Auto-affection, within the metaphysical tradition, as well as in Heidegger, has never meant anything but presence, self-presence, presence of the self to itself, what Derrida also calls a *self-touching*, a touching of one's own presence. Yet Derrida does not criticise the notion of auto-affection itself. In *Of Grammatology*, he recognises that auto-affection is 'a universal structure of experience. All living things are capable of auto-affection' (1997: 165). He shows, however, that auto-affection is never pure. In *On Touching: Jean-Luc Nancy*, instead of affirming the existence of an originary auto-affection, he asks: 'shouldn't one rather distinguish between several types of auto-hetero-affection without any pure, properly pure, immediate, intuitive, living, and psychical auto-affection at all?' (2005: 180). It would accordingly be impossible to identify the feeling of existence with the feeling of oneself, with the originary temporal address of the subject to itself.

Hetero-affection may be defined as *the affect of the other* in two senses: first, the one who is affected in me is always the other in me – never the 'I' conceived as an infrangible identity; and second, the other in me is always affected by the wholly other of this other. The other who is affected in me and the other who is affecting me are definitely not one and the same. Derrida declares, again in *On Touching*: 'No sooner does "I [touch] itself" than it is itself – it contracts itself, it contracts with itself, but as with another [. . .] *I* self-touches spacing itself out, losing contact with itself, precisely in touching itself' (2005: 34). The feeling of existence is thus never present to itself, but always disarticulated. It is not the feeling of my existence, but of the other's existence in me. The temporal difference that lies at the heart of the 'I' is the difference between me and the 'intruder', the other of me in me, 'the heart of the other': 'touching, in any case, touches the heart and on the heart, but inasmuch as it is *always* the heart of the other' (2005: 67). Love, for example, like any other affect, would proceed from a disarticulation – and not from an intuitive synthesis – of the ego. Hetero-affection, more exactly 'auto-hetero-affection', would then be the real source of all affects.

Damasio brings to light the existence of what he calls the neural self, which is the elementary form of our subjectivity. It consists in a series of homeostatic processes or regulating devices that maintain life in check and produce a relatively stable and endlessly repeated biological state. Curiously, emotions play a central role in these homeostatic processes: 'Emotions are curious adaptations that are part and parcel of the machinery with which organisms regulate survival. Old as emotions are in evolution, they are a fairly high-level component of the mechanisms of life regulation' (Damasio 1995: 54). Homeostatic emotions produce an elementary form of attachment of the self to itself and to its own life. Damasio thus acknowledges the existence of a primary form of auto-affection.

However, this emotional elementary auto-affection never becomes conscious. Rather, it constitutes the unconscious part of subjectivity. 'The focus on self', Damasio says, 'does not mean that I am talking about self-consciousness' (1995: 238). If there is an originary auto-affection, it does not amount to a conscious self-touching of the neural self. Right from the start, neural auto-affection appears to be a kind of hetero-affection to the extent that there is no possible experience of it, that it stays alien to the feeling of oneself. There is a gap between homeostatic emotions and conscious feelings, and we will see that this divorce manifests itself as such in many forms of brain damage, as if the possibility of the subject's dislocation were originally inscribed in the neural system.

The Hetero-Affection of the Subject: Neurobiological or Deconstructive?

With these four terms – affects, auto-affection, hetero-affection and emotions – now briefly defined, I will address, in outline, the problem that concerns me: who brings to light hetero-affection in the most radical way?

In order to address this issue, I will confront three texts. Each presents an essential aspect of hetero-affection. The first one might be given the title 'The two lovers', the second, 'Non-human becoming', and the third, 'I am in pain – but I don't feel it'. First, 'The two lovers', from Derrida's *On Touching*:

> Imagine: lovers separated for life. Wherever they may find themselves and each other. On the phone, through their voices and their inflection, timbre, and accent, through elevations and interruptions in the breathing, across moments of silence, they foster all the differences necessary to arouse a sight, touch, and even smell – so many caresses, to teach the ecstatic climax from which they are forever weaned – but are never deprived. They know that they will never find ecstasy again, ever – other than across the cordless cord of their entwined voices. A tragedy. But intertwined, they also know themselves, at times only through the memory they keep of it, through the spectral phantasm of ecstatic pleasure – without the possibility of which, they know this too, pleasure would never be promised. They have faith in the telephonic memory of a touch. Phantasm gratifies them. Almost – each in monadic insularity. Even the shore of a 'phantasm', precisely, seems to have more affinity with the *phainesthai*, that is, with the semblance or shine of the visible. (2005: 112–13)

Next, 'Non-human becoming', from Deleuze and Guattari's *What is Philosophy?*

> The affect goes beyond affections no less than the percept goes beyond perceptions. The affect is not the passage from one lived state to another but man's nonhuman becoming. Ahab does not imitate Moby Dick [. . .] It is not resemblance, although there is resemblance [. . .] It is a zone of indetermination, of indiscernibilty, as if things, beasts and persons [. . .] endlessly reach that point that immediately precedes their natural differentiation. This is what is called an

affect. In *Pierre; or The Ambiguities,* Pierre reaches the zone in which he can no longer distinguish himself from his half-sister, Isabelle, and he becomes woman [. . .] This is because from the moment that the material passes into sensation as in a Rodin sculpture, art itself lives on this zone of indetermination. (1994: 173)

Finally, from Damasio's *The Feeling of What Happens,* pain without a subject:

> In short, pain and emotion are not the same thing.
>
> You may wonder how the above distinction can be made, and I can give you a large body of evidence in its support. I will begin with a fact that comes from direct experience, early in my training, of a patient in whom the dissociation between *pain as such* and *emotion caused by pain* was vividly patent. The patient was suffering from a severe case of refractory trigeminal neuralgia, also known as tic douloureux. This is a condition involving the nerve that supplies signals for face sensation in which even innocent stimuli, such as a light touch of the skin of the face or a sudden breeze, trigger an excruciating pain. No medication would help this young man who could do little but crouch, immobilized, whenever the excruciating pain stabbed his flesh. As a last resort, the neurosurgeon Almeida Lima [. . .] offered to operate on him, because producing small lesions in a specific sector of the frontal lobe had been shown to alleviate pain and was being used in last-resort situations such as this.
>
> I will not forget seeing the patient on the day before the operation, afraid to make any movement that might trigger a new round of pain, and then seeing him two days after the operation, when we visited him on rounds; he had become an entirely different person, relaxed, happily absorbed in a game of cards with a companion in his hospital room. When Lima asked him about the pain, he looked up and said quite cheerfully that 'the pains were the same', but that he felt fine now. I remember my surprise when Lima probed the man's state of mind a bit further. The operation had done little or nothing to the sensory patterns corresponding to local tissue dysfunction [. . .] The mental images of that tissue dysfunction were not altered and that is why the patient could report that the pains were the same. And yet the operation had been a success [. . .] Suffering was gone [. . .]
>
> This sort of dissociation between 'pain sensation' and 'pain affect' has been confirmed in studies of groups of patients who underwent surgical procedures for the management of pain. (2000: 74–5)

These three texts all share something in common: each of them challenges the possibility of the self touching or coinciding with itself. They all state the impossibility of what Merleau-Ponty calls the 'touching-touched' relationship between me and myself. Derrida quotes this passage from *Phenomenology of Perception,* in which Merleau-Ponty writes: 'When my right hand touches my left . . . I touch myself touching: my body accomplishes a "sort of reflection" and becomes a "subject-object"' (Derrida 2005: 187). In each case, we find in a way two subjects: the two lovers, first of all, who can also be read as two expressions of the same subject, as a staging of the impossibility of its auto-affection; second, the difference between the subject and his own affects, which always escape him; and finally, the subject who feels pain but is not affected by it. We always find two subjects in one, but there is an infinite distance between them, contrary to what occurs in Kantian auto-affection.

The 'telephonic memory of touch' presupposes the existence of a touch without presence. If two lovers can stay together without ever being able to see each other, beyond joy and sorrow, it is because there is no presence of the self to itself, no mirror, no self-reflection. There is no difference between the feeling of myself and the feeling of the other; in both cases, I experience 'sharing, parting, partitioning, and discontinuity, interruption, caesura – in a word, syncope' (Derrida 2005: 156). No *phainestai*. The opening of the self to itself or the other does not signify autonomy or auto-affection.

We know that Deleuze is not concerned with the problem of the deconstruction of metaphysics. Yet there is a Deleuzian concept of auto-affection. Deleuze makes use of it when he characterises what Spinoza calls ideas of the third kind:

> Ideas of the third kind are affections of essence, but it would have to be said, following a word that will only appear quite a bit later in philosophy, with the Germans for example, [that] these are auto-affections. Ultimately, throughout [. . .] the ideas of the third kind, it is essence that is affected by itself. (Deleuze 1978)

This auto-affection appears, from the onset, to be a hetero-affection.

Deleuze gives three examples of affects, which correspond to the three kinds of ideas in Spinoza. First, the affect caused by the effect of the sun on the body; second, the affects caused by the effect of the sun on a painter's canvas; and third, the affect caused by the essence of the sun on the mind, which is the example of auto-affection. In each case, there is no reflection: the sun – the affecting or touching power – is not reflected by the surface that it touches. The touching and the touched are driven out of themselves; they form a block exceeding the material locus of their contact – body, canvas or mind. This is why Deleuze says that percepts go beyond perceptions, affects beyond affections, and that subjects become non-human subjects. Deleuze repeats, a little further on: 'Affects are precisely the nonhuman becomings of man' (1978).

Affects, including auto-affection, separate the human subject, the 'I', from itself. I am not affected. The affect exists in my place. Curiously, we also find a critique of phenomenology in *What is Philosophy?* under the name of what Deleuze there calls 'fleshism'.

> The being of sensation, the block of percept and affect, will appear as the unity or reversibility of feeling and felt, their intimate intermingling like hands clasped together [. . .] In fact, flesh is only the thermometer, not the frame of becoming. The difficult part is not to join hands but to join planes. (1994: 178–9)

According to Damasio, the most intimate and elementary part of our neural self is what he calls the proto-self. The proto-self is made of the interconnected and coherent collection of neural patterns, which, moment by moment, represent the internal state of the organism, the neural 'map', that is, that the organism forms of itself. This map helps the organism to regulate and maintain its homeostasis, which is continuously disturbed by intruding objects. Homeostasis is not a merely mechanistic or logical process. As I said, it produces the first form of attachment of the self to itself.

To the extent that this attachment is non-conscious, the subject is anonymous. If we could take a tour though our neural processes, Damasio says, it would always be from the third-person perspective. In the case of the suffering patient, what occurs is not exactly the loss of emotion but the loss of *conscious* emotion. The surgery effectuates a dissociation between two strata of the subject that typically remain unified: the proto-self and the conscious self. The third person, which is involved in homeostatic processes, and the first person, involved in conscious procedures, are disconnected and can thus look at each other from a distance.

Sometimes, the opposite situation occurs. After incurring certain kinds of profound brain damage, some patients lose their feelings and emotions but not their first-person perspective, their consciousness. These people, as Damasio says, act in cold blood. Because of their disease, they are led to indifference, coldness and a lack of concern, to 'a marked alteration of the ability to experience feelings' (Damasio 1995: xvi).

Being No One: 'Deconstruction' on its Neurobiological Path

It is time now to go back to the initial question: who thinks auto-affection in the most radical way? All the questions that Derrida raises – the impossibility of a presentation of the self to itself, the impossibility of regarding the affects as rooted in conscious auto-affection – seem precisely to coincide with the problems that are addressed by the neurobiological redrawing of the self. We also know that Deleuze devotes a whole chapter to the brain at the end of *What is Philosophy?*

In fact, this apparent proximity hides a genuine discrepancy. It seems that both the thought of affects in Deleuze and the thought of hetero-affection in Derrida always require a thought of a hetero-body, that is, of a non-organic body or a body without organs (BwO). In order to bring to light the originary process of hetero-affection, Derrida and Deleuze need to delocalise the natural body. The absence of organs, for Deleuze, means the lack of organisation. As if our flesh, our blood, our brain were suspected to be the material expressions of metaphysics: like substance, system, presence, teleology. The BwO remains a body, but it only presents itself as a surface, a plane, to slip over or bounce off. Derrida also needs to think of a kind of non-natural surface, a non-biological bodily extension that allows for an encounter with the other. The subjectile is such a surface, since it 'stretches out under the figures that are thrown upon it' and lies 'between the subject and the object', without any biological determination (Derrida and Thévenin 1998: 74–5). This exclusion of the body returns in *On Touching*:

> No one should ever be able to say 'my heart', my own heart, except when he or she might say it to someone else and call him or her this way [. . .] There would be nothing and there would no longer be any question without this originary exappropriation and without a certain 'stolen heart'. (2005: 273)

Why this? Why shouldn't we say 'my heart'? Why this moral injunction, this 'shouldn't'? Is it really necessary to transcend biology in order to articulate a concept of affects that would not be related to subjectivity or to its self-touching? Or doesn't it appear, on the contrary – and this would be one of the most striking lessons of neurology today – that organic neural organisation is radically deconstructive? That a deconstruction of subjectivity is at work in our neurons?

I certainly do not intend to pit biology against philosophy. I am just wondering whether the critique of phenomenology, of the phenomenological body, of 'flesh' and 'fleshism', does not lead Derrida and Deleuze to dematerialise, in their turn, the real processes that are affects. When I clasp my hands, is it really two planes that I join? Can one be sure that two lovers can resist the absence of bodily pleasure, and be satisfied with a phantasm? Why is it necessary to look for the outside outside the body? Why put the body at a distance, at a distance from its own organs?

Again, I am by no means attempting to defend some kind of biological reductionism against philosophical thinking, but to elaborate a new (continental) philosophical position on neurobiology, a bridge connecting the humanities and the empirical sciences of the brain or mind. Such a bridge could be found in the fact that, instead of proposing a substantial vision of subjectivity, current neurobiology is exploring the absence of the self to itself. There could be no power of acting, no feeling of existence, no temporality, without this originary delusion of the first person.

Being No One. That is the title of a book. Not a work of Derrida's or Blanchot's, but one by a cognitive neuroscientist by the name of Thomas Metzinger (2003). 'Nobody ever was or had a self.' Those are its first, destabilising words. We should no longer be sure that deconstruction and neighbouring philosophies have a monopoly on uttering such phrases or conceiving their stakes.

Note

1 This essay presents in outline form problems developed in a seminar entitled 'On Wonder – From the Passionate Soul to the Emotional Brain: Affects in Philosophy and Neurobiology Today', which was given in the Rhetoric Department of the University of California, Berkeley, in the spring of 2008.

20

Floating Signifiers Revisited: Poststructuralism Meets Neurolinguistics

'Floating signifier': all of a sudden I started to see this term everywhere. As if this famous denomination, coined by Claude Lévi-Strauss in his *Introduction to the Work of Marcel Mauss*, had literally invaded the whole field of critical theory – philosophy, political theory, gender studies, race studies, all domains that have paradoxically challenged structuralism over the last fifty years. Whatever the critiques of structuralism, the concept of 'floating signifier' has remained continuously central in poststructuralist discourses, in all sorts of contradictory and unperceived ways.

In his *Introduction*, Lévi-Strauss develops his conception of language through his discussion with Mauss. Language, he says, has to be approached from two inseparable perspectives: an evolutionary and genetic one, and a linguistic and synchronic one. The first perspective is vertical. It deals with the origin and development of language through time. The second is systematic and horizontal. It studies the relations between the elements of language: signs (signifieds and signifiers), phonemes and morphemes. Lévi-Strauss's theory of the floating signifier, the meaning of which I will recall in a moment, follows both lines: it has an evolutionary and a structural dimension.

I want to argue here that, instead of maintaining these two dimensions, diachronic and synchronic together, poststructuralist thinkers have only retained the second one. They have taken for granted the existence of an empty square, a void or blank space, a signifier zero in the symbolic chain of language without ever interrogating its empirical and biological origin. The floating signifier has become a ready-made, indefinite element, able to play all possible parts, a critical skeleton key whose origin, once again, has remained unquestioned.

What is this origin? What does it say about language – and poststructuralism itself? Such are the issues I intend to deal with here. First, after resituating Lévi-Strauss's argument and recalling his definition of the floating signifier, I give examples of the proliferation of the concept of 'floating signifier' in various theoretical contexts. Second, I return to the aforementioned double take on language – evolutionary and structural – with the help of current trends of research in neurolinguistics. I am referring in particular to the 'microgenetic' theory of language brought to light by the neurologist Jason Brown and analysed by the neuro-anthropologist Terence Deacon. I then examine how the concept of 'floating signifier' finds itself transformed by this approach that brings neurology and structural linguistics together, and why such a transformation is important for critical thinking today. Severing floating signifiers from their biological roots, displacing them from their initial structural birthplace, was clearly an attempt to dismantle all essentialist visions of language and bring to light the contingent, transformable status of cultural values. Nevertheless, such gestures have ended up conferring on meaninglessness a hyper-meaningful status, thus undermining their own critical force. I intend to demonstrate that such a deconstructive gesture has to be deconstructed in its turn.

What is a Floating Signifier?

In the *Introduction to the Work of Marcel Mauss*, Lévi-Strauss proposes an interpretation of the presence, across a wide range of languages, of certain enigmatic signifiers which are invested with great importance in the ritual life of certain 'primitive' societies, but whose specific reference or meaning is mysterious and variable. One of the best examples, borrowed from Polynesian culture by Marcel Mauss himself, is the signifier *mana* and its related terms, apparently capable of signifying a magical property, that of reciprocity in the process of exchange (Lévi-Strauss 1987: 51). The same thing goes for terms such as *wakan*, *orenda* or *manitou* (1987: 51). This phenomenon also concerns Western societies. Let's think of words such as *truc* or *machin* in French, or *oomph* in American English (1987: 55). Such terms, Lévi-Strauss says, can be considered 'floating signifiers' (1987: 63), empty squares 'in themselves devoid of meaning' (1987: 55) that allow for all other signifiers to circulate. How can we explain their presence in language?

Here is Lévi-Strauss's answer: 'Whatever may have been the moment and the circumstances of its appearance in the ascent of animal life, language can only have arisen all at once' (1987: 59). The world became meaningful all of a sudden, which created the following problem: 'man has from the start had at his disposition a signifier-totality which he is at a loss to know how to allocate to a signified, given as such, but no less unknown for being given [. . .] There is always a non-equivalence or inadequation between the two' (1987: 62).

Consequently, in all languages, there exists a surplus of signifiers over the number of signifieds to which they can be fitted.

By failing to signify anything specific, floating signifiers function as a kind of supplementary intra-systematic manifestation of this permanent excess of signifiers. Their sole function is thus to fill a gap between the signifier and the signified. They possess no specific referential function, appear as a 'zero symbolic value' (1987: 64), and only stand within the system for the surplus of signifiers over the signified.

As mentioned earlier, Lévi-Strauss's analysis is twofold: diachronic and vertical, and systemic or horizontal. The latter explores the biological origin of language, as the former explores its actual functioning. Therefore, anthropology, Lévi-Strauss says, is never only 'sociological', but also 'physical and physiological' (1987: 26). It seems, however, that only the synchronic line has survived the structuralist conception of language.

This synchronic line corresponds to what Lévi-Strauss calls the *symbolic function*, which designates the capacity of certain systems to form closed and self-referential entities.[1] Language is the archetype of such systems: in language, the meaning of a word is not fixed according to an external reference or 'real' object, but only though its articulation with other words. It is even possible to say that language is the symbolic function per se, from which all other symbolic domains derive, such as myths, rituals, art, etc. And this for the reason that language possesses a unique, specific characteristic: it is a symbolic system that designates itself as such. Floating signifiers are markers of the self-referentiality of language. They entirely depend on the context in which they appear and the relationships they form with other words at a given moment.

A Few Examples

Let me now offer a few examples of such an interpretation, voluntarily juxtaposed without explanation. The first three examples insist upon the positive, creative resources of floating signifiers, the others upon their possible ideological, abusive reattachments to a supposed reality.

Deleuze. Gilles Deleuze sees floating signifiers as indefinite possibilities of creation, tangible inscriptions of poetry in language. Unforgettable chapters of *Logic of Sense* bring together Lévi-Strauss, Lewis Carroll and Nietzsche. Deleuze says that these authors have opened the space of nonsense within sense by producing 'surface effects in language': 'sense', Deleuze writes, 'regarded not at all as appearance but as surface effect and position effect, [is] produced by the circulation of ['non-sense', that is] the empty square in the structural series (the place of the dummy, the place of the king, the blind spot, the floating signifier, the value degree zero, the off-stage or absent cause, etc)' (1990b: 71). Non-sense is not the absence of sense, but something other than sense in sense, an unlimited gliding or detachment from reference that appears to be the very possibility of literature.

Balibar. The liberating and generative value of floating signifiers is also manifest when it comes to political concepts, that, even if sometimes very old, remain to be born. Such is the case of 'communism', for example. As Étienne Balibar declares, 'we recognize that "communism" has become a floating signifier, whose fluctuations incessantly traverse the complete range of [. . .] epistemological, but also political, difference[s]' (2011: 5). This fluctuating status comes from the fact that even if 'communism has existed', it 'has never yet existed' (2011: 4).

Lyotard. If communism is a floating signifier, it may also allow for a floating – that is, a non-dogmatic and intermittent – relationship with Marxism itself. Jean-François Lyotard affirms the necessity to 'let relationships with Marxism be free and floating [*laisser libre et flottant le rapport avec le marxisme*]' (1990: 105).[2]

Butler. Let us now move to contexts in which floating signifiers designate a type of socially constructed reality that cannot be assigned a 'natural' or ontologically 'essential' signified and referent. I am thinking here of Judith Butler's well-known definition of gender in *Gender Trouble* as a 'free-floating artifice' (2007: 10), impossible to bring back into alignment with biological sex. Gender and desire are plastic and do not obey pre-given and stable factors.

Hall. The two last examples are borrowed from critical race studies, contexts in which floating signifiers are seen as possible sites for pure ideological constructions. Race, according to Stuart Hall, is a floating signifier, as explicitly indicated in his 1997 documentary, *Race: The Floating Signifier*. Racism presupposes that race is a natural, essential 'fixed biological characteristic' (Hall 1997: 4). In reality, race is 'a discursive construct, that is a sliding signifier' (1997: 5). Hall adds,

> What do I mean by a floating signifier? Well, to put it crudely, race is one of those major concepts, which organize the great classificatory systems of

difference, which operate in human society. And to say that race is a discursive category recognizes that all attempts to ground this concept scientifically, to locate differences between the races, on what one might call scientific, biological, or genetic grounds, have been largely shown to be untenable. We must therefore, it is said, substitute a socio-historical or cultural definition of race, for the biological one. (1997: 6)

The meaning of 'race' is 'relational, and not essential', and is 'subject to the constant process of redefinition and appropriation', the 'endless process of being constantly re-signified' (1997: 8).[3] We need a politics 'without guarantee' (1997: 16).

Wright. In his article 'What Has Cultural African Studies Done for You Lately?', Handel Kashope Wright, referring to Stuart Hall, asks what the specific object of African studies is: 'So, what of our object of study, African Studies?' (Wright 2016: 479). It has no signified: 'are we speaking strictly about continental Africa or does the concept spill over beyond the continent into its globally dispersed diaspora?' (2016: 479). The concept of African studies floats in between a 'homogeneous Black Africa' and a 'complexity of multiple Black ethnicities and cultures' (2016: 482) – what Paul Gilroy identifies as the conceptual frame of 'creolization, metissage, *mestizaje* and hybridity' (qtd. in Wright 2016: 482). It is a 'historical and political construction' (2016: 485).

Wright adds:

> I don't mean to suggest that African cultural studies is a floating signifier in Claude Lévi-Strauss' original literal sense (i.e. a signifier without a referent or without a signified), but rather in Ernesto Laclau's overtly political sense of the floating signifier having a signified which is in fact the result of a hegemonic process that has appropriated (and obfuscated) various unsatisfied demands. An empty signifier in Laclau's sense is necessarily open to contestation, with claims made upon it by various differing, opposing or allied political stances and causes. In this sense, then, though it might appear to be known, what we are calling African cultural studies should more accurately be identified as multiple (reflective of various positions on Africa, African studies and cultural studies) and should be contested over in the struggle for what it can and should become. (2016: 490)

Laclau and Mouffe. It would take much too long to develop Ernesto Laclau's and Chantal Mouffe's theory of the floating signifier, understood as what reveals the 'opentexturedness of social relations' (Wright 2016: 491),[4] the existence of antagonistic political forces, as well as the instability and flexibility of the frontiers that divide them. I will just mention that they explicitly acknowledge their debt to Lévi-Strauss.

Once again, these different approaches are concerned with the synchronic perspective on language only. From such a perspective, floating signifiers are said to operate in a system with no outside. The 'free-floating dispersion of signifiers', as Žižek puts it (2008: 118), is paradoxically closed on itself. At this point, we can pinpoint the subtle transition from language to the symbolic order. The closure of language, the absence of all external relation to nature, paradoxically allows for the symbolic order to be indefinitely open, 'simultaneously "finite" [. . .] and "infinite"' (Žižek 2008: 119). Floating signifiers are the tricksters, the go-betweens of the linguistic and the symbolic.

All the authors I mentioned have strongly challenged Lévi-Strauss, denouncing his rationalism, his positivism, his anthropocentrism. Yet the category of 'floating signifier' is still a central concept in their thinking. No deconstruction of structuralism has deconstructed the floating signifier. The concept of floating signifier has escaped the decline of structuralism.

The only philosopher to have cast some doubt on this situation is Giorgio Agamben, who interestingly characterises in *Homo Sacer* the contemporary privilege conferred upon the category of floating signifiers as an unperceived 'linguistic "state of exception"' (Agamben 1998: 25). The 'Lévi-Strauss' entry in *The Agamben Dictionary* reads as follows: 'The deconstruction of the primacy of the signified in the metaphysical tradition results in a paradoxical preservation of the form of signification itself beyond any determinate contents' (Murray and White 2011: 123). To talk about the absolutisation of the floating signifier is a very sound critique. Unfortunately, however, Agamben does not develop this and never interrogates the neglected dimension of Lévi-Strauss's theory of language.

The Neurolinguistic Approach

This neglected dimension concerns the issue of the origin of language and the evolutionary view that sustains it. For many thinkers, as we just saw with Stuart Hall's declarations, biology inevitably entails determinism, naturalisation, essentialisation or 'political guarantees'.

Can there exist another approach to biology that would serve the concept of the 'floating signifier' instead of naturalising it? Let us turn to the neurolinguistic theory of language called 'microgenetic theory'. Not only does this theory help strengthen Lévi-Strauss's evolutionary view of language; it also sheds a new light on the status of floating signifiers.

In his article, 'Language as an Emergent Function: Some Radical Neurological and Evolutionary Implications', Terrence W. Deacon rightly states that it may be 'time to reflect on why neurobiology and formal linguistics have not converged' (2005: 269). Deacon thematises the split that took place over the second half of the twentieth century between formal linguistics and neurobiology. The 'development of formal generative linguistic analysis', he goes on, 'has been the most important advance in the study of language in the last half century' (2005: 269). Formal linguistics has helpfully discovered the 'open-ended generativity' of language (Deacon 2005: 269). Floating signifiers obviously represent a central element of this generativity. The problem is that formal or structural linguistics has studied language from its components (signs, signifieds, signifiers, letters), treating language as a mechanism and thus hiding or dismissing the fact that 'sentence structure is produced analogous to the way embryos develop, not as machines are built' (Deacon 2005: 274).

The time has come to reunify the evolutionary and neurological perspective on language with the structural synchronic approach, that is, to reconcile language with life. Let us quote Lévi-Strauss's famous affirmation more extensively:

> Whatever may have been the moment and the circumstances of its appearance in the ascent of animal life, language can only have arisen all at once. Things cannot have begun to signify gradually. In the wake of a transformation which is not a subject of study for the social sciences, but for biology and psychology, a shift occurred from a stage when nothing had a meaning to another stage when everything had meaning. (1987: 59–60)

Such a conception of a sudden appearance of language is now labelled by neurologists and neurolinguists the 'theory of emergence'.[5] According to this theory, language, exactly as Lévi-Strauss presupposed it, is the result of a spontaneous, self-organised dynamism that entirely pertains to brain activity. Deacon declares: 'Language has an emergent architecture to the extent that its structure is a product of spontaneous bottom-up self-organizing interactions' (2005: 274).

This spontaneity is not, as one might think at first, without memory or a past. Language, of course, did not appear out of nothing. Its sudden emergence was the result of a long genesis, implying successive processes of neural differentiation taking place along an evolutionary line – a line that led from the primitive brain to the appearance of the neocortex. Emergence does not mean erasure. Jason Brown affirms that the human brain recapitulates this evolution in miniature: such is the core tenet of microgenesis. In *Microgenetic Theory and Process Thought* (2015), Brown argues that the brain replicates in miniature the evolutionary process that leads from the reptilian brain to the higher cortical functions.[6] In Brown's view, Deacon writes, 'brain development resembles a kind of micro-evolution in many important respects' (2005: 272). Further, according to Deacon: 'language is a neurologically emergent function because its structure is a product of the complex synergy that develops between [the] multiple systems and through levels of progressive neural differentiation. Each stage of differentiation involves correlated processing in corresponding levels of anterior (intention-action) and posterior (attention-sensory) cortical systems' (2005: 280). This genesis finds itself reiterated in every individual mental act.

The unfolding of a mental state (such as the utterance of a sentence, for example) at a given moment in time passes through the same phases – phylogenetic as well as ontogenetic – as the evolution and development of our brain. Microgenetic theory is, then, an account of the phases in brain process through which successive mind/brain states arise and perish in a succession of psychological moments measured in milliseconds, and yet containing within themselves the whole evolutionary past and the life history of the individual. As Brown strikingly puts it: 'eons in evolution, decades in maturation, milliseconds in microgenesis' (1996: 3).

Mental processes flow from the archaic to the recent in forebrain evolution, from the continually reactivated past to the present moment. Each moment disappears and leaves a trace that shapes the next one. The crucial point is the paradoxical duration or 'thickness' of the 'now': instants are very short but 'thick' (Pachalska and MacQueen 2005: 96). Emergence and spontaneity are surprisingly not instantaneous, but contain an accelerated history, a temporal density.

Now, what is the link between microgenesis and floating signifiers? It is true that microgenetic theory does not deal with the relationship between signifiers and signifieds. At the same time, it sheds light on it in a very particular way. The evolutionary perspective of language also reveals the existence of a blank or empty square in language, a non-speaking origin of language. Because of neurological microgenesis, the recent speaking brain communicates with the very old non-speaking brain every time a sentence or a word is uttered. Language constantly, continuously remembers its non-linguistic origin.

This blank is not that of the symbolic void of the floating signifier, but the blank of an absence. The absence of the subject. The absence of the speaking subject. The blank time when there were no subjects, only elementary, reptilian brains. No human beings. No locutors. No interlocutors.

The internal exchange of our brain reminds it that the missing signified, in the first place, is precisely that of humanity. This also explains why there is no dramatic structural difference between primate and human brains. As Deacon argues,

> Despite the obvious human uniqueness of language, no unprecedented new brain structures distinguish human from nonhuman primate brains. Even the so-called language areas of the cerebral cortex (e.g. Broca's and Wernicke's areas) have been shown to derive from primate homologues sharing positional, cytoarchitectonic, and connectional patterns with their human counterparts, despite not subserving language or even vocal control [. . .] So language processing is ultimately carried out with the same brain structures and functional logic that other primates use for nonlinguistic functions. (Deacon 2005: 270)

The merging of neurology and linguistics brings to light the fact that there is no anthropological specificity of language. We thus have to suppose that language – language in general as well as every particular utterance – is 'the tip of an iceberg that *floats* to the surface' (Pachalska and MacQueen 2005: 97). This originary floating of language is the moving ground of all symbolic floating signifiers. Language floats on the ocean of its non-linguistic origin. Floating signifiers are the paradoxical memories of such an origin.

Conclusion

The process of hominisation produces through language the cerebral memory of the non-human. Therefore, Deacon claims, '[t]he questions "What is a concept before it is expressed in words and phrases?" and "What is a proposition or request before it is phrased as a sentence?" must eventually be given serious attention as linguistic issues' (2005: 274).

Because of a massive paradigm shift in biology, critical theory should definitely pay attention to the 'neurological embryos' of speech acts. Instead of providing 'guarantees', evolutionary biology allows for a new deconstruction of 'human nature' as it reveals the non-human origin of the human, inscribed in a history that constantly reactualises itself and repeats its speechless point of departure. Today, a non-essentialist turn in biology is taking place that needs to be acknowledged in order to understand what 'non-essentialism' is. Signifiers are able to float *because*, not in spite of, their biological, neurological origin.

Floating signifiers have to be considered expressions of this origin.

Communism, gender, race, African studies ... all 'floating' determinations or categories are frontier concepts situated at the limit between the two meanings of the term 'cortical': cortex and bark, neural envelope and symbolic surface.

We have to admit definitely that evolutionary changes can be revolutionary transformations.

Notes

1 On this point, see Lévi-Strauss (1963).
2 The English translation of Lyotard's text is Malabou's own – Editor.
3 Hall continues on this point with the following: 'The meaning of a signifier can never be finally or trans-historically fixed. That is, it is always, or there is always, a certain sliding of meaning, always a margin of not yet encapsulated in language and meaning, always something about race left unsaid, always someone as a constitutive outside, whose very existence the identity of race depends on, and which is absolutely destined to return from its expelled and rejected position outside the signifying field to trouble the dreams of those who are comfortable inside' (1997: 8).
4 See Laclau and Mouffe (2014), especially pages 141–50.
5 Emergence, in evolutionary theory, characterises the rise of a system that cannot be predicted or explained from antecedent conditions.
6 See also Brown (1979).

Part Four

Destructive Forms

21

Is Retreat a Metaphor?

I initially intended to talk about Martin Heidegger.[1] I wanted to explain the reason why, according to him, there can be no retreat without a retreat of the retreat itself, no retreat without a redoubling, to the extent that the only gesture or move retreating can perform is to perform nothing, that is, to retreat. The only thing which retreating can do, and mean, is to retreat. *Retreat retreats*. I would have liked to explain that this sentence, *retreat retreats*, can also be formulated as 'retreat is', and recall that, for Heidegger, Being originarily coincides with its own retreat or withdrawal (*Entziehung*). For this very reason, retreating is a synonym for Being. Every time we say something like *s is p*, it means *s* retreats from *p*, as well as *p* retreats from *s*, because the copula *is* is nothing but its own withdrawal.

Being, affirms Heidegger, has always already retreated, has always meant its own withdrawal in withdrawing, but has also hidden this retreat, it has always retreated from its retreat. It has retreated a first time from its own retreat to give way to metaphysics. Metaphysics is this long tradition, also called philosophy, through which or within which Being hides itself under beings, and appears as what it is not, that is, as a form of presence, be it God, substance, or reality – as something eternal which never withdraws. Ontological withdrawing has veiled or covered itself behind what never retreats. In that sense, Being, through or within metaphysics, has always appeared as its own opposite, as a substantial referent, as something towards which everything tends, thus as the proper name or the proper meaning for every particular being. Every particular being became a metaphor for Being, a transfer, a way towards it.

But I've become a stranger since I was wounded [. . .] Everything that I learned or experienced in life has just dropped out of my mind and memory, vanished for good, leaving behind nothing but an atrocious brain ache (Luria 1987: 100, trans. modified).

This would have led me to comment on Heidegger's powerful statement in his book *The Principle of Reason*: 'the metaphorical exists only within metaphysics' (1996: 48).² This would have led me also to explain that the first retreat of the retreat, metaphysics, has come to an end, has come to *its* end. This would have led me to show that the distinction between proper and metaphorical meaning has also disappeared, that there is no longer any such thing as a 'metaphor'. The metaphorical exists only within the borders of metaphysics and ceases to be when metaphysics comes to its end and reveals the achievements of its own destruction or deconstruction. The meaning of Being, then, is neither proper nor figured; Being cannot be understood as a referent any longer. Being is retreating or withdrawing from its metaphysical meaning. It is withdrawing from its previous retreat. It retreats from its retreat again. And if retreat has retreated a second time, this time from both its proper and metaphorical status, then what does retreat mean?

Simply, naively, if I decide to retreat from others, to look for some seclusion, or solitude, or shelter, and if retreat has retreated from the distinction between its proper and its metaphorical meaning, what can I reach where and when I retreat? Nothing proper, no authenticity, I can't obtain any truth, any essential way of being, because the difference between the proper and the figurative, between authenticity and inauthenticity, between truth and falsity, between what is essential and what is not has withdrawn. If I can't get anything like a more proper kind of existence from my withdrawal, if getting into the wild does not give me anything else but the very absence of wilderness, if everywhere I go is like everywhere else, then staying where I am, here, there, with the others, consuming, logging on, playing all sorts of games, enjoying this good capitalist global nothingness, doing all this, then, amounts to living in the woods. Is this no less authentic, that is, no more inauthentic, than living in a retreat?

I would have liked to dwell on these ideas but

She had suddenly become motionless and speechless [. . .] She would lie in bed, often with her eyes open but with a blank facial expression [. . .] The term neutral helps convey the equanimity of her expression [. . .] She was there but not there (Luria 1987: 101–2).

I also intended to extend this reflection with Jacques Derrida's analysis of retreat and withdrawal in his powerful text, 'The *Retrait* of Metaphor' (2007). Derrida recalls the Heideggerian trajectory, the double double retreat, the metaphysical and the deconstructive one, where the metaphorical and the proper withdraw in the end. Derrida agrees that retreating or withdrawing is always a failure, and that the frontier between authenticity and inauthenticity has become absolutely porous. Derrida shows, nevertheless, that this aporia does not equate to an impossibility. We can still invent a new meaning for retreat, we can open a new possibility of withdrawing, something yet to come. One cannot distinguish between authenticity and inauthenticity, the proper and the metaphorical, but one can make a difference between them. Retreat is always retreat of the retreat, retreat from the retreat, but between retreat and retreat a difference hides itself, which silently asks to be made. Derrida says *traced*. There is always a possibility of retracing the retreat, of insisting upon the secret difference that dwells within the retreat, which opens the space of the trace. Derrida plays with the French *trait*, *zug* (which you hear in *Entziehen*, or *retrait*), saying that we have to retrace the retreat in order to invent a different way to retreat, to open a gap between retreat and retreat, and so invent a new meaning of retreat, a poetic one. Poetry, Derrida says, is language freed from the distinction between the metaphorical and the proper meaning, a language that traces itself, retraces itself to make the difference between retreat and retreat appear without designating or imaging it. Foucault calls this retracing 'the thought from outside' (1987).

Retreating, then, would equate to travelling to the outside, an outside deprived of any contrary, of any inside.

Let me still go on mentioning what I would have said if I hadn't retreated from my project, from my own outside. If I. . .

No less dramatic than the oblivion that anosognosic patients have regarding their sick limbs is the lack of concern they show for their overall situation, the lack of emotion they exhibit, the lack of feeling they report when questioned about it. The news that there was a major stroke [. . .] is usually received with equanimity, sometimes with gallows humor, but never with anguish or sadness, tears or anger, despair or panic (Damasio 1995: 64).

I would have liked to present three great figures of the retreat, three heroes, my three heroes: Maurice Blanchot, Alexander Grothendieck and Thomas Bernhard. Each of them retraces the retreat: in not appearing (Blanchot), in disappearing (Grothendieck) and in about-turning (Bernhard).

Not appearing. For Blanchot, a writer has no proper existence. Which leads literature to its own disappearance, and the book to its definitive withdrawal.

> Writing marks but leaves no trace; it does not authorize us to work our way back from some vestige or sign to anything other than itself as (pure) exteriority – never given, never constituting or gathering itself in a relation of unity with a presence (to be seen, to be heard), with the totality of presence or the Unique, present-absent. (Blanchot 1993: 424)

Disappearing. Grothendieck, born on 28 March 1928, was a mathematician who made pivotal contributions to the modern theory of algebraic geometry, particularly by incorporating into it commutative algebra, homological algebra and category theory. As a result, due in no small part to his influence on various aspects of pure mathematics, Grothendieck is often credited as being among the most revolutionary of twentieth-century mathematicians. He formally retired from his professorship in 1988 and within a few years moved to the Pyrenees, where he lived in isolation from human society until his death in 2014.

He refused several prizes.

In January 2010, Grothendieck wrote a letter to a fellow mathematician, Luc Illusie. In this letter, known as the '*Déclaration d'intention de non-publication*', Grothendieck denies having given authorisation for the publication of any of his works during his prolonged absence. A crucial part of his seclusion, Grothendieck announces a prohibition against all future republication of his work, whether partially or in its entirety, and requests that libraries containing copies of his works remove them.

About-turning. Bernhard's autobiography is a collection of five separate volumes: *A Child, An Indication of the Cause, The Cellar, Breath* and *In the Cold*.³ The subtitle of *The Cellar* [*Der Keller*] is *Eine Entziehung, Une retraite* in French, and strangely translated into English as *An Escape*, which is not quite accurate. *Entziehung* is the same word as the one Heidegger uses about Being, which is translated as withdrawal. When he was fifteen, Bernhard left school and became an apprentice in a grocery store in the poorest area of Salzburg. He called this his *retreat*.

> [O]ne day as I was walking to school – a walk which took me along the Reichenhaller Strasse – I decided not to go to the grammar school but to go to the labour exchange instead. The labour exchange sent me that very morning to Podlaha's grocery store on the Scherzhauserfeld Project, where I began a three-year apprenticeship without saying a word about it to my family. I was now fifteen years old. (2011b: 141)

Bernhard presents this *Entziehung* as a move '*in the opposite direction*' (2011a: 145). 'I did not just want to go in a *different* direction – it had to be the *opposite* direction, a compromise being no longer possible' (2011a: 150). And again: 'that morning I did an about-turn and ran for dear life in the direction of Mülln and Lehen. I ran faster and faster, leaving the whole deadly routine of recent years behind me, leaving absolutely everything behind me, once and for all' (2011a: 153).

These three turns to the negative have oriented my intellectual life for a long time: *desœuvrement*, or 'unworking' in Blanchot, 'nothingness' in Grothendieck, and 'contradictory negativity' in Bernhard. Or, to use other names: neutrality, nihilisation, dialectics. I would have liked to expose here the tension between these tensions, making three different versions of the retreat emerge in conflict and unity with one another: sending words without a face, stopping conceptual activity and transforming oneself into someone else, into the very opposite of oneself – for instance, transforming a writer into a grocer's apprentice.

I would have liked to tell you how much I hoped I would be able to withdraw from my own ideas. Will I one day be able to withdraw? To cease writing? To do my about-turn? Will I find my way of retracing the retreat, just like my three heroic figures?

Why am I unable to do what I initially intended to do?

[W]hat would I do, what could I do, all day long, I mean between the bell for waking and the bell for sleep? [Pause.] Simply gaze before me with compressed lips. [Long pause while she does so. No more plucking.] Not another word as long as I drew breath, nothing to break the silence of this place (Beckett 1989: 23).

Blanchot's, Grothendieck's and Bernhard's retreats are voluntary ones. They all proceed from a decision, however difficult and painful. In order to make a difference, to invent, create or retrace the retreat, you have in a certain sense to decide it. In order to enter neutrality or burn your works, or become an apprentice in going the opposite way, you still have to want it. To be powerful enough to want it.

It is true that Blanchot makes a strong distinction between withdrawing and taking one's own life. The latter, he says, is a matter of will.

> He who kills himself says, 'I withdraw from the world, I will act no longer.' And yet this same person wants to make death an act; he wants to act supremely and absolutely. This illogical optimism which shines through voluntary death – this confidence that one will always be able to triumph in the end by disposing sovereignly of nothingness, by being the creator of one's own nothingness and by remaining able, in the very midst of the fall, to lift oneself to one's full height – this certitude affirms in the act of suicide the very thing suicide claims to deny. (1989: 102–3)

The contradiction that lies at the heart of suicide – 'you don't *want* to die, you cannot make of death an object of the will' (1989: 105) – is precisely what separates it from the writer's withdrawal. Withdrawal is apparently alien to any voluntary decision.

Yet, when Blanchot declares that he has no proper existence, he asks his readers to respect this absence as a *will*, in the dual sense of the term. Respect my will; don't take pictures of me; don't try to render me visible. Invisibility is my decision. In that sense, retreating is perhaps akin to this 'illogical optimism which shines through voluntary death – this confidence that one will always be able to triumph in the end by disposing sovereignly of nothingness' (1989: 103).

Grothendieck presents retreat as a political gesture. He declares that he does not see any interest in going on doing mathematical research if it doesn't address poverty, exploitation and injustice. To stop doing maths, as admirable and respectable as it is, is nevertheless an act of power.

Bernhard admits it: 'Two possibilities had been open to me, as I can still see clearly today: one was to kill myself – and I was not brave enough for that; the other was to quit the grammar school without further ado. I did not kill myself but got myself an apprenticeship. Life went on' (2011a: 146). 'I did not want to throw myself off the Mönschberg – I wanted to live', Bernhard writes. 'And so that morning I did an about-turn and ran for dear life in the direction of Mülln and Lehen' (2011a: 153).

I *wanted* to talk about all this. And then. . .

As I was preparing this paper, I felt my arm falling. I felt that someone or something in me *didn't want* any more. Didn't want to retreat. Couldn't retreat, couldn't want to retreat any longer.

I couldn't forget what I had learned while exploring the neuroscientific field, the domain of neuropatholologies in particular. All brain lesions, neurobiologists say, provoke to different degrees disturbances in the inductors of emotion, and the identities of neurological patients are characterised by disaffection or coolness. A bottomless absence. To the extent that every trauma induces disturbances within the core of the 'self', all post-traumatic changes of personality present such disaffection or desertion.

Such a disaffection appears as a non-voluntary retreat. So, I wonder if retreat can mean anything else but this unintentional indifference. Unconcern. Absence of care.

'Eliott [was] [. . .] thoroughly charming but emotionally contained [. . .] He was cool, detached, unperturbed even by potentially embarrassing discussion of personal events' (Damasio 1995: 34–5). *When he is confronted with images designed to provoke strong emotions – 'for instance, pictures of buildings collapsing in earthquakes, houses burning,*

people injured in gory accidents or about to drown in floods' (1995: 45) – *Eliott flatly declares that he does not feel anything. The images cause no reaction whatsoever.*

The emotional life of brain patients is extremely impoverished. Most striking is their cold-blooded manner of reasoning – a phenomenon that, according to neurologists, directly threatens their ability to *decide*, that is, to evaluate the different options in play when it comes to making a choice. Only the emotional apparatus makes it possible to lend weight to various solutions that call for a decision. If this apparatus remains mute, decisions become a matter of indifference: everything is just as good as everything else, so nothing is worth anything. The disturbance of cerebral auto-affection produces a sort of nihilism in the patient, an absolute indifference, a coolness that visibly annihilates all difference and all dimensionality.

The difference between brain patients and the three heroic figures of retreat I mentioned previously is abysmal.

The stroke suffered by this patient, whom I will call Mrs. T, produced extensive damage to the dorsal and medial regions of the frontal lobe in both hemispheres. She suddenly became motionless and speechless, and she would lie in bed with her eyes open but with a blank facial expression; I have often used the term 'neutral' to convey the equanimity – or absence – of such an expression.

After recovering the ability to speak, she was certain about not having felt anguished by the absence of communication. Nothing forced her not to speak her mind. Rather, as she recalled, 'I really had nothing to say.'

To my eyes Mrs. T had been unemotional. To her experience, all the while, it appears she had had no feelings (Damasio 1995: 72–3).

No less dramatic than the oblivion that anosognosic patients have regarding their sick limbs is the lack of concern they show for their overall situation, the lack of emotion they exhibit, the lack of feeling they report when questioned about it. The news that there was a major stroke . . . is usually received with equanimity, sometimes with gallows humor, but never with anguish or sadness, tears or anger, despair or panic (Damasio 1995: 64).

The only authentic retreat is the one that is totally deprived of authenticity, that is, of any relationship to will. The only possible retreat is the non-conscious one.

On many occasions, Antonio Damasio compares the disorientation of his patients to that of Winnie in Beckett's *Happy Days*. She is the incarnation of *wakefulness without consciousness* (Damasio 2000: 90–2). 'Patients with some neurological conditions [. . .] are awake and yet lack what core consciousness would have added to their thought process: images of knowing centered on a self' (2000: 90). The theatre of absence is the privileged expression of affective impoverishment and destructive metamorphosis. Its rhetoric comprises figures of interruption, pauses, caesuras – the blank spaces that emerge when the network of connections is shredded or when the circulation of energy is paralysed.

I wish I could have told you about Heidegger, about Derrida, Blanchot, Grothendieck and Bernard. I wish I were able to talk about difference. The way in which difference helps retrace the retreat and prevent its redoubling to equate pure failure.

But indifference suddenly fell upon me, from the other side of my retreat, the non-different one, the neurobiological one. Indifference appeared to me as the contemporary form of retreat, a retreat which is undecided, unvoluntary, non-chosen. A retreat within coolness and unconcern. A retreat indifferent to itself. It also appeared to me that such an indifference is not proper to brain patients only, but that we all share it, in one way or another.

We have always already involuntarily retreated into indifference, our own and the indifference in which we are held. Indifference to ourselves is our strange answer to the world's indifference to us.

Once upon a time, there were famous retired people like Blanchot, Grothendieck or Bernard. There were famous thinkers of the withdrawal of being and of the end of metaphysics. There were famous thinkers of the retreat of metaphor and of the poetry to come, and of the difference a little trace can make.

I wish I could still believe in the trace, and go in the opposite direction; I wish I could still invent something out of the disappearance of proper and figurative meaning. . . But all this has already sunk in oblivion.

Jimmie suffers from Korsakov's syndrome, which entails a profound and irreversible loss of memory. This pathology is sometimes also called 'transient global amnesia' (TGA). Jimmie 'both was and wasn't aware of this deep, tragic loss in himself, of himself' (Sacks 1998: 35). He had the very strong feeling of 'something missing' but did not know what precisely it was and, for this reason, displayed a strange and profound indifference to his own 'disappearance' ('"Are you miserable?" – "I can't say that I am." "Do you enjoy life?" – "I can't say I do. . ."' [1998: 36]). At a certain point, Sacks wondered whether it would be valid to conclude that Jimmie had lost his soul: 'was it possible that he had really been "desouled" by a disease?' (1998: 37).

Notes

1 Malabou originally prepared this chapter as a lecture delivered in 2012 at the Banff Research in Culture (BRiC). Imre Szeman's introduction to Malabou's BRiC lecture appeared as follows: 'In this talk, Malabou takes the significance of the concept of "retreat" and the theoretical operations it performs head on, by probing what retreat and withdrawal tells us about our ontological and epistemological condition. The performance of these words is significant to their meaning: by telling us what she was planning, intending or hoping to do, Malabou reveals her own ideas about retreat as she retreats from them, making them available to us even as she refuses to affirm them, or does so only with suspicion at her motives. And as she interrogates the metaphysics of retreat, we are reminded repeatedly of the significance of the physical and neurobiological in the philosophical, an area of research in which Malabou has played a critical framing role, and which is represented here in the form of italicised asides (from A. R. Luria and Antonio Damasio, among others). The double voice of Malabou's talk both repeats and challenges the double character of retreat, while Malabou's own struggle with retreat alerts us to to the difficulty of thinking – and performing – it. Malabou's drift towards indifference is a productive ruse that challenges the reader to think the Being of philosophy alongside the very different Being of the brain' – Editor.
2 This text also appears in Jacques Derrida's reading and translation of Heidegger's *Der Satz vom Grund* in *Margins of Philosophy* (Derrida 1982: 226, n. 29).
3 In English, these five separate volumes appear in a single volume entitled *Gathering Evidence* (2011) – Editor.

22

Plasticity and Elasticity in Freud's
Beyond the Pleasure Principle

If there is anything beyond the pleasure principle, it can only be a certain time. 'A certain time' means first of all a particular moment. If there is anything beyond the pleasure principle, it can only be a certain moment of time. 'A certain time' also means a determined category of time. If there is anything beyond the pleasure principle, it can only be a certain category or concept of time.

The moment of time that Freud is looking for beyond the pleasure principle appears to be the very first, the earliest and most originary moment. This moment precedes the emergence of life, or of what Freud calls the living substance. Consequently, it precedes also the emergence of death. We must not forget that 'death is a *late* acquisition' of organisms (*SE* XVIII: 47). The very first moment is not the beginning but comes just before the beginning of life and death. It is the last stage of matter before it becomes animate. The very first moment is the last moment of inorganic matter.

The concept of time that Freud is looking for beyond the pleasure principle thus coincides with the notion of a pre-organic temporality, which appears as a post-organic temporality as well. If every living being departs from that age of inorganic matter, it returns to it when it dies. 'In this way the first instinct came into being: the instinct to return to the inanimate state' (*SE* XVIII: 38). Inorganic matter is both past and future. It is both the past and future of life and death.

This pre- and post-organic temporality is structured by the dual rhythm of life drives and death drive. 'One group of instincts', Freud writes in chapter 5, 'rushes forward' inorganic matter towards life (*SE* XVIII: 41). The other group seeks '*to restore an earlier state of things* which the living entity has [. . .] abandon[ed]' (*SE* XVIII: 36). They seek to return to inanimate matter. This 'earlier state of things'

> must be an *old* state of things, an initial state from which the living entity has at one time or other departed and to which it is striving to return [. . .] If we

are to take as a truth that knows no exception that everything living dies for *internal* reasons – becomes inorganic once again – then we shall be compelled to say that '*the aim of all life is death*' and, looking backwards, that '*inanimate things existed before living ones*'. (*SE* XVIII: 38)

The time of materiality would then characterise for Freud the temporal mode of being of the non-living and the non-dying, which in a way surrounds the pleasure principle and goes beyond it as, again, its past and its future, its before and its after. There would thus be something more primitive, more elementary than the pleasure principle, which would shake its mastery. The time of materiality would be prior to the time of pleasure.

How can that be? Freud reminds us, at the very beginning of the text, the first paragraph of chapter 1, that

[i]n the theory of psycho-analysis we have no hesitation in assuming that the course taken by mental events is automatically regulated by the pleasure principle. We believe, that is to say, that the course of [. . .] events is invariably set in motion by an unpleasurable tension [*unlustvolle Spannung*], and that it takes a direction such that its final outcome coincides with a lowering of that tension – that is, with an avoidance of unpleasure or a production of pleasure. (*SE* XVIII: 7)

The psychic apparatus seeks to maintain its quantity of excitation at a level as low, or at least as constant, as possible. This regulation of psychic tension is said to be the fundamental law of the psyche. In this sense, it seems that we are not allowed to speak of a 'beyond' of the pleasure principle.

At the same time, Freud admits that one objection to the mastery of the pleasure principle has to be taken seriously: an objection concerning the existence of unpleasant traumatic experiences that may be caused by an external threat or danger. Such experiences would be irreducible to the pleasure principle. Freud writes, 'A condition has long been known and described which occurs after severe mechanical concussions, railway disasters and other accidents involving a risk to life; it has been given the name of "traumatic neurosis"' (*SE* XVIII: 12). What threatens the mastery of the pleasure principle in such neuroses is the compulsion to repeat. The time of materiality is the time of repetition.

In traumatic neuroses, the accident and the situation of fright tend to repeat themselves mostly in dreams. 'Now dreams occurring in traumatic neuroses have the characteristic of repeatedly bringing the patient back into the situation of his accident, a situation from which he wakes up in another fright' (*SE* XVIII: 13). These dreams no longer bring back the hallucinatory satisfaction of desire; they reproduce the traumatic situation.

A dream that reproduces a situation of violent unpleasure clearly escapes the pleasure principle. 'We may assume, rather', says Freud,

> that dreams are here helping to carry out another task, which must be accomplished before the dominance of the pleasure principle can even begin [...] They thus afford us a view of a function of the mental apparatus which, though it does not contradict the pleasure principle, is nevertheless independent of it and seems to be more primitive than the purpose of gaining pleasure and avoiding unpleasure. (*SE* XVIII: 32)

Once again, this 'more primitive element', which takes place before the pleasure principle and goes beyond it, is characterised as the compulsion to repeat. '[I]f a compulsion to repeat *does* operate in the mind', Freud says,

> we should be glad to know something about it, to learn what function it corresponds to, under what conditions it can emerge [*hervortritt*] and what its relation is to the pleasure principle – to which, after all, we have hitherto ascribed dominance [*Herrschaft*] over the course of the processes of excitation in mental life. (*SE* XVIII: 23)

We may reduce the different characteristics of this compulsion to one, which is underscored all through the text: what goes beyond always tends to come back. Such is the time of inorganic materiality. In *Beyond the Pleasure Principle*, Freud articulates the first and to my knowledge a unique concept of time in all Western thought in which the very notions of origin and end, of past, present and future, are merely referred to inorganic matter. The temporality of the soul, the temporality of finitude, the temporality of existence, life and death themselves would be derived only from this primitive material time. They would definitely be secondary. What goes beyond and what comes back through the compulsion to repeat is not the threat of death, not the image of endangered life, not the situation of a being-towards-death faced with her fragility. Such situations are not irreducible to pleasure. Freud would certainly have considered that the existential analysis developed in *Being and Time* would perhaps be able to supersede metaphysics, but not pleasure. What goes beyond the pleasure principle as the originary temporality is not the temporality of Dasein but the pure neutrality of inorganic matter. By pure neutrality, I mean a state of being which is neither life nor death but their very similarity.

The question I would like to address here is whether Freud succeeds in bringing to light the specific form of this material time. Does this form resist the pleasure principle, or is it still, despite Freud's insistence, subordinated to it? Is there eventually anything beyond the pleasure principle, or is matter, whatever its form, always dominated by it?

To develop these issues, I will examine Freud's concept of plasticity, which characterises the relationship between matter and form in psychic life. I will show that this concept is constantly threatened by another, the concept of elasticity, which is apparently close to it but functions in reality as its opposite. Another version of the previously asked question – is there finally anything beyond the pleasure principle? – might then be: is the time of materiality plastic or elastic?

I

Let us first point out two distinguishing features of the Freudian concept of plasticity. First of all, plasticity characterises for Freud the fact that psychic life is indestructible. Second, plasticity designates the fluidity of the libido. We will see that these two meanings are strongly linked with one another.

In *Thoughts for the Times on War and Death*, Freud states that, in the development of the mind,

> every earlier stage of development persists alongside the later stage which has arisen from it; here succession also involves co-existence, although it is to the same materials that the whole series of transformations has applied. The earlier mental stage may not have manifested itself for years, but none the less it is so far present that it may at any time again become the mode of expression of the forces in the mind, and indeed the only one, as though all later developments had been annulled or undone. This extraordinary plasticity of mental developments is not unrestricted as regards direction; it may be described as a special capacity for involution – for regression – since it may well happen that a later and higher state of development, once abandoned, cannot be reached again. But the primitive stages can always be re-established; the primitive mind is, in the fullest meaning of the word, imperishable. (*SE* XIV: 285–6)

The 'extraordinary plasticity of mental developments' is thus linked with the permanence of the form. Once formed, the psychic matter cannot go back to its previous state. We must remember that 'plasticity' generally describes the nature of that which is plastic, being at once capable of receiving and of giving form. The psyche is plastic to the extent that it can receive the imprint and impose this earlier form upon the most recent developments.

But we know that plasticity also means the power to annihilate form. 'Plastic' is the name of an explosive material. Plasticity may be used to describe the crystallisation of form as well as the destruction of all form (as suggested by the term *plastic explosive* for a bomb). This destructive meaning of plasticity is also present in Freud's characterisation of psychic life. Paradoxically, the permanence of form and the impossibility of forgetting appear to be specific means of destruction of this same form. If it is true that a conservative instinct exists in the psyche that tends to restore an earlier state of things, that is, the inorganic passivity of matter before it came to life, then the status of the plasticity of psychic life is properly undecidable. The impossibility of erasure or disappearance in mental life expresses equally the liveliness of the trace as well as the inertia proper to the death drive. That is why this liveliness is also the mask of mental disease. 'What are called mental diseases inevitably produce an impression in the layman that intellectual and mental life have been destroyed. In reality, the destruction only applies to later acquisitions and developments. The essence of mental disease lies in a return to earlier states of affective life and functioning' (*SE* XIV: 286).

The impossibility of oblivion coincides with the inability to change, with the tendency to restore an earlier state of things, and with the deadly mechanism of the compulsion to repeat. We remember this passage from *Beyond the Pleasure Principle*, in which Freud declares:

> The elementary living entity would from its very beginning have had no wish to change; if conditions remained the same, it would do no more than constantly repeat the same course of life [. . .] Every modification which is thus imposed upon the course of the organism's life is accepted by the conservative organic instincts and stored up for further repetition. Those instincts are therefore bound to give a deceptive appearance of being forces tending towards change and progress, whilst in fact they are merely seeking to reach an ancient goal by paths alike old and new. (*SE* XVIII: 38)

To say that the primitive mind is imperishable means that the originary form of the psyche both resists death and is the very expression of death. Preservation is thus the mark of vitality as well as the characteristic of inorganic passivity. The 'extraordinary plasticity of mental developments' thus suspends the psyche between life and death, between the emergence and the destruction of form.

But what is the form of this in-between state itself? What is the form of this matter? Perhaps Freud seeks to answer this question throughout his work. In *Civilization and its Discontents*, he shows that all possible comparisons between the psyche and other cases of development are faulty. The plasticity of mental life is first compared with the past of the city of Rome.

> [L]et us, by a flight of imagination, suppose that Rome is not a human habitation but a psychical entity with a similarly long and copious past – an entity,

that is to say, in which nothing that has once come into existence will have passed away and all the earlier phases of development continue to exist alongside the latest one. (*SE* XXI: 70)

But this comparison is not satisfactory. 'There is clearly no point in spinning our phantasy any further', Freud goes on, 'for it leads to things that are unimaginable and even absurd. If we want to represent historical sequence in spatial terms we can only do it by juxtaposition in space: the same space cannot have two different contents. Our attempt seems to be an idle game' (*SE* XXI: 70–1).

The time of materiality, between life and death, cannot be represented in 'spatial terms'. The same thing occurs with the comparison of the plasticity of mental life with the plasticity of 'the body of an animal or a human being'. 'But here, too', says Freud,

> we find the same thing. The earlier phases of development are in no sense still preserved; they have been absorbed into the later phases for which they have supplied the material. The embryo cannot be discovered in the adult. The thymus gland of childhood is replaced after puberty by connective tissue, but is no longer present itself; in the marrow-bones of the grown man I can, it is true, trace the outline of the child's bone, but it itself has disappeared, having lengthened and thickened until it has attained its definitive form. The fact remains that only in the mind is such a preservation of all the earlier stages alongside of the final form possible, and that we are not in a position to represent this phenomenon in pictorial terms. (*SE* XXI: 19–20)

The time of materiality, between life and death, cannot be represented in 'pictorial terms'. Organic life strangely suffers from the same defect as architecture: space is the privileged metaphor for its development. But the plasticity of mental life implies an unpicturable state of things in which emergence and preservation, life and inertia, vitality and passivity coincide in time – not in space. This simultaneity between the two meanings of plasticity – the creation of form and the destruction of form – is the main characteristic of the time of materiality that goes beyond the pleasure principle.

Is there a way to set up a proper representative model for this temporality? If pictorial representation is not satisfactory, can we think of another kind of representation, that is, of form? And again, what is the form of the simultaneity of life and death? It is clear that Freud is looking for a kind of form that would be neither architectural nor organic. And it is also clear that he fails on this point.

In *Beyond the Pleasure Principle*, Freud invokes Hering's theory:

PLASTICITY AND ELASTICITY IN *BEYOND THE PLEASURE PRINCIPLE*

> According to E. Hering's theory, two kinds of processes are constantly at work in living substance, operating in contrary directions, one constructive or assimilatory and the other destructive or dissimilatory. May we venture to recognize in these two directions taken by the vital processes the activity of our two instinctual impulses, the life instincts and the death instincts? (*SE* XVIII: 49)

Eros, or the life drive, creates forms. The death drive destroys them. Life drives and death drive are two plastic tendencies that coincide in time. But Freud does not succeed in bringing to light the actual form of this temporal and material coincidence. He fails because he is led insidiously to dissociate this simultaneity. At the very moment when he defines the plasticity of mental life as a coexistence of life and death, as an undecidable state between life and death, he introduces a distinction between plasticity and elasticity that breaches this undecidability or this coexistence.

If we read *Beyond the Pleasure Principle* carefully, we discover that only the life drives are eventually said to be plastic. The death drive is 'elastic'. The destructive tendency, the compulsion to repeat, and the restoration of an earlier state of things are eventually driven out of the field of plasticity.

Freud never uses the words 'plastic' or 'plasticity' to characterise the work of the death drive. In *Beyond the Pleasure Principle*, the death drive is said to be 'a kind of organic elasticity, or, to put it in another way, the expression of the inertia inherent in organic life' (*SE* XVIII: 36). An elastic material is able to return to its initial form after undergoing a deformation. Elasticity is thus opposed to plasticity to the extent that a plastic material retains the imprint and thereby resists endless polymorphism. As we recall, what is said to be imperishable in psychic life is the permanence of form, not the absence of form. But instead of bringing into play the two opposite meanings of plasticity within the same phenomenon – the permanence of form – Freud sets to work, contradictorily to what he is looking for, a pure opposition between plasticity and elasticity. Instead of a fascinating face-to-face between creative plasticity and destructive plasticity, we have a disappointing contrast between plasticity and elasticity. Form means life. Death is without form. Life and death lose their similarity.

Freud states, however, that the profound meaning of the death drive is that death is immanent to life. It means that life forms its own destruction. That is why Freud affirms that 'the organism wishes to die only in its own fashion' (*SE* XVIII: 39). The organism fashions or forms its own death. There may be an elasticity of inorganic matter, but it is attained only as the result of a formative process: the process of repetition. But Freud does not succeed in characterising the proper – the temporal – form of the death drive. There is finally no plastic work of the death drive.

This impossibility of characterising the form of the death drive constitutes the main objection against its existence. Freud is well aware of that when he writes, '[t]he difficulty remains that psychoanalysis has not enabled us hitherto to point to any instincts [or drives] other than the libidinal ones'. For the moment, we can only prove the existence of erotic drives, that is, of life drives, which do not exceed the realm of the pleasure principle. He tries to find what he calls an 'example', that is to say, a form, of a death instinct in sadism. 'From the very first', he says, 'we recognized the presence of a sadistic component in the sexual instinct. As we know, it can make itself independent and can, in the form of a perversion, dominate an individual's entire sexual activity' (*SE* XVIII: 53, 53–4). The form of the sadistic instinct when it 'separates' from the life drives or when it 'has undergone no mitigation or intermixture' may be considered as the possible form of the death drive. 'If such an assumption as this is permissible, then we have met the demand that we should produce an example of a death instinct' (*SE* XVIII: 54).

However, Freud is clearly not satisfied with this 'example'. Sadism and masochism are still derived from love and proceed from the transformation of love into hatred. In this sense, they still belong to the pleasure principle and express 'the familiar ambivalence of love and hate in erotic life' (*SE* XVIII: 54). Sadism and masochism ultimately are and can only be forms of pleasure.

Because he introduces a non-plastic element in his definition of the plasticity of mental life – elasticity – Freud ruins the possibility of thinking what he precisely wishes to think: the plastic coincidence between creation and destruction of form. The characterisation of the death drive as 'elastic' deprives it of its plastic power and of its capacity to resist the pleasure principle. If we are not able to prove that the destruction of form has and is a form, if form is always on the side of Eros and of pleasure, it becomes impossible to prove that there is anything beyond the pleasure principle.

Let us turn to the second main signification of the Freudian concept of plasticity in order to clarify this difficulty: the fluidity of the libido. Here too appears the same inexplicable and insidious splitting of plasticity into plasticity and elasticity.

The libido is defined as an energy of strange material consistency. It is often presented as a substance that is neither liquid nor solid but something in between. 'Fluid' or, precisely, 'plastic' are terms often used by Freud to characterise this type of amazing materiality. The libido is sometimes compared to a river: '*die Libido wie ein Strom*' (*SE* VII: 170). At other times, Freud uses the metaphor of protoplasmic liquid, which is a little thicker than sheer water. These metaphors help us understand that a healthy libido has the power to fix and solidify itself in cathexis, but that it may easily give up previous objects to move to new ones.

The plasticity of the libido thus designates the double ability to cling to the object and to abandon it. Plasticity is a medium state between elasticity – the impossibility of preserving a form – and rigidity – the excess of attachment to a form. In *A Difficulty in the Path of Psychoanalysis*, Freud writes,

> For complete health it is essential that the libido should not lose this full mobility [*Beweglichkeit*]. As an illustration of this state of things we may think of an amoeba [*Protoplasmatierchen*], whose viscous substance [*zählflüssige Substanz*] puts out pseudopodia, elongations into which the substance of the body extends but which can be retracted at any time so that the form [*die Form*] of the protoplasmic mass is restored [*wieder hergestellt wird*]. (*SE* XVII: 139)

Again, a healthy libido has to situate itself between two non-plastic excesses: 'adhesiveness [*Klebrigkeit*], ability to fixation [*Fähigkeit zur Fixierung*]', on the one hand, and elasticity on the other.

Both adhesiveness and elasticity constitute major obstacles to therapy. The first is encountered in the Wolf Man's case. Freud says,

> Any position of the libido which he had once taken up was obstinately defended by him from fear of what he would lose by giving it up and from distrust of the probability of a complete substitute being afforded by the new position that was in view. This is an important and fundamental psychological peculiarity, which I have described in my *Three Essays on the Theory of Sexuality* (1905) as a susceptibility to 'fixation'. (*SE* XVII: 115)

Freud evokes the second case, concerning the elasticity of the libido, in *Analysis Terminable and Interminable*, in which he concludes:

> The processes which the treatment sets in motion [in certain subjects] are so much slower than in other people because, apparently, they cannot make up their minds to detach libidinal cathexes from one object and displace them onto another, although we can discover no special reason for this cathectic loyalty. One meets with the opposite type of person, too, in whom the libido seems particularly mobile; it enters readily upon the new cathexes suggested by analysis, abandoning its former ones in exchange for them. The difference between the two types is comparable to the one felt by a sculptor, according to whether he works in hard stone or soft clay. Unfortunately, in this second type the results of analysis often turn out to be very impermanent: the new cathexes are soon given up once more, and we have an impression, not of having worked in clay, but of having written on water. In the words of the proverb, 'Soon got, soon gone'. (*SE* XXIII: 241)

It appears that plasticity can only characterise the good shape of the form, if I may say so. Plasticity means health, the ability to cling to a form without getting destroyed by it. As soon as the libido loses the right measure between attachment and detachment, it also loses its plasticity. Once again, there is no plastic work of negativity. Elasticity appears as the natural limit, or boundary, of plasticity.

Freud asserts that the degree of psychic plasticity varies from one individual to another and that we can't explain the origin of this variability. It depends on a 'psychical factor of unknown origin [. . .] pertinacity or susceptibility to fixations' (*SE* VII: 242). It is given by nature. Some individuals are plastic, and some others are not.

Another example of the natural elastic limits of plasticity is the problem of age. Freud writes,

> Great mobility or sluggishness of libidinal cathexes [. . .] are special characteristics which attach to many normal people [. . .] They are, as it were, like prime numbers, not further divisible. We only know one thing about them, and that is that mobility of the mental cathexes is a quality which shows striking diminution with the advance of age. This has given us one of the indications of the limits within which psycho-analytic treatment is effective. There are some people, however, who retain this mental plasticity far beyond the usual age-limit, and others who lose it very prematurely [. . .] So that in considering the conversion of psychical energy no less than of physical, we must make use of the concept of an *entropy*, which opposes the undoing of what has already occurred. (*SE* XVII: 116)

Entropy (*entropia* in Greek signifies the return to an original state) is clearly not plastic. Freud dissociates once again the unity of the concept of plasticity. In the end, this concept can only mean the creation of form, the vitality and the suppleness of attachments – in other words, erotic activity. Loss of vitality, destruction of objects, repeated impossibility of loving are analysed in terms of tenacity, adhesiveness or elasticity. They never appear as negative plastic tendencies, as destructive forms. The intermediary state between life and death that Freud is looking for dissolves itself in what appears to be a poor opposition between life and death. Deprived of its form, the tendency to restore a previous state of things, to return to the very first moment, remains inexplicable. A mysterious natural elasticity contaminates the plasticity of life. We understand why, in *The Ego and the Id*, Freud can state in the end that '[t]he erotic instincts appear to be altogether more plastic [. . .] than the destructive instincts' (*SE* XIX: 44–5). The destructive instincts are not plastic at all.

We can perhaps explain Freud's failure to bring to light the form of material time by his inability to think of a plasticity that would go beyond the archetype of the plastic arts. We recall that Freud insists upon the impossibility of representing the plasticity of psychic life in spatial or pictorial terms. He nevertheless continues to describe plasticity in spatial and pictorial terms. The psychoanalyst is compared to a sculptor, the patient to a plastic material. In other texts, the libido is compared to a painting ink. The figures of sadism and masochism come from literature. The understanding of plasticity as an aesthetic category remains pregnant throughout Freud's work. Instead of finding a non-artistic kind of form, a non-creative form, a non-picturable one – which would be the form of the destruction of all forms – Freud turns to another spatial model, a spatial non-plastic model: elasticity. We can represent the work of elasticity – but not the contradictory work of plasticity – in space. The plastic materiality of time and the plastic metaphor of this materiality remain to be found.

At the end of *Beyond the Pleasure Principle*, Freud shows that the compulsion to repeat is a tendency that binds the excess of energy threatening the psyche. In the last chapter, we are told that this activity of binding does not finally oppose the pleasure principle. On the contrary, it depends on it. Binding can cause displeasure, says Freud, but this does not imply the suspension of the pleasure principle (*SE* XVIII: 62). It rather occurs 'in its service'. Because binding prepares the work of the pleasure principle, it opens the way for it. '[B]inding is a preparatory act which introduces and assures [*sichert*] the dominance of the pleasure principle.' Binding is an operation which transforms the free traumatic energy into a quiescent energy. It gives the elastic destructive energy a form, the form of Eros. In this sense, the 'transformation [the transformation of energy, binding] occurs on *behalf* of the pleasure principle' (*SE* XVIII: 62). The operation of binding is also very close to an artistic practice. It consists in shaping, moulding the scattered energy to unify and gather it.

II

In conclusion, I would like to insist upon the ambiguity of the compulsion to repeat in Freud. On the one hand, it appears opposed to the pleasure principle but, for want of its own form, that is, for want of plasticity, it can only be tamed in the end by the good plasticity of pleasure.

As Derrida writes in 'To Speculate—On Freud', 'There is only pleasure which itself limits itself, only pain which itself limits itself' (1987: 401). There is no beyond of the pleasure principle, only pleasure which occurs twice: once in the form of mobile energy, secondly in its bound form. The repetition compulsion is that of pleasure. There is only pleasure binding itself. Elasticity binding itself.

23

Are There Still Traces? Memory and the Obsolescence of the Paradigm of Inscription

I

The most recent discoveries in contemporary neurobiology have revealed that no single memory centre exists in the brain where complete memories could be stored.[1] In their book *Memory: From Mind to Molecules*, Eric Kandel and Larry Squire write: '*Memory* does *not* exist in a *single* site or region of the central nervous system' (2008: 10). Memory occurs through a distributed economy of storage instead of being stocked in a single, localisable preservation site. There exist several memory systems, involving different parts of the brain, mainly the amygdala, the hippocampus, the cerebellum and the prefrontal cortex. It follows that memory itself is fragmented: scientists distinguish between declarative memory, episodic memory, semantic memory, procedural memory, to name only the best-known ones. The amygdala is involved in fear and traumatic memories. The hippocampus is associated with declarative and episodic memory as well as recognition memory. The cerebellum plays a role in processing procedural memories, such as the knowledge of piano playing. The prefrontal cortex is involved in remembering semantic tasks. All these memory systems work together and collaborate within what is now called the 'global neuronal workspace',[2] but they remain different in their specificity. Therefore, they can also be dissociated and function independently from each other. Brain diseases show the extreme consequences of such dissociations. Injuries to the hippocampus area, for example, leave the patient unable to process new declarative memories, even if they can still remember information and events that occurred prior to the wound or surgery.

Another striking fact is that memories are not encoded as images. They do not have any material presence in the brain, nor leave any mark on neural connections. They rather produce modifications of the forms of these connections. Repeated neuronal activity leads to a modification in size and volume of the connections. For a long time, memories were said to imprint

287

the connections, like a writing stylus on a wax tablet. Such a model has now become obsolete. The substitution of plasticity – change of form – for inscription and trace constitutes one of the fundamental shifts in the contemporary neurobiology of memory. Conceptualising the obsolescence of the writing metaphor has become one of the most urgent philosophical tasks.

Is such a shift sufficient to challenge the concept of trace, though? After all, why should we identify trace only with the written sign? Can't inscription itself be understood beyond writing? Can't there be plastic inscriptions? That is also a plasticity of trace and inscription themselves?

How are memories preserved? Eric Kandel has spent decades working on the synapse, the basic structure of the brain, and its role in controlling the flow of information through neural circuits needed to encode and store memories. Such a control first operates as a selection between memories that will be consolidated and classified long-term, and those that will be discriminated as short-term. Long-term memories, as we said, are not stored in just one part of the brain but are widely distributed and preserved throughout the brain as groups of neurones primed to fire together in the same pattern that created the original experience. Connections are said to be potentialised when frequently solicited, and depressed when seldom solicited. These modifications are made possible by neurotransmitters that allow communication among neurones and whose action is critical for developing new memories. Frequent neural activity leads to increased neurotransmitters in the synapses and more efficient synaptic connections. This is how memory consolidation occurs.

II

Again, why should such a consolidation process challenge or impact the concept of trace? There is absolutely no reason why we should reduce the trace to an inscription, and the inscription itself to a graphic mark. At this point, we should remember Jacques Derrida's 'grammatological' lesson. A trace is not necessarily 'graphic' in the usual sense of the term: '*The (pure) trace is differance*. It does not depend on any sensible plenitude, audible or visible, phonic or graphic' (Derrida 1997: 62). A trace can be a stain, a breath, or a form precisely. If differance is the 'being-imprinted of the imprint', it can also be 'the formation of form' (Derrida 1997: 63). A trace can, then, be considered plastic. Writing itself, Derrida pursues, should not be reduced to the act of writing, that is using letters in order to compose a sentence or a text. Writing can also mean '"to scratch," "to engrave," "to scribble," "to scrape," "to incise"' (1997: 123).

Nevertheless, Derrida's careful enlargement of the concept of writing, scratching, scribbling, scraping still presupposes an inscription, something that remains and breaks a path – a line on a sheet of paper, or on a wax tablet, a scratch on a rock, a road in a wild forest, some condensation on a surface:

> one should meditate upon all of the following together: writing as the possibility of the road and of difference, the history of writing and the history of the road, of the rupture, of the *via rupta*, of the path that is broken, beaten, *fracta*, of the space of reversibility and of repetition traced by the opening, the divergence from, and the violent spacing, of nature, of the natural, savage, salvage, forest. The *silva* is savage, the *via rupta* is written, discerned, and inscribed violently as difference, as form imposed on the *hylè*, in the forest, in wood as matter; it is difficult to imagine that access to the possibility of a road-map is not at the same time access to writing. (Derrida 1997: 107–8)

One of the major issues of deconstruction is that, while announcing the irreducibility of the trace to any determined material modality, it has never been able to extend the trace beyond the paradigm of inscription. Plasticity, in Derrida, remains dominated by such a paradigm. The formation of form is not the simple flip side of the being-imprinted of the imprint; it designates a dramatically different economy than that of the imprint. Something grammatology never accounted for.

III

Coming back to the brain: one might object that scientists still use the term 'engram' to designate the outcome of the process of consolidation of a memory. It is clear that the notion of 'engram' still belongs to the inscription lexicon. Nevertheless, a very puzzling paradox lies in its neurobiological definition: 'An engram [. . .] is a hypothetical biophysical or biochemical change in the neurons of the brain, hypothetical in the respect that no-one has ever actually seen, or even proved the existence of, such a construct.'[3] That nobody has ever 'seen' an engram means that, despite its name, an engram is not engrammed, so to speak.

It is difficult, if not impossible, to isolate a particular memory in the innumerable neural networks at work in the 'global neuronal work space'. Besides, the three processes of memory encoding, memory storage and memory retrieval are not operated by the same networks. Therefore, in the end, a stored memory and a retrieved memory are always unfaithful to the original.

All memories change the form of what is remembered. Again, this is not only a matter of writing and erasing; it is a matter of transvestment and neurobiological alternative facts.

I do believe that our era of 'post-truth' is linked to the disappearance of inscription. In an article titled 'Blame Derrida for Donald Trump', S. D. Kelly writes,

> The world is no longer logocentric, words no longer mean anything, and this is not Trump's fault. Trump is not to be held solely responsible for the fact that, when he is front of a crowd, or in a debate, or in an interview, telling it like it is, there is no longer an is. Our politicians make a practice of speaking words into the void and seeing what happens next. If the madness that follows the political rhetoric at a rally demonstrates the dismantling of society itself, don't blame the practitioners. Blame the theoreticians for a change. Blame Derrida. (Kelly 2016)

Such a conclusion is erroneous, I think. Donald Trump is not a deconstructionist, and post-truth is not a product of deconstruction. Contrary to what Kelly tends to think, deconstruction has faith in the trace; deconstruction has faith in the inscription. Post-truth can start when there are no more traces; post-truth does not belong to the graphic era. It is a post-deconstructive phenomenon.

IV

The paradigm of inscription is highly dependent upon the Freudian category of *Bahnung*, 'facilitation', as exposed in the *Project for a Scientific Psychology*. 'Facilitation' designates the opening of a path in the neural flesh, a breach that renders a passage easier. The opening of the path and its reiterative use facilitate the retrieval of memories. As Derrida explains, 'there would be two kinds of neurones' according to Freud: 'the permeable neurones (*phi*), which offer no resistance and thus retain no trace of impression [. . .] [and] other neurones (*psy*), which would oppose contact-barriers to the quantity of excitation, would thus retain the printed trace' (Derrida 1978: 201). These printed traces themselves can be rearranged, reinscribed elsewhere. This is the palimpsest principle, so important in the definition of the unconscious. In a letter to Fliess, Freud declared: 'As you know, I am working on the assumption that our psychic mechanism has come into being by a process of stratification; the material present in the form of memory-traces being subjected from time to time to a *rearrangement* in accordance with fresh circumstances to a *retranscription*' (qtd in Derrida 1978: 206). Such a transvestment, a displacement, does not impact the fact that memories, differently inscribed in different layers of the system, constitute an archive. Reinscription in Freud is the very condition of possibility of the archive. We know now not only that there are no *psy* neurones, but also that neuronal networks do not form a palimpsest or a *Wunderblock*, a mystic writing pad.

Neural materiality does not obey the archaeological principle. The different cortical layers of the brain do not constitute a multi-dimensional text in which a message is encrypted. Memories are not deposited in the depth of a palimpsest. Memories are abstractions, the result of chemical processes that sculpt the forms of the neurones but do not endow them with any iconic content.

This fact has dramatic consequences. Because they are processed by different memory systems, because they are not inscribed or archived anywhere, memories are fragile, alterable, changeable; they can also be false. False memories are recollections that feel real but are not based on actual experience. The great specialist of false memories, Dr Elizabeth Loftus, says that we need independent evidence to corroborate memories:

> The one take home message that I have tried to convey in my writings, and classes [. . .] is this: Just because someone tells you something with a lot of confidence and detail and emotion, it doesn't mean it actually happened. You need independent corroboration to know whether you're dealing with an authentic memory, or something that is a product of some other process. (qtd in Shaw 2016)

Just because we are absolutely confident, the fact that we remember something accurately does not mean it is true. We not only distort memories of events we have witnessed; we may also have completely false memories of events that never occurred at all. Such false memories are particularly likely to arise in certain contexts, such as (unintentionally) through the use of certain dubious psychotherapeutic techniques or (intentionally) in psychology experiments. There is currently no way to distinguish, in the absence of independent evidence, whether a particular memory is true or false. Even detailed and vivid memories held with an adamant conviction can be completely false. And neither is there convincing evidence to support the existence of the psychoanalytic concept of repression to help explain the emergence of false, disguised or distorted memories. Memory, to summarise, is highly malleable, to such a degree that truth based on recollection is highly challengeable. No inscription can guarantee the authenticity of a memory.

I was mentioning the phenomenon of false memories; I could also mention that of the trauma-erasing molecules. Neuroscientific research on the removal of unpleasant and traumatic memories is at a very early stage, although in recent years there has been significant progress in the understanding of the mechanisms of memory and their possible alterations. The main purpose of such practices is to give relief to those who have experienced or witnessed negative events (accidents, assaults, natural disasters, terrorist attacks) that have caused serious psychological consequences and, in severe cases, even led to post-traumatic stress disorder.

Here also, erasure isn't simply the erasure of a trace; it is not like wiping a board. The different processes involved in the erasing operation all pertain to plasticity insofar as they act on neural connections and neurotransmitters. When a protein synthesis inhibitor is given after retrieval, molecular and cellular mechanisms of reconsolidation are disrupted and long-term memories are significantly impaired on subsequent tests. Although this technique has only been used in animal models, it may be feasible for use in humans. Theoretically, patients could be brought into a clinical setting, presented with a stimulus that retrieves the fearful memory, given a drug, and the memory would be weakened. A reorganisation of neural networks would follow, allowing the neural architecture to reshape istelf.

V

The whole history of philosophy, even deconstruction, has never challenged the paradigm of inscription. Be it in Heideggerian or Derridean deconstruction, what was challenged and critically explored was essentially an order, an order of succession. The paradigm of the inscription of the idea in the soul has determined an order of priority, according to which the idea is prior to its inscription. The trace therefore is only a result, the consequence of this precedence. The act of imprinting comes first, and the trace appears as its outcome. For Derrida, more strongly perhaps than in Heidegger, the trace is older than that of which it is the trace. First comes the trace, then the presence, or the passage. Understood in this sense, the trace would always be originary. The past to which the trace refers is a past that never happened, a past that was never present. Yet the past remains as a trace, even if it is written under erasure. The inscription model remains pregnant, allowing the eternal return of interpretation, reading, infinite conversation. Even when Deleuze and Guattari challenge psychoanalysis in *A Thousand Plateaus*, they still do so in the name of the trace, contrasting Freud's psychic imprint with the multitude of animal traces scattered in snow. The trace never ceases to inscribe itself, even in the form of its erasure. It lasts, persists, as a ghost, indestructible. 'Long-term memory (family, race, society, or civilization) traces and translates, but what it translates continues to act in it, from a distance, off beat, in an "untimely" way, not instantaneously' (Deleuze and Guattari 1987: 16).

Neural memory processing, on the contrary, resists hermeneutics. Plasticity renders the trace illegible because there is no trace. This explains why, for example, psychoanalysts so often resist the possibility that there exists a cerebral unconscious. Such an unconscious dismisses all attempts at interpreting it. Experience plastically sculpts or fashions the brain and yet it does not inscribe it. This does not imply that psychoanalysis of the cerebral unconscious is impossible, but it definitely has to re-elaborate its main concepts and method.[4] Plasticity raises two issues at the same time: the first is a paradigm shift, the second is an ontological problem.

Plasticity not only designates a new modality of memorisation or healing; it also characterises the way the subject is excluded from these modalities themselves. Because of the way the brain and regeneration function, the possibility for a subject, be it individual or collective, to appropriate or reappropriate their own wounds or traumas, to constitute and read their own archive, finds itself profoundly and definitely challenged.

The recent success of 'speculative realism' in philosophy can be partly explained by the current demise of inscription. Contemporary realists, like Quentin Meillassoux in *After Finitude* (2009), also and rightly affirm the ontological impossibility of inscribing the world. What Meillassoux calls the 'real' is precisely what resists the human attempts to leave traces in or on it. The ecological crisis renders manifest such an incompatibility, as it shows the deep incompatibility between the earth and 'our' traces on the earth, the catastrophe of our 'imprints'. The earth, the world in general, the realists declare, is perfectly indifferent to the possibility of being thought, remembered, deciphered, read or interpreted.

Meillassoux redefines the very definition of what a 'fossil' is. The 'archefossil' refers to an event anterior to 'life as consciousness', this anteriority being characterised as 'fossil time':

- date of the origin of the universe (13.5 billion years ago)
- the date of the accretion of the earth (4.56 billion years ago)
- the date of the origin of life on earth (3.5 billion years ago)
- the date of the origin of humankind (*Homo habilis*, 2 million years ago) (Meillassoux 2009: 9)

The becoming obsolete of the trace opens a desert ontology, a void, which can be characterised as a space of non-response. The world does not respond to us as we thought it did, through traces, that is, through artefacts; the subject does not respond to itself as we thought it did, through traces, that is, through memories and history. Traumas, wounds, scars would just be formed and reformed in a continuous fluidity without leaving any trace anywhere. We would have to think of 'a world where humanity is absent; a world crammed with things and events that are not the correlates of any manifestation' (Meillassoux 2009: 26). The demise of the trace then opens a space of absolute opaqueness, which is also, paradoxically, of absolute transparence.

One will object that the brain – or the nervous system in general – does not exactly belong to such a space insofar as its appearance in evolution marks the emergence of life. Nevertheless, Daniel Lord Smail, in his book *On Deep History and the Brain*, expresses a different point of view. In the brain, he says, some modules are precisely 'like fossils', and remain unchangeable. 'Like fossils, modules were laid down in the strata of the brain a long time ago and preserved against the ravages of time' (2008: 139). Further:

> Some modules, like basic fears, urges, and other predispositions, are identical to those found in primate or mammalian brains and indeed derived from them. Other modules, like deep grammar, emerged more recently and are unique to humans. According to evolutionary psychologists, all have remained largely unchanged since the origin of the species some 140,000 years ago. (2008: 139)

What is 'deep history'? Let us recall the definition proposed by Edward Wilson, in his book *In Search of Nature*: 'Human behavior is seen as the product not just of recorded history, ten thousand years recent, but of deep history, the combined genetic and cultural changes that created humanity over hundreds of [thousands of] years' (1996: ix–x).

For Smail, deep history is inseparable from an archaeology of the brain, that is, a study of the brain that compares it to a geological formation. For Smail, deep history substitutes itself for prehistory. According to the usual view, history starts with the rise of civilisation, and departs from a 'buffer zone' between biological evolution and history proper – such a buffer zone is what precisely is called prehistory. If history must be understood, as Wilson suggests, as the originary intimate interaction between the genetic and the cultural, it would start at the beginning of hominisation, with no 'pre' zone.

Smail declares:

> To abandon prehistory [. . .] would be to postulate continuity between the biological descent of hominids and the 'ascent of civilization' of the abstract 'mankind' of humanistic historical writing. Prehistory is a buffer zone.

A deep history of humankind is any history that straddles this buffer zone, bundling the Paleolithic and the Neolithic together with the Postlithic – that is, with everything that has happened since the emergence of metal technology, writing and cities some 5,500 years ago. The result is a seamless narrative that acknowledges the full chronology of the human past. Although the themes of a deep history can coalesce around any number of narrative threads, the one I propose in this book centers on biology, brain, and behavior. (2008: 2–3)

The relationship between the three terms (biology, brain and behaviour) set up here – we notice that the brain is situated as a crossing point between the two others – is clearly an *epigenetic* approach. Epigenetics is a branch of molecular biology that studies the mechanisms that modify the function of genes by activating or deactivating them without altering the DNA sequence in the formation of the phenotype. Epigenetic modifications depend on two types of causes: *internal* and *structural* on the one hand, *environmental* on the other. First, it is a matter of the physical and chemical mechanisms described (RNA, nucleosome, methylation). Secondly, epigenetics also supplies genetic material with a means of reacting to the evolution of environmental conditions. The definition of phenotypical malleability proposed by the American biologist Mary Jane West-Eberhard is eloquent in this respect: it is a matter of the 'ability of an organism to react to an environmental input with a change in form, state, movement, or rate of activity' (2003: 34). Contemporary epigenetics reintroduces the development of the individual into the heart of evolution, opening a new theoretical space called 'evolutionary developmental biology' or 'evo-devo' (West-Eberhard 2003: 34).

The paradoxical situation of this 'archaeological', 'epigenetic', 'deep-historical' brain is that it is the incarnation – in the proper sense – of a very ancient memory, the bearer of old traces, that is, of arche-inscriptions. At the same time, and this is what interests me, to the extent that those inscriptions *cannot be made conscious*, because they are biological, they cancel themselves as such. Memory is too deep to be written. It appears, I said to start with, in the way neural connections change form, develop or decrease.

In conclusion, I think we are confronted with the following alternative. Either we state, as contemporary realists do, that the disappearance of the trace means that everything is radically contingent, that nothing is stable, not even laws, not even rules, and that consequently truth itself is definitely aleatory, to such a degree that no memory can ever be trusted – the world can be considered a decorrelated desert from which something like subjectivity has disappeared and has only a delusionary presence. Or we affirm, and such is my contention, that the non-inscribable essence of memory determines a new structure of responsibility. A responsibility for the non-response. If subjectivity is just a window through which we see, if there is no possibility for us to turn on ourselves and decipher with certainty the past of our neural system, if there is no ground, no encrypted secret, no palimpsest, then we have to remain at the surface. The prefix *epi* in *epigenesis* and *epigenetics* precisely means 'at the surface' (epigenetics is said to operate at the surface of the DNA). We have to remain at the epicentre, in the middle, at the crossing point between the ground and the sky, with the task of producing an understanding of the impossibility of referring to any origin or even trace of the origin. Such an understanding would constitute this plastic responsibility, this capacity to respond to the absence of any preliminary question, to witness in the absence of witnesses. To go on reading and writing when there are no texts any more, no books even, nothing to read, but still a lot to say.

Notes

1 This essay is a prolongation of the discussion developed in 'Grammatology and Plasticity', the second chapter in *Changing Difference: The Feminine and the Question of Philosophy* (Malabou 2011a: 41–66).
2 See Mashour, Roelfsema, Changeux and Dehaene's recent article, 'Conscious Processing and the Global Neuronal Workspace Hypothesis' (2020).
3 See 'Memory encoding', in *The Human Memory,* online edition, September 2020.
4 A perspective hopefully opened by 'neuro-psychoanalysis'.

24

Phantom Limbs and Plasticity: Merleau-Ponty and Current Neurobiology

At the end of chapter 3 of *Phenomenology of Perception*, Merleau-Ponty summarises his recent research on the relationship between body and motricity. He declares: 'What we have discovered through the study of motricity is, in short, a new sense of the word "sense"' (2012: 148). By 'we', Merleau-Ponty means we phenomenologists. And by 'the study of motricity [*motricité*]', Merleau-Ponty means 'the neurobiological study of motricity'. This new meaning of the word 'meaning [*sens*]' clearly emerges from the crossing between a phenomenological and a biological approach to the body's spatiality, to the body's specific orientation in space and movement, in other words to 'being in the world'. When it comes to the body, to life, to the issue of being this living body in this world, it is of primary importance to give up what Merleau-Ponty calls 'intellectualist psychology' as well as 'idealist philosophy', and to stress the empirical biological dimension of our existential situation. He insists on the necessity of taking into account the most recent biological and neurobiological discoveries. This double approach constitutes as we know the singularity and uniqueness of the *Phenomenology of Perception*.

My first issue here is to interrogate what currently remains from this approach. It seems that with the most recent neurobiological discoveries concerning bodily motricity, we are also witnessing the emergence of a new meaning of the word 'meaning'. To what extent is this new meaning still indebted to Merleau-Ponty? To what extent is it not? At first sight, as is practically always the case, the confrontation between the domain of continental philosophy and that of strict neurobiology seems unbalanced. In the first part of this chapter, I will show that the current neurobiological meaning of the word 'meaning' appears to be poorer and much less differentiated than the one Merleau-Ponty was talking about. Again, for Merleau-Ponty, the novelty of the word 'meaning' results from the crossing of several approaches. It seems on the contrary that the neurobiological definition of the new meaning of the word 'meaning' currently reduces it to a mere empirical and objective set of data, deprived of any phenomenological or existential dimension.

The problem is of great importance, as the issues at stake here (body, motricity, being in the world), as Merleau-Ponty exposes in chapter 4 of part II entitled 'Others and the Human World', concern the intertwining between nature and the human world, between our biological existence and the way it projects itself into the community – this projection appearing to be the political translation of the bodily naturality. In fact, and this will be my second part, the discrepancy between two new meanings of the word 'meaning [*sens*]' is only apparent, and it will become clear that a genuine dialogue between Merleau-Ponty and current neurobiology is possible, which transforms Merleau-Ponty's bio-phenomenological conclusions in a most promising and interesting way.

I will situate the confrontation in the specific context of two neural pathologies that cause profound modifications of the body schema: first, phantom pains and phantom limbs; second, a pathology called 'anosognosia'. Anosognosia is a condition in which a person who suffers disability seems unaware of or denies the existence of his or her disability. This may include unawareness of quite dramatic impairments, such as blindness or paralysis.[1] This pathology only appears when the right hemisphere is injured, the patient then becoming unaware of the left side of his or her body.

Why these examples? First, because Merleau-Ponty announces the emergence of the new meaning of the word 'meaning' just after his analysis of such pathologies. Second, because the divergence between his approach and the current neurobiological one is quite manifest on these points.

This divergence concerns the way of interpreting the kind of negation or negativity involved in phantom pains and anosognosia. Merleau-Ponty considers phantom pains or anosognosia to be cases of what Freud calls 'psychic refusal' or disavowal. Phantom pains or phantom limbs would express the patient's refusal of her own mutilation. According to Merleau-Ponty, the subjects suffering from anosognosia would not say, 'I cannot see that my left side is paralysed', but 'I don't want to see that my left side is paralysed'. Because being in the world necessarily implies a double situation of the body, a biological one and an existential one, these pathologies have two sides: they are both objective medical facts and hermeneutical modes of being. The body, as Merleau-Ponty puts it, 'interprets itself' (2012: 151). It interprets itself as non-mutilated or as non-suffering, because it cannot regard itself other than as a significant whole despite its fragmentation:

> What refuses the mutilation of the deficiency in us is an I that is engaged in a certain physical and inter-human world, an I that continues and tends toward

> its world despite deficiencies or amputations that to this extent does not *de jure* recognize them. The refusal of the deficiency is but the reverse side of our inference in a world, the implicit negation of what runs counter to the natural movement that throws us into our tasks, our worries, our situation, and our familiar horizons. To have a phantom limb is to remain open to all of the actions of which the arm alone is capable and to stay within the practical field that one had prior to the mutilation. The body is the vehicle of being in the world, and, for a living being, having a body means being united with a definite milieu, merging with certain projects, and being perpetually engaged therein. (2012: 83–4)

Or:

> Here the phenomenon of the phantom limb is clarified through the phenomenon of anosognosia, which clearly demands a psychological explanation. Subjects who systematically ignore their right hand, and who rather offer their left hand when asked for their right, nevertheless speak of their paralyzed arm as a 'long and cold serpent', which excludes the hypothesis of a genuine anaesthesia and suggests the hypothesis of a refusal of the deficiency. (2012: 79)

The refusal must, then, be understood as an act of *Sinngebung*, meaning bestowing. The body maintains its integrity through negation. What hides behind the fear of having lost a part of oneself is the fear of being excluded from the realm of social and political life. Merleau-Ponty often describes this fear in the war-wounded who have lost an arm. His fear is that of being excluded from the human community, held back to childhood or primitivity, that is, to pre-political and pre historical life, a life in which movement, motor actions, are not yet signs. The brain, in particular the motor cortex, reorganises the body schema after the accident or the lesion in order to sustain the refusal of the deficiency and the need for the political meaning of being in the world.

The refusal is, then, both a neural and a phenomenological phenomenon. To differentiate it from the mere Freudian disavowal, Merleau-Ponty calls it 'a repression or an organic suppression [*refoulement organique*]' (2012: 80). Such 'terms, which are hardly Cartesian, force us to form the idea of an organic thought by which the relation between the "psychical" and the "physiological" could become conceivable' (2012: 80). The unity of the psychic and the physiological forms a shield against the loss of the historical meaning of being in the world. '[T]he refusal of the deficiency, which is an overall attitude of our existence, needs this highly specialized modality which we call a sensorimotor circuit in order to actualize itself' (2012: 83), which maintains the amputated limb in existence in order to 'maintain a void that the history of the subject will fill in' (2012: 88).

When we now turn towards the current neurobiological analysis of the same pathologies, we can only be struck by what appears almost as an incompatibility with Merleau-Ponty's approach. It seems that the new meaning of the word 'meaning', brought to light by such analyses, is purely and simply a loss of meaning. A loss of meaning or a regression compared to the rich and complex description of the phenomenon of being in the world. A loss of the political meaning that phantom limbs and anosognosia are, according to Merleau-Ponty, supposed to protect. Most neurologists currently consider these pathologies to be deprived of any psychological or existential signification. The 'inability to acknowledge disease in oneself', as Damasio characterises anosognosia in *Descartes' Error*, would not have any psychological causes:

> Imagine a victim of a major stroke, entirely paralyzed in the left side of the body, unable to move hand and arm, leg and foot, face half immobile, unable to stand or walk. And now imagine that same person oblivious to the entire problem, reporting that nothing is possibly the matter, answering the question, 'How do you feel?' with a sincere 'Fine' [. . .]
>
> Someone unacquainted with anosognosia might think that this 'denial' of illness is 'psychologically' motivated, that it is an adaptive reaction to the previous affliction. I can state with confidence that this is not the case. (1995: 62)

It is not the case: the inability to regard oneself as disabled would only be a non-dialectic kind of 'no', with only one meaning: the patient, for objective and medical reasons, would be absolutely unable to see that she is impaired. There is no refusal in such a fact, only a physical cognitive incapacity. 'The "denial" of illness results from the loss of a particular cognitive function. This loss of cognitive function depends on a particular brain system which can be damaged by stroke or by various neurological diseases' (Damasio 1995: 63).

Damasio's approach to phantom limbs and phantom pain is extremely rapid and manifests the same abstract negativity: 'patients with the phantom-limb condition may report that they feel their missing limb is still there, but they realize that it clearly is not' (1995: 154).

It seems that we are facing two opposite conceptions of pathological negativity. A first one, full of sense, of hermeneutical and political resources, that tends to establish the psychological meaning of this negativity. And a second one, hardwired and reductionist, that reduces negativity to a one-sided objective reaction. The dimensions of being in the world, being in the community, the effort to maintain social networks by means of 'organic repression', would have purely and simply disappeared.

In reality, as I announced at the beginning, a secret dialectical relationship links these two negativities: disavowal, on the one hand, and abstract factual negativity, on the other. This secret dialectical link organises every kind of encounter or confrontation between continental philosophy and neurobiology or cognitive psychology in general. We gradually discover that the neurobiological point of view concerning phantom limbs, phantom pains and anosognosia conceals not a reduction but a radicalisation of Merleau-Ponty's position, a deconstruction of certain rigid definitions of being in the world, and that it addresses a genuine political issue in the *Phenomenology of Perception*.

Before I expose this reversal, I will briefly develop two neurobiological arguments that achieve and accomplish in a way Damasio's reductionist position.

The first comes from V. S. Ramachandran, who, in his book *Phantoms in the Brain*, insists upon the impossibility of considering phantom pains and limbs or anosognosia to be psychic refusals or denials. These phenomena, he says, of course express the need to preserve the body schema's stability. In that sense, the 'Freudian defences (denials, repressions, confabulations. . .)' are useful to understand the nature of this need for stability. Rapidly, though, Ramachandran comes to the same conclusions as Damasio: first, Freud says that all of us use defence mechanisms every day of our lives. What, then, is the difference between a normal and a pathological defence mechanism or psychic refusal? 'One problem with the Freudian view is that it doesn't explain the difference in magnitude of psychological defence mechanisms between patients with anosognosia and what is seen in normal people' (Ramachandran and Blakeslee 1998: 131). It is true that Merleau-Ponty does not seem to offer an answer to this question.

Second, anosognosia only appears when the right hemisphere is impaired: 'The second problem with the Freudian view is that it doesn't explain the asymmetry of this syndrome [. . .] When people suffer damage to the left brain hemisphere, with paralysis on the body's right side, they almost never experience denial' (Ramachandran and Blakeslee 1998: 132). Merleau-Ponty does not seem to have an answer to this problem either.

In order to distinguish these pathologies from psychic refusals, Ramachandran proposes to characterise them as 'neglect syndromes', without genuine hermeneutical dimensions.

The other argument goes even further. It is developed by Shaun Gallagher in his book, *How the Body Shapes the Mind*. Focusing on phantom limbs and pain phenomena, Gallagher notices that Merleau-Ponty never takes into account the pathology called 'aplasia', that is, the existence of phantoms related to congenital absence of a limb or following early amputations (prior to age six).

PLASTICITY

> The psychological and neurological literature stretching from the early twentieth century to the early 1960s indicated that in cases of aplasia and in most cases of early amputation no phantoms develop. This was the established scientific doctrine and it was the view held in the overwhelming majority of studies up until the early 1960s. (Gallagher 2005: 87)

Merleau-Ponty is, of course, part of this list.

What is at stake? The refusal to consider the existence of aplasia is founded on the fact that most psychologists, including Merleau-Ponty himself, held that no body schema exists at birth. Even less can there be for them something like an innate body schema.

> The studies conducted by Simmel confirmed this view. There is no phantom in aplasia because the limb in question is never experienced, and thus never incorporated into a body schema or body image. This view of the phantom was also expressed by Merleau-Ponty in connection with its acceptance of the received doctrine that the body schema is a product of the development. (Gallagher 2005: 87)

We encounter 'plasticity' at this point. According to Merleau-Ponty, the body schema is plastic, and this plasticity has two characteristics. First, it means that the body schema forms itself under the influence of experience and development. It is supple and open to change (that is why it cannot be innate). Second, this plasticity is also to be understood as a compensatory power. When the body schema is impaired (as in the case of the missing limb, for example, but this works also for anosognosia), it reconstitutes its integrity and reforms itself, hence the vivid sensation of the missing limb experienced by the amputee.

Gallagher shows that taking early amputation or aplasia into account challenges this accepted vision of the body schema. The body schema, states Gallagher, is innate. 'The more recent data on aplasics indicate that aplasic phantoms do exist, and it is sometimes inferred on this basis that this is evidence for an innate body schema' (2005: 93). Aplasia would be the expression of a flaw in this innate body schema. The body schema is innate: Such a statement produces at first sight a terrible effect.

It seems to negate the definition of existence as being in the world, as a way to construct one's relationship with the world through experience, as this intertwining between biological, historical and political life. In other words, it seems to negate all plasticity.

Damasio, Ramachandran and Gallagher would then share the same position: no hermeneutics, no being in the world, no political meaning of the wounds, of the negativity involved in the refusal of one's own pathology. Just objective facts mounted on a deterministic vision of the body schema. Genetics against phenomenology.

It is precisely at this point, where everything seems to condemn neurobiology, to accuse it of reductionism, to regard it as a regression, that everything turns upside down and the situation reverses. This reversal concerns the status of plasticity. According to Merleau-Ponty, as I just said, plasticity means the ability of the body schema to reform itself and to compensate after wounds or impairments. Thanks to the neurobiological approach, such a conception of plasticity suddenly appears as something that has to be discussed and perhaps even deconstructed. What is compensation for Merleau-Ponty? What does 'compensate' mean here, in the pathological context? Plasticity sculpts our being in the world and our body schema in the following sense: 'for the normal person, the subject's intentions are immediately reflected in the perceptual field: they polarize it, put their stamp on it, or finally, effortlessly give birth there to a wave of significations" (Merleau-Ponty 2012: 133). When a pathology occurs, this first, primordial plasticity is disrupted, interrupted: 'For the patient, the perceptual field has lost this plasticity [. . .] [T]he world no longer suggests any significations to him and, reciprocally, the significations that he considers are no longer embodied in the given world' (2012: 133). We see that a second plasticity, the compensatory one, replaces the first, formative one, and tries to repair the loss. This is what occurs in phantom limbs and anosognosia cases. According to Merleau-Ponty, it is clear that this repairing plasticity is secondary. The fragmented body schema always comes after the originary one. Once reconstituted, it works much less well. The way in which it preserves the patient's being in the world is itself paralysed, incomplete. In other words, Merleau-Ponty considers compensatory plasticity to be itself a pathology:

> Illness, like childhood or like the 'primitive' state is a complete form of existence, and the procedures that it employs in order to replace the normal functions that have been destroyed are themselves pathological phenomena. The normal cannot be deduced from the pathological [. . .] through a mere change of sign. The substitutions must be understood as substitutions, as allusions to a fundamental function that they attempt to replace, but of which they do not give us the direct image. (2012: 110)

Again, we find the comparison between illness and childhood or primitiveness, and it appears that compensatory plasticity itself acts like a clumsy child. 'The substitutions must be understood as substitutions', as copies, shams, imitations: how far away from the deconstructive understanding of the substitute or of the supplement such a concept of substitution is!

Phantom limbs or anosognosia appear, then, to be defective substitutions for a definitively lost originary integrity. Merleau-Ponty says that these phenomena express the patient's incapacity to project himself into the future, his pathological attachment to the present time and tense.

> The phantom arm must be the same arm that was torn apart by shrapnel – whose visible envelope had at some point burned or decayed – and that now comes to haunt the present body by merging with it. The phantom limb is thus, like a repressed experience, a previous present that cannot commit to becoming past. (2012: 88)

Further: in traumatic experience, 'the subject still remains open to the same impossible future' (2012: 85). The patient suffering from anosognosia would then not only say, 'I don't want to see that my left arm is paralysed', but 'I won't ever see that it is. My refusal is permanent, a permanent present.'

This arguable vision of compensation and plasticity would be totally different if we were to consider substitutions not to be substitutions in the traditional sense, not as responses to a loss, not as secondary, but as originary instances, instances that would be as primordial, in their virtuality, as 'normal functions'. Compensation would then appear as a creative moment, as a source, a resource of 'first time', and not as a replica-making process. There would then be no hierarchy between the normal and the pathological, between normal and replacing or compensatory plasticity.

What if formation were always to be a compensation? What if creation and substitution, originary movement and reorganisation were to become synonymous? What if the body schema's 'remapping' were to be contemporary with its 'mapping'? These issues surprisingly arise from the neurobiological approach of compensation and plasticity.

What does Gallagher say exactly when he insists on the innate character of the body schema? Let's go back to aplasia and the phenomenon of phantom limbs in patients who have never had amputations. The phantom arm, for example, is linked with the impairment of the neural hand–mouth pattern:

> In the non-plastic case, hand–mouth coordination is an automatic movement [in foetal life]. In the case of aplasia the same movement pattern may be initiated, but without the hand, there is no tactile reinforcement of that experience. Lacking such reinforcement, it is possible that the neural matrix underlying the schema begins to reshape itself even *in utero*. Depending on individual differences and circumstances, the phantom may disappear or be reactivated, much as behavioural studies indicate. (2005: 98)

We clearly see here that, in the case of aplasia, phantom limbs are not phantoms of a lost limb, but phantoms of a phantom, phantoms of a compensation. In the innate body schema, there is already an attempt at replacing the hand, and the phantom is and will be the phantom of this attempt. This idea of an innate reformation, reorganisation or restructuration of a neural matrix is fascinating. The conception of an innate body schema does not amount, contrary to what I suggested earlier, to a conception of a non-plastic body schema. On the contrary, it introduces plasticity into innateness. Such an introduction obviously displaces the frontiers between bare life, understood here as foetal life, or even infantile life, pre-political life, and life understood as being in the world.

Gallagher uses Ramachandran's book *Phantoms in the Brain* as a basis to infer his conception of an originary neural reorganisation or reorganisibility. Ramachandran shows that most phantom pains proceed from neural restructurations. After a hand amputation, for example, some neural structures from the somato-sensorial cortex may invade other areas. In this case, the sensory fibres originating from the face invade the territory of the missing hand. 'Therefore, when I touched Tom's face, he also felt sensations in his phantom hand' (Ramachandran and Blakeslee 1998: 29). The phantom does not exist in the hand area:

> it exists in most central parts of the brain, where the remapping has occurred. To put it crudely, the phantom emerges not from the stump but from the face and jaws, because every time Tom smiles or moves his face and lips, the impulse activates the 'hand' area of his cortex, creating the illusion that the hand is still there [. . .] If so, the only way to get rid of the phantom would be to remove his jaw. (1998: 33)

> The implications are staggering. First and foremost, they suggest that brain maps can change, sometimes with astonishing rapidity. This finding flatly contradicts one of the most widely accepted dogmas in neurology – the fixed nature of connections in the adult human brain. (1998: 31)

Of course, in such cases reorganisation comes after birth and after amputation. Nevertheless, Gallagher declares, '[a]s several studies have shown, amputation may cause a disinhibition or unmasking of pre-existing synaptic connections that allow for the simultaneous transmission of information from the face to both the face and the hand area of the cortex' (2005: 99). One can thus acknowledge the originary and innate existence of compensation, virtually present in the body schema, that can be activated in foetal life in cases of aplasia, and in life in general after an amputation. Compensation works as a substitution mechanism, but this substitution is as old, in its possibility, as the normal function it is determined to substitute for. We may then consider that the originary formative plasticity and the compensatory plasticity are both, on equal footing, existential possibilities. Following this conception, we may also consider that phantom limbs and anosognosia are not exactly psychical refusals or disavowals, but the results of a remapping of ourselves that does not have much resemblance with a first mapping – a first mapping that in some cases never took place and never happened. A phantom replacing a phantom. We might even say that the body schema itself is a phantom. As Ramachandran puts it:

> The experiments I've discussed so far have helped us understand what is going on in the brains of patients with phantoms and given us hints as to how we might help alleviate their pain. But there is a deeper message here: *Your own body is a phantom*, one that your brain has temporarily constructed purely for convenience. (1998: 58)

The dialectical confrontation at work here between phenomenology and neuroscience, between two approaches of negativity, refusal and neglect, produces a final reversal. What seemed to be reductionist and regressive positions appear in the end to be deconstructive tools that radicalise the meaning of the substitute or supplement. There is no hierarchy between the two meanings of plasticity: formative and compensatory. The neurobiological approach helps us to understand substitution as an originary existential, and in this sense as an ontological, possibility. This is an example of how supple, thin and improbable the frontiers between ontology and biology are currently becoming – or perhaps always have been.

In *Phenomenology of Perception*, defending his idea of a culturally constructed body schema, Merleau-Ponty assimilates foetal life, neonate life and childhood itself to what he calls 'unformed' or 'amorphous' (that is, non-plastic) modes of living.

> If my first years are behind me like some unknown land, this is not through some fortuitous breakdown of memory or the lack of a complete exploration: there is nothing to be known in these unexplored lands. For example, nothing was perceived in intra-uterine life, and this is why there is nothing to remember. There was nothing but the sketch of a natural self and of a natural time. This anonymous life is merely the limit of the temporal dispersion that always threatens the historical point of view. (2012: 362)

We saw, with Gallagher in particular, how difficult, even impossible it was to consider the prenatal existence as an amorphous state of things, to consider the natural self to be non-historical. The idea of an innate plasticity, as well as the idea of a plastic innateness, challenges the distinction between nature and history. I will give two brief quotes. First, from Gallagher: 'In this context the concept of innateness is not a philosophical threat to the concept of experience' (2005: 171). Second, from Ramachandran: 'I mention these bizarre examples because they imply that phantom limbs emerge from a complex interplay of both genetic and experiential variables' (1998: 58). The idea of a historical organicity challenges all ideas of bare or pre-political life. What is originary in biopolitics is the substitutive and transposable character of our neural maps, that is, of our nature. Subjective identity is erasable and replaceable from the start. There could not be any community without the natural community that we are, from the beginning, forming with ourselves, with the different mapping of ourselves.

Note

1 *Anosognosia* was first named by neurologist Joseph Babinski in 1914, although relatively little has been discovered about the cause of the condition since its initial identification. The word comes from the Greek words *nósos* (disease) and *gnosis* (knowledge). In Greek, as in English, *an-* or *a-* is a negative prefix.

25

The Example of Plasticity

Tyler M. Williams: You are often presented as a philosopher 'of' neuroscience, or at least more generally a philosopher 'of' science, since your work is so devoted to bridging the historical gap that continental philosophers have maintained between the philosophical and the scientific. Plasticity provides you precisely such a bridge, as you elaborate in your many books, essays, lectures and interviews. Despite the fact that neuroplasticity takes up significant portions of your attention, the range of approaches to the concept of plasticity exhibited in *Plasticity: The Promise of Explosion* shows that it is erroneous to equate 'plasticity' solely with its neurological – or even its scientific – dimensions. Plasticity is, after all, as you say in *Plasticity at the Dusk of Writing*, a 'motor scheme' for a new era of philosophy. But this raises a question of *exemplarity*. How exactly do you situate 'plasticity' in your work? Is the brain an *example*, one example among others, of plasticity? Or is the exemplarity of neuroplasticity inseparable from plasticity?

Catherine Malabou: This is a very interesting and difficult question. First of all, no, I do not identify myself as a philosopher of science because philosophy of science is a specialisation I do not have. Plasticity only makes sense because of its plurality – of fields, of meanings, and of empirical occurrences. Regarding neuroscience, I would say that what I do is bring to light the philosophical impact of neuroscience, which is not the same thing as building a philosophy of neuroscience. For a long time, contemporary neuroscience and contemporary philosophy ignored each other and, as a result, the brain never became a philosophical object comparable to the mind, the spirit or the soul. What was important for me was to dig out the importance of the brain for understanding contemporary subjectivities, contemporary identities, selves, etc. It occurred to me that it was no longer possible to act as if the most recent research in neurology and the most recent definitions of the brain had no impact on our way of thinking – particularly in critical theory. But, of course, this does not mean that I define myself as a specialist in neuroscience.

Now, regarding your question about plasticity and how I situate it among its many meanings and empirical occurrences: one of my main tasks is to find a way between three main philosophical directions. These directions link directly with the philosophers that interest me most and have had the strongest influence on my thinking.

First of all, the partition between the transcendental and the empirical (Kant), which needs to be fluidified today, if not erased. My concept of plasticity does not act as a transcendental concept that would be exemplified by many empirical occurrences. Because it is itself plastic, that is, exposed to change both by external influences and internal modifications, plasticity is in a certain sense the exemplification of itself. Therefore, it cuts through the divide between the transcendental and the empirical.

The second direction is Hegel. Even though I characterise my own method as dialectical, I do not assimilate plasticity with what Hegel calls the pure movement of the concept. For Hegel, the transcendental and the empirical function together without any hierarchy, and this is what is so fascinating in his philosophy, but they are gathered in the end in the Absolute Idea, which is the logical translation of the Absolute Knowing as it appears in the *Phenomenology of Spirit*. 'Plasticity' may characterise a certain meaning of the absolute, that is dissolution, solitude (*Ab-solvenz*, absolutus), but not that of totality, exclusivity and infinity.

The third direction is deconstruction: Derrida. Even if strongly influenced by it, plasticity opposes the idea of the trace, of something ungraspable that constantly differs and defers from itself and escapes all *Setzung*, all position. Plasticity is a motor scheme that determines the obsolescence of the inscription paragraph, the end of writing, as I demonstrate in *Changing Difference*. Coming back to these three directions, I would say that I tried to keep them all while moving away from them at the same time. Plasticity organises a circulation between these three paths.

The brain acts as a metaphor for this methodological interaction. The brain is not one object among others. Its plasticity incarnates and manifests the concept of plasticity itself. That is why I use it as a model, a model of a network that gathers many logics at the same time. Reciprocally, plasticity acts as a metaphor for the brain, so that, in this interplay between plasticity and the brain, neither of them is really the proper sense or image of the other. It is this constant interplay that helps me circulate around and within the three philosophical directions I just mentioned.

THE EXAMPLE OF PLASTICITY

TMW: As you put it, this logic of exemplarity is indistinguishable from a metaphoricity. If something like the brain is not just the empirical example of a transcendental idea, does this mean that the very logic of exemplarity is itself plastic?

CM: The question for me is not a matter of exemplifying plasticity with different objects or phenomena. It is to show that plasticity designates the exemplarity itself, conceptually, so that, as I just mentioned, it makes the distinction between the transcendental and the empirical explode. The brain is plastic because, like plasticity, it functions by exemplifying and metaphorising itself. There is no possible subjective approach to the brain. Nobody feels their own brain, as I said in *What Should We Do With Our Brain?* The only possible personal approach to the brain is impersonal because it is mediated by technical imagery. We do not have a phenomenalisation of our brain outside the different examples, if I can put it that way, with which it manifests itself. This is what Bernard Stiegler would call the 'exorganisation' of the brain: the fact that it has no subjective presence outside its different projections. Like, for example, the capacity to play, to think, to move from one activity to another. These are what I call 'examples'. So, in a certain sense, yes, there is mirroring between the two exemplarities. The brain exhausts itself in its phenomena. It exists, of course, as an organ. But, critically speaking, it doesn't have an archepresence outside of its different exteriorisations.

TMW. Considering the brain's exorganisation, its availability as a phenomenon through metaphoricity and exemplarity, you have said before that plasticity is plastic. If plasticity is itself plastic, such that the concept of plasticity remains dynamic and open to future transformation, then this would mean that one always says more – and also less, too soon and too late – about plasticity than one intends. How should we understand this 'promise', to use Derridean language, at the heart of an understanding of plasticity?

CM: There are, of course, some common traits between plasticity and *différance*. In his essay 'Différance' in *Margins of Philosophy*, Derrida says that *différance* 'is' not, but is always erasing its own trace, thus constantly promising itself, being more and less than itself at the same time. The same could be said about plasticity. Nevertheless, at the end of this same essay, Derrida announces that *différance* will one day be replaced by something else, though such a replacement never occurred in Derrida's writing. On the contrary, this mobility – that is, this promise of being more than oneself – had become for *différance* a kind of fixity, a kind of permanence. Writing, or the trace, in Derrida, is paradoxically permanent, always acting in the same way. Plasticity, by contrast, is absolutely finite. I know that, very soon, plasticity will no longer be adequate. It functions at a certain moment of our culture; it is obvious that, for example, there are so many references in cellular biology to plasticity (of the genome, of vaccines, etc.). But at some point, another model, another paradigm, will replace it. For me, plasticity always promises more than itself but it is also constantly diminishing, if I may say so. It is witnessing its own obsolescence.

TMW: Is this diminution an essential aspect of the logic of plasticity, or is it the result of the epochal movement of a science that would technologise something to replace plasticity?

CM: I think it is both. We cannot make such a distinction; the logic of plasticity and the dynamics of epochality go together. Plasticity is diminishing because it is a fragile concept – and a concept of fragility. It does not have the force of big, massive concepts like the transcendental, etc. But epochality is also fragile; we can only speak of it in terms of finitude and transience. The diminution will happen on both sides.

TMW: Including the historical retrospect with which we read plasticity into texts and discourses that predate the rise of our current paradigms regarding plasticity?

CM: It may wake up or reanimate certain texts, it can shed light on certain contexts, it may help reread texts from the past in a certain way, it may remain helpful in the future, but it will certainly bear the mark of its finitude, yes.

TMW: Earlier, you identified Derrida as the third figure in the trilogy of your major influences, and you just explained the distance and proximity shared between plasticity and *différance*. Does this proximity and distancing bear upon the philosophical interventions that neuroscience allows for your work and the philosophical interventions that literature enables for Derrida? On a variety of occasions, Derrida remarked that his early career aspirations amounted to a search for the 'literary event'. Part of this search would include his aborted thesis project on the 'ideality of the literary object', but a pivotal part appears in his crucial pairing of Joycean-literary equivocity with Husserlian-phenomenological univocity. Derrida describes this 'desire to go in the direction of the literary event' as a search for the 'outside' of philosophy that works eccentrically within philosophy. Is your attention to neuroscience a type of recalibration of deconstruction's turn to literature, since you so often identify the biological sciences as a 'literary' frontier for/within philosophy, as an adventure to the outside of philosophy from within philosophy?

CM: There is a literary element in neuroscience and in plasticity, since they mirror each other. Plasticity is itself an old term; it is not a term I invented. It existed in language before I tried to make something out of it. So, I also play with language in this story. I play with the idea that, though it is an old term that had existed, for example, in Hegel or Goethe, no one had really conceptualised it and no one had really exploited its potential. I am interested in the fact that, all of a sudden, an old word can proliferate and become an event – and I would call that 'literary', even if it is not 'literary' in Derrida's sense. It is very important to me that I did not have to invent the concept but instead played with the resources of language.

I am doing the same right now with the concept of anarchy and anarchism, since everyone seems to have forgotten the meaning of these terms. I like it when an old word, an apparently banal and uninteresting word, appears as loaded with literary promise. And I would say that, in biology, the most interesting research is based on reactivating old possibilities inscribed in the living being (e.g. stem cells, or how the Pfizer vaccine [for Covid-19] reanimates something that is already inscribed within us, etc.). If there is something literary in neuroscience, neuroplasticity and the biological sciences in general today, it is that, contrary to popular belief, it is not so much to invent new technologies but rather to use new technologies to reactivate this potential and to make an event out of very ancient things.

I will also note that I was a bit disappointed by Derrida's turn to literature because I sometimes thought it was a way to avoid engaging with recent scientific and technological developments. As you know, Derrida affirms that literature has the right to say everything. The problem is that this affirmation allowed Derrida to say that something is contrary all the time; it allowed him to play this constant game with deconstruction: 'I never said that', 'I could have said the contrary', etc. I don't think literature is that. I don't think you can 'say everything' in literature, and constantly deny yourself. I think this appeal to 'everything' is a bit of an escape. So, why not try to situate literature at the heart of truth?

TMW: You use that famous quotation from Joyce's *A Portrait of the Artist as a Young Man* ('To live, to err, to fall, to triumph, to recreate life out of life') as an epigraph to your chapter, 'Philosophers, Biologists: Some More Effort if You Wish to Become Revolutionaries!' At the end of that quotation, you note that the biotechnologist J. Craig Venter inscribed this line into the genome of a synthetic microbe. I recall you mentioning Venter's bio-literary citation of Joyce on more than one occasion during one of your seminars at the University at Buffalo. In light of your remarks a moment ago on Derrida's tendency to turn to literature to avoid engagement with technoscientific discourses, can you explain the role that an 'event' such as Venter's citation plays in your understanding of plasticity?

CM: Recently, when dealing with epigenetics in particular, I wrote an article entitled 'One Life' in which I challenge the distinction between symbolic life and biological life. I discovered that the symbolic – for example, this sentence by Joyce; everything that deals with sense or meaning – cannot be separated from the heart of, let's say, the matter. To distinguish between two kinds of bodies is so frequent in philosophy. The most striking example is Deleuze's concept of the 'body without organs' – as if we would have two lives or two bodies. One purely 'existential' and the other purely 'organic', or, to speak like Agamben, a *bios* and a *zoe* – a qualified life and an obscure biological one. It does not work like that. Even in the most elementary cell, even in the most elementary organism, there is already something like a Joyce phrase inscribed in it. I mean, biology has an essential symbolic dimension: codes, letters, etc. Look at the names given to the Covid-19 variants today: Greek letters!

TMW: Though you are not known as a philosopher of literature, or as a literary theorist, literature features prominently in your work. The figures who most frequently appear in your work span from the early to late modernists, particularly writers such as Proust, Kafka, Beckett, Mann, Duras. In one sense, this presence of literature is unsurprising, since your elaboration of plasticity allows for a *material* revaluation of the *symbolic* tendencies in poststructuralist philosophy. And, after all, many poststructuralists demonstrate the 'literary' excesses within philosophical discourse. In another sense, though, this presence of literature in your work is harder, and thus more interesting, to account for because, even while you distance yourself from some of the symbolic tendencies in poststructuralism, you still marshal literature to your side.

If literature participates in your materialist/biological/scientific treatment of plasticity, then in your work the traditional boundaries that separate the scientific from the literary begin to falter. I would even argue that articulating these fault lines between 'science' and 'literature' comprises one of the major contributions of your thought. But this requires some elaboration, still on the topic of exemplarity. You will often use, for example, a Beckett play or a Kafka story to demonstrate a symptomatology of neurobiological trauma, but literature clearly works for you more conceptually than as a set of available examples to reiterate scientific conclusions. We have already discussed the exemplarity of neuroscience in your work, but how exactly do you position 'literature' within your thought?

CM: This is a very interesting question. Yes, literature is not for me one example among others. The problem of plasticity, ontologically speaking, is that it is a movement that defines itself as a priority of fashioning over being. Plasticity has to invent itself and never depends on pre-set or pre-defined principles. It has to become the forms that it creates, as it creates itself through these forms.

This is where literature intervenes for me. The kind of literary examples I use are all about the emergence of forms. Be it Kafka's metamorphoses or Duras's transformations, I always refer to the moment of the emergence of a form as an event. I think that plasticity and literature share this common destiny: they invent the form that they are. This at least resonates with another of my main philosophical problems, which is that two giants are competing with each other: being and life. It is very clear that, since Heidegger, being has occupied the foreground; in *Being and Time* he says that what is important is being and not life. But we see that life is reintroducing itself in philosophy through many doors. This interplay between being and life is crucial for me because it is precisely in this in-between that something like a form can emerge. I would say that the space of literature is precisely this in-between. It is not ontological or biological; it is in-between, just like Gregor Samsa's metamorphosis. It is from this space that the forming of an invention and the invention of a form can emerge.

I wouldn't read just any kind of literature. I am not sensitive to certain kinds of literature. For me, a text in which there is no logic of form would not be of interest. For example, I was rereading recently Claude Simon and forms emerge in every line – this is the kind of literature to which I am particularly sensitive.

TMW: This makes all the difference between treating literature as the staging of metamorphoses and conceptualising the literariness of literature as itself metamorphic.

CM: Exactly. This is why I do not agree at all with Deleuze's interpretation of Kafka's *Metamorphosis*. He says that this text is the phenomenology of the Oedipal triangle – father, mother, sister, who leave the monster (Gregor) behind. No, you cannot interpret *Metamorphosis* out of a pre-existing model like that. I think he totally misses the meaning of this text.

TMW: Along similar lines, I am curious about the relationship between the *rupture* of destructive plasticity and any perceivable *precedent* for such rupture. Across your work, from the various examples you are able to provide of the destructively plastic transformations in the subject, there appears to be a spectrum of the severity of this rupture. In *The New Wounded* and *Ontology of the Accident*, you provide examples of those who suffer traumatic brain injuries that completely transform the subject. The wound, in this sense, severs the pre-traumatic from the post-traumatic subject. Yet in other instances, this destruction appears to retain evidence of a trace. For example, in 'Is Retreat a Metaphor?' you cite Thomas Bernhard's impulsive decision to abandon his schooling and undertake a grocery-store apprenticeship in a notoriously dangerous part of Salzburg. It is true that Bernhard describes this change as an abrupt, spontaneous and unalterable 'about-turn' that annihilates a former life by adopting a new one, but this change is not – at least in the novel – a complete surprise. As the title of Bernhard's novel indicates (the German title of which – *Die Ursache* – is the same word Heidegger uses in 'The Question Concerning Technology' for *cause*), this rupture has a comprehensible precedent and articulating this precedent comprises the entirety of what in English bears the title *An Indication of the Cause*. How are we to understand this relationship between plasticity's destructive ruptures and its indicative traces?

CM: Freud says somewhere that when a crystal falls to the floor it breaks according to pre-existing lines of fracture. I don't think that's the case – at least not always. There was perhaps something in Bernhard's identity that was expecting such a change. It is a dialectical exchange, his transformation is dialectical and operates according to a kind of *Aufhebung*. At the same time, in *Breath*, the novel that comes after *The Cellar*, Bernhard explains that working in this cellar destroyed his health because he got tuberculosis there. So, the change narrated in *The Cellar* as something constructed appears as really destructive as well in the subsequent book. His 'U-turn' almost killed him in the end.

TMW: Are we to take this, then, as a distinction to be drawn between the plastic transformation itself and the hermeneutic with which this transformation gets assimilated as an analytic criteria? After all, Bernhard's epigraph to *The Cellar* comes from Montaigne: 'It is an irregular uncertain motion, perpetual, patternless and without aim'. In this sense, the destructive metamorphosis Bernhard describes at the end of *An Indication of the Cause* would produce in *The Cellar*, at the moment of rupture, the criteria by which to comprehend it.

CM: What is difficult in this story of destructive plasticity is the issue of the witness. Who can witness it? Most of the time, the subject of transformation is not really able to produce any kind of awareness. Great writers like Bernhard or Duras attempt to do so, but this awareness is always flickering. Let's take the case of Alzheimer's patients, for example. Some members of the family will say, 'It is always the same person. I know; I can recognise them' and others will say, 'No, they have become someone else'. I think that there is this problem of the witness in destructive plasticity and it resonates with what Lyotard says about the witness in many of his texts. Some truths cannot be expressed in any way other than via witnessing or testimony. But testimonies are never 'objective'. I think this is the problem with destructive plasticity: it cannot reflect on itself as self-consciousness would.

TMW: The plastic transformation and its correspondence to the transformation of the analytic criteria to make sense of that criteria also leads directly to the third major part of your work. We have already discussed the aesthetic and scientific dimensions of your philosophical work, but we have not yet discussed the political. The criteria by which we judge and commit ourselves to judgement (for example, according to what you call 'social selection') are not set teleologically in advance but are produced through the very process of transformation – this is a big part of how you challenge political orthodoxies in your work.

CM: Until now, I had never really produced any kind of political thinking outside of what I say about capitalism in *What Should We Do With Our Brain?*. Now, I am writing about anarchism because it seems to me, at my age and experience, and when I think about everything I have done, it seems like the meaning of plasticity is anarchism. That is, anarchism is the only political form that follows the same movement as the one you were describing: self-invention and the invention of the self. One of the main difficulties with plasticity is how to think the compatibility of plasticity with ethics. If everything is in constant transformation, how can we have anything like a value or something like justice? This is a problem that traditional, classical anarchists decided to take seriously: how, in the absence of any kind of pre-existing schema, of any kind of government (if 'government' means the difference between commanding and obeying, since every kind of government is based on that difference and dissymmetry), is something like that order, community, or coherent mode of management possible? If it can be demonstrated that it is possible to invent political forms that can be transformed, that don't have to be fixed but just have to adapt to reality, then we would be allowed to think plasticity – that is, transformation – as being compatible with community, with being-with-others. What is important for me is the extent to which we can live without being governed. I know this was Foucault's question in particular, but I think he did not go as far as he could have gone. In the end, something of the government always remains – like the government of the self. When there is no institutional government, we still have the government of the self. . .

TMW: In your essay 'Anarchism and Philosophy', you describe this movement at the ontological level – in defence of an anarchic ontology. This same logic, even though you do not articulate it as such, operates as the animating principle of your essay 'Whither Materialism?', where you use Althusser to demonstrate the illegitimate hierarchy in which principles of natural and social selection are typically rigidified. You show in that essay that there is a de-hierarchised way to understand natural and social selection, which you attribute to Althusser's 'materialism of the encounter'. Yet the implications of this materialist encounter seem to be precisely an anarchic ontology by another name.

CM: Regarding natural selection and social selection, remember that Nietzsche says that a fair selection would be one in which the criteria appear after the selection and not before. In this text by Althusser, there's this affirmation of the contingency of the political order, but we cannot fix criteria before – this is the illusion that everybody has, as if we are expecting what we select. And then, we do not even have a chance to select because we know already in advance what we are looking for. Look at what happens in universities: in France, for example, we already know in advance who will get the jobs! I think that Althusser is trying to deconstruct this model.

TMW: Let's conclude by discussing your work at the level of the breadth with which we started. At the end of 'Floating Signifiers Revisited', you describe the plastic, floating nature of language as a type of surface. You frequently point to the 'plastic arts' to highlight the function of malleability within the concept of 'plasticity'. Also, the sculptural power of masks and masking plays a prominent role in *Plasticity at the Dusk of Writing*. But for a concept as closely related to the sculptural, to the visual, to the figure of the surface as plasticity is, literature dominates your aesthetic attention. My question is whether, for this reason, you think that this distinction between the literary and the sculptural is an untenable distinction.

In *On the Name*, Derrida remarks that he is not particularly interested in literature in its own right; he is instead interested in 'making literature out of' works of history, biography, philosophy, religion and so on. This suggests, even in Derrida's own terms, a kind of sculptural power to literature. Are you likewise invested in such a gesture? If we maintain for a moment the classic association of the sculptural with the material and the literary with the symbolic, then, insofar as your work remains so invested in challenging these borders by highlighting the material within the symbolic, does this amount ultimately to making sculpture out of literature?

CM: This is a beautiful question. If I had had the wonderful opportunity to become an artist, I would have been a sculptor. For sure. Sculpture is my favourite artistic practice and domain; I am totally fascinated by it. But, then again, I am much more comfortable with the work of concepts: give me an abstract work and I am much more able to play with it than a piece of earth. If I am sculpting anything, I think it comes more from an intellectual, conceptual place than from an artistic, literary place.

In fact, to address your question, the sculptural element of literature is what stands out to me. Rather than, say, something more neutral. By 'neutrality' I mean something like Blanchot's concept, a non-appearance.

TMW: Even Gregory Chatonsky's digital images appear to be very sculptural – and hence the decision to use one of his images as the cover for *Plasticity: The Promise of Explosion*.

CM: Yes, exactly, and that is why he and I get along quite well.

Perhaps, if there is a big mistake in my work, a big flaw, it is that I cannot help but think that everything important is and has a form. For me, everything that counts is related to this process of formation, sculpting, etc. This is perhaps unconvincing. I remember, when I defended my PhD, that this was something about which Derrida reproached me: 'So, for you, everything is about form. What about formless things? What about the non-plastic dimension of the real?' It is true that I'm not really able to respond to that. I think I go quite far in a thinking of destruction. Even destruction, for me, pertains to sculpture as a sense of formation.

This is how thinking is given to me.

Works Cited

Abensour, Miguel. 2011. *Democracy Against the State: Marx and the Machiavellian Moment*, trans. Max Blechman and Martin Breaugh. Cambridge: Polity.
Agamben, Giorgio. 1998. *Homo Sacer: Sovereign Power and Bare Life*, trans. Daniel Heller-Roazen. Stanford, CA: Stanford University Press.
—. 2015. *The Use of Bodies: Homo Sacer IV, 2*, trans. Adam Kotsko. Stanford, CA: Stanford University Press.
Althusser, Louis. 2006. The Underground Current of the Materialism of the Encounter. In *Philosophy of the Encounter: Later Writings, 1978–87*, ed. François Matheron and Olivier Corpet. London: Verso.
Ameisen, Jean-Claude. 1999. *La Sculpture du vivant. Le Suicide cellulaire ou la mort créatrice*. Paris: Seuil.
Annas, Julia. 1981. *An Introduction to Plato's Republic*. Oxford: Clarendon.
—. 1982. Plato's Myths of Judgment. *Phronesis* 27, no. 2: 119–43.
Apollinaire, Guillaume. 2004. *Selected Poems*, trans. Oliver Bernard. London: Anvil.
Arendt, Hannah. 1970. *On Violence*. New York: Harcourt.
Aries, Philippe. 1981. *The Hour of Our Death: The Classic History of Western Attitudes toward Death over the Last One Thousand Years*, trans. Helen Weaver. New York: Vintage.
Atlan, Henri. 1999. *La Fin du 'tout génétique'? Vers de nouveaux paradigmes en biologie*. Paris: Institut National de la Recherche Agronomique.
—. 2009. Programme de Recherche Inter-Centres Biologie et société. *Annuaire de l'EHESS*. <https://journals.openedition.org/annuaire-ehess/20375>. Accessed 10 June 2021.
Badiou, Alain. 1969. Marque et manque: a propos de zero. *Cahiers pour l'Analyse* 10, no. 8: 150–73.
—. n.d. Mark and Lack: On Zero, trans. Zachary Luke Fraser and Ray Brassier. *Concept and Form: The Cahiers pour l'Analyse and Contemporary French Thought*. <http://cahiers.kingston.ac.uk/pdf/cpa10.8.badiou.translation.pdf>. Accessed 14 September 2021.
Balibar, Étienne. 1985. *Spinoza et la politique*. Paris: Presses Universitaires de France.
—. 2011. Occasional Notes on Communism. *Krisis: A Journal for Contemporary Philosophy*, 1: 4–13.
Baracchi, Claudia. 2002. *Of Myth, Life, and War in Plato's Republic*. Indianapolis, IN: Indiana University Press.
Barnett, Derek C. 2016. The Primacy of Resistance: Anarchism, Foucault, and the Art of Not Being Governed. PhD dissertation, University of Western Ontario.
Barthes, Roland. 1979. Lecture in Inauguration of the Chair of Literary Semiology, Collège de France, 7 January 1977, trans. Richard Howard. *October* 8: 3–16.

Bateson, Gregory. 2000. *Steps to an Ecology of Mind: Collected Essays in Anthropology, Psychiatry, Evolution, and Epistemology*. Chicago: University of Chicago Press.
Baudelaire, Charles. 1974. *Paris Spleen*, trans. Louis Varèse. New York: New Directions.
Baugh, Bruce. 2003. *French Hegel: From Surrealism to Postmodernism*. London: Routledge.
Beckett, Samuel. 1989. *Happy Days: A Play in Two Acts*. New York: Grove.
Benardete, Seth. 1992. *Socrates' Second Sailing: On Plato's* Republic. Chicago: University of Chicago Press.
Benveniste, Emile. 1973. Religion and Superstition. In *Indo-European Language and Society, (Study in General Linguistics)*, trans. Elizabeth Palmer. London: Faber.
Bernhard, Thomas. 2011a. *The Cellar*, in *Gathering Evidence: A Memoir*, trans. David McLintock. New York: Vintage.
—. 2011b. *An Indication of the Cause*, in *Gathering Evidence: A Memoir*, trans. David McLintock. New York: Vintage.
Blanchot, Maurice. 1987. *Michel Foucault as I Imagine Him*, trans. Jeffrey Mehlman. New York: Zone.
—. 1989. *The Space of Literature*, trans. Ann Smock. Lincoln, NE: University of Nebraska Press.
—. 1993. *The Infinite Conversation*, trans. Susan Hanson. Minneapolis, MN: University of Minnesota Press.
Bloom, Allan. 2016. *The Republic of Plato*, 2nd edn. New York: Basic Books.
Bonneuil, Christophe, and Jean-Baptiste Fressoz. 2016. *The Shock of the Anthropocene: The Earth, History, and Us*, trans. David Fernbach. London: Verso.
Borck, Cornelius. 2018. *Brainwaves: A Cultural History of Electroencephalography*, trans. Ann M. Hentschel. London: Routledge.
Bourdieu, Pierre, and Jean-Claude Passeron. 1979. *The Inheritors: French Students and their Relation to Culture*, trans. Richard Nice. Chicago: University of Chicago Press.
Braudel, Fernand. 1973. *Capitalism and Material Life, 1400–1800*, trans. Miriam Kochan. New York: Harper and Row.
—. 2001. *The Mediterranean and the Ancient World*, trans. Siân Reynolds. London: Penguin.
Braver, Lee. 2007. *A Thing of This World: A History of Continental Anti-Realism*. Evanston, IL: Northwestern University Press.
Brekke, Øystein. 2013. On the Subject of Epigenesis. An Interpretive Figure in Paul Ricœur. In *Impossible Time: Past and Future in the Philosophy of Religion*, ed. Marius Timmann Mjaaland, Ulrik Houlind Rasmussen and Philipp Stoellger. Tübingen: Mohr Siebeck.
Brochard, Victor. 2013. *Le Dieu de Spinoza*. Paris: Éditions Manucius.
Brown, Jason W. 1979. Language Representation in the Brain. In *Neurobiology of Social Communication in Primates: An Evolutionary Perspective*, ed. Horst D. Steklis and Michael J. Raleigh. New York: Academic Press.
—. 1996. *Time, Will, and Mental Process*. New York: Plenum.
—. 2015. *Microgenetic Theory and Process Thought*. Exeter: Imprint Academic.
Buffon, Georges-Louis Leclerc, comte de. 1830. Expériences au sujet de la generation. In *Œuvres complètes, Histoire des animaux*, vol. 11. Paris: F.D. Pillot.
Butler, Judith. 2002. What is Critique? An Essay on Foucault's Virtue. In *The Political*, ed. David Ingram. Oxford: Blackwell.
—. 2007. *Gender Trouble: Feminism and the Subversion of Identity*. London: Routledge.
Canetti, Elias. 1984. *Crowds and Power*, trans. Carol Stewart. New York: Farrar, Straus and Giroux.
—. 1990. The Torch in My Ear. In *The Memoirs of Elias Canetti*, trans. Joachin Neugroschel. New York: Farrar, Straus and Giroux.
Canguilhem, Georges. 1994. *A Vital Rationalist: Selected Writings from Georges Canguilhem*. New York: Zone.

—. 2008. *Knowledge of Life*, ed. Paola Marrati and Todd Meyers, trans. Stefanos Geroulanos and Daniela Ginsburg. New York: Fordham University Press.
Castel, Robert. 2003. *From Manual Workers to Wage Laborers: Transformation of the Social Question*. New Brunswick, NJ: Transaction.
Centre National de Ressources Textuelles et Lexicales (CNRTL). 2012. Prison, etymologie. <https://www.cnrtl.fr/etymologie/prison>. Accessed 12 May 2021.
Chakrabarty, Dipesh. 2009. The Climate of History: Four Theses. *Critical Inquiry* 35, no. 2: 197–222.
—. 2012. Postcolonial Studies and the Challenge of Climate Change. *New Literary History* 43, no. 1: 1–18.
Changeux, Jean-Pierre. 1985. *Neuronal Man: The Biology of Mind*, trans. Laurence Garey. New York: Pantheon.
—. 2012. *The Good, the True, and the Beautiful: A Neuronal Approach*, trans. Laurence Garey. New Haven, CT: Yale University Press.
Damasio, Antonio. 1995. *Descartes' Error: Emotion, Reason, and the Human Brain*. New York: Avon.
—. 2000. *The Feeling of What Happens: Body and Emotion in the Making of Consciousness*. New York: Harcourt.
Darwin, Charles. 2008. *On the Origin of Species*, rev. edn. Oxford: Oxford University Press.
Deacon, Terence W. 2005. Language as an Emergent Function: Some Radical Neurological and Evolutionary Implications. *Theoria: An International Journal for Theory, History and Foundations of Science* 20, no. 3: 269–86.
Deleuze, Gilles. 1978. Lecture Transcripts on Spinoza's Concept of *Affect*: Cours Vincennes 24 January 1978, trans. Timothy S. Murphy. <www.gold.ac.uk/media/images-by-section/departments/research-centres-and-units/research-centres/centre-for-invention-and-social-process/deleuze_spinoza_affect.pdf>. Accessed 22 December 2020.
—. 1984. *Difference and Repetition*, trans. Paul Patton. New York: Columbia University Press.
—. 1990a. *Expressionism in Philosophy: Spinoza*, trans. Martin Joughin, New York: Zone.
—. 1990b. *The Logic of Sense*, ed. Constantin V. Boundas, trans. Mark Lester and Charles Stivale. New York: Columbia University Press.
—. 1997. The Exhausted. In *Essays Critical and Clinical*, trans. Daniel W. Smith and Michael A. Greco. Minneapolis, MN: University of Minnesota Press.
—. 2000. *Proust and Signs*, trans. Richard Howard. Minneapolis, MN: University of Minnesota Press.
Deleuze, Gilles, and Félix Guattari. 1987. *A Thousand Plateaus: Capitalism and Schizophrenia*, trans. Brian Massumi. Minneapolis, MN: University of Minnesota Press.
—. 1994. *What is Philosophy?*, trans. Hugh Tomlinson and Graham Burchell. New York: Columbia University Press.
Delumeau, Jean. 1990. *Sin and Fear: The Emergence of a Western Guilt Culture, Thirteenth to Eighteenth Centuries*, trans. Eric Nicholson. Chicago: University of Chicago Press.
Deneen, Patrick J. 2003. *The Odyssey of Political Theory: The Politics of Departure and Return*. Lanham, MD: Rowman and Littlefield.
Derrida, Jacques. 1978. *Writing and Difference*, trans. Alan Bass. Chicago: University of Chicago Press.
—. 1981. *Dissemination*, trans. Barbara Johnson. Chicago: University of Chicago Press.
—. 1982. *Margins of Philosophy*, trans. Alan Bass. Chicago: University of Chicago Press.
—. 1986. *Glas*, trans. John P. Leavey Jr and Richard Rand. Lincoln, NE: University of Nebraska Press.
—. 1987. *The Post Card: From Socrates to Freud and Beyond*, trans. Alan Bass. Chicago: University of Chicago Press.
—. 1993. Circumfession. In Geoffrey Bennington and Jacques Derrida, *Jacques Derrida*, trans. Geoffrey Bennington. Chicago: University of Chicago Press.

—. 1995a. *The Gift of Death*, trans. David Wills. Chicago: University of Chicago Press.
—. 1995b. Passions: An Oblique Offering. In *On the Name*, trans. David Wood et al. Stanford, CA: Stanford University Press, 3–31.
—. 1995c. Kh ra. In *On the Name*, trans. David Wood et al. Stanford, CA: Stanford University Press, 87–127.
—. 1996. 'Il courrait mort': salut, salut. Note pour un courier aux *Temps Modernes*. *Les Temps modernes*, 587: 22.
—. 1997. *Of Grammatology*, trans. Gayatri Chakravorty Spivak. Baltimore, MD: Johns Hopkins University Press.
—. 2000. *The Instant of My Death/Demeure: Fiction and Testimony*, trans. Elizabeth Rottenberg. Stanford, CA: Stanford University Press.
—. 2001. A Silkworm of One's Own. In Hélène Cixous and Jacques Derrida, *Veils*, trans. Geoffrey Bennington. Stanford, CA: Stanford University Press, 17–92.
—. 2002. Faith and Knowledge: Two Sources of 'Religion' at the Limits of Reason Alone, trans. Samuel Weber. In *Acts of Religion*, ed. Gil Anidjar. New York: Routledge, 42–101.
—. 2005. *On Touching: Jean-Luc Nancy*, trans. Christine Irizarry. Stanford, CA: Stanford University Press.
—. 2006. *Specters of Marx: The State of Debt, the Work of Mourning and the New International*, trans. Peggy Kamuf. New York: Routledge.
—. 2007a. The *Retrait* of Metaphor. In *Psyche: Inventions of the Other, vol. 1*, ed. Peggy Kamuf and Elizabeth Rottenberg. Stanford, CA: Stanford University Press.
—. 2007b. A Certain Impossibility of Saying the Event, trans. Gila Walker. *Critical Inquiry* 33: 441–61.
—. 2008a. *The Animal That Therefore I Am*, ed. Marie-Louise Mallet, trans. David Wills. New York: Fordham University Press.
—. 2008b. How to Avoid Speaking: Denials. In *Psyche: Inventions of the Other, vol. 2*, ed. Peggy Kamuf and Elizabeth Rottenberg. Stanford, CA: Stanford University Press.
—. 2008c. Marx & Sons, trans. G. M. Goshgarian. In *Ghostly Demarcations: A Symposium on Jacques Derrida's* Specters of Marx, ed. Michael Sprinkler. London: Verso.
—. 2009. *The Beast and the Sovereign, volume 1*, trans. Geoffrey Bennington. Chicago: University of Chicago Press.
—. 2010. *Athens, Still Remains*, trans. Pascale-Anne Brault and Michael Naas. New York: Fordham University Press.
—. 2011. *Voice and Phenomenon: Introduction to the Problem of the Sign in Husserl's Phenomenology*, trans. Leonard Lawlor. Evanston, IL: Northwestern University Press.
Derrida, Jacques, and Paule Thévenin. 1998. *The Secret of Antonin Artaud*, trans. Mary Ann Caws. Cambridge, MA: MIT Press.
Détienne, Marcel, and Jean-Pierre Vernant. 1978. *Cunning Intelligence in Greek Culture and Society*, trans. Janet Lloyd. New York: Harvester.
Dosse, François. 1987. *L'histoire en miettes: Des Annales à la 'nouvelle histoire'*. Paris: La Découverte.
Dussel, Enrique. 1985. *Philosophy of Liberation*, trans. Aquilina Martinez and Christine Morkovsky. Eugene, OR: Wipf and Stock.
Ehrenberg, Alain. 2010. *The Weariness of the Self: Diagnosing the History of Depression in the Contemporary Age*, trans. Enrico Caouette, Jacob Homel and Don Winkler. Montreal: McGill-Queen's University Press.
Epigenetic Inheritance: 'What Genes Remember'. 2009. *Institute of Science in Society*. <https://www.i-sis.org.uk/epigeneticInheritance.php>. Accessed 10 June 2021.

WORKS CITED

Esposito, Roberto. 2013. *The Terms of the Political: Community, Immunity, Biopolitics*, trans. Rhiannon Noel Welch. New York: Fordham University Press.

Földényi, László. 2020. *Dostoyevsky Reads Hegel in Siberia and Bursts into Tears*, trans. Ottilie Mulzet. New Haven, CT: Yale University Press.

Foucault, Michel. 1977. *Discipline and Punish: The Birth of the Prison*, trans. Alan Sheridan. New York: Vintage.

—. 1984. What is Enlightenment?, trans. Catherine Porter. In *The Foucault Reader*, ed. Paul Rabinow. New York: Pantheon.

—. 1987. *Maurice Blanchot: The Thought from Outside*, trans. Brian Massumi. New York: Zone.

—. 1990. *The History of Sexuality: An Introduction*, vol. 1, trans. Robert Hurley. New York: Vintage.

—. 1994. *The Birth of the Clinic: An Archaeology of Medical Perception*, trans. A. M. Sheridan Smith. New York: Vintage.

—. 1996. The Question of Culture. In *Michel Foucault Live: Collected Interviews, 1961–1984*, ed. Sylvère Lotringer. New York: Semiotext(e).

—. 1998. On the Archaeology of the Sciences: Response to the Epistemology Circle. In *Aesthetics, Method, and Epistemology: Essential Works of Foucault, 1954–1984, Volume Two*, ed. James D. Faubion. New York: New Press.

—. 2001. La vérité et les forms juridiques. In *Dits et écrits I. 1954–1975*, ed. Daniel Defert, François Ewald and Jacques Lagrange. Paris: Gallimard.

—. 2003a. The Ethics of the Concern of the Self as a Practice of Freedom. In *The Essential Foucault: Selections from the Essential Works of Foucault, 1954–1984*, ed. Paul Rabinow and Nikolas Rose. New York: New Press.

—. 2003b. *Society Must Be Defended: Lectures at the Collège de France, 1975–76*, trans. David Macey, ed. François Ewald and Alessandro Fontana. New York: Picador.

—. 2003c. What is Critique? In *The Essential Foucault: Selections from the Essential Works of Foucault, 1954–1984*, ed. Paul Rabinow and Nikolas Rose. New York: New Press.

—. 2007. *Security, Territory, Population: Lectures at the College de France, 1977–78*, trans. Graham Burchell. New York: Picador.

—. 2010. *Archaeology of Knowledge*, trans. A. M. Sheridan Smith. New York: Vintage.

—. 2014. *On the Government of the Living: Lectures at the Collège de France, 1979–1980*, trans. Graham Burchell, ed. Michel Senellart. New York: Picador.

Fowler, Thomas. 1869. *The Elements of Deductive Logic*, 3rd edn. Oxford: Clarendon.

Frank, Joseph. 1987. *Dostoevsky: The Years of Ordeal: 1850–1859*. Princeton, NJ: Princeton University Press.

Frege, Gottlob. 1980. *The Foundations of Arithmetic*, trans. J. L. Austin. Evanston, IL: Northwestern University Press.

Freud, Sigmund. A Difficulty in the Path of Psychoanalysis. In *The Standard Edition of the Complete Psychological Works of Sigmund Freud*, vol. XVII, trans. James Strachey et al. London: Hogarth.

—. Analysis Terminable and Interminable. In *The Standard Edition of the Complete Psychological Works of Sigmund Freud*, vol. XXIII, trans. James Strachey et al. London: Hogarth.

—. Beyond the Pleasure Principle. In *The Standard Edition of the Complete Psychological Works of Sigmund Freud*, vol. XVIII, trans. James Strachey et al. London: Hogarth.

—. Civilization and its Discontents. In *The Standard Edition of the Complete Psychological Works of Sigmund Freud*, vol. XXI, trans. James Strachey et al. London: Hogarth.

—. The Ego and the Id. In *The Standard Edition of the Complete Psychological Works of Sigmund Freud*, vol. XIX, trans. James Strachey et al. London: Hogarth.

—. From the History of an Infantile Neurosis. In *The Standard Edition of the Complete Psychological Works of Sigmund Freud*, vol. XVII, trans. James Strachey et al. London: Hogarth.
—. Inhibitions, Symptoms, and Anxiety. In *The Standard Edition of the Complete Psychological Works of Sigmund Freud*, vol. XX, trans. James Strachey et al. London: Hogarth.
—. Negation. In *The Standard Edition of the Complete Psychological Works of Sigmund Freud*, vol. XIX, trans. James Strachey et al. London: Hogarth.
—. Project for a Scientific Psychology. In *The Standard Edition of the Complete Psychological Works of Sigmund Freud*, vol. I, trans. James Strachey et al. London: Hogarth.
—. Thoughts for the Times on War and Death. In *The Standard Edition of the Complete Psychological Works of Sigmund Freud*, vol. XIV, trans. James Strachey et al. London: Hogarth.
—. Three Essays on the Theory of Sexuality. In *The Standard Edition of the Complete Psychological Works of Sigmund Freud*, vol.VII, trans. James Strachey et al. London: Hogarth.
Gallagher, Shaun. 2005. *How the Body Shapes the Mind*. New York: Oxford University Press.
Goldman, Emma. 1917. The Tragedy of Woman's Emancipation. In *Anarchism and Other Essays*, 3rd rev. edn. New York: Mother Earth.
Graeber, David. 2006. Interview. *Charlie Rose*. <https://charlierose.com/videos/10730>. Accessed 15 June 2021.
Grosfoguel, Ramón. 2011. Decolonizing Post-Colonial Studies and Paradigms of Political-Economy: Transmodernity, Decolonial Thinking, and Global Coloniality. *Transmodernity: Journal of Peripheral Cultural Production of the Luso-Hispanic World* 1, no. 1: 1–38.
—. 2012. Decolonizing Western Uni-versalisms: Decolonial Pluri-versalism from Aimé Césaire to the Zapatistas. *Transmodernity: Journal of Peripheral Cultural Production of the Luso-Hispanic World* 1, no. 3: 88–104.
Gutting, Gary. 2001. *French Philosophy in the Twentieth Century*. Cambridge: Cambridge University Press.
Hall, Dale. 1977. The *Republic* and the 'Limits of Politics'. *Political Theory* 5, no. 3: 293–313.
Hall, Stuart. 1997. Race: The Floating Signifier. *Media Education Foundation*. <https://www.mediaed.org/transcripts/Stuart-Hall-Race-the-Floating-Signifier-Transcript.pdf>. Accessed 10 June 2021.
Halliwell, Stephen. 2007. The Life-and-Death Journey of the Soul: Interpreting the Myth of Er. In *The Cambridge Companion to Plato's Republic*, ed. G. R. F. Ferrari. Cambridge: Cambridge University Press, 445–73.
Hardt, Michael. 1997. Prison Time. *Yale French Studies* 91: 64–79.
Hardt, Michael, and Antonio Negri. 2000. *Empire*. Cambridge, MA: Harvard University Press.
—. 2004. *Multitude: War and Democracy in the Age of Empire*. New York: Penguin.
Harper, Douglas. 2021. *Online Etymology Dictionary*. <https://www.etymonline.com/word/captive#etymonline_v_53199>. Accessed 12 May 2021.
Harvey, William. 1847. *Exercises on the Generation of Animals*. In *The Works of William Harvey*, trans. Robert Willis. London: Sydenham Society.
Hegel, Georg Wilhelm Friedrich. 1977. *Phenomenology of Spirit*, trans. A.V. Miller. Oxford: Oxford University Press.
—. 1991a. *Elements of the Philosophy of Right*, ed. Allen W. Wood, trans. Hugh Barr Nisbet. Cambridge: Cambridge University Press.
—. 1991b. *The Encyclopaedia Logic*, trans. T. F. Geraets, W. A. Suchting and H. S. Harris. Indianapolis, IN: Hackett.
Heidegger, Martin. 1988. *Basic Problems of Phenomenology*, trans. Alfred Hofstadter. Bloomington, IN: Indiana University Press.

—. 1992. *Parmenides*, trans. André Schuwer and Richard Rojcewicz. Bloomington, IN: Indiana University Press.

—. 1996. *The Principle of Reason*, trans. Reginald Lilly. Bloomington, IN: Indiana University Press.

—. 1997. *Kant and the Problem of Metaphysics*, trans. Richard Taft. Bloomington, IN: Indiana University Press.

—. 1998. On the Question of Being, trans. William McNeil. In *Pathmarks*, ed. William McNeil. Cambridge: Cambridge University Press.

—. 1999. *Contributions to Philosophy: From Enowning*, trans. Parvis Emad and Kenneth Maly. Bloomington, IN: Indiana University Press.

—. 2001. *Phenomenological Interpretations of Aristotle: Initiation into Phenomenological Research*, trans. Richard Rojcewicz. Bloomington, IN: Indiana University Press.

—. 2010. *Being and Time*, trans. Joan Stambaugh, rev. Dennis J. Schmidt. Albany, NY: State University of New York Press.

—. 2015. *Hegel*, trans. Joseph Arel and Niels Feuerhahn. Bloomington, IN: Indiana University Press.

Henry, Brian. 2010. Loaves, Light, Chalice: Pablo Neruda's *Alturas de Macchu Picchu*. *The Best American Poetry*. <https://blog.bestamericanpoetry.com/the_best_american_poetry/2010/07/loaves-light-chalice-pablo-nerudas-alturas-de-macchu-picchu-by-brian-henry.html>. Accessed 19 May 2021.

Henry, Michel. 1983. *Marx: A Philosophy of Human Reality*, trans. Kathleen McLaughlin. Bloomington, IN: Indiana University Press.

—. 2009. *Marx*. Paris: Gallimard.

Heraclitus. Fragment 29. *Heraclitus Fragments*. <http://www.heraclitusfragments.com/files/ge.html>. Accessed 28 June 2021.

Ho, Mae-Wan. 2003. *Living with the Fluid Genome*. London: Institute of Science in Society.

Jablonka, Eva, and Marion Lamb. 2014. *Evolution in Four Dimensions: Genetic, Epigenetic, Behavioral, and Symbolic Variation in the History of Life*, rev. edn. Cambridge, MA: MIT Press.

Jacob, François. 1973. *The Logic of Life: A History of Heredity*, trans. Betty E. Spillmann. New York: Pantheon.

James, Ian. 2012. *The New French Philosophy*. Cambridge: Polity.

—. 2016. (Neuro)-Plasticity, Epigenesis and the Void. *Parrhesia* 25: 1–19.

—. 2019. *The Technique of Thought*. Minneapolis, MN: University of Minnesota Press.

Jameson, Fredric. 1972. *The Prison-House of Language: A Critical Account of Structuralism and Russian Formalism*. Princeton, NJ: Princeton University Press.

Jenuwein, Thomas, C. David Allis, Marie-Laure Caparros and Danny Reinberg, eds. 2007. *Epigenetics*. Cold Spring Harbor, NY: Cold Spring Harbor Laboratory.

Joughin, Martin. 1990. Translator's Preface. In Gilles Deleuze, *Expressionism in Philosophy: Spinoza*, trans. Martin Joughin. New York: Zone, 5–11.

Joyce, James. 2007. *A Portrait of the Artist as a Young Man*, ed. John Paul Riquelme. New York: W. W. Norton.

Kandel, Eric, and Larry Squire. 2008. *Memory: From Mind to Molecules*. Greenwood Village, CO: Roberts.

Kant, Immanuel. 1996. *Religion within the Boundaries of Mere Reason*, trans. George di Giovanni. In *Religion and Rational Theology*, ed. Allen W. Wood. Cambridge: Cambridge University Press.

—. 1998. *Critique of Pure Reason*, trans. Paul Guyer and Allen W. Wood. Cambridge: Cambridge University Press.

—. 2000. *Critique of the Power of Judgement*, trans. Paul Guyer and Eric Matthews, ed. Paul Guyer and Allen W. Wood. Cambridge: Cambridge University Press.

Keller, Evelyn Fox. 2000. *The Century of the Gene*. Cambridge, MA: Harvard University Press.

Kelly, S. D. 2016. Blame Derrida for Donald Trump. *Mere Orthodoxy*. <https://mereorthodoxy.com/blame-jacques-derrida-for-donald-trump/>. Accessed 22 December 2020.

King, Jr, Martin Luther. 1965. Remaining Awake Through a Great Revolution. *Oberlin College Archives*. <https://www2.oberlin.edu/external/EOG/BlackHistoryMonth/MLK/CommAddress.html>. Accessed 12 May 2021.

—. 2000. Letter from Birmingham Jail. In *Why We Can't Wait*. New York: Signet, 85–112.

Koopman, Colin. 2010. Historical Critique or Transcendental Critique in Foucault: Two Kantian Lineages. *Foucault Studies* 8: 100–21.

Kropotkin, Pëtr. 1902. Mutual Aid: A Factor of Evolution. In *The Anarchist Library*. <https://theanarchistlibrary.org/library/petr-kropotkin-mutual-aid-a-factor-of-evolution>. Accessed 15 June 2021.

Kuhn, Thomas. 1962. *The Structure of Scientific Revolutions*. Chicago: University of Chicago Press.

Laclau, Ernesto, and Chantal Mouffe. 2014. *Hegemony and Socialist Strategy: Towards a Radical Democratic Politics*, 2nd edn. London: Verso.

Laplanche, Jean, and Jean-Bertrand Pontalis. 2018. *The Language of Psychoanalysis*, trans. Donald Nicholson-Smith. New York: Routledge.

Lawtoo, Nidesh. 2017. The Plasticity of Mimesis. *Modern Language Notes* 132, no. 5: 1201–24.

Le Douarin, Nicole. 2007. *Les Cellules souches, porteuses d'immortalité*. Paris: Odile Jacob.

Le Robert Dictionary. 1994. Paris: Le dictionnaire Robert SNL.

Lévi-Strauss, Claude. 1963. *Structural Anthropology*, trans. Claire Jacobson and Brooke Grundfest Schoepf. New York: Basic Books.

—. 1985a. A Small Mythico-Literary Puzzle. In *The View from Afar*, trans. Joachim Neugroschel and Phoebe Hoss. New York: Basic Books.

—. 1985b. Race and Culture. In *The View from Afar*, trans. Joachim Neugroschel and Phoebe Hoss. New York: Basic Books.

—. 1987. *Introduction to the Work of Marcel Mauss*, trans. Felicity Baker. London: Routledge.

Levinas, Emmanuel. 1969. *Totality and Infinity: An Essay on Exteriority*, trans. Alfonso Lingis. Pittsburgh, PA: Duquesne University Press.

—. 1994a. On the Jewish Reading of Scripture. In *Beyond the Verse: Talmudic Readings and Lectures*, trans. Gary D. Mole. London: Continuum.

—. 1994b. Revelation in the Jewish Tradition. In *Beyond the Verse: Talmudic Readings and Lectures*, trans. Gary D. Mole. London: Continuum.

—. 1994c. Spinoza's Background. In *Beyond the Verse: Talmudic Readings and Lectures*, trans. Gary D. Mole. London: Continuum.

—. 1997a. Have You Reread Baruch? In *Difficult Freedom: Essays on Judaism*, trans. Sean Hand. Baltimore, MD: Johns Hopkins University Press.

—. 1997b. Israel and Universalism. In *Difficult Freedom: Essays on Judaism*, trans. Sean Hand. Baltimore, MD: Johns Hopkins University Press.

—. 1997c. The Spinoza Case. In *Difficult Freedom: Essays on Judaism*, trans. Sean Hand. Baltimore, MD: Johns Hopkins University Press.

—. 1998. *Otherwise Than Being, Or, Beyond Essence*, trans. Alfonso Lingis. Pittsburgh, PA: Duquesne University Press.

—. 1999a. Beyond the State in the State. In *New Talmudic Readings*, trans. Richard A. Cohen. Pittsburgh, PA: Duquesne University Press.

—. 1999b. The Prohibition Against Representation and 'The Rights of Man'. In *Alterity and Transcendence*, trans. Michael B. Smith. New York: Columbia University Press.

—. 2003. *Humanism of the Other*, trans. Nidra Poller. Urbana, IL: University of Illinois Press.

—. 2009. *Carnets de captivité*. In *Œuvres complètes, tome 1: Carnets de captivité et autres inédits*, ed. Rodolphe Calin and Catherine Chalier. Paris: Grasset. 1

Ludwig, Pascal, and Thomas Pradeu, eds. 2008. *L'Individu, perspectives contemporaines*. Paris: Vrin.

Luria, A. R. 1987. *The Man with a Shattered World: The History of a Brain Wound*, trans. Lynn Solotaroff. Cambridge, MA: Harvard University Press.

Lyotard, Jean-François. 1990. *Pérégrinations. Loi, forme, événement*. Paris: Galilée.

—. 2010. *Discourse, Figure*, trans. Anthony Hudek and Mary Lydon. Minneapolis, MN: University of Minnesota Press.

MacLeod, Norman. 2016. Response to Catherine Malabou, 'One Life Only: Biological Resistance, Political Resistance'. *Critical Inquiry* 43, no. 1: 191–9.

Malabou, Catherine. 2004a. *Le Change Heidegger*. Paris: Léo Scheer.

—. 2004b. *Que faire de notre cerveau?* Paris: Bayard.

—. 2005. *The Future of Hegel: Plasticity, Temporality and Dialectic*, trans. Lisabeth During. London: Routledge.

—. 2008. *What Should We Do With Our Brain?*, trans. Sebastian Rand. New York: Fordham University Press.

—. 2010. *Plasticity at the Dusk of Writing: Dialectic, Destruction, Deconstruction*, trans. Carolyn Shread. New York: Columbia University Press.

—. 2011a. *Changing Difference: The Feminine and the Question of Philosophy*, trans. Carolyn Shread. Cambridge: Polity.

—. 2011b. *The Heidegger Change: On the Fantastic in Philosophy*, trans. Peter Skafish. Albany, NY: State University of New York Press.

—. 2012. *The New Wounded: From Neurosis to Brain Damage*, trans. Steven Miller. New York: Fordham University Press.

—. 2016. *Before Tomorrow: Epigenesis and Rationality*, trans. Carolyn Shread. Cambridge: Polity.

—. 2019. *Morphing Intelligence: From IQ Measurement to Artificial Brains*, trans. Carolyn Shread. New York: Columbia University Press.

Malabou, Catherine, and Judith Butler. 2010. *Sois mon corps: Une lecture contemporaine de la domination et de la servitude chez Hegel*. Paris: Bayard.

Malabou, Catherine, and Xavier Emmanuelli. 2009. *La grande exclusion*. Paris: Bayard.

Malafouris, Lambros. 2010. Metaplasticity and the Human Becoming: Principles of Neuroarcheology. *Journal of Anthropological Sciences* 88: 49–72.

—. 2013. *How Things Shape the Mind: A Theory of Material Engagement*. Cambridge, MA: MIT Press.

Maldonado-Torres, Nelson. 2006. Post-continental Philosophy: Its Definition, Contours, and Fundamental Sources. *Worlds and Knowledges Otherwise* 1, dossier 3: 1–29. <https://globalstudies.trinity.duke.edu/projects/wko-post-continental>. Accessed 19 May 2021.

Mallet, Marie-Louise, ed. 2004. *La démocratie à venir. Autour de Jacques Derrida*. Paris: Galilée.

Marchant, Patricio. 1987. En qué lengua se habla hispanoamérica? In *Ecritura y temblor*, ed. Pablo Oyarzún and Willy Thayer. Santiago: Cuarto Proprio.

Martinon, Jean-Paul. 2007. *On Futurity: Malabou, Nancy and Derrida*. New York: Palgrave.

Marx, Karl. 1977. *Critique of Hegel's 'Philosophy of Right'*, ed. Joseph O'Malley. Cambridge: Cambridge University Press.

Mashour, George A., Pieter Roelfsema, Jean-Pierre Changeaux and Stanislaus Dehaene. 2020. Conscious Processing and the Global Neuronal Workspace Hypothesis. *Neuron* 105, no. 5: 776–98.

Maturana, Humberto R., and Francisco L. Varela. 1991. *Autopoiesis and Cognition: The Realization of the Living*. London: Reidel.

Maupertuis, Pierre-Louis. 1754. *Essai sur la formation des corps organisées*. Berlin.
McLuhan, Marshall. 1990. *Understanding Media: The Extensions of Man*. New York: St Martin's.
McVittie, Brona. 2006. Definition of Epigenetics. *Epigenetics?* <http://epigenome.eu/en/1,1,0.html>. Accessed 22 December 2020.
Meillassoux, Quentin. 2009. *After Finitude: An Essay on the Necessity of Contingency*, trans. Ray Brassier. London: Continuum.
Merleau-Ponty, Maurice. 2012. *Phenomenology of Perception*, trans. Donald A. Landes. New York: Routledge.
Metzinger, Thomas. 2003. *Being No One: The Self-Model Theory of Subjectivity*. Cambridge, MA: MIT Press.
Mignolo, Walter D. 2000. *Local Histories/Global Designs: Essays on the Coloniality of Power, Subaltern Knowledges and Border Thinking*. Princeton, NJ: Princeton University Press.
—. 2011. *The Darker Side of Western Modernity: Global Futures, Decolonial Options*. Durham, NC: Duke University Press.
Miller, Jacques-Alain. 1965. La Suture (Elements de la logique de significant). In *Concept and Form: The* Cahiers pour l'Analyse *and Contemporary French Thought*. <http://cahiers.kingston.ac.uk/pdf/cpa1.3.miller.pdf>. Accessed 17 May 2021.
—. 1977. Suture (Elements of the Logic of the Signifier), trans. Jacqueline Rose. *Screen* 18, no. 4: 37–49.
Morgan, Thomas H. 2018. The Relation of Genetics to Physiology and Medicine. Nobel Prize Lecture, 4 June 1934. <www.nobelprize.org/uploads/2018/06/morgan-lecture.pdf>. Accessed 22 December 2020.
Murray, Alex, and Jessica Whyte, eds. 2011. *The Agamben Dictionary*. Edinburgh: Edinburgh University Press.
Nau, Jean-Yves. 1999. Quand les cellules du cerveau se mettent à produire du sang. *Le Monde*, 23 January. <www.lemonde.fr/archives/article/1999/01/23/quand-les-cellules-du-cerveau-se-mettent-a-produire-du-sang_3533393_1819218.html>. Accessed 22 December 2020.
Negri, Antonio. 2008. Towards an Ontological Definition of the Multitude. In *Reflections on Empire*, trans. Ed Emery. Cambridge: Polity.
Nietzsche, Friedrich. 1989. *On the Genealogy of Morals*, trans. Walter Kaufmann and R. J. Hollingdale. New York: Vintage.
Noys, Benjamin. 2008. Through a Glass Darkly: Alain Badiou's Critique of Anarchism. *Anarchist Studies* 16, no. 2: 107–20.
Pachalska, Maria, and Bruce Duncan MacQueen. 2005. Microgenetic Theory: A New Paradigm for Contemporary Neuropsychology and Neurolinguistics. *Acta Neuropsychologica* 3, no. 3: 89–106.
Philbin, Nora. n.d. Towards an Understanding of Stereotypic Behaviour in Laboratory Macaques. *Animal Welfare Institute*. <https://awionline.org/content/towards-understanding-stereotypic-behaviour-laboratory-macaques>. Accessed 12 May 2021.
Plato. 1997. *Republic*, trans. G. M. A. Grube and C. D. C. Reeve. In *The Complete Works*, ed. John M. Cooper and D. S. Hutchinson. Indianapolis, IN: Hackett, 971–1223.
Proudhon, Pierre-Joseph. 2011. What is Property? In *Property is Theft! A Pierre-Joseph Proudhon Anthology*, ed. Iain McKay. Edinburgh: AK Press.
Proust, Marcel. 1993. *In Search of Lost Time vol. 5: The Captive and The Fugitive*, trans. C. K. Scott Moncrieff and Terence Kilmartin, rev. D. J. Enright. New York: Modern Library.
Ramachandran, V. S., and Sandra Blakeslee. 1998. *Phantoms in the Brain: Probing the Mysteries of the Human Mind*. New York: Quill.
Ravaisson, Félix. 2008. *Of Habit*, trans. Clare Carlisle and Mark Sinclair. London: Continuum.

Ricoeur, Paul. 1970. *Freud and Philosophy: An Essay on Interpretation*, trans. Denis Savage. New Haven, CT: Yale University Press.
—. 1974. *The Conflict of Interpretations*, ed. Don Ihde. Evanston, IL: Northwestern University Press.
Rockmore, Tom. 2006. *In Kant's Wake: Philosophy in the Twentieth Century*. Malden, MA: Blackwell.
Sacks, Oliver. 1998. *The Man Who Mistook His Wife for a Hat and Other Clinical Tales*. New York: Touchstone.
Sartre, Jean-Paul. 2012. *Saint Genet, Actor and Martyr*, trans. Bernard Frechtman. Minneapolis, MN: University of Minnesota Press.
Saussure, Ferdinand de. 2011. *Course in General Linguistics*, trans. Wade Baskin, ed. Perry Meisel and Haun Saussy. New York: Columbia University Press.
Schrift, Alan D. 2006. *Twentieth Century French Philosophy: Key Themes and Thinkers*. Oxford: Blackwell.
Schürmann, Reiner. 1987. *Heidegger On Being and Acting: From Principles to Anarchy*, trans. Christine-Marie Gros. Bloomington, IN: Indiana University Press.
Shaw, Julia. 2016. What Experts Wished You Knew About False Memories. *Scientific American*. <https://blogs.scientificamerican.com/mind-guest-blog/what-experts-wish-you-knew-about-false-memories/>. Accessed 22 December 2020.
Smail, Daniel Lord. 2008. *On Deep History and the Brain*. Berkeley, CA: University of California Press.
Spinoza, Baruch. 1996. *Ethics*, trans. Edwin Curley. New York: Penguin.
—. 2001. *Theological-Political Treatise*, 2nd edn, trans. Samuel Shirley. Indianapolis, IN: Hackett.
Starobinski, Jean. 1989. *The Living Eye*, trans. Arthur Goldhammer. Cambridge, MA: Harvard University Press.
Verter, Mitchell. 2010. The Anarchism of the Other Person. In *New Perspectives on Anarchism*, ed. Nathan J. Jun and Shane Wahl. Plymouth: Lexington.
Villalobos-Ruminott, Sergio. 2017. Anarchy as the Closure of Metaphysics: Historicity and Deconstruction in the Work of Reiner Schürmann. *Política Común* 11. <https://doi.org/10.3998/pc.12322227.0011.004>. Accessed 10 June 2021.
Waddington, C. H. 1968. The Basic Ideas of Biology. In *Prolegomena: Towards a Theoretical Biology, vol. 1*. Edinburgh: Edinburgh University Press.
West-Eberhard, Mary Jane. 2003. *Developmental Plasticity and Evolution*. New York: Oxford University Press.
Wilderson III, Frank B. 2010. *Red, White and Black: Cinema and the Structure of U.S. Antagonisms*. Durham, NC: Duke University Press.
Williams, Tyler M. 2013. Plasticity, in Retrospect: Changing the Future of the Humanities. *Diacritics* 41, no. 1: 6–25.
Wilson, Edward. 1996. *In Search of Nature*. Washington, DC: Island.
Wood, James. 2020. The Scholar Starting Brawls with the Enlightenment. *The New Yorker*. <https://www.newyorker.com/magazine/2020/06/01/the-scholar-starting-brawls-with-the-enlightenment>. Accessed 24 May 2021.
Wormald, Thomas, and Isabell Dahms, eds. 2018. *Thinking Catherine Malabou: Passionate Detachments*. Lanham, MD: Rowman and Littlefield.
Wright, Handel Kashope. 2016. What Has African Cultural Studies Done for You Lately? Autobiographical and Global Considerations of a Floating Signifier. *Critical Arts* 30, no. 4: 478–94.
Yovel, Yirmiyahu. 1989. *Spinoza and Other Heretics: The Adventures of Immanence*. Princeton, NJ: Princeton University Press.
Žižek, Slavoj. 2008. *Enjoy Your Symptom!* New York: Routledge.
—. 2012. Hegel versus Heidegger. *e-flux journal* 32. <https://www.e-flux.com/journal/32/68252/hegel-versus-heidegger/>. Accessed 25 May 2021.

Index

Abensour, Miguel, 220–1
Addiction, 196, 197–8, 202
Affect, 43, 54, 126, 196, 198, 243–9
    Auto-affection, 94, 243–6, 248–9, 271
    Hetero-affection, 243, 245–6, 248, 250
Agamben, Giorgio, 132, 141–2, 146–8, 152–3, 156, 215, 227–9, 237, 258, 314
Alienation, 106, 131, 135–6, 216
Alterity, 24, 57, 74, 93–4, 96–8, 198
Althusser, Louis, 111, 203–14, 318
Alzheimer's disease, 7, 317
Ameisen, Jean-Claude, 234
Anarchism, anarchy, 57, 215–25, 313, 317–18
Anarchaeology, 222–3
Annales School, 190, 200, 202
Annas, Julia, 144–5, 155
Anosognosia, 298–304, 306, 307n1
Anthropocene, 189–91, 197, 199–200, 202
Anzaldúa, Gloria, 182
Apollinaire, Guillaume, 27–32, 36
Archaeology, 91, 161, 192–3, 222–3, 294
Aries, Philippe, 201
Aristotle, 154, 157, 158, 165n2, 218–19
Atlan, Henri, 5, 163, 164, 165n6, 241
Aufhebung, 40, 316
Augustine, 21

Babinski, Joseph, 307n1
Badiou, Alain, 101–2, 105–12, 215
Bakunin, Mikhail, 215, 219
Balibar, Étienne, 256
Bare life, 148–9, 154, 229–30, 305, 307
Barnett, Derek C., 222–3
Barthes, Roland, 131, 133, 136, 139
Bataille, Georges, 184

Baudelaire, Charles, 115–16, 119, 123, 125–6
Beckett, Samuel, 269, 271, 314, 315
Benjamin, Walter, 229
Benveniste, Émile, 55, 83
Bergson, Henri, 4, 5, 55
Bernhard, Thomas, 267–70, 316–17
Bible, 66, 74, 77, 78, 85
Biopolitics, 1, 10, 155, 227–9, 230, 235, 237–40, 242, 307
Black Lives Matter, 138
Blanchot, Maurice, 15, 18–20, 22, 124, 179–81, 183, 251, 267, 269–70, 272, 319
Bloom, Allan, 144, 151
Bookchin, Murray, 215
Bourdieu, Pierre, 210, 240
Braudel, Fernand, 199–202
Brochard, Victor, 68–9, 71–2, 75
Brown, Jason, 254, 260, 262n6
Butler, Judith, 12n8, 224, 256
Buffon, Comte de, 157, 165n3

Canetti, Elias, 115–23, 125–6, 128–9
Canguilhem, Georges, 4–5, 208, 230
Canto-Sperber, Monique, 237
Castel, Robert, 128–9
Chakrabarty, Dipesh, 190–1, 193–5, 197–202
Changeux, Jean-Pierre, 164, 241, 296n2
Chatonsky, Gregory, 319
Climate change, 189, 197–200, 202
Clone, cloning, 29–33, 35–8, 228, 230, 233–4, 238–9, 240
Contingency, 94–8, 156, 203–6, 209, 318
Correlation, correlationism, 92–5, 193–4, 199, 213
Croce, Benedetto, 199

332

Damasio, Antonio, 243, 245, 247, 249, 267, 270–1, 273, 300–2
Darwin, Charles, 4, 203–8, 214, 221
Deacon, Terence, 254, 259, 260, 261
Deconstruction, 1, 3, 5, 6, 7, 28, 29, 35–6, 47–9, 52, 58, 90, 94, 97, 99, 153, 182–3, 191, 218–19, 235, 243, 245, 247, 249–50, 258, 261, 266, 289, 290, 292, 301, 310, 313
Decorrelation, 194, 295
Deleuze, Gilles, 5, 12n3, 15, 127, 204, 215, 240, 243, 244, 248, 250, 314, 315–6
  Difference and Repetition, 18, 19, 25n3, 212
  Expressionism in Philosophy, 63–8, 70–1, 73–5, 84, 86
  Logic and Sense, 255–6
  Proust and Signs, 242n2
  Thousand Plateaus, 129n5, 292–3
  What is Philosophy?, 246–7, 249, 250
Delumeau, Jean, 201
Democracy, 56, 58, 70, 86, 115, 116, 118–19, 121, 123–6, 128–9
Deneen, Patrick, 144, 145, 150, 151, 156
Derrida, Jacques, 3, 5, 10, 11, 12n4, 15, 22, 35–6, 49, 52, 58, 90, 91, 97, 99, 115–16, 118, 119, 127, 183, 184, 204, 215, 218, 240, 243, 251, 272, 290, 292, 310, 313, 314
  'A Certain Impossibility of Saying the Event', 50
  Animal that therefore I am, 128
  Athens, Still Remains, 51
  'Circumfession', 50, 124, 128
  Demeure, 123–4, 126
  Dissemination, 37
  'Faith and Knowledge', 50, 54–9, 61
  The Gift of Death, 22–3
  Glas, 39–48, 100n8
  'How to Avoid Speaking: Denials', 50, 52, 57
  'Khōra', 50
  Margins of Philosophy, 311–12
  'Marx & Sons', 50
  Of Grammatology, 35–6, 59, 91, 182, 244, 288–9
  On the Name, 319
  On Touching, 118, 245–50
  'Passions', 101–2, 109–11
  Post Card, 31, 32, 112n7, 126, 127, 225, 285
  '*Retrait* of Metaphor', 266–7
  Specters of Marx, 50, 124, 125, 203
  'Violence and Metaphysics', 54
  Voice and Phenomenon, 91
  Writing and Difference, 290
Descartes, René, 104, 181
Desert, desertion, 57–8, 94, 96, 162, 166n7, 171, 180, 270, 293, 295
Détienne, Marcel, 126–7
Dialectic, 3, 11, 40, 42, 44–6, 112, 160, 161, 165, 171, 174–5, 204, 215, 227, 234, 269, 300, 301, 306, 310, 316
Dostoyevsky, Fyodor, 167–77
Duras, Marguerite, 314, 315, 317
Dussel, Enrique, 181–3, 186

Epigenesis, epigenetics, 2, 4, 6–8, 10, 157–66, 166n11, 191–2, 228, 230–3, 238–9, 241–2, 295–6
Enantiomorphosis, 122, 129n5
Engram, 289
Epicurus, 204
Epimenides, 179, 180
Er (myth of), 141–50, 152, 154–6
Erection, 39–48
Esposito, Roberto, 228, 237
Evolution
  In anarchism, 221
  In biology, 10, 191–2, 205, 206, 208, 221, 231–2, 234, 241, 245, 260, 294–5
  In geology, 200–1, 202
  In philosophy, 3, 4, 5, 90
  In psychoanalysis, 161
Example, exemplarity, 282, 309, 311, 315
Expressionism, 64–7, 70, 76, 82, 86

Face, 18–25, 122, 123, 128, 247, 269, 305
Faith, 37, 49–61, 63, 66, 68, 71, 76, 86, 136, 246, 290
Fascism, 3, 131–2, 171
Fetish, 43–7
Filiation, 24, 32, 128, 206, 235, 239, 240, 242
Flight, 15–25, 25n4, 34, 57, 120, 121, 123, 127–8, 129n5, 130n10, 165, 205, 250, 318
Földényi, László, 167–77

INDEX

Form, 2–4, 6–9, 11, 12n4, 15, 17, 18, 21–5, 29, 33, 36, 44, 63, 68–72, 91, 93, 104, 122, 123, 127, 134, 146, 148–9, 156, 157, 159, 161, 164–5, 175, 184, 185, 190, 191, 200–1, 204–6, 208–9, 211–13, 223–4, 242, 244–5, 272, 277–85, 288–92, 295, 315, 317, 319
Formation, 25, 27, 112n6, 157, 158, 191, 194, 204–6, 209, 288, 289, 294, 295, 304, 319
Fossil, arche-fossil, 111, 193–4, 201, 293–4
Foucault, Michel, 4, 90–2, 111, 132, 179–84, 215–6, 218, 222–5, 227–30, 237–8, 240, 267, 318
Frank, Joseph, 168
Frege, Gottlob, 102–6, 108, 112n3
Freud, Sigmund, 10, 11, 52–4, 58, 60–1, 116–17, 161, 173–4, 225, 275–85, 290–1, 292, 298, 299, 301, 316

Gallagher, Shaun, 301–2, 304–7
Genet, Jean, 39–42, 44–8, 132, 135–6, 139, 172
Gilroy, Paul, 257
Glissant, Édouard, 186n2
God, 21, 23, 33, 35–6, 52, 63–72, 74–7, 79, 82–3, 85–7, 127, 148, 156, 170–1, 181, 256
Gödel, Kurt, 106, 107
Goldman, Emma, 215, 217
Graeber, David, 217
Grosfoguel, Ramón, 181–3, 186
Grothendieck, Alexander, 267–8, 269, 270, 272
Guattari, Félix, 129, 246, 292, 293

Hall, Stuart, 256–7, 262n3
Halliwell, Stephen, 144
Hardt, Michael, 132–3, 135–9
Harvey, William, 157, 165n3
Hegel, G.W.F., 1, 2, 3–4, 7, 9, 10, 11, 12n3, 21–2, 29, 39–40, 42, 43–8, 60, 90, 109, 135, 161, 167–76, 184, 210, 310, 313
Heidegger, Martin, 1, 6–7, 29, 56, 90–1, 94, 97, 99, 134, 136, 147, 154, 172, 174–5, 204, 218–20, 244, 265, 266, 268, 272, 292, 315, 316
Henry, Michel, 132, 135–6, 139n2

Heraclitus, 211
Hobbes, Thomas, 204, 221, 223
Hume, David, 95–6
Husserl, Edmund, 5–6, 90, 108, 312

Immanence, 59, 63–6, 74–6, 84–5, 87, 134–6, 138, 149, 204, 221, 281

Jablonka, Eva, 231–2, 241
Jacob, François, 208, 240
Jameson, Fredric, 131
Jenuwein, Thomas, 232, 241
Joyce, James, 237, 213, 313–14
Judaism, 59, 71–3, 77, 80
Jünger, Ernst, 175

Kafka, Franz, 176, 314–15
Kandel, Eric, 287, 288
Kant, Immanuel, 1, 2, 5–6, 10, 15, 44, 49, 55–6, 89–95, 98–9, 108, 157–8, 160, 162, 168, 175, 184, 244, 248, 310
Keller, Evelyn Fox, 241
Kierkegaard, Søren, 173
King, Martin Luther, 132, 137
Korsakov's syndrome, 272
Kropotkin, Peter, 215, 221
Kuhn, Thomas, 164

Lacan, Jacques, 46, 102, 104–5, 108, 112, 239–40
Laclau, Ernesto, 257, 262n4
Lamb, Marion, 231–2, 241
Laplanche, Jean, 52
Le Douarin, Nicole, 233–4
Leibniz, Gottfried Wilhelm, 86, 103, 108
Lévi-Strauss, Claude, 27–37, 126, 237, 239–40, 253–5, 257–9
Levinas, Emmanuel, 10, 15, 19, 23–4, 25n4, 54, 63, 65–7, 71–7, 79–80, 84, 97, 132, 215, 218, 220–2, 224
Lewontin, Richard, 240
Literature, 39, 44, 48, 101–2, 110, 123–4, 137, 138, 139, 167, 172, 176, 179, 180, 184, 256, 267, 285, 312–5, 319
Loftus, Elizabeth, 291
Luria, A. R., 265, 266, 273n1
Lyotard, Jean-François, 10, 15–18, 23–4, 256, 317

INDEX

Machiavelli, Niccolò, 204, 208, 211, 212
MacLeod, Norman, 237–8, 241, 242
McLuhan, Marshall, 197–8, 202
Malafouris, Lambros, 192–3
Mann, Thomas, 314
Marchant, Patricio, 184–6
Marx, Karl, 124, 135, 203, 204, 210, 212–13
Marxism, 101, 111, 138, 202, 203, 215, 216, 256
Mask, 20, 52, 106, 115–16, 119–23, 124–8, 151–2, 154, 279, 305, 318
Materialism, 1, 7, 92, 203–14, 235, 318
Maturana, Humberto, 240
Maupertuis, Pierre Louis, 157
Mauss, Marcel, 253, 254
Meillassoux, Quentin, 89–99, 111, 193–5, 293
Melville, Herman, 152–3
Memory, 189, 230, 232, 234, 246, 248, 259, 261, 265, 272, 287–93, 295, 306
Merleau-Ponty, Maurice, 247, 297–307
Messianic, messianism, 50, 52, 56, 59, 61, 97, 221
Metamorphosis, 29, 98, 118, 119, 120–3, 125–7, 128, 129n3, 272, 315, 317
Metaphor, 34, 47, 93, 132, 176, 190, 265–7, 272, 280, 282, 285, 288, 310–11, 316
Metzinger, Thomas, 251
Mignolo, Walter, 186n2
Miller, Jacques-Alain, 101–6, 108
Montaigne, Michel de, 316–17
Morgan, Thomas, 158, 231
Mouffe, Chantal, 257–8, 262n4
Mutability, 82, 118, 123, 199, 206, 239

Nancy, Jean-Luc, 44
Natural selection, 206–8, 210, 212, 221, 318
Nazism, 228
Negri, Toni, 117, 136–7
Neruda, Pablo, 185
Neutrality, neutral, 10, 20, 44, 52, 93, 94, 145, 150, 152, 180, 189–90, 193–5, 197–8, 200, 202, 266, 269, 271, 277, 319
Nietzsche, Friedrich, 136, 184, 204, 211, 255, 318
Nussbaum, Martha, 237

Odysseus, 141–56
Orpheus, 22, 149

Other, 3, 16, 21, 23–4, 38, 39, 42, 49–61, 64, 93–5, 97, 104, 106, 119, 121, 146, 173, 174, 182, 186, 220–1, 245, 248, 250
Outside, 16–18, 23, 44, 52, 64–5, 79, 85, 86, 104, 128–9, 133, 135, 136–8, 146–8, 152, 153, 163–5, 179–186, 186n1, 204, 224, 250, 258, 262n3, 267, 311, 312–13

Passeron, Jean-Claude, 210
Petrashevsky Circle, 167
Phantom, 60, 124, 305, 306
Phantom limb, 297–307
Plato, 16, 31, 108–9, 134, 141–3, 146–7, 149, 151–6, 219
Poetry, 18, 38, 110, 119, 123, 185, 255, 267, 272
Promise, 11, 15, 49, 55, 58, 97, 129, 207, 211–12, 246, 311–12, 313
Proudhon, Pierre-Joseph, 215, 219, 220
Proust, Marcel, 20–1, 126, 314

Ramachandran, V.S., 301–2, 305–7
Rancière, Jacques, 215, 218
Ravaisson, Félix, 4, 12n5
Rembrandt, 41–2
Retreat, 265–73, 316
Revelation, 22, 24, 55–7, 63–76, 82, 84, 86, 163, 165, 204
Ricoeur, Paul, 159–62, 165
Rousseau, Jean-Jacques, 209, 211

Sartre, Jean-Paul, 41, 127, 137–8, 225n1
Schürmann, Reiner, 215, 218–20, 224
Sculpture, 120, 208, 247, 283, 285, 291, 293, 303, 318–19
Secret, 22–4, 35, 49, 52, 60, 110–11, 116, 119, 122–7, 170, 203, 225, 240, 267, 296, 301
Set-theory, 96
Sign, 34–6, 60, 64, 70, 107, 133–4, 288, 303
Signification, 17, 33, 35, 66, 73, 76, 78–9, 90, 104, 258, 282, 300
Simon, Claude, 315
Smail, Daniel Lord, 190–1, 193–7, 202, 294
Social Darwinism, 207
Social Selection, 205, 207, 210, 211, 317–18
Socrates, 31, 51, 141–5, 147, 149–54, 156

Solovyov, Vladimir, 171
Sovereignty, 10, 125, 141, 146–50, 153–5, 181, 214, 222, 227, 238
Spinoza, Baruch, 10, 63–87, 197, 204, 243–4, 248
Squire, Larry, 287
Stiegler, Bernard, 311
Suicide, 41, 269
Symbolic, 2, 4, 7, 30, 32, 34, 36, 44, 63, 65–6, 73–6, 80, 82, 84–7, 148, 214, 228–9, 235, 238–42, 253, 255, 258, 260, 261–2, 314, 319

Teleology, 161, 203–4, 206–7, 212, 250
Thom, René, 34–5
Todorov, Tzvetan, 240
Torah, 72–4, 87n5
Trace, 3, 50, 52, 57, 59, 106–8, 161, 194, 234, 260, 267, 272, 279, 288–90, 292–6, 310, 311–12, 316
Transcendence, 16, 59, 65–6, 74–6, 84–5, 136, 139, 170–1, 221, 240
Transcendental, 2, 5–6, 10, 36, 39–40, 42–7, 49–50, 75, 89–99, 100n8, 116, 157–60, 162, 164–5, 174–6, 195, 197, 204, 214, 244, 310–12
Trump, Donald, 290

Varela, Francisco, 240
Venter, J. Craig, 242n1, 314
Vernant, Jean-Pierre, 127
Verter, Mitchell, 221
Violence, 17, 45, 120, 141, 146, 152, 154, 155, 224
Vrangel, Aleksander Yegorovich, 168–9

Waddington, Conrad, 158, 231
Weber, Max, 216
West-Eberhard, Mary Jane, 164, 191, 295
Wilderson, Frank, 132, 138
Wilson, Edward, 190–1, 294
Wood, James, 167, 170
Wright, Handel Kashope, 257

Yovel, Yirmiyahu, 85

Zero, 102–7, 205, 253, 255, 256
Žižek, Slavoj, 175, 258

EU representative:
Easy Access System Europe
Mustamäe tee 50, 10621 Tallinn, Estonia
Gpsr.requests@easproject.com

www.ingramcontent.com/pod-product-compliance
Lightning Source LLC
Chambersburg PA
CBHW052044220426
43663CB00012B/2441